The State of Population Theory

SACRED TO THE MEMORY
OF THE REV. **THOMAS ROBERT MALTHUS**
LONG KNOWN TO THE LETTERED WORLD
BY HIS ADMIRABLE WRITINGS ON THE SOCIAL BRANCHES OF
POLITICAL ECONOMY

PARTICULARLY BY HIS ESSAY ON POPULATION

ONE OF THE BEST MEN AND TRUEST PHILOSOPHERS
OF ANY AGE OR COUNTRY
RAISED BY NATIVE DIGNITY OF MIND
ABOVE THE MISREPRESENTATIONS OF THE IGNORANT
AND THE NEGLECT OF THE GREAT
HE LIVED A SERENE AND HAPPY LIFE
DEVOTED TO THE PURSUIT AND COMMUNICATION
OF TRUTH
SUPPORTED BY A CALM BUT FIRM CONVICTION OF THE
USEFULNESS OF HIS LABORS
CONTENT WITH THE APPROBATION OF THE WISE AND GOOD

HIS WRITINGS WILL BE A LASTING MONUMENT
OF THE EXTENT AND CORRECTNESS OF HIS UNDERSTANDING

THE SPOTLESS INTEGRITY OF HIS PRINCIPLES
THE EQUITY AND CANDOUR OF HIS NATURE
HIS SWEETNESS OF TEMPER URBANITY OF MANNERS
AND TENDERNESS OF HEART
HIS BENEVOLENCE AND HIS PIETY
ARE THE STILL DEARER RECOLLECTIONS OF HIS FAMILY
AND FRIENDS

BORN FEB:14.1766.   DIED 29.DEC:1834.

Malthus's memorial in Bath Abbey

The State of Population Theory

Forward from Malthus

Edited by
David Coleman
and
Roger Schofield

Basil Blackwell

©Basil Blackwell Ltd 1986

First published 1986

Basil Blackwell Ltd
108 Cowley Road, Oxford OX4 1JF, UK

Basil Blackwell Inc.
432 Park Avenue South, Suite 1505,
New York, NY 10016, USA

British Library Cataloguing in Publication Data

The State of population theory: forward from Malthus.
1. Demography
I. Coleman, David   II. Schofield, Roger
307.2   HB871

ISBN 0-631-13975-3

Library of Congress Cataloging in Publication Data

Main entry under title:

The State of population theory.

Includes index.
1. Population – Addresses, essays, lectures.
2. Demography – Addresses, essays, lectures.
I. Coleman, David.   II. Schofield, Roger.
HB849.4.S73 1986   304.6′ 01   85-26668
ISBN 0-631-13975-3

Phototypeset by Dobbie Typesetting Service, Plymouth, Devon
Printed in Great Britain by T. J. Press (Padstow) Ltd, Cornwall

Contents

Acknowledgements

With the exception of those by Coleman, Kunitz, Schofield and von Tunzelmann, the papers in this volume were given in their first form at a conference entitled 'Forward from Malthus: the state of population theory in 1984' organized by the British Society for Population Studies at Gonville and Caius College, Cambridge on 17–19 September 1984. The editors wish to express their appreciation of grants from the Office of Population Censuses and Surveys, and the Royal Society, and contributions from the Royal Economic Society, the International Association of Human Biologists and the Galton Foundation, which helped to make the conference possible.

Introduction: The State of Population Theory

Roger Schofield and David Coleman

Any subject which finds it necessary, or indeed possible, to consider its material divorced from an appropriate body of theory must be in trouble. This seems to be the case with demography at present, and it raises many questions about the maturity and nature of the subject and about its standing in relation to other disciplines, especially the directions in which it is developing or failing to develop.

Keyfitz (1984) has recently observed that

demography, far from being imperialistic, has withdrawn even from its own frontiers and left a no-man's land which other disciplines have infiltrated. Economists have turned their attention to marriage and fertility, with interesting results. The classical question of population and food supplies is part of farm economics, world modellers have taken on the relation of population to its ecological setting.

Only recently is there evidence of a revival of interest in these matters in demography, as opposed to the practical concerns of agricultural economists (McNicoll 1984, Grigg 1980, Gilland 1984). However, the methods of inquiry which are appropriate in demography and the structure of demography as a subject are seldom considered.

The most fundamental problem is knowing what the problems really are and how to formulate them. At the most general and problematic, the integration of ideas at the same scale and at different scales remains a major difficulty. The idea of an internally coherent population system, defined in social as well as in formal demographic terms, is embodied in the notion of a 'demographic regime', but its specification often remains vague, especially the nature of its adaptation to external (environmental) pressures. A crucial question is how it can change without losing the ability to function or its capacity to adapt.

Integration of ideas and models at the same scale

Some models in demography, operating at the level of total population size and growth, and which consider the relation of population to welfare, poverty

1

and technology, appear to be mutually contradictory – for example, the views of Malthus and Boserup on the consequences of population growth (see Lee, this volume). Both theories present an opportunity for testing ideas against experience (Wrigley and Schofield 1981, Spooner 1972), but they have not been cast in the form of contrasting statistical models and tested competitively against population data. On the one hand, as Lee's paper shows, there are circumstances where both theories may be true, in that population growth may be an important cause of the persistence or worsening of poverty while at the same time stimulating technical innovation which may alleviate problems of subsistence and welfare at least in the longer run. Boserup's model takes population growth as a given, being concerned with its consequences, and to that extent is incomplete (Cowgill 1974).

Reconciliation of Malthus and Marx on population presents a greater problem, partly because Marx's views were expressed as reactions against Malthus, but also because Marx insisted that population models are 'culture-specific', denying the validity of any general theoretical statements about population processes. Recently Woods (1983) has tried to integrate both systems into a model where the predominance of the influence of each component depends on the level of development.

Relation of ideas and models at different scales

Demography abounds in ideas, such as the 'child-survival hypothesis' or 'minority-status hypothesis', which are plausible and even testable in isolation, however inconclusive the results. But for the most part these exist on an almost-continuous scale of comprehensiveness from the micro to the macro, without any frame of reference to relate one to the other. The development of ideas relating family structures and intermediate institutions to demographic response is a promising exception (McNicoll 1984). The fundamental importance of different family and household structures in determining the nature of demographic regimes is now realized: not just as between Western Europe and the rest (Hajnal 1982, Smith 1981), but also in the contrast between, for example, the extreme version of the extended family found among the Yoruba, and the more nucleated structures of the family in rural Bangladesh (Caldwell 1977, Cain 1982). In particular, it is now realized that nucleated family structures require the support of institutional means of welfare and risk insurance if they are to survive critical periods in their life-cycle (Smith, this volume), while high fertility serves this function elsewhere even when subsistence problems make this otherwise irrational (Cain 1982). This is a major step towards the definition of particular population systems as working wholes, and the analysis of the pathological dissonances which may arise when rationality at the large and the small scale works in different directions during periods of change, as in many contemporary Third-World situations.

These new theoretical developments bridge the scales between the family and the institution, but their relation to the total population scale remains unclear except in the case of Western Europe. The theory of wealth-flows and fertility, for example, can be criticized because it is insufficiently quantified and because its population consequences, and their feedback through land and economy to the family system, have not been formally set out. Thus it is impossible to see if the whole system could work, either in modern or in traditional circumstances, for more than a few years or a generation. Its failure to do so in the economic circumstances of present-day urban West Africa (especially Ghana) is forecast in Boserup's discussion (this volume) of a poverty-led demographic transition even in that area of recalcitrantly high fertility.

Methods of inquiry in demography

When theory is weak or disparate, a subject's contents and aims remain ill defined. Little consideration may be given to the most appropriate methodology, with the result that empirical work is poorly structured and the subject fails to develop its full potential. Accordingly, it may be useful to reflect first on what kind of subject demography is; what intellectual property might be said to be its distinctive possession; and where and how it can make its most effective contribution.

Methods of inquiry may be considered first because they are rarely addressed in the literature. Indeed, Wunsch (1984) is somewhat a pioneer in this regard, commenting that, while limited hypotheses are subjected to the trial of real data, they are rarely falsified or checked and few ideas are linked to broad or underlying theory. *Ex post facto* explanations seem inevitable, so that a large part of the work done in demography remains remote from the canons of scientific inquiry. Furthermore, the multiple nature of demographic explanation complicates the interpretation of predictive failure; there is always a temptation for investigators to add further statistical epicycles to try to make their system work, rather than think afresh.

Without being self-conscious about it, Malthus himself realized the crucial importance of empirical evidence to support his originally more theoretical structure, as Wrigley shows elegantly in this volume. Malthus preferred the complexity of an actual to the simplicity of a purely logical structure, sharply distinguishing his own work from the ideologies which he criticized. But it cannot be said that he specifically deployed his facts in a manner calculated to test, rather than support, his own hypotheses, although it provided the theoretical framework for the biggest-ever demographic reconstruction and trial (Schofield 1985). Unfortunately, we still lack sufficient long runs of data to test his ideas on more than one or two examples. While the English historical experience lends some support to Malthus's theory, the Dutch pattern, in a different economic context, is less accommodating (de Vries 1985).

The scientific pursuit of asking and answering questions about populations cannot usually be conducted experimentally. In this respect demography resembles astronomy, geology and some aspects of ecology, ethology and population genetics. Quasi-experimental designs – the random scattering of subjects over treatments – do occur, if rather infrequently, in natural populations. One of the few such is the recent arrival in Western European and North American environments of large populations from the Third World.

These unusual combinations of subject and treatment have not been exploited systematically to further the general explanation of fertility transitions. Instead, attention has been captured by race-relations aspects and by the specific question of 'minority status', admittedly an important extra interaction variable, generated by the quasi-experimental process itself. No attempt has been made to integrate the 'characteristics' model of ethnic-minority fertility with the broader 'demographic-transition' model to which it seems related, another example of the problem of integrating theory across different scales. Nor has the alternative 'minority-status' hypothesis been integrated with the ideas of Davis (1963), Coale (1973), or even Caldwell (1979), with which it has more in common (Coleman 1983). Population policies can produce situations which come closer to an experimental design. But while most 'treatments' are relatively weak, recent stronger treatments, as when policies are vigorously or ruthlessly pursued and socially pervasive (as in China and Vietnam) or represent sharp reversals of previous policy (as in Malaysia), may produce results which challenge conventional theory, providing suitable 'controls' can be identified in a world of unique nations.

Universal theory or generalizations which link small-scale with large-scale processes, such as 'grand unified theories' in physics or evolutionary theory in biology, may not be possible in demography. Especially in the social sciences, such generalizations may not even be falsifiable. One of the few attempts to bring together ideas in demography – Sauvy's 'General Theory of Population' (1969) – is an adventurous compilation of generalizations on a broad front, but there is no central paradigm which links all the ideas together. Sometimes, of course, ambitious statements on populations may be difficult to falsify not because they are inadequately specified but because, being synthetic rather than experimental, their replication would require the reassembling, adjudication and processing of vast amounts of data. Flinn (1982) comments that it is inconceivable that anyone could ever repeat all the operations which went into Wrigley and Schofield's formidable reconstruction (1981) of English population history from 1541 to 1871, even though the operations involved have been specified to an intimidating degree. In the search for a central paradigm general biological models have sometimes proved popular in demography. The mathematics of population processes is the same for all two-sex species, and the biological facts of reproduction and death have inevitable physiological similarities. But whether human population processes are usefully modelled by general biological models, whether ecological or genetical, is a more controversial matter (see Howell in this volume, Keyfitz 1984).

In the end, demography without numbers is waffle, an amiable kind of social natural history. Fuzzy causation in demography, and the probabilistic nature of individual events, require a statistical model as a testable interface between theory and data. Unplanned events in human life, and the varied interpretation of reality of the human actors themselves, even in the same circumstances, introduce a major stochastic element into the distribution of measured demographic behaviour. But demographic models rarely have statistical distributions or confidence limits built into them, so the statistical criteria for rejection or acceptance are seldom known in advance. An interest in this problem has been forced upon the related subject of population genetics, because biological anthropologists are characteristically interested in small-scale societies where stochastic population processes are paramount (Cavalli-Sforza and Bodmer 1971). Keyfitz (1981) has made the first substantial analysis of errors in past population forecasts to estimate the size of errors *a priori* for future population forecasts, and Murphy's statistical experiments to judge alternative forecasting-models (1980) were also concerned with the measurement of error. New techniques of time-series analysis (Box and Jenkins 1970), while by no means specific to demography, can give error estimates, given the hypothesis, by a different route (Raeside in press). If proof of hypothesis is prediction, we still have a lot to learn.

The irritating failure of most attempts to forecast population (especially its fertility component) is a humbling example of the limitations even of restricted working hypotheses, although at least some of the blame can be shared with other subjects (notably economics) which are incapable of forecasting the future values of their variables, that demographers then use as independent variables.

THE STRUCTURE OF DEMOGRAPHY AS A SUBJECT

The subject matter of demography may be imagined as being arranged within a sphere with a hard mathematical core and a softer socio-economic and biological rind. The core represents the specific technical property of demography; the mathematical theory which deals with statics and dynamics of population; vital rates in relation to the age structure, dynamics, growth and their perturbations, and all the techniques of measurement, analysis and substitution that follow. Mathematical statements of the equilibrium position of population under specified circumstances form the basis of population dynamics rather as the Newtonian laws of motion provide one of the bases for classical physics and the Hardy–Weinberg rule is the foundation of the mathematical models of change in population genetics. And these, too, are generalizations of dynamic systems with a tendency to return to an equilibrium state.

But this hard core of demography does not touch the surface of the real world directly, except through measurement and reconstruction. It does so only when the population is made specific. An outer structure of theory and fact is then necessary to explain and predict that population's response, through the specific agencies of independent biological, social and economic causes and consequences of population trends. In this outer region of demography, the numerical techniques and ideas of demography act as an interdisciplinary common currency. Demography, which deals with the hardest (biological) facts in social science, enables material from one subject to be used in conjunction with material drawn from another. This permits the risks of the fundamental human events of birth and death to be analysed interchangeably by ideas which may draw on sociology, geography, history, biology and other subjects. How far demography develops its own interdisciplinary theory, to explain major changes or continuities in demographically measurable events, is still debated. But it suggests that demography in its broader sense is necessarily an eclectic and multi-disciplinary approach.

In this wider meaning, the identity of 'demography' as a subject is less definable. Many who would not call themselves demographers use demographic material and contribute to demographic ideas. It is not just a question of labels, more one of aims and purposes – for example, demographers are generally concerned with the working of demographic systems and the definition of demographic regimes. In practice, however, most research is with more manageable components of these systems, such as the socio-economic determinants of fertility or mortality trends, rather than with whole population systems.

None of this high-level demography can operate without the dynamics and the limits imposed by the central core of demographic mathematics. Research into the way that population systems work and into their consequences in the real world always needs numerical demographic models to set limits and give patterns to the empirical phenomena. At the beginning of modern population theory, Malthus needed to go some way towards the development of stable-population theory (Coale 1979) in order to advance his argument. The absence of any such interest by Graunt 250 years earlier (Kreager, 1980) may help to explain why his work remained at the level of 'Observations' rather than ascending to the pretension of a 'Principle'. Furthermore, the underlying long-run stable population structure with constant vital rates presupposes a coherent and stable social system which can generate and maintain the balanced vital rates. The two are not distinct, but reciprocally dependent. A society's demography is a formalization of the risks of its membership.

THE ORIGIN AND PURPOSE OF THE PRESENT VOLUME

In the course of these brief remarks on the nature of demography and population theory the name of Robert Malthus has been mentioned several times. Malthus was the first to develop a total population system operating on specified, if elementary, rules relating population behaviour to the social, economic and moral context. Although the idea of such systems, together with the nature of their feedback mechanisms and their effect on human society and economic development, was raised so long ago, we are still very far from answering all the questions which Malthus posed. Since 1984 marked the 150th anniversary of Malthus's death it seemed an opportune moment to review the current state of population theory. Accordingly, the British Society for Population Studies organized a conference at Cambridge under the title, 'Forward from Malthus: The State of Population Theory in 1984'. The conference was convened neither to praise Malthus, nor indeed to bury him; but to take stock of developments in population theory since his death, and especially to see how far they could be unified. Eight papers were presented at the conference, which have formed the basis of the contributions to this volume, supplemented by four additional papers.

Since the conference assembled only for two days it was clearly impossible to consider all aspects of population theory. In the circumstances it seemed advantageous to concentrate on 'external' theory relating population processes to the real world rather than the 'internal' theory of the hard mathematical core, and to pay special attention to the questions of scale and coherence in population theory. For example, the papers at the conference addressed questions such as how large-scale population processes can be related to individual actions and perceptions, and whether these relations can be generalized across societies of different degrees of organizational complexity.

Wrigley's paper in this volume shows that Malthus gave a clear lead on both these critical issues, proposing a theoretical framework which provides an excellent basis for re-evaluating population theory today. Malthus's theory was wide-ranging, positing general relationships for the animal kingdom as well as for human society. On the other hand his theory was not cast in a blindly universal mould; in this respect Marx and many other commentators have misunderstood the nature of Malthus's thought. Malthus certainly posited certain 'laws', such as the 'passion between the sexes', and insisted on rigorous logical deduction as a method of reasoning; but he was well aware that population processes were powerfully influenced by economic structures and social value systems. Indeed, in the language of modern scientific discourse, Malthus regarded the latter as 'initial boundary conditions' which limited the range of applicability of the posited 'laws' and profoundly affected their outcome. Malthus's theory, therefore, embraced both the core and the rind of demography. It showed the need both for an 'internal' mathematical theory to guarantee the logical consistency of deduction, and for an 'external' theory of 'initial conditions' which could do justice to the complexity of the real world by systematically relating population processes to the social, economic and moral context.

Through its combination of 'laws' and 'initial conditions' Malthus's theoretical formulation accords well with the canons of scientific inquiry. Furthermore, as Wrigley's paper shows, Malthus was personally committed to the view that the test of theory lay in verification against the empirical record. Nor was Malthus's intellectual activity confined to population theory; as the first professor of political economy in England he wrestled with many central problems in the social sciences. His writings on economics are generally less well known than his population theory (see Eltis 1984); but his ideas on the roles of consumption, savings and investment as stimulants to demand, and hence to employment, have made their mark on economic theory through their influence on Keynes. Malthus brought to economics, as he did to population theory, a desire to formulate rigorous theoretical propositions, combined with an awareness of the complexity of the real world, and an appreciation of the need for empirical verification. The qualities of Malthus the economist and Malthus the man are discussed in a paper contributed by Richard Stone, the text of which was originally given as an after-dinner speech at the Cambridge conference.

Ironically, Malthus's attempt to be both rigorous and realistic may well have lessened the impact of his work amongst both demographers and economists, but for opposite reasons. While demographers have reproached

Malthus for the abstract universalism of his 'laws', economists have tended to discount his attempts to incorporate features of the real world in his theories, preferring the more abstract and universal formulations of Ricardo. On the other hand, the power of Malthus's theories has long been recognized in the biological sciences through their contribution to the development of evolutionary theory by Darwin and Wallace, its mathematical formulation by Fisher (1930) and in the context of the regulation of animal populations (Lack 1954). And there are signs that demographers and economists are now becoming aware of the potential of Malthus's theoretical approach to some fundamental issues in the social sciences.

In this volume, for example, von Tunzelmann argues that Malthus should be distinguished from other classical economists, such as Smith and Ricardo, in that he approached the theory of economic equilibrium not in the usual 'comparative-static' manner, but as a problem in dynamics. For Malthus, what was important was analysing the properties of a system 'out of equilibrium', and tracing the paths by which equilibrium might be approached. Von Tunzelmann explores the dynamic properties of Malthus's demographic–economic theory, showing how Malthus tried to go beyond the simplifying assumptions of other economists of the day and incorporate into his theory systematic features of the economic and moral systems of the real world. Combining aspects of this dynamic theory with recent data on demographic and economic indicators in the late eighteenth and early nineteenth centuries, von Tunzelmann reconsiders the classical Malthusian problem of the interactions between population growth, economic change, and welfare in the era in which Malthus himself lived.

Lee's paper in this volume also tackles the central question of the relationship between population dynamics and economic dynamics. He analyses the two most influential macro theories in demography: the first due to Malthus – that population equilibrates with resources at a level mediated by technology and a conventional standard of living; the second, due to Boserup – that technological change is itself spurred by increases in population. Lee shows how the relations between population, technology and the standard of living predicted by Malthus and Boserup can be synthesized into a joint theory of considerable power and scope. His extension of macro-demographic theory affords valuable insights into several questions concerning population development. For example, his 'phase diagrams', which show the directions of forces operating in a joint population – technology field, help to explain why populations may have experienced such widely differing rates of development. Certain combinations of rates of growth of population and technology will lead to populations equilibrating at a low population size and with low technological development, while other combinations will lead to stable equilibria with much larger population sizes and higher levels of technology.

Some of the factors which help determine the course that a population might follow through the population – technology field may be exogenously determined, as in the case of mortality due to infectious disease. However, Lee argues that many of the predisposing factors are cultural or institutional, since the latter govern key intermediate variables, such as the rate of reproduction, and the rate of extraction of economic surplus and the uses to which it is put.

In his contribution to this volume Kreager also argues that population development is critically mediated by cultural systems, and that population theory must consequently pay careful attention to the cultural and institutional context. He notes how some influential population theories in the past – for example, 'transition theory' – have been seriously flawed by their assumption that the organizing principles of social and personal life are immaterial to population development. More recently population theories have begun to incorporate models of institutional forms, and to distinguish between different value systems, as a means of explaining variations in demographic behaviour. Kreager suggests that this approach could with advantage be pressed even further, so that demographic processes are viewed as one of the ways in which societies can adapt to changing circumstances within a wider institutional context. In this perspective, the concept of the adaptive capacity of a society, both demographically and institutionally, becomes a critical element in population theory.

Several of the remaining contributors in this volume employ this larger appreciation of population theory to investigate population development in societies of differing degrees of complexity and economic development. Howell shows how the small, sparse and stable populations of hunter–gatherer societies were the product of their style of life: they moved frequently, owned few possessions, shared widely, and ate little despite an abundance of available food. Consequently they were thin and had low fertility; and their populations showed no tendency towards exponential growth. This characteristic demographic regime presupposes a cultural context specific to hunter–gatherer societies; whole areas of population theory which assume the values and institutions of settled agriculture are irrelevant to these populations.

By contrast, Smith examines how the population development of the settled agricultural society of pre-industrial England was dependent on a very different cultural and institutional context, one in fact which formed the background to Malthus's formulation of the preventive check. Attitudes in pre-industrial England comprised an unusual combination of individualistic and collectivistic elements. For, while economic and residential independence at marriage was the norm, there was also an apparatus of community welfare which compulsorily transferred wealth between unrelated families to provide support for normally independent households at critical points in their demographic development when income was insufficient to cover expenses. In such a society both individual and social attitudes to such matters as age at marriage and the desired number of children differed from those in other societies, where resources flowed within, rather than between, families. Thus, population theory also needs to take into account the nature of familial obligation and local political structures in modelling the relations between demographic and economic change.

A similar point is emphasized in Lesthaeghe's discussion of the adaptability of different societies in sub-Saharan Africa to recent economic and demographic changes. Although the area is characterized by high population growth rates, there are considerable differences between societies. Lesthaeghe shows that the degree to which societies have responded to the problems of rapid population growth produced by a decline in mortality has depended on the nature of agricultural production and social organization, which vary considerably from region to region. Moreover, the response to recent social and economic changes, such as the introduction of cash crops, the expansion of formal education, and urbanization has been uneven. As a result, in some societies aspects of social behaviour which affect fertility have been changing rapidly, while in others there has been a high degree of resistance to change.

Boserup also discusses the question of the determinants of fertility today, drawing evidence from the developing world. In evaluating the relative importance of environmental, technological, economic and cultural factors in determining fertility behaviour, she lays particular emphasis on the degree to which social and economic institutions afford individuals some form of economic security. Like Smith she draws a distinction between societies in which individual security may be obtained through the ownership of land, or through communal welfare systems; and those in which individuals are dependent on their family, or wider kin group, for economic or other support. Boserup's paper underlines, once again, the importance of the social and institutional context in mediating the interactions between demographic and economic change.

Much the same conclusion emerges from Simons's study of variations in fertility in Europe today. In contrast to members of some other societies, European parents do not give birth to children as a means of increasing their wealth or power, nor because they do not know how to avoid them. Accordingly, Simons analyses recent survey data in a number of European countries to discover the cultural values which impel modern Europeans to have children, and to estimate the strength of the relationship between these values and fertility behaviour. He distinguishes between two main sets of values: the external moral authority of traditional attitudes emphasizing the desirability of parenthood, and the internal personal satisfaction that can be gained from self-expression and self-realization as a parent. Simons finds that much of the present-day variation in fertility between different countries in Europe can be explained in terms of the degree of acceptance of external moral authority, whether religious or secular. This does not mean that economic factors are irrelevant; rather that the perceived implications of the costs and benefits of children are culturally mediated. It might be added to Simons's comments that the fertility of European countries responds remarkably similarly to economic trends – in this respect they have converged; but they remain set at different levels.

Most of the contributors to this volume who have explored the application of population theory to the real world have concentrated on fertility and nuptiality, treating mortality as an exogenous variable. Kunitz, however, addresses the important question of the extent to which a theory can be constructed to account both for differences in the mortality levels of populations, and for change over time. Distinguishing between death from infectious, and from non-infectious, disease, Kunitz analyses the way that mortality has evolved in Europe, North America and Latin America from historical times until the present day. He concludes, with Malthus, that there is no universal law of mortality. On the contrary, both the nature and the level of mortality depend upon the capacity of individual societies to adapt to their ecology, which as societies develop and grow becomes increasingly modified by their own activities. Furthermore, the ability to adapt depends in turn on the organization of political, economic and social institutions. Some societies can adapt and learn by monitoring themselves and by scientific progress; others utterly fail to do so.

The contributors to this volume show clearly that, after decades of concentration on the 'internal' mathematical theory of demography, much greater attention is now being paid to the 'external' theory of the 'initial conditions' imposed by the social, economic and moral context. This development brings both methodological and substantive advantages. In relating population processes to the social context demographers can draw on theories derived from several disciplines, notably biology, economics, sociology and history. When combined with the logical rigour of internal demographic theory, the insights of these disciplines can be used to develop hypotheses in a form which enables them to be subjected to the standard procedures of scientific inference. In this way demographers may hope to put their house in order and avoid the charge recently levelled by Wunsch that a substantial proportion of their research has lacked an adequate theoretical orientation (Wunsch 1984, p. 1).

Furthermore, an approach which treats the social context not merely as a descriptive background, but as an integral part of the theory of population processes, can provide a means to link hypotheses which have been formulated at very different scales of analysis. Since both macro and micro theories are likely to invoke contextual factors as 'initial conditions', the latter occupy critical nodes in a theoretical structure enabling hypotheses that have been framed at very different levels of aggregation to be related meaningfully to each other. Indeed the recent use of family and household structures in theoretical writings at both the macro and micro scale furnishes a prominent example of an 'organizing principle' capable of integrating theories of the population behaviour of individuals and of society as a whole (Hajnal 1982, Caldwell 1977, Smith 1981).

Demography is still far from possessing a central paradigm linking small-scale and large-scale processes. Yet the papers contributed to this volume suggest that considerable progress is being made in identifying and articulating the elements of an 'external' population theory which can widen and deepen our understanding of population processes by relating them systematically to the social, economic and moral context. By integrating the new insights of 'external' theory with the 'internal' theory of mathematical demography, population theory today can develop into a more rigorous and realistic discipline. This was Malthus's method, and his agenda: the way ahead lies 'Forward from Malthus'.

REFERENCES

Birdsell, J. B. 1978: Spacing mechanisms and adaptive behaviour among Australian aborigines. In F. J. Ebling and D. M. Stoddart (eds), *Population Control by Social Behaviour*. London: Institute of Biology, pp. 213–34.

Box, G. E. B. and Jenkins, G. M. 1970: *Time Series Analysis Forecasting and Control* (San Francisco: Holden-Day).

Cain, M. 1981: Risk and insurance: perspectives on fertility and agrarian change in India and Bangladesh, *Population and Development Review* 7, 435–74.

Caldwell, J. C. 1977: The economic rationality of high fertility: an investigation illustrated with Nigerian survey data. *Population Studies*, 31, 5–28.

—— (ed.) 1979: Introduction. The persistence of high fertility: population prospects in the third world. Canberra: Australian National University Press.

Cavalli-Sforza, L. L. and Bodmer W. 1971: *The Genetics of Human Populations*. San Francisco: Freeman.

Coale, A. J. 1973: The demographic transition reconsidered. *International Population Conference, Liège, 1973*, 1, Liège: IUSSP, pp. 53–72.

—— 1979: The use of modern analytical demography by T. R. Malthus. *Population Studies*, 33, 329–32.

Coleman, D. A. 1983: The demography of ethnic minorities, in *Biosocial Aspects of Ethnic Minorities*, Supplement No. 8, *Journal of Biosocial Science*, 43–90.

Cowgill, G. L. 1975: On causes and consequences of ancient and modern population changes. *American Anthropologist*, 77, 505–25.

Davis, K. 1963: The theory of change and response in modern demographic history, *Population Index*, 21 (4), 345–66.

De Vries, J. 1985: Population and economy of the pre-industrial Netherlands. *Journal of Interdisciplinary History*, 15, 661–82.

Ebling, F. J. and Stoddart, D. M. (eds) 1978: *Population Control and Social Behaviour*. London: Institute of Biology.

Eltis, W. A. 1984: *The Classical Theory of Economic Growth*. London: Macmillan.

Fisher, R. A. 1930: *The Genetical Theory of Natural Selection*. Oxford: Clarendon Press.

Gilland, B. 1984: Considerations on world population and food supply. *Population and Development Review*, 9, 203–11.

Grigg, D. B. 1980: *Population Growth and Agrarian Change: an historical perspective*. Cambridge: Cambridge University Press.

Hajnal, J. 1982: Two kinds of preindustrial household formation system. *Population and Development Review*, 8, 449–94.

Keyfitz, N. 1981: The limits of population forecasting. *Population and Development Review*, 7, 579–94.

—— (ed.). 1984: Introduction: population and biology. *Biology and Demography*. Liège: Editions Ordina, pp. 1–8.

Kreager, P. 1980: Anthropological considerations for a theory of fertility (unpublished D.Phil Thesis, Oxford University).

Lack, D. 1954: *The Natural Regulation of Animal Numbers*. Oxford: Clarendon Press.

McNicoll, G. 1980: Institutional determinants of fertility change. *Population and Development Review*, 6, 441–62.

—— 1984: Consequences of rapid population growth: overview and assessment. *Population and Development Review*, 10, 177–240.

Murphy, M. 1980: Extrapolation of current trends for forecasting populations. *Centre for Population Studies Working Paper, no. 80–2*. London: London School of Hygiene and Tropical Medicine.

Raeside, R. in press: The logistic curve as a means of forecasting human populations. *Journal of Forecasting*, forthcoming.

Sauvy, A. 1969: *General Theory of Population*. London: Weidenfeld and Nicolson, New York: Basic Books.

Schofield, R. S. 1985: Through a glass darkly: the 'Population History of England' as an experiment in history. *Journal of Interdisciplinary History*, 15, 571–93.

Spooner, B. 1972: *Population Growth, Anthropological Implications*. Cambridge, Mass.: MIT Press.

Smith, R. M. 1981: Fertility, economy, and household formation in England over three centuries. *Population and Development Review*, 7, 595–622.

Woods, R. I. 1983: On the long-term relationship between fertility and the standard of living. *Genus*, 39, 21–36.

Wrigley, E. A. and Schofield, R. S. 1981: *The Population History of England 1541–1871: a reconstruction*. London: Edward Arnold.

Wunsch, G. J. 1984: Theories, models and knowledge: the logic of demographic discovery. *Genus*, 40, 1–18.

Population Regulation: A Long-Range View

David Coleman

As well as the problems discussed in the introduction, there are many other important topics in the dynamics of populations which it has not been possible to include in this volume. Some, especially those concerning the socio-economic analysis of fertility change and household economics, have received considerable attention elsewhere and so will not be considered here (Hohn and Mackensen 1982, Bulatao and Lee 1983).

Instead, this chapter will discuss, although by no means resolve, some relatively neglected problems in contemporary demography. They mainly concern the ways in which populations adapt – or fail to adapt – their numbers and growth rate to their environment, and they fall under four main heads:

1 the uncoupling of fertility and mortality trends from population size and growth rates – the dissociation of demographic response from population pressure;
2 the evolution of systems of population feedback and regulation and the adaptive nature of changes – the development of population systems;
3 the existence of a variety of feedback mechanisms, both positive and negative, including some relatively neglected causes of mortality such as warfare and infanticide, and their development in different kinds of society;
4 absolute limits to population size, on a regional and global scale, and exogenous factors affecting them.

THE DISSOCIATION OF DEMOGRAPHIC RESPONSE FROM POPULATION
PRESSURE – A QUESTION OF SCALE

Most modern theory treats fertility trends and mortality trends as autonomous: contributing to population growth and structure, but not in turn being influenced by them. Even in demographic transition theory it is notable that while population growth is seen as potentially leading to economic deterioration and hence a reason why fertility *should* decline, it is no longer usually presented as a reason why it *does* decline through, for example, Malthusian effects on wages and on available land. The

14

historically coincident process of economic development is usually preferred as an explanation, although part of its operation, of course, is to create a threat to family welfare by changing the utility and cost of children, while at the same time providing the notion and the means for limiting their number in absolute terms.

It is clearly important to consider the scale at which factors operate. Population pressures at any given level of land tenure and technique may be shown to be reducing the size of landholding below subsistence needs. But of itself the pressure does not initiate adoption of fertility control. Such response requires in addition a shift in occupation and an emancipation of ideas permitting a fall in the need for children and in the perception of that need (Boserup, this volume, Lesthaeghe 1983). On the large scale, feedback from population growth to fertility decline here is usually seen as the 'artificial' one of population policy itself. However the notion of a poverty-led demographic transition, discussed by Boserup in this volume (e.g. in Ghana or Bangledesh), may mark a return to a more Malthusian model of total population thinking.

Feedbacks – or their absence – at the level of the family rather than the population have tended to predominate in the analysis of fertility in developed societies since the nineteenth century. The opposite is true of the analysis of the populations of prehistoric or simple societies, where biological or whole-population models are paramount (e.g. Cohen, Malpass and Klein 1980). A transition from population pressures to family or household pressures is apparent in the literature on fertility control from the nineteenth century on-wards. Both the qualitative sociological analysis of Banks, for example (1954, 1981), and the more quantitative work of his successors (Teitelbaum 1985, Woods and Smith 1983) concentrate upon family level pressures and the attitudes and aggregate socioeconomic attributes of the individual. Population feedbacks play no part in the analysis, in contrast to the treatment of earlier periods of population growth and its failure (Postan 1966, Grigg 1980).

Generalized theories which can incorporate responses from any of the major components of population growth such as the theory of change and response (Davis 1963) are in fact usually concerned with only a section of the population response system: with the process of the reduction of fertility. It does not explicitly recognize population growth itself as a major challenge. The New Home Economics approach to twentieth-century fertility trends treats family and household almost as quasi-individuals (Smith, this volume) and focuses exclusively on their response to exogenous economic trends, in which population trends play no part. This is in line with the general neglect accorded to population growth by modern economists (Ohlin 1976). Smith (this volume) points out that the microeconomic analysis of fertility by the household theorists has little in common with Malthus's notion of relationships between income, marriage and fertility, however appropriate they may be to other, earlier societies. In some respects Malthus was ahead of them, regarding the specific form of preventive check from marriage in Western societies as a response intimately connected with population response, while the New Home Economics theorists take little interest in the family, regarding it as a 'given'.

Easterlin's model (1968) is something of an exception. It preserves a strong if unacknowledged Malthusian element in its emphasis on the effects of cohort size on individual life-chances and their corresponding feedback on to subsequent fertility. Malthus in fact discussed the excess labour supply provided by the large Napoleonic War birth cohorts as a contributory cause of post-war economic difficulties, including low wages (von Tunzelmann, this volume). To some extent, neglect of the influence of the population dimension in modern societies arises from the relative immobility of the whole, as opposed to its components – population growth rates are low or negative in industrial societies and have great inertia. Interest would certainly revive if population growth were to approach 1 per cent per year (Population Panel 1973, Select Commission on Science and Technology 1971) or, as is perhaps more likely, if its decline were to approach 1 per cent per year (Royal Commission on Population 1949, Council of Europe 1978).

Since Malthus's death it is in these areas of total population theory that there has been the least interest, despite the popularity of the ideas of Carr-Saunders (1922) earlier in the century, and the adventurous but over-bold work of the world modellers a decade or two ago (Meadows 1972, Cole 1973). The greatest strides have been made either in the harder inner technical core or, if more general, in theory related to specific components of population systems, notably fertility, rather than in population consequences as a whole. This relative failure seems to be the crucial point at issue; its resolution determines whether there really is demography beyond mathematics.

MECHANISMS OF EQUILIBRIUM AND FEEDBACK

Relative constancy of population numbers is often produced as *prima facie* evidence of the existence of some mechanism of population regulation. Malthus took this for granted in his work, and in biology it is a basic observation underlying most models of animal population regulation (Lack 1954, 1966, Anderson 1984). In the short run at least, over a small number of generations, for most of human history and prehistory the pace of change in the capacity to exploit the environment (technological growth) has been slow in relation to potential population growth, as indeed Malthus assumed in his postulata. Earlier biological models tend to emphasize the direct role of positive, density-dependent, checks upon numbers; either from the direct effects of starvation or the effects of predators consuming their most common available food source, depending on the species' position in the food chain (Lack 1954, Cragg and Pirie 1955). Although even here the effects are seen to be mediated through social structure and the age-structure, so that the most serious impact is upon the weakest or non-reproducing members of the population.

More subtle models, especially those derived from studies of the higher vertebrates, recognize the intervening effects of the social structure upon fertility as well as mortality. The most adventurous of these ideas are owed to Wynne-Edwards (1963) who proposed that one of the main functions of social organization and communication was population control to a target optimum. Despite its sometime vogue in social anthropology (Douglas 1966) and in historical demography (Wrigley 1966), Wynne-Edwards's model has never found general favour with zoologists (Crook 1965) and was unnecessarily based on a fallacious evolutionary model and still remains unspecified demographically (but see Ebling and Stoddart 1978). Hierarchies and intra-specific competition may restrict reproduction to a small set of organisms of reproductive age, limit reproduction where predation is ineffective, or raise mortality rates in response to intra-specific competition or other social interactions, keeping population size well below the level at which positive checks become paramount or irreversible environmental damage may be caused (Wilson 1975). In man, concentration of reproduction at any time to a small subset of males (not females) is characteristic of many tropical African populations through polygyny (Lesthaeghe, Howell, this volume), and also by the arrogation to themselves of younger females by older males in many gerontocratic patriline societies, not only in tropical Africa but also among Australian aboriginals and American Indians.

There has been some speculation that the human species may have inherited a phylogenetic mechanism to relate its fecundity, or its mortality, to its environmental circumstances. Frisch's notions of 'critical fat' levels (1978) fit well into this scheme of things, especially as modified by Howell in this volume in relation to the !Kung hunter–gatherers. But such ideas have been very critically received (Menken, Trussell and Watkin 1980) and the mechanisms, if they exist, are clearly no longer effectively functional in today's nutritional environment, although fecundity does appear to be environmentally sensitive in other animal species. Although the !Kung may be the most intensively studied of hunter–gatherer societies, they may be also one of the most unusual. Their low mortality, rarity of fighting, abortion and infanticide and unusually long birth intervals are not so characteristic of other hunters and gatherers, such as the Hadza of Tanzania and the aborigines of Australia (Dyson 1977, Birdsell 1978).

Many biologists have speculated that there may be biologically determined limits to population density (set by the proximity of neighbours or the frequency or variety of interaction) which human beings, having evolved in small-scale hunting and gathering groups, can withstand before manifesting behavioural, endocrine, or other clinical pathology (Boyden 1970, Harrison and Gibson 1977, Ebling and Stoddart 1978). Much of this interest arises as an extension from animal studies, where failure of fecundity, and infanticide, became common at high density in captivity (Calhoun 1963). But it is very difficult, for example in urban environments, to isolate the effects of crowding from the poverty and other deprivations which usually accompany it. While there do seem to be adverse effects of overcrowding on health, other things being equal (Gath 1974, Galle and Gove 1978), normal human populations appear to be able to function well over several orders of magnitude of population density (Freedman 1980).

In the analysis of modern human populations, non-density-dependent models are favoured, negative feedback being initiated and operating entirely at the family level. Here it is family size and its growth rates that matter, not population size or its growth rates. Non-density-dependent models may be appropriate in considering modern human population questions, providing that technological change is not adversely affected by human population growth.

ADAPTABILITY OF POPULATION SYSTEMS

The range of demographic parameters within which a given population system will 'work' – keeping within sustainable rates of growth or decline, for example – can be specified using stable population theory. But any such demographic system must be compatible with a social system which will also work. The question arises: how do compatible social and demographic components emerge and how are they sustained as a coherent regime? Not for the first time in such problems, demographic and social components here depend on forces not demographically measurable: in this case human needs and their satisfaction, and human intellectual capacities and their limits. In part, the maintenance of social systems depends on a structure (hierarchies, territory, property) which produces 'losers' (Kreager, this volume); but mechanisms must ensure that the losers are not too numerous and have some expectation of ceasing to be losers (by ageing, or succession to niches).

The production of adaptable social forms raises the question of 'unconscious rationality' (Wrigley, this volume). Kreager's 'societies that work well most of the time' may well cease to do so when their circumstances start to change rapidly: a reduction in death rate may increase family size or change its composition, population growth may put new pressures on land and inheritance. If the social system cannot cope with the consequences, then the fall in death rate cannot be sustained but, interestingly, this has rarely happened. A conspicuous example of a deliberate attempt to cope with the consequences of rapid demographic change is furnished in the form of family planning policies, a forced social change not much studied in sociology. And as Kunitz shows later in this volume, attempts to avoid mortality, although more or less deliberate, were based until recently on a very imperfect understanding of what 'caused' disease symptoms.

EXTINCTION AND ITS AVOIDANCE

In the long run equilibrium fails. Almost all populations and most species that have ever existed have become extinct. Stochastic simulations (e.g. Cannings and Skolnick 1975, MacCluer and Dyke 1976) show the need for small human populations (less than 1,000) to employ some form of density-dependent mechanism to adjust mortality, fertility or migration to random changes in numbers. They also show that 'low pressure' demographic systems, where both fertility and mortality are low, are less vulnerable to these random changes than high pressure systems at any given population size. For these reasons completely *closed* populations of small effective size are probably not viable in primitive circumstances. Moreover, avoidance of close consanguinity in a small closed population further reduces its survival chances. Indeed, density-dependent migration and out-marriage are necessary to preserve any semblance of the maintenance of incest-avoiding marriage rules and to protect against undue inbreeding (Wobst 1976, Yengoyan 1968) which is important for survival in the longer run. In precontact Australia, for example, about 15 per cent of marriages were exogamous between tribal groups in each generation (Birdsell 1978), although it is not known if the rate varied in a density-dependent fashion.

These facts may serve to remind us that migration, usually regarded as the weak sister of fertility in population dynamics, may for the greater part of human existence have been a most important determinant of population homoeostasis and insurance against extinction, being capable of much more rapid and flexible response than fertility. Indeed, in studies of the population genetics of simple societies and prehistoric populations much more emphasis has typically been placed on patterns of migration and mating than on fertility differentials (Crawford and Mielke 1983, Boyce 1984). And in later prehistory through to the early medieval period in Eurasia, and later elsewhere, migration of nomadic people beyond their usual home range (Huns, Avars, Seljuks, Ottomans, Mongols) has dominated historical accounts of the destruction, displacement and establishment of human population over wide areas (Diesner 1982). These population movements are habitually attributed to the overpopulation of their homeland or the instability of its marginal climate and productivity. But no worthwhile demographic data are available – or likely to be found – to test these dramatic ideas.

THE DEVELOPMENT OF POPULATION SYSTEMS

How have population feedbacks and homoeostatic systems changed as societies and economies have developed? For the population systems themselves must be adaptive, their key regulators reacting to new developments either occurring within society (e.g. urbanization) or originating from outside (e.g. new epidemics). The notion of an evolving population system is essential in order to comprehend past patterns (e.g. Wrigley and Schofield 1981) and present variety. If the evolution of human population regulation systems over different kinds of economy, size of population and complexity of society could be reconstructed, it would provide a most helpful guide for predicting how different societies might respond to future events.

The evolution of population systems is the idea at the base of this volume and may be evidenced to some degree in its structure. To present such an evolutionary scheme it is necessary to know how changes have developed in several dimensions: the positive/preventive, the biological/learned, whether mediated by marriage or otherwise, whether under exogenously high mortality or not. Malthus believed that systems typically began in a 'crude' state where the positive check was paramount at low levels of social organization. The anthropologist Weiss (1976) has developed this further, attempting to assign numerical values to the relative magnitude of positive and preventive checks in an ascending scale of societies. But a simple linear scale seems unlikely in view of the probable increase of the burden of mortality on the transition from nomadic to settled population, which is discussed later. The biological basis of human reproduction and lifespan has probably remained constant since the rise of anatomically modern man, perhaps from 70,000 years ago. There is no evidence for any major genetical change affecting the population parameters of natural fertility and longevity (Ward and Weiss 1976), although it is likely that the immune system has generally advanced since those days, and inherited antigenic variation has certainly increased (Anderson 1984), most of it probably in the last few thousand years. If this is so then common biological features (but not necessarily social ones) of human population response derived from ethnographic studies may be applied to past populations, according to the principle of uniformity (Howell 1976).

The constancy of the underlying biological material contrasts with the short-term variability of human populations' vital rates and the uneven pace of social and technical change. Nowadays in biology the notion of punctuated equilibria in evolutionary systems is popular. According to this view evolutionary change occurs in short bursts of rapid development which quickly transform species. In between, longer periods of stability obtain. A cursory examination of any long-term human population graph suggests a similar pattern. Large-scale human population change is characterized by a small number of quantum leaps in size, especially associated with agriculture and industrialization, although these, especially the former, occurred at different times in different places (Deevey 1960, Hassan 1980). At this level of generalization, it is only orders of magnitude of population size in the past that can be distinguished. Where more detailed data are available, local populations show trends and plateaux over centuries, and in the short run the noise of crisis mortality and the adjustments of marriages and births on a yearly and seasonal basis.

In the very long term, population growth must have been very slow indeed; perhaps 0.001 per cent per year in the Palaeolithic, and up to 0.1 per cent in the Neolithic (Binford 1968, Carneiro and Hilse 1966). In the short run periods of rather more rapid growth (up to 1 per cent) may alternate with periods of decline, in response to density-dependent environmental feedback, internal stochastic population processes in small-scale societies and exogenous effects such as climatic variability. Indeed, it is difficult to imagine how a constant very low rate of population growth, adding only a few individuals per decade to average group size, could be maintained (Weiss 1976). As far as we can tell, hunters and gatherers have until recently shown no trend towards an increase in numbers. On the other hand, relatively rapid growth of total population, though not necessarily of density, seems likely in the initial peopling of uninhabited continental areas. For example, population growth rates of just 1 per cent per year would be sufficient to people the Americas and Australia within a thousand years (Birdsell 1957, Martin 1973, Hassan 1973), and in Europe, Ammerman and Cavalli-Sforza (1985) have proposed a 'demic diffusion' model of the spread of agricultural change through logistic population growth and small-scale local mobility – a 'colonisation without colonists'. But this view has its critics (Barker 1985).

In areas of settled population, however, the natural cyclical or random changes in the habitat would impose recurrent stresses on the population, tending to keep it well below maximum carrying capacity most of the time, and imposing periods of population decline and subsequent recovery. Local, relatively rapid recolonization would have followed the extinction of neighbouring groups by warfare or epidemics. Under such circumstances it may not be very useful to regard 'carrying capacity' as a fixed quantity over long periods of time (Hayden 1981).

The second general trend, visible especially over the last two millenia insofar as the data permit us to say, is that the pace of growth was higher after the first of these transitions; indeed in general the rate of growth accelerates over time although it is often severely checked. This is apparent even in such apparently unpromising areas as nineteenth-century India and China (McEvedy and Jones 1978).

MODELLING STEADY STATES AND TRANSITIONS

Different models of population systems are appropriate for the steady-state phase as opposed to the transitional phases of human populations. Almost all the demographers that have ever lived have experienced only our present unusual phase of rapid transition. Malthus is the one major exception. It was his misfortune to be writing just at the end of a long period of oscillation in population size, without any clear general upward trend, which he so successfully analysed. The bad timing of his birth ensured his declining popularity after his death in the nineteenth and earlier twentieth century. Now, the advent of more and more post-transitional societies is bringing him back into fashion.

For whatever reason, transition models have tended to capture most interest, even though sustained growth and a change of regime are unusual events. A steady-state or cyclical model is more appropriate for most times in the past, and probably for the future. Simple transition models, such as the logistic, are currently enjoying a revived fashion in demography and have always been regarded as useful in more general ecological modelling, although the excessive enthusiasm of early biological advocates (Pearl 1921) certainly needed correction (Andrewartha and Birch 1954). Such models and their derivatives can provide at least the basis for modelling the movement from one reasonably stable position to another in a simple and generalized system of feedback (Leach 1981, Murphy 1980, Raeside 1985). Lee's paper elsewhere in this book shows how populations may sustain different kinds of population and technological homoeostasis according to their different starting points in the spaces he describes.

The logistic model was developed by Verhulst (Schtickzelle 1981) as a reasoned rebuff to what was mistakenly thought to be the catastrophic nature of the Malthusian model of population regulation through positive checks. A negative feedback operating in proportion to the proximity of population size to some assumed maximum at a given technology was felt to represent a more humane and realistic model of events. Attempts can be made to justify use of the logistic model as a form of population projection on purely empirical grounds (Murphy 1980). But especially in earlier usage it was favoured because of its supposed correspondence to the dynamics of regulation of human populations. It remains a commonplace in animal population dynamics, from Pearl (1921) to the present day. Because it assumes that growth in population could exceed by orders of magnitude any imaginable rates of growth in technology, and therefore in subsistence, it is in fact a Malthusian model. The logistic feedback itself has been inferred from Malthus's formulation of his total population system (Samuelson 1966, von Tunzelmann, this volume, Minami 1961), irrespective of whether it is deemed to operate in a 'positive' or 'preventive' mode.

Like Malthus's model, that of Verhulst is imagined primarily in terms of population and land and the progressive diminution of returns to further inputs of labour. Malthus, however, although he does not use such terms, admits the possibility of raising the carrying capacity by technical change, though not rapidly and certainly not indefinitely; and in this respect his model is the more responsive and subtle.

Nevertheless, logistic models of population growth and their projections can perform well and may bear re-examination. For example, Verhulst's second model (1847) projected a final population total (9.4 million) for Belgium very close to the present almost stationary figure (9.9 million), compared to the exponential projection from 1847 of about 18 million. Asymptotes determined from various points in the early twentieth century population growth of England and Wales give less variable population totals than more recent Registrar General's projections (Leach 1981), especially if modified forms of the logistic model are used (Murphy 1980).

Logistic pictures of human populations feature one-way feedback only. The carrying capacity affects the population but the population does not affect the carrying capacity, although Murphy's (1980) asymptotic model enables the asymptote to be determined by more recent growth trends. The Boserup model treats the relation between population and technology explicitly. According to her views (1965), intensification and innovation are stimulated by increasing population pressure so that population growth drives cultural change, at least episodically, although the source of the growth is not specified.

However, it is notorious that the explanation of the beginning and end of periods of change present serious problems for demography. Catastrophe theory (Thom 1975, Zeeman 1976) is one of the few generalized models that deal with radical discontinuities in quantifiable phenomena. It has not yet been applied to population questions (but see Raeside, in press) but might have a role in the analysis of sharp changes in population behaviour, provided the latter are the consequences of measurable trends crossing some definable threshold and not merely random events. Crises and cyclical population changes, discussed later on, might be reconsidered from this viewpoint.

POPULATION REGULATION AND ECOLOGICAL RELATIONS
WITH OTHER SPECIES

The feedbacks from the environment mostly involve other organisms either as a base for human subsistence, or themselves using human populations as a subsistence base. Hence biological models of population regulation have often been used in addressing human demographic questions, from Malthus onwards. The mathematics of demography and the physiology of subsistence, reproduction and death in sexually reproducing species ensure some similarities in population processes and feedback mechanisms, although many argue strongly against animal models in a human context (Callan 1970, see also Keyfitz 1984). Models of the regulation of numbers of the higher vertebrates, like those of human numbers, have increasingly tended to emphasize the predominance of preventive checks over positive checks (Ebling and Stoddart 1978).

From the earliest times, human social organizations and material cultures have successfully suppressed or evaded competition from other species, through co-operation in the division of labour for the hunting of food, in protection from predators, and driving other predators off their own prey. No rival species for a remotely similar ecological niche has been in sight for the past few million years, although two, or even three, species of hominoid co-existed in the Plio-pleistocene era, about 5 million years ago. Nonetheless, with a human population of only about 5 million at the end of the Palaeolithic, the human species was just one of several mammalian species of comparable size and, with a few exceptions given below, was not yet in a position to make much impact on the environment.

Since then, competition from other large organisms has been effectively eliminated. But even today, insects and small mammals have reduced the effective carrying capacity of many human environments by a substantial but unknown fraction, particularly in mono-cultures. Total world-wide food losses from biological causes are estimated at 45 per cent:30 per cent pre-harvest losses, 10–20 per cent post-harvest losses (Pimentel 1978). Simple agricultural societies may lose up to 60 per cent of stored food such as tubers to moulds, rodents and insects (Schulten 1982). Occasionally, epidemic crises can bring overwhelming competition to agriculturalists in the form of locust swarms or irruptions of mice. Such crises occur anyway in natural environments; agricultural monocultures encourage them further. However, competition does not seem to be a major problem for hunters and gatherers. Most such as the !Kung (Howell, this volume) are not directly constrained by food supplies and their ecological niche is so varied that almost any competition can be evaded. Other gatherers, fishers and hunters in harsher and less varied environments may have been less fortunate.

As far as predation is concerned, man is more dining than dined against. Human body size and social organization, as well as natural longevity, argue against any major impact of predation on the regulation of human numbers at any stage in human history. Certainly great apes are seldom subject to predation; and savannah baboons who live in a much more dangerous and open habitat, probably more similar to that of early man, are usually able to take collective action to see off any predators from which they cannot escape by flight.

As far as food species are concerned, in most recent societies of hunters and gatherers most of which now inhabit marginal arid environments (Lee and DeVore 1968) 80 per cent of diet comes from plant sources of many species, and 20 per cent comes from animal species, also of several kinds. But in other circumstances meat has formed a very much larger part of the diet, especially in climatically harsh areas where vegetable foodstuffs may not be readily processed directly by the human digestion, but can be accessed indirectly via large mammals. The latter are likely to have been favoured food sources in pre-agricultural times when they were abundant everywhere. The highest hunting technology is not needed to catch them and they are a much more efficiently packaged source of food than small game and other animal sources (at the other extreme, mussels may be easy to collect, but it takes the protein of 83,000 mussels to reach the equivalent of one deer – Osborn 1977). Most of these large, easy-to-kill, species of animals and birds were 'K-selected' (Pianka 1974); that is, they were characterized by large size, slow growth and reproduction, low mortality and low productivity and their survival was easily jeopardized by a new predation threat.

Our present-day fauna of large mammals and birds is highly impoverished compared to the variety of the Pleistocene. Human competition and predation may be primarily responsible (Martin and Wright 1967). Archaeological evidence shows an enormous slaughter of elephants, rhinoceroses and horses by Palaeolithic hunters in North–Western Europe and of grazing animals in Africa. Hunting may have extinguished most of the cold-climate Pleistocene fauna about 10,000 years ago, leading to the different culture of the succeeding Mesolithic period. South America suddenly became accessible to human hunters and other predators when the isthmus of Panama became dry land; the extinction of the large, varied but archaic South American mammal fauna soon followed, leaving it in the impoverished state we see today (Krantz 1970). Elsewhere, human predation has eliminated many food or competitor species in historical times: in the Mediterranean, and in the South and North Pacific, especially on islands, although it has also been argued that human activity may merely have finished off relict populations already diminished by adverse climatic change (Grayson 1977). The feedback this may have had on colonizing human populations is likely to have been considerable, both on population and culture. Attention would perforce shift to less convenient but more abundant 'r-selected' species of small game and invertebrates, and more plant sources. With a much higher turnover these species can support more dense populations with less nomadic habits (Hayden 1981). Even here there may be limits: abandoned Pacific islands probably owe their uninhabited status to the extinction by hunting of the native bird fauna (Steadman and Olson 1985).

Especially in simple ecosystems, human populations may become involved in cyclical population changes such as the remarkable four- or eleven-year cycles recorded for Arctic mammals over a period of almost 200 years. In certain circumstances, which may exist more easily on paper than in reality, predator and prey regulate each other's numbers in a cyclical fashion as Lotka and Volterra showed (Hassell 1976). But while the fluctuations in the prey species may limit the predators, the opposite is not true. The prey, for example small mammals, do not 'eat out' their habitat; instead their fecundity declines and their mortality rises in relation to population density. This may occur because pathological endocrine changes, leading to infecundity or premature death, are triggered by increased frequencies of individual interaction (Christian and Davis 1964, Christian 1980), or by changes in the population genetic structure (Chitty 1967). Anderson (1984) claims that prey are limited by parasite/prey oscillations from recurrent infections, for example the plague-like bacterium of tularemia. So although the predators do not regulate the prey, the prey numbers may regulate the predators. Human generation length and low rates of reproduction make short-run cycles of this kind impossible, but longer-range cycles such as the 70-year caribou cycle might have a detectable cyclical effect on human numbers (Harpending and Bertram 1975).

At a much more general level it has been suggested that the cyclical interaction of wages and population generalized from Malthus's system can be likened to a Lotka–Volterra predator–prey cycle (von Tunzelmann, this volume). Long periods of inertia seem to characterize human social responses to new conditions (Cooke and Renfrew 1978); for example in the population responses of the early modern period, and in the adoption of fertility limitation in nineteenth-century Europe and in the modern developing countries. This wages–population cycle described by Wrigley and Schofield (1981) has such a long period that only 1.5 complete cycles have elapsed from the sixteenth to the nineteenth century. This does not give much confidence in the estimation of its parameters (Lee 1985). Over a period of half a millennium or more the system itself is likely to change, although recent evidence supports the presence of one of its fundamental features – late marriage – even in medieval times (Hallam 1985). Modern economic interest in long-term (Kondratieff) cycles, which are thought to be driven by phases of technical innovation (Freeman et al. 1983), has not yet been extended to their demographic connections. Recent thinking on Roman Britain (Salway 1981) suggests a much higher population peak for Britannia than previously accepted – perhaps 5 million people. If so, it would suggest that the peak was reached three times in the last two millennia, at unequal intervals ($c200$, 1300, 1650), before being finally breached in the eighteenth century.

Human populations used to be thought unique in the animal kingdom because their high burden of mortality from infectious disease had undoubtedly caused the majority of human deaths up to the present. This of itself does not make infectious disease the key to population regulation; for that to be true it must be shown that human disease operates in a sufficiently responsive, density-dependent fashion.

In fact, the human species may not be so distinctive in this regard as has been commonly thought. Studies of populations of insects, birds and small mammals have all revealed cyclical changes in antibody rates, infestation rates of parasites, and population numbers (Anderson and May 1979, 1980). Some species (e.g. red grouse) appear to have their numbers regulated by parasites and wild ungulate populations are known to have suffered catastrophic mortality from epidemics (e.g. the African rinderpest epidemic

In the long run, these burdens have not stopped human population growth in Western Europe, although it certainly helped to make it irregular. Where growing populations have been checked by rising death rates, notably in Europe in the early fourteenth and later seventeenth centuries, it is difficult to find evidence that this was the direct effect of density-dependent mortality from disease. At least in the seventeenth century, the preventive check through greatly reduced nuptiality had a greater effect on the growth rate. Relatively few people seem to have died of famine in European history, especially in Britain. This is quite different from the higher-pressure regimes in contemporary India or China (Charbonneau and Larose 1979).

In such areas the burden of infectious disease has been chronically higher than in Europe, partly for reasons of climate and altitude, often greatly increased by radical environmental changes from human activity (Goudie 1981). Deforestation for agriculture has made falciparan malaria the most important tropical disease of all, so much so that it has forced evolutionary change on human populations in hyperendemic areas within a couple of millennia. A number of harmful recessive genes (the abnormal haemoglobins, especially HGS or 'sickle cell', Thalassaemia, G6PDD), elsewhere very rare because of their lethal effects in double dose, have become common in tropical Africa, the Mediterranean and the Far East. This is because the physiological changes they provoke in haemoglobin or other aspects of blood physiology discourage the falciparan malaria parasite. Furthermore, two variants of the Duffy blood group system, common only in Africa, appear to confer almost complete immunity from the milder *vivax* form of malaria.

In considering whether density-dependent disease mortality was sufficiently elastic to check any population growth arising from changes in other factors, the time-scale and speed of response are important matters. Mortality can rise almost immediately to any level, including extinction of the population, faster than any increase or decline from fertility. Migration can be almost as flexible, without involving the destruction of the population. A mortality check from pressure of subsistence will tend to reduce population only to the subsistence maximum. The equilibrium position in response to epidemic disease alone, however, is not immediately obvious. Since human populations are usually subject to the attentions of several important lethal diseases, the dynamic equilibrium, if it exists, would be complex and perhaps seldom attained.

Until recently, this question has received little theoretical treatment. However, analysis of parasite–host interaction in animal systems suggests that there is not just one stable population position of a host in relation to a parasite but at least two (e.g. low infestation–low mortality and high infestation–high mortality), depending on the characteristics of the parasite, especially the complexity of its life-cycle. According to this view, cyclical changes in host numbers may often be due to switches across an unstable transitional population-density level between two relatively stable equilibrium positions (May 1977). It has been speculated that the density dependence of mortality from disease may not arise primarily from increased transmission probabilities, but through a fall in nutritional status at high population densities, which depletes the immune system and permits higher parasite loads and easier infestation (Anderson and May 1979), but empirical evidence is still quite inadequate to support the model in human populations.

DESTABILIZATION OR REGULATION – WARFARE AND VIOLENCE

Malthus (1826) considered that warfare was a predominant check to the populations of 'savage' nations, citing (admittedly inadequate) early ethnographic evidence and travellers' tales concerning the constant and sometimes annihilating character of local warfare among North American Indians, South Sea Islanders, Maoris and others. He suggested that the destruction from this cause required fertility to be kept particularly high. Despite its considerable demographic consequences, whether catastrophic or endemic, warfare has been relatively ignored in demography since Malthus's time, usually being regarded as an exogenous or catastrophic random event. But some more recent writings have returned to the view that population density may act through warfare to influence population aggregation, and that warfare may act to limit population size in some societies (Vayda 1971). Population growth in environmentally circumscribed areas conducive to agriculture may provoke armed conflict over territory and lead to the amalgamation of population units into states (Carneiro 1970). States continue to suffer epidemic warfare between (but not within) themselves but usually have political mechanisms for ending it. Endemic feuding and warfare is particularly characteristic of nomadic or long-fallow simple societies, which are not states, and which appear to have no social or political mechanism for ending chronic conflict. Such significant effects on male mortality have been described as inevitable pathological consequences of undeveloped societies (Hallpike 1973), and it is difficult to see how they could be 'adaptive'. But the best-described hunting and gathering groups, the !Kung bushmen (Howell, this volume), show a remarkably low frequency of violent deaths, whether from warfare or from infanticide. Opinions differ as to how typical their behaviour can be of hunters and gatherers in the past (Birdsell 1968, Ripley 1980).

In some societies deaths in battle may account for 14–25 per cent of each cohort of males. For example, in the Eipo of West New Guinea, 0.3 per cent of males still die in fighting each year. This current figure is thought to be much less than pre-contact mortality (Schiefenhovel 1984) which has been estimated at 1 per cent per year mortality of adult males, a figure which has also been estimated for the more serious warfare of the Plains Indians. Australian aboriginal hunters may have lost 15 per cent of each male cohort in fighting; the Murngin, up to 28 per cent (Livingstone 1968). In the areas of Yanomamo settlement (Amazon basin) where fighting is chronic, as much as 30 per cent of mortality of adult males may be due to violence (Chagnon 1974). Furthermore, at least in some of these societies, such as the Eipo, adult female mortality from witch-killings and suicide is apparently common.

Agricultural society cannot be continuously at war. Unlike hunters and gatherers farmers do not have year-round leisure. Neither, with their higher levels of mortality, do they have the surplus natural increase. But their economic surplus can support small populations of permanent soldiers; a specialization denied simpler levels of society. Warfare then turns from being endemic and uncontrollable to being epidemic and occasionally controllable at least in the short run. Under these circumstances there is more likely to be a 'winner' and a 'loser' on a large scale, who may suffer severe demographic losses affecting the geographical distribution of population, even to the extent of obliteration over large areas. Severe examples can be found in the Mongol invasions of Russia in the twelfth century, the Thirty Years War in Germany in the seventeenth century, and the depopulation of Cambodia after 1975 (Meng-Try 1981). Despite the very severe casualties suffered by civilian populations in wars of conquest, religion or ideology, the pattern of mortality seems to be more episodic and exogenous, less related to population characteristics and more to social and political processes and to the changeable 'bellicist' characteristics of states (Howard 1983). Most modern historians of warfare have paid no attention to population characteristics at all in discussing the causes of wars.

Other forms of deliberate violent death, notably infanticide, are also common in simple societies with high male mortality from warfare. Infanticide is most common in hunting and gathering and nomadic cultivating societies – in the former, at least, for spacing reasons. At the other end of the scale of development, in advanced societies which have not yet developed contraception, infanticide may become common at some levels of society to space births or to avoid illegitimacy (eighteenth-century Europe; Langer 1972, Sauer 1978) although only in Japan at a more general level sufficient to regulate growth of the whole population (Eng and Smith 1976).

Ethnographic studies suggest that infanticide can consume a significant part of each birth cohort, equivalent to a doubling of natural infant mortality. Among the Eipo, an unusually careful study shows that between a quarter and a third of all live births are killed, especially births of girls (Schiefenhovel 1984). Reasons quoted include extramarital pregnancy, boy preference, malformation, a wish to terminate childbearing, a reluctance to begin childbearing or an unduly short birth interval. Earlier accounts of infanticide of such severity (e.g. among the Netsilk Eskimo, Balikci 1970) were regarded as abnormal responses in extreme circumstances, but more evidence now supports comparable levels of infanticide (10–30 per cent of births) in other societies without settled agriculture; hunters and gatherers and swidden agriculturalists, notably in Papua New Guinea, the Amazon basin (Chagnon 1974) and in Australia (Birdsell 1978). The !Kung described by Nancy Howell in this volume seem to be a remarkable exception, with a very small (0–5 per cent) level of infanticide. As she describes, the !Kung have very long birth intervals, and it may be that they enjoy a unique phylogenetic adaptation (they have others, notably steatopygia) enabling them to link their fertility through lactation, fat levels and ovulation, with the productivity of their rather sparse environment. If so, it is no longer shared by anyone else.

Infanticide is common among animal populations, notably monkeys and apes (Hrdy 1980) as well as among nomadic humans. In other mammal species, mothers commonly abort or resorb litters if they are disturbed or if a strange male controls their group. Newborns will also be destroyed and eaten if the nest is disturbed. These are taken to be responses to prevent the mother as well as infants perishing in new or uncertain circumstances. Takeovers of groups by males often leads to the destruction of existing infants, especially in species where a few males are responsible for most reproduction. This behaviour is interpreted as maximizing inclusive fitness of the new dominant male at the expense of unrelated ones. None of these processes in primates seem particularly related to population control; they are much more readily understood in terms of inclusive fitness as part of a male reproductive strategy (Ripley 1980).

Infanticide in humans is usually performed by women (which may explain its under-enumeration) although male sanction may be needed. It is not associated with group takeovers in one-male groups, neither of which is a characteristic human social pattern (although it is true that stepfathers more often mistreat their stepchildren than do natural fathers their own children; Creighton 1984).

Human reproductive capacities are relatively high compared with apes: human birth intervals under natural fertility are usually shorter than those of the chimpanzee, for example (McKinley 1973), even though the chimpanzee is the smaller animal. It is generally accepted that the human species separated from the other primates in the Plio-pleistocene by becoming adapted to life in the more open savannah (Fox 1967, Stringer 1983). This environment, less stable and more hazardous than the forest, might require a more r-selected reproductive physiology to compensate for higher mortality. Subsequent social and technical developments, especially in tools, fire and personal care (see Howell, this volume), might reduce mortality to such an extent that infanticide might become necessary in the absence of social preventive checks (Ripley 1980). But, if this is so, it is not clear why intervening evolutionary change did not reduce fecundity; the pace of sexual maturation certainly slowed subsequently (Bromage and Dean 1985).

Finally it is appropriate to mention here that Malthus (1826) expressed some modern-sounding ideas relating to simple societies in the sixth edition of the Essay, despite very poor ethnographic data. Although he mistakenly assumed that most populations are close to their maximum, with consequent high levels of 'distress', he also discusses infanticide, warfare and vendettas and 'want of fecundity among women'. He emphasized the importance of child spacing to nomads (Australians). He also notes, 130 years before Sahlins, that 'the only advantage of savage over civilized life is the greater leisure of the mass of the people' and also suggests that 'distress' may in the end 'generate certain customs, which operate sometimes with greater force on the prevention of a rising population than in its subsequent destruction'.

LIMITS TO POPULATION SIZE

Most models of human population regulation envisage at least some temporary environmental limit on population size imposed by climate and technology.

Beyond the maximum population, resources for subsistence may degrade from overhunting, soil erosion, laterization of ancient soils in tropical areas, desertification and other responses to overcropping while such changes are in progress – and they may last a long time – the population will have overshot its carrying capacity and its numbers will be living on borrowed time before inevitably falling to a lower density (Birdsell 1968 Harpending and Bertram 1975). Late Imperial Roman populations (Russell 1958), fourteenth- and seventeenth-century European populations (Grigg 1980), and the Maya populations of the seventh century AD (Spooner 1972) have been claimed as historical examples of such pressures, as well as many contemporary tropical populations, especially in the arid tropical zones of Africa.

It may seem perverse not to discuss in more detail in this volume the terrible famines currently in progress in Ethiopia, the Sudan and elsewhere, as they appear to be unusually powerful and acute examples of misery following overpopulation. It is certainly true that population growth in tropical Africa has generally overtaken food production, and that the region is in economic decline with mortality and fertility both remaining stubbornly high. Here rapid population growth makes much worse a situation already made difficult by artificially high exchange rates, collectivization of land in some areas and the disruption of traditional land use patterns. Recent severe droughts may mark a climatic change which will lower local carrying capacities and force population redistribution. All these problems, compounded by warfare, are present to complicate our picture of the famine areas and the poverty of data on demography, climate, soils and agriculture has so far prevented any systematic analysis of the relative importance of all the factors. While the importance of over-population greatly worsening misery and mortality in famine areas seems apparent, external aid and other factors may prevent the death rate imposing any kind of major positive check on population growth. The mortality from an earlier, milder Sahel famine proved no great obstacle to continued growth in the few areas where it could be measured.

Malthusian population analysis assumes that the capacity of populations in simple societies to grow up to and beyond the sustainable level of their environment is greater than the ability of their population pressure – or any other factor – to stimulate technical change which might change that sustainable level. But rates of technological change grow exponentially with the volume of technology (Freeman 1983). In advanced societies these rates are very much faster – by at least an order of magnitude – than maximum rates of population growth. Modern scientific knowledge is self-accelerating, and industrial capitalism has always had an increasing tendency to invest in technical changes which improve productivity. Given the large population sizes attained by industrial societies, and the even larger populations which form their export markets, neither of these processes of technological growth is any longer obviously connected with population growth. If this is so then the phase diagrams of Lee (this volume) are closed at the far end of technical development. Population growth is in any case near zero in most industrial countries, precisely where scientific and industrial change is at its fastest. Although carrying capacity may still have some meaning in terms of amenity or of self-sufficiency for strategic reasons, it is not at present a major focus of the contemporary demography of industrial populations. The failure of population growth, and the unlikelihood of its resumption, has quelled the environmental excitement of just fifteen years ago (e.g. Taylor 1970, Meadows 1972). Only at simpler levels of human culture might it make sense to talk of only one carrying capacity at any one point in time.

The distance between real and supposed maximum population will determine the likely magnitude of feedback effects. The preventive check is assumed to be more sensitive to these differences and start operating first, the positive checks becoming paramount as K approaches (Wrigley 1966). Some lag and some leeway would be expected in all societies; Mary Douglas (1966) elaborated Malthus's point that human ambitions are not confined to mere subsistence if there is any choice, but are focussed on the symbolic and the prestigious, so that maximum numbers will usually be well below physiological limits. How far this is true will depend upon the social and economic level of the society and also on the equality of its inhabitants (Sauvy's (1969) 'power maximum' satisfies the luxury tastes of the elite only, not the masses, who live close to subsistence). Daly (1985), for example, suggests that population policy in Brazil – which has very high social fertility differentials – is hampered because a number of special interest groups perceive advantage to themselves in the high fertility of the Brazilian poor.

There are many estimates of K from empirical considerations of natural productivity or of the maximum yield which crops under a given technology could produce without degradation. Allan (1965) computed 'critical population densities' for agricultural societies some of which, especially those based on short fallow or continuous cropping, were quite close to the maximum. But most estimates place actual populations, especially of hunters and gatherers, at about 20–70 per cent of the carrying capacity. Hunters and gatherers, garden cultivators and long-fallow agriculturalists often show population densities at these percentages of the sustainable maximum (Lee and DeVore 1968, Sahlins 1972), although recent reports claim some are close to the maximum (Schiefenhovel 1984) or are having to shorten fallow because of population growth to a degree which the land cannot support (Gilland 1984). Allan suggested that his 'critical population densities' could be greatly exceeded for long periods – up to twenty years – in certain circumstances, but after that the land would begin to deteriorate in a way difficult to reverse. The frequency of famines and the high mortality in densely-settled intensive agricultural populations up to this century (India, China, Middle East; e.g. Barclay et al. 1976) suggest that they have tended to be close to the sustainable maximum.

Over the longer term, changes in the human environment suggest that carrying capacity has been exceeded from time to time. Several millennia of continuous cultivation, especially the deforestation of hills, has seriously degraded environments until they are incapable of supporting the original pattern of agriculture (most of the Mediterranean basin and Middle East, Tropical Africa on lateritic soils, West Asia; e.g. Goudie 1981, Meiggs 1982) unless the soil is renewed by regular alluvial flooding (valleys of the Yangtse, Yellow River, Ganges, Nile) or by artificial means. In our present state of rapid population growth and the wide extension of cultivation to most accessible areas, soil runoff now exceeds new soil creation by severalfold even in many developed areas. It has been estimated that food output is unlikely to be continuously sustained above the level sufficient to feed 7.5 billion people adequately (Gilland 1984). But the past experience of such forecasting is not favourable.

EXOGENOUS CHANGES IN CARRYING CAPACITY

A major problem underlying discussions of carrying capacity is the natural variability of the latter as a result of climatic changes or human interference (Hayden 1975). Carrying capacity can, and has, changed quite independently of population pressures. In the long run, this is a major feature of evolutionary pressures and extinctions in other species. Seasonal variability affects simple societies with limited capacity to store and pushes long-term sustainable population even further down from the maximum. The time-scale is important here, because more severe fluctuations are less frequent than small ones. It would not make sense for populations to remain so low so that they could cope easily with bottlenecks which only occurred every century or so. Climatic vagaries over a shorter time-scale may tempt population into expansion in good periods, only for numbers to be forced down in bad ones. In the past at least, the expansion of the pastoral Samburu of East Africa followed that of their cattle numbers, followed by collapse in unusually dry years producing a sawtooth population profile. But their culture encouraged optimism and expansion like a perpetual bull market, unlike their Rendille neighbours who inhabited a more arid area which supported domestic animals (camels) with lower reproduction rates than the cattle of the Samburu (Spencer 1973) and who limited and spaced families much more severely than the Samburu. The Samburu may perhaps be regarded as having a more r-selected demographic regime and culture than their neighbours. Other nomads in simple ecosystems may have followed a similar pattern of growth and crash, for example the Eskimo in relation to caribou, which have a 70-year cycle (Burch 1972). The longer the cycle, the bigger impact it would make on the variability of human numbers, and the more difficult it would be to talk of a carrying capacity of any permanence (Harpending and Bertram 1975). Hayden (1975) has suggested that for practical enquiry a measure of resource exploitation based on the level of protein-energy malnutrition, mortality rates and other supposedly overpopulation-related measures would be a more logical, reverse approach – to measure the feedback rather than attempt to envisage the carrying capacity itself.

The longer term brings other problems. Since the last retreat of the glaciers about 10,000 years ago there have been a number of climatic reversals over a time scale of centuries (Goudie 1983), possibly caused by changes in solar radiation associated with regular deviations in the Earth's orbit (Lamb 1982). Whatever their cause, these climatic fluctuations, preserved in the layered structure of ice and mud, in diatoms, tree rings, pollen and beetles' exoskeletons, indicate major changes in historical and prehistoric climate and environment. There seems little doubt that some of the population crises of history – the extinction of the Greenland colony, the decline of the marginal Icelandic population, the end of medieval expansion, and at least some of the problems of the late seventeenth century, for example – are due to episodes such as colder periods that which lasted from the fourteenth to the nineteenth century, with its worst point in the seventeenth (Wrigley and Schofield 1981, Tomasson 1977, Lamb 1982, but also Sauer 1968). Most accounts of these crises posit demographic or economic causes of a traditional Malthusian kind; climatic changes are not integrated into the explanation even though these factors which changed the level of resource may have been more important at some stages than the relation between population growth and resources.

Finally, human populations have now reached the position where they are capable of changing environmental conditions – and therefore carrying capacity – on a global scale. A recent change associated both with population and its recent enormous energy consumption is the rise in carbon dioxide concentration in the atmosphere, which has risen from about 280 parts per million in about 1750 to about 345 in 1984 (Neftel et al. 1985). In view of the temperature-enhancing effect of this change, and the possibility that the Earth's climate may be able to flip into different stable states than the present one – by no means all favourable to the good life – this may be an important development (Broecker et al. 1985).

CONCLUSIONS

There is still far to go in the development of theory in population, even in the limited scope discussed here. As Marx suggested, detailed generalizations applicable to all societies seem out of the question. But we may hope to develop a scheme of the development of population feedback systems so that the demographic regime of a society might be predicted from its economic type and environment. The notion of such a relationship dates in outline from Malthus's writings, though as a simple linear progression it falls down in detail even at the beginning in the contrast between the !Kung and other hunter–gatherers, for example. Although all societies can suffer problems of excess population size or growth, nonetheless at least in transitional stages the rationality of fertility at the microdemographic level may be diametrically opposite to that at the larger scale, even though such a contrast cannot be sustained indefinitely. A developed model of dynamic development of population regimes and their feedback systems is needed, which for its rationale demands an adaptable model of culture sensitive to environmental pressures. In such a sequence the salience of population size and growth as a source of feedback for large- and small-scale family and household systems will vary greatly. In demographically stagnant industrial society the connections at the level of the whole population appear to have diminished to an all-time low; attention must now focus on the family as the effective population unit on which feedbacks operate. It was hoped to present a sequence of diagrams to summarize the several sequences of population regulation shown by human societies (there is unlikely to be *one* sequence;

Lee's paper suggests several kinds of equilibrium). This would usefully follow the model of the developing sequence of feedback mechanisms described in the diagrams of the Conclusions chapter of Wrigley and Schofield's (1981) reconstruction of English population history. So far, lack of empirical data keeps a precise reconstruction in the realm of the speculative; in the end it has not been attempted. All this paper has done has been to outline some of its more neglected or less fashionable dimensions.

REFERENCES

Acsádi, G. and Nemeskéri, J. 1970: *History of Human Life Span and Mortality*. Budapest Akadémiai Kiadó.

Allan, W. 1967: *The African Husbandman*. New York: Barnes and Noble.

Ammerman, A. J. and Cavalli-Sforza, L. L. 1985: *The Neolithic Transition and the Genetics of Populations in Europe*. Princeton: Princeton University Press.

Anderson, R. M. 1984: Vertebrate populations, pathogens and the immune system. In N. Keyfitz (ed.), *Population and Biology*. Liège: Editions Ordina, pp. 249–68.

—— and May, R. M. 1979: Population biology of infectious disease. *Nature*, 280, 361–7, 455–61.

—— and May, R. M. 1980: Infectious diseases and population cycles of forest insects. *Science*, 210, 658–61.

Andrewartha, H. G. and Birch, L. C. 1954: *The Distribution and Abundance of Animals*. Chicago: University of Chicago Press.

Balikci, A. 1970: *The Netsilik Eskimo*. New York: Natural History.

Banks, J. A. 1954: *Prosperity and Parenthood*. London: Routledge.

—— 1981: *Victorian Values: secularism and the size of families*. London: Routledge and Kegan Paul.

Barclay, G. W., Coale, A. J., Stoto, M. A., and Trussell, T. J. 1976: A reassessment of the demography of traditional rural China. *Population Index*, 42, 606–35.

Barker, G. 1985: *Prehistoric Farming in Europe*. Cambridge: Cambridge University Press.

Billewicz, W. Z. and McGregor, I. A. 1981: The demography of two West African (Gambian) villages 1951–1975. *Journal of Biosocial Science*, 13, 219–40.

Binford, L. R. 1968: Post-pleistocene adaptations. In S. R. Binford and L. R. Binford (eds), *New Perspectives in Archeology*. Chicago: Aldine.

Birdsell, J. B. 1957: Some population problems involving pleistocene man. *Cold Spring Harbor Symposia in Quantitative Biology*, 22, 47–69.

—— 1968: Some predictions for the pleistocene based on equilibrium systems among recent hunter–gatherers, in R. B. Lee and I. DeVore (eds), *Man the Hunter*. Chicago: Aldine, pp. 229–40.

—— 1978: Spacing mechanisms and adaptive behaviour of Australian aborigines. In F. J. Ebling and D. M. Stoddart (eds), *Population Control by Social Behaviour*. London: Institute of Biology, pp. 213–44.

Boserup, E. 1965: *The Conditions of Agricultural Growth*. London: George Allen and Unwin.

Boyce, A. J. (ed.) 1984: Migration and mobility: biosocial aspects of human movement. *Symposia of the Society for the Study of Human Biology*, vol. 23. London: Taylor and Francis.

Boyden, S. (ed.) 1970: *The Impact of Civilisation on the Biology of Man*. Toronto: Toronto University Press.

Bromage, T. G. and Dean, M. C. 1985: Re-evaluation of the age at death of immature fossil hominids. *Nature*, 317, 525–7.

Broecker, W. S., Peteet, D. M. and Rind, D. 1985: Does the ocean–atmosphere system have more than one stable mode of operation? *Nature*, 315, 21–6.

Bulatao, R. A. and Lee, R. D. (eds) 1983: *Determinants of Fertility in Developing Countries.* New York: Academic Press.

Burch, E. S. 1972: The caribou/wild reindeer as a human resource. *American Antiquity,* 37, 339–68.

Caldwell, J. C. 1977: The economic rationality of high fertility: an investigation illustrated with Nigerian survey data. *Population Studies,* 31, 5–28.

Calhoun, J. B. 1963: Population density and social pathology. In L. J. Duhl (ed.), *The Urban Condition.* New York: Basic Books.

Callan, H. 1970: *Ethology and Society: towards an anthropological view.* Oxford: Clarendon Press.

Cannings, C. and Skolnick, M. 1975: Homeostatic mechanisms in human populations – a computer simulation. *Theoretical Population Biology,* 1, 39–54.

Carneiro, R. L. 1970: A theory of the origin of the state. *Science,* 169, 733–8.

—— and Hilse, R. F. 1966: On determining the probable rate of population growth during the Neolithic. *American Anthropologist,* 68, 177–81.

Carr-Saunders, A. 1922: *The Population Problem: a study in human evolution.* London: Clarendon Press.

Chagnon, N. A. 1974: *Studying the Yanomama.* New York: Holt, Rinehart and Winston.

Charbonneau, H. and Larose, A. (eds) 1979: *The Great Mortalities: methodological studies of demographic crises in the past.* Liège: Editions Ordina.

Chitty, D. 1967: The natural selection of self-regulatory behaviour in animal populations. *Proceedings of the Ecological Society of Australia,* 2, 51–78.

Christian, J. J. 1980: Endocrine factors in population regulation. In M. N. Cohen, R. S. Malpass and H. G. Klein (eds), *Biosocial Mechanisms of Population Regulation.* New Haven: Yale University Press, pp. 55–116.

—— and Davis, D. E. 1964: Endocrines, behaviour and population. *Science,* 146, 1550–60.

Coale, A. J. 1974: The history of the human population. *Scientific American,* September 1974, 41–51.

Cockburn, A. 1963: *The Evolution and Eradication of Infectious Diseases.* Baltimore: Johns Hopkins.

Cohen, M. N. 1977: *The Food Crisis in Prehistory.* New Haven: Yale University Press.

—— and Armelagos, G. J. (eds) 1984: *Paleopathology at the Origins of Agriculture.* London: Academic Press.

—— Malpass, R. S. and Klein, G. (eds) 1980: *Biosocial Mechanisms of Population Regulation.* New Haven: Yale University Press.

Cole, H. S. D. 1973: *Thinking about the Future: a critique of the limits to growth.* London: Chatto and Windus.

Cooke, K. L. and Renfrew, C. A. (eds) 1978: *Transformations: mathematical approaches to culture change.* London: Academic Press.

Council of Europe 1978: *Population Decline in Europe.* London: Edward Arnold.

Cragg, J. B. and Pirie, N. W. 1955: *The Numbers of Man and Animals.* Edinburgh: Oliver and Boyd for the Institute of Biology.

Crawford, M. H. and Mielke, J. H. (eds) 1983: *Current Developments in Anthropological Genetics,* Vol. 2: *Ecology and Population Structure.* New York: Plenum Press.

Creighton, S. 1984: *Trends in Child Abuse.* London: National Society for the Prevention of Cruelty to Children.

Crook, J. H. 1965: The adaptive significance of social organisation and visual communication in birds. *Symposia of the Zoological Society of London,* 14, 181–218.

Daly, H. E. 1985: Marx and Malthus in north-east Brazil: a note on the world's largest class difference in fertility and its recent trends. *Population Studies,* 39, 329–38.

Davis, K. 1963: The theory of change and response in modern demographic history. *Population Index,* 21, 4.

Deevey, E. S. 1960: The human population. *Scientific American,* 203, 195–204.

Diesner, H-J. 1982: *The Great Migration.* London: Orbis.

Dobson, M. 1980: 'Marsh Fever' – the geography of malaria in England. *Journal of Historical Geography,* 6, 357–89.

Douglas, M. M. 1966: Population control in primitive groups. *British Journal of Sociology*, 17, 263–73.

Dumond, D. E. 1975: The limitation of human population – a natural history. *Science*, 187, 713–21.

Dyson, T. 1977: *The Demography of the Hadza – in historical perspective*, Proceedings of a conference on African Historical Demography. Edinburgh: Centre for African Studies (mimeo, 19pp).

Easterlin, R. A. 1968: *Population, Labor Force and Long Swings in Economic Growth*. New York: National Bureau of Economic Growth.

Ebling, F. J. and Stoddart, D. M. (eds) 1978: *Population Control by Social Behaviour*. London: Institute of Biology.

Eng, R. Y. and Smith, T. C. 1976: Peasant families and population control in eighteenth-century Japan. *Journal of Interdisciplinary History*, 6, 417–45.

Flinn, M. 1982: Book review of Wrigley and Schofield 1981: The Population of England 1541–1871: a reconstruction. *Economic History Review*, 35, 443–57.

Fox, R. 1967: In the beginning: aspects of hominid behavioural evolution. *Man*, 2, 415–33.

Freedman, J. C. 1980: Human reactions to population density. In M. N. Cohen, R. S. Malpass and H. G. Klein (eds), *Biosocial Mechanisms of Population Regulation*. New Haven: Yale University Press, pp. 189–308.

Freeman, C. et al. 1983: *Long Waves in the World Economy*. London: Heinemann.

Frisch, R. 1978: Population, food intake and fertility. *Science*, 109, 22–30.

Galle, O. R. and Gove, W. R. 1978: Overcrowding, isolation and human behaviour: exploring the extremes in population distribution. In K. E. Taeuber, L. L. Bumpass and J. A. Sweet (eds), *Social Demography*. London: Academic Press, pp. 95–132.

Gath, D. 1974: Mental Health and Population Change. In H. B. Parry (ed.), *Population and its Problems – a plain man's guide*. Oxford: Clarendon Press, pp. 256–85.

Gilland, B. 1984: Considerations on world population and food supply. *Population and Development Review*, 9, 203–11.

Goudie, A. S. 1981: *The Human Impact: man's role in environmental change*. Oxford: Basil Blackwell.

—— 1983: *Environmental Change*, 2nd edn. Oxford: Clarendon Press.

Grayson, D. R. 1977: Pleistocene avifaunas and the overkill hypothesis. *Science*, 195, 691–3.

Grigg, D. B. 1980: *Population Growth and Agricultural Change: an historical perspective*. Cambridge: Cambridge University Press.

Hallam, H. E. 1985: Age at first marriage and age at death in the Lincolnshire Fenland 1252–1478. *Population Studies*, 39, 55–70.

Hallpike, C. R. 1973: Functionalist interpretations of primitive warfare. *Man*, 8, 451–70.

Harpending, H. and Bertram, J. 1975: Human population dynamics in archaeological time: some simple models. In A. C. Swedlund (ed.), *Population Studies in Archaeology and Biological Anthropology: a symposium*. *American Antiquity*, 40, pp. 82–91.

Harrison, G. A. and Gibson, J. B. (eds) 1976: *Man in Urban Environments*. London: Oxford University Press.

Hassan, F. A. 1973: On mechanisms of population growth during the Neolithic. *Current Anthropology*, 14, 535.

—— 1980: The growth and regulation of human populations in prehistoric time. In M. N. Cohen, R. S. Malpass and H. G. Klein (eds), *Biosocial Mechanisms of Population Regulation*. New Haven: Yale University Press, pp. 305–19.

—— 1981: *Demographic Archaeology*. London: Academic Press.

Hassell, M. 1976: The dynamics of competition and predation. *Studies in Biology*, no. 72. London: Edward Arnold.

Hatcher, J. 1977: *Plague, Population and the English Economy 1348–1530*. London: Macmillan.

Hayden, B. 1975: The carrying capacity dilemma: an alternative approach. In A. C. Swedlund (ed.), *Population Studies in Archaeology and Biological Anthropology: a symposium*. *American Antiquity*, 40, Memoir 30, 11–21.

—— 1981: Research and development in the Stone Age: technological transitions among hunter–gatherers. *Current Anthropology*, 22, 519–48.

Hohn, C. and Mackensen, R. (eds), 1982: *Determinants of Fertility Trends: theories re-examined*. Liège: Editions Ordina.

Howard, M. 1983: Weapons and peace. In *The Causes of War*. London: Allen and Unwin, pp. 151–70.

Howell, N. 1976: Towards a uniformitarian theory of human paleodemography, in R. H. Ward and K. M. Weiss (eds), *The Demographic Evolution of Human Populations*. London: Academic Press, pp. 25–40.

Hrdy, S. B. 1979: Infanticide: a review. *Ethology and Sociobiology*, 1, 13–40.

Hutchinson, G. Evelyn 1978: *An Introduction to Population Ecology*. New Haven: Yale University Press.

Isaac, G. 1971: The diet of early man: aspects of archaeological evidence from lower and middle Pleistocene sites in Africa. *World Archaeology*, 2, 279–99.

Keyfitz, N. (ed.) 1984: *Population and Biology*. Liège: Editions Ordina.

Knodel, J. 1977: Breast-feeding and population growth. *Science*, 198, 1111–15.

Krantz, G. S. 1970: Human activities and megafaunal extinctions. *American Scientist*, 58, 164–70.

Lack, D. 1954: *The Natural Regulation of Animal Numbers*. Oxford: Clarendon Press.

—— 1966: *Population Studies of Birds*. Oxford: Clarendon Press.

Lamb, H. H. 1982: *Climate, History and the Modern World*. London: Methuen.

Langer, W. L. 1972: Checks in population growth 1750–1850. *Scientific American*, February 1972, 3–9.

Leach, D. 1981: Re-evaluation of the logistic curve for human populations. *Journal of the Royal Statistical Society* A, 144, 94–103.

Lee, R. B. and DeVore, I. (eds) 1968: *Man the Hunter*. Chicago: Aldine.

Lee, R. D. 1979: New methods for forecasting fertility: an overview. In *Prospects of Population: Methodology and Assumptions*, Papers of the Ad Hoc group of experts in Demographic Projections, UN Population Studies No. 67. New York: United Nations, pp. 215–21.

Lesthaeghe, R. 1983: A century of demographic and cultural change in Western Europe: an exploration of underlying dimensions. *Population and Development Review*, 9, 411–36.

Livingstone, F. B. 1968: The effects of warfare on the biology of the human species, in M. Fried, M. Harris and R. Murphy (eds), *War: the anthropology of armed conflict and aggression*. New York: Natural History Press.

Livingstone, F. B. 1980: Natural selection and the origin and maintenance of genetic marker systems. *Year Book of Physical Anthropology*, 23, 25–42.

Lovejoy, C. O. 1981: The Australopithecines. *Science*, 211, 341–50.

McClaren, I. A. (ed.) 1971: *Natural Regulation of Animal Numbers*. New York: Atherton Press.

MacCluer, J. W. and Dyke, B. 1976: On the minimum size of endogamous populations. *Social Biology*, 23, 1–12.

McEvedy, C. and Jones, R. 1978: *Atlas of World Population History*. Harmondsworth: Penguin.

McKinley, K. R. 1973: Survivorship in gracile and robust australopithecines: a demographic comparison and a proposed birth model. *American Journal of Physical Anthropology*, 34, 417–26.

McNeill, W. H. 1977: *Plagues and Peoples*. London: Basil Blackwell.

Malthus, T. R. 1826: *An Essay on the Principle of Population, or a View of its Past and Present Effects on Human Happiness*, 6th edn. G. T. Bettany (ed.) 1890. London: Ward, Lock and Co.

Martin, P. S. 1973: The discovery of America. *Science*, 179, 969–74.

—— and Wright, H. E. (eds) 1967: *Pleistocene Extinctions*. New Haven: Yale University Press.

May, R. M. 1977: Thresholds and breakpoints in ecosystems with a multiplicity of stable states. *Nature*, 269, 471–8.

Meadows, D. H. 1972: *The Limits to Growth*. London: Earth Island Press.

Meiggs, R. 1982: *Trees and Timber in the Ancient Mediterranean World*. Oxford: Oxford University Press.

Meng-Try, E. 1981: Kampuchea: a country adrift. *Population and Development Review*, 7, 209–28.

Menken, J., Trussell, J. and Watkin, S. 1981: The nutrition fertility link: an evaluation of the evidence. *Journal of Interdisciplinary History*, XI, 425–41.

Mimms, C. A. 1977: *The Pathogenicity of Infectious Disease*. London: Academic Press.

Minami, R. 1961: An analysis of Malthus' population theory. *Journal of Economic Behavior*, 1, 53–63.

Murphy, M. 1980: Extrapolation of current trends for forecasting population, *Centre for Population Studies* Working Paper, no. 80-2. London: London School of Hygiene and Tropical Medicine.

National Academy of Sciences 1971: *Rapid Population Growth*, vols 1 and 2.

Neftel, A., Moor, E., Oeschger, H. and Stauffer, B. 1985: Evidence from polar ice cores for the increase in atmospheric CO_2 in the past two centuries. *Nature*, 315, 45–7.

Ohlin, G. 1976: Economic theory confronts population growth. In A. J. Coale (ed.), *Economic Factors in Population Growth*. London: Macmillan, pp. 3–28.

Osborn, A. 1977: Strandloopers, mermaids and fairy tales. Ecological determinants of marine resource utilisation – the Peruvian case. In L. Binford (ed.), *For Theory Building in Archaeology*. New York: Academic Press, pp. 157–205.

Parry, H. B. (ed.) 1975: *Population and its Problems – a plain man's guide*. Oxford: Clarendon Press.

Pavlovsky, E. N. 1966: *Natural Nidality of Transmissible Disease*, tr. F. K. Plous. Urbana: University of Illinois Press.

Pearl, R. 1921: The biology of death, V. *Science Monthly*, 13, 206.

—— and Reed, L. J. 1920: On the rate of growth of the population of the United States since 1790 and its mathematical representation. *Proceedings of the National Academy of Sciences USA*, 6, 275–88.

Pianka, E. R. 1974: *Evolutionary Ecology*. New York: Harper.

Pimentel, D. (ed.) 1978: *World Food, Pest Losses and the Environment*. American Association for the Advancement of Science, Selected Symposium No. 13. Boulder, Colorado: Westview Press.

Population Panel 1973: Report. Cmnd 5258. London: HMSO.

Postan, M. M. (ed.) 1966: *Cambridge Economic History of Europe*, vol 1: *The agrarian life of the middle ages*. Cambridge: Cambridge University Press, ch. 7, pp. 549–76.

Preston, S. H. (ed.) 1982: *Biological and Social Aspects of Mortality and the Length of Life*. Liège: Editions Ordina.

Raeside, R. in press: The logistic curve as a means of forecasting human populations. *Journal of Forecasting*, forthcoming.

—— in preparation: Modelling and forecasting human populations using sigmoid models. PhD thesis, Napier College, Edinburgh.

Ripley, S. 1980: Infanticide in langurs and man: adaptive advantage or social policy? In M. N. Cohen, R. S. Malpass and H. G. Klein (eds), *Biosocial Mechanisms of Population Regulation*. New Haven: Yale University Press, pp. 349–90.

Royal Commission on Population 1949: Report. Cmnd 7695. London: HMSO.

Russell, J. C. 1958: Late ancient and mediaeval populations. *Transactions of the American Philosophical Society*, 48, 1–152.

Sahlins, M. 1972: *Stone Age Economics*. London: Tavistock.

Salway, P. 1981: *Roman Britain*. Oxford: Clarendon Press.

Samuelson, P. A. 1966: *The Collected Scientific Papers of P. A. Samuelson*, ed. J. E. Stiglitz, vol. 1. Cambridge, Mass.: MIT Press.

Sauer, C. O. 1968: *Northern Mists*. California: University of California Press.

Sauer, R. 1978: Infanticide and abortion in 19th century Britain. *Population Studies*, 32, 81–94.

Sauvy, A. 1969: *General Theory of Population*. London: Weidenfeld and Nicolson.

Schiefenhovel, W. 1984: Preferential female infanticide and other mechanisms regulating population size among the Eipo, in N. Keytitz (ed.), *Population and Biology*. Liège: Editions Ordina, pp. 169–92.

Schtickzelle, M. 1981: Pierre-François Verhulst (1804–1849). La première découverte de la fonction logistique. *Population*, 36, 540–55.

Schulten, G. 1982: Post-harvest losses in tropical Africa and their prevention. *UN Food and Nutrition Bulletin*, 4, 2–9.

Scrimshaw, N. S., Taylor, C. E. and Gordon, J. E. 1968: *Interactions of Nutrition and Infection*, World Health Organisation Monograph Series, 57, Geneva.

Select Committee on Science and Technology 1971: *First Report, Population of the United Kingdom*. London: HMSO.

Solimano, G. R. and Vine, M. 1982: Malnutrition, infection and infant mortality, in S. H. Preston (ed.), *Biological and Social Aspects of Mortality and the Length of Life*.

Spencer, P. 1973: *Nomads in Alliance: Symbiosis and Growth among the Rendille and Samburu of Kenya*. London: Oxford University Press.

Spooner, B. (ed.) 1972: *Population Growth: anthropological implications*. Cambridge, Mass: MIT Press.

Stanley, N. F. and Joske, R. A. (eds) 1980: *Changing Disease Patterns and Human Behaviour*. London: Academic Press.

Steadman, D. W. and Olson, S. L. 1985: Bird remains from an archaeological site on Henderson Island, South Pacific: man-caused extinctions on an 'uninhabited' island. *Proceedings of the National Academy of Sciences*, 82, 6191–5.

Stringer, C. B. (ed.) 1983: *Aspects of Human Evolution*. London: Taylor and Francis.

Taylor, L. R. (ed.) 1970: *The Optimum Population for Britain*. London: Academic Press.

Teitelbaum, M. S. 1985: *The British Fertility Decline*. Guildford: Princeton University Press.

Thom, R. 1975: *Structural Stability and Morphogenesis*, tr. D. H. Fowler. Reading, MA: W. A. Benjamin.

Tomasson, R. F. 1977: A millennium of misery: the demography of the Icelanders. *Population Studies*, 31, 405–28.

Vayda, A. P. 1971: Phases of war and peace among the Marings of New Guinea. *Oceania*, 42, 1–24.

Verhulst, P. F. 1847: Deuxième mémoire sur l'accroissement de la population. *Nouveaux Mémoires de l'Academie Royale des Sciences et Belles Lettres de Bruxelles*, 20, 1–32.

Ward, R. H. and Weiss, K. M. 1976: *The Demographic Evolution of Human Population*. London: Academic Press.

Weiss, K. M. 1972: A general measure of human population growth regulation. *American Journal of Physical Anthropology*, 37, 337–44.

—— 1976: Demographic theory and anthropological inference. *Annual Reviews of Anthropology*, 5, 351–81.

Wigley, T. M. L., Ingram, M. J. and Farmer, G. 1981: *Climate and History*. Cambridge: Cambridge University Press.

Wilson, E. O. 1975: *Sociobiology: the modern synthesis*. San Francisco: Freeman.

Wobst, H. M. 1976: Locational relationships in palaeolithic society. In R. H. Ward and K. M. Weiss (eds), *The Demographic Evolution of Human Populations*. London: Academic Press.

Woods, G. I. and Smith, C. W. 1983: The decline of marital fertility in the late 19th century; the case of England and Wales. *Population Studies*, 37, 207–25.

Wrigley, E. A. 1966: Family limitation in pre-industrial England. *Economic History Review*, 19, 82–109.

—— 1969: *Population and History*. London: Weidenfeld and Nicolson.

—— and Schofield, R. S. 1981: *The Population History of England 1541–1871: a reconstruction*. London: Edward Arnold.

Wynne-Edwards, V. C. 1963: *Animal Dispersal in Relation to Social Behaviour*. Edinburgh: Oliver and Boyd.

Yengoyan, A. 1968: Demographic and ecological influences on Australian aboriginal marriage sections. In R. B. Lee and I. DeVore (eds), *Man the Hunter*. Chicago: Aldine.

Zeeman, E. C. 1976: Catastrophe theory. *Scientific American*, 234, 65–83.

Zinsser, H. 1935: *Rats, Lice and History*. New York: Little, Brown; repr. New York: Bantam, 1967.

Robert Malthus:
An Appreciation

Richard Stone

I have long had a great affection and admiration for Malthus on a number of counts. In the first place I like him because he was the most good-natured, sympathetic and kindly man, very different from the heartless fiend his enemies made him out to be. His writings, his diaries, his letters, his behaviour to friends and adversaries alike would make this clear even if we did not have the testimony of so many of his friends and acquaintances, whose unanimity on this point is practically deafening.

In the second place I like him because he was intellectually free, impervious to cant of either the right or the left. This scientific detachment, to me wholly admirable, was probably the main cause of the fury his writings aroused in his opponents in both camps. Certainly it is the trait that shows uppermost in Peacock's portrait of him in *Melincourt*. At the beginning of the chapter entitled 'The principle of population' a post-chaise rattles up to the door of Redrose Abbey, the home of the amiable Mr Forester. When the glass is let down,

a tall, thin, pale, grave-looking personage peeped from the aperture. 'This is Mr Fax,' said Mr Forester, 'the champion of calm reason, the indefatigable explorer of the cold clear springs of knowledge, the bearer of the torch of dispassionate truth, that gives more light than warmth. He looks on the human world, the world of mind, the conflict of interests, the collision of feelings, the infinitely diversified developments of energy and intelligence, as a mathematician looks on his diagrams, or a mechanist on his wheels and pulleys, as if they were foreign to his own nature, and were nothing more than subjects of curious speculation.'

Which had not prevented his saving a destitute family from eviction by a prompt and generous financial intervention, as is revealed later on in the book.

In the third place I like him because he could 'connect', in Forster's sense of the word. He had received a good formal education, ending as ninth wrangler in the mathematical tripos of 1788. Through his father, who was a friend and follower of Rousseau, he had acquired while still very young a familiarity with the currents of advanced thought of his time. By his own choice he was in orders, a conscientious Christian who accepted the tenets of the Church. In his early manhood as a country curate he had seen with

Given as an after-dinner speech at the conference 'Forward from Malthus' organized by the British Society for Population Studies at Gonville and Caius College, Cambridge on 17–19 September 1984.

his own eyes what life was like among the English poor, and, as a traveller in search of knowledge, what it was like among the poor of other countries. All these ingredients were ground together in his speculative mill.

In the fourth place I like him because his field of investigation is conterminous with mine, though he and I found our way into it from opposite directions: he reached economics through social demography; my inroads into social demography have been excursions from economics. Don't misunderstand me: I am not suggesting that the results of the two explorations are of equal importance, but merely saying that my feeling for Malthus springs not only from respect but also from an affinity of interests.

In the fifth place I like him because he had an empirical turn of mind. He believed that ideas should not be erected into theories without being tested against facts, and this is exactly what I believe and how I have tried to deal with my own ideas, such as they are. Besides being himself an assiduous collector of facts, he materially helped the cause by promoting the formation of the Statistical Section of the British Association and the subsequent foundation of the Statistical Society of London, now the Royal Statistical Society.

In the sixth place I like him for two qualities which are not often allied to a reforming zeal such as his was and which I find very refreshing, namely tolerance and an almost unshakeable equanimity. 'His temper was so mild and placid,' says his friend Bishop Otter,

> his allowances for others so large and so considerate, his desires so moderate, and his command over his own passions so complete, that the writer of this article, who has known him intimately for nearly fifty years, scarcely ever saw him ruffled, never angry, never above measure elated or depressed. Nor were his patience and forbearance less remarkable – no unkind word or uncharitable expression, respecting anyone either present or absent, ever fell from his lips; and though doomed to pass through more censure and calumny than any other author of his or perhaps any other age, he was little disposed to advert to this species of injury, still less to complain of it, and least of all to retort it.

Malthus himself told Harriet Martineau, who visited him towards the end of his life, that he had suffered in spirits from the abuse lavished upon him 'only just at first' and that it had never kept him awake a minute 'after the first fortnight'.

Finally, I like him very much as an economist, and this for many reasons, first among which is his open-mindedness. He warned us against generalizations based on insufficient premises, be these theoretical or factual; against the complacent acceptance of established views; against the suppression of uncomfortable exceptions that contradict the general rule; against the short-sighted mistrust of pure research; against the danger of mistaking chance coincidences for fundamental economic laws; and against the hasty application of imperfect knowledge. In his own words, 'To know what can be done, and how to do it, is beyond a doubt, the most valuable species of information. The next to it is, to know what cannot be done, and why we cannot do it.' His creed is contained in the Introduction to his *Principles of Political Economy* and should be required reading for all first-year students of economics.

His theory of population arose from discussions with his father on Godwin's *Political Justice* and the idea of a future age of equality and prosperity. Daniel Malthus, who was a believer in the perfectibility of mankind, supported Godwin's thesis but Robert demurred, principally on the ground that the tendency of population to increase faster than the means of subsistence was likely to lead to more rather than less poverty. The father encouraged the son to put his arguments on paper. This Robert did, and *An Essay on the Principle of Population* appeared anonymously in 1798.

Malthus's thesis was not new. Without going further back than the Renaissance, it had been stated in 1589 by Giovanni Botero in his book *Della ragione di Stato*; the idea that populations tended to increase in geometric progression was suggested by Petty in 1686; and that they would increase up to the limits set by the available means of subsistence was urged by many eighteenth-century writers, among them Mirabeau with his dictum, 'men will multiply to the limits of subsistence like rats in a barn'. But Malthus did not lean on these authorities; the *Essay* of 1798 was deductive, lively and short, and it created a sensation.

We all know how his reasoned plea against overpopulation was interpreted by his critics as an advocacy of misery and vice. Malthus rode the storm without being unduly upset; but, being Malthus, he felt the need to validate his opinions by more extensive reading and a wider knowledge of facts. The second edition, which appeared in 1803, was a very different book. It was about five times as long and contained a great deal of factual material collected in a tour through Scandinavia and part of Russia in 1799, and another through France and Switzerland during the short peace of 1802, when he had his famous conversation with his Swiss driver. His conclusion, that what he called 'moral restraint' was the only effective preventive to misery and vice, created another furore, being taken by many as an encouragement to contraception in spite of his express condemnation of the practice.

More top people were convinced by his arguments than were antagonized by them, however. Paley accepted them. Pitt was induced by them to scrap his intended legislation for the encouragement of large families; and the Poor Law of 1834 was to a large extent inspired by them. We know how the theory of the survival of the fittest was suggested to both Darwin and Wallace independently by a reading of the *Essay*. And may we not owe to it Quetelet's interest in population growth curves?

Economics being a less emotional subject than birth control and requiring more esoteric knowledge to be understood, Malthus's economic writings did not generate so much heat among the general public, although they did provoke much debate among his fellow economists. His most distinguished opponent was Ricardo. A remarkable feature of the controversy between Malthus and Ricardo is its total freedom from acrimony. On the contrary, a firm and long-lasting friendship was built on it.

Among the numerous points on which they disagreed, the most interesting to us now, because it was brought into prominence by Keynes's *General Theory*, is the role of consumption and accumulation as stimulants to demand and hence to employment. It was commonly held that, just as current outlays constitute a demand for consumption goods, saving constitutes automatically a demand for capital goods, so that a demand for commodities is always ensured no matter whether income is consumed or saved. Malthus argued that a decision to save is not the same as a decision to buy capital goods and that it is possible for a community to wish to save too much: since the main purpose of investment is to maintain and increase the supply of consumption goods, and since money saved is money withheld from the purchase of such goods, it follows that if saving is carried too far it will reduce the demand for consumption goods to the point where there will be no incentive for additional capital expenditure. Thus the equality of saving and investment may be brought about not by the investment of all the money people wish to save but by a reduction in the demand for consumption goods, which leads to unemployment, which reduces aggregate income, which in turn reduces aggregate saving to the level dictated by this depressed and depressing situation.

Ricardo was not persuaded. The two went hammer and tongs at each other on this and other questions from their first exchange of letters in 1811 until Ricardo's death in 1823. Curiously, the kind, even-tempered Malthus loved a good fight. When he was still at school his master, Robert Graves, reported to his father,

Don Roberto, though most peaceably inclined, and seeming even to give up his just rights, rather than to dispute with any man, yet, paradox as it may seem, loves fighting for fighting's sake and delights in bruising. . . . Yet he and his antagonist are soon the best friends in the world, learn together, assist each other, and I believe, love each other better than any two boys in the school.

And, throughout his friendship with Ricardo, Malthus seems to have sought every occasion for an exchange of intellectual blows. Both men did, for that matter: as often as not, their letters end by proposing a meeting at each other's house to continue the argument. Maria Edgeworth wrote of them, 'They hunted together in search of truth, and huzzaed when they found her, without caring who found her first.'

On this edifying picture I shall conclude. Let us raise our glasses to Malthus and the pursuit of truth.

Elegance and Experience:
Malthus at the Bar of History

E. A. Wrigley

It may be held that there is a tension in Malthus's writings between the types of insight gained by the construction of a simple deductive model of the functioning of society as an economic–demographic system on the one hand, and the painstaking assembling of heterogeneous empirical data on the other, especially as Malthus, though sometimes castigated for arguing deductively, showed a firm preference for factual evidence as the only safe basis for the establishment of knowledge. He valued elegance but gave pride of place to experience. Because he laid so much emphasis upon experience, as he termed it, or what might today be called empirical evidence, I have attempted in this essay to subject some of the fundamental assumptions he made in the first *Essay*, his postulata, to the test of modern historical knowledge of the behaviour of economic and demographic variables in England in the centuries immediately before he wrote. By his own criteria this is the most appropriate and searching test to be made. In the main Malthus stands the test well, though there are grounds for questioning some of the elements in his model which he believed to be sound: for example, the reality of declining marginal returns on the land, at least in the time scale of early modern history.

The opening passages of the first edition of the *Essay on the Principle of Population* suggest that Malthus's characteristic habit of mind in seeking to analyse society owed much to the principles of deductive logic. In a manner which appears directly to reflect his mathematical background, and using a terminology appropriate to it, he invites his readers to accept the truth of two postulata – 'that food is necessary to the existence of man'; and 'that the passion between the sexes is necessary, and will remain nearly in its present state' – and then proceeds to infer what must follow from the postulata and from certain associated assumptions (1798, p. 11). Among the latter the most important was the inability of societies to expand food supply at more than an arithmetic ratio in contrast to the tendency of population to rise at a geometric ratio unless checked. He refers to 'fixed laws of our nature' which, short of divine intervention, must always continue to operate in the same way (pp. 11–12). And in the penultimate sentence of the first chapter he asserts, 'Consequently, if the premises are just, the argument is conclusive against the perfectibility of the mass of mankind' (p. 17).

Some of the sharp hostility with which his writings have been greeted, both in his lifetime and since, was due to the belief that Malthus had attempted to develop an analytic system and a set of conclusions derived from it which were impervious to criticism if his assumptions, his postulata, were granted. Such an approach to the study of social behaviour may be regarded as improper both on methodological grounds and because, maddeningly, it appears to try to pre-empt much of the criticism which might otherwise find the mark against it.

Undoubtedly it is possible to read Malthus's opening chapter in the first *Essay* in this way, yet it would be entirely at variance with Malthus's thinking as a whole to take such a view of his epistemology. Indeed, both in his early controversy with Godwin and in his later exchanges with Ricardo, it is highly characteristic of Malthus to place an appeal to empirical evidence higher than any other authority in determining an issue. So much is this the case that, to appreciate the strengths and weaknesses of his demographic and economic work, there is no better starting-point than to examine his understanding of the empirical complexities of the world in which he lived and of its development over the preceding two or three centuries.

Even at the beginning of the first *Essay*, in the last sentence of the first chapter, Malthus qualified the view expressed in the penultimate sentence quoted above, when he referred to 'experience, the true source and foundation of all knowledge' (p. 17). The same attitude of mind was to be echoed repeatedly. For example, later in the first *Essay*, in the course of seeking to dispose of Godwin's conjectures about the possibility of man attaining immortality on earth, he wrote,

I expect that great discoveries are yet to take place in all the branches of human science, particularly in physics; but the moment we leave past experience as the foundation of our conjectures concerning the future; and still more, if our conjectures absolutely contradict past experience, we are thrown upon a wide field of uncertainty, and any one supposition is then just as good as another. (p. 232)

More than twenty years later, in the introductory sections of the *Principles*, he set out clearly and firmly his reservations about sweeping assertions and his preference for discussions which remained closely grounded in the empirical. Of contemporary economic writings he wrote, 'The principal cause of error . . . appears to me to be a precipitate attempt to simplify and generalize' (1820, pp. 5–6). And, again,

The same tendency to simplify and generalize, produces a still greater disinclination to allow of modifications, limitations and exceptions to any rule or proposition, than to admit the operation of more causes than one. . . . yet there is no truth of which I feel a stronger conviction than that there are many important propositions in political economy which absolutely require limitations and exceptions. (pp. 7–8)

Malthus, therefore, was more predisposed to be eclectic in the range of arguments he would employ to elucidate a problem than many social scientists of his own day or since; more insistent upon constant reference to the empirical to test any theoretical formulation; and more apt to accept that even the most successful formulation would fail to 'save the phenomena' in many cases. To use modern jargon, he was happy to build conceptual models but vividly aware of their limitations and with no expectation that they would prove universally applicable. Since both then and later this attitude ran counter to the expectations and assumptions of many of his readers, he has suffered no less from the impatience of those out of sympathy with the complex, tentative and conditional nature of much of his analysis than from the condemnations of those outraged by what they saw as the starkness of his postulata and the simplistic inferences deduced from them.

In view of the importance he attributed to what he termed 'experience', it may be of interest to compare his view of the workings of the socio-economic system in which he lived, his model of reality, with the findings of recent research into the same range of topics. Malthus regarded 'experience' as the touchstone for judging theoretical schemes and the safest basis for any discussion of the future. He was greatly interested in the dynamics of social systems, in characteristic paths of change, in cyclical phenomena, and in what would today be called feedback mechanisms. How well had he understood the English economy and demography of his day and their recent evolution?

It is convenient to begin with his two basic postulata. Both might be described as biological rather than sociological or historical in character. Malthus hoped that they would be recognized as invariant features of all societies. In this he may have been too sanguine, at least in regard to the second of the two, since patterns of sexual behaviour vary substantially between different societies, though not perhaps in ways that would seriously affect the arguments he advanced.[1] However, Malthus annexed to his postulata certain associated assumptions which he clearly believed also to be essentially outside the realm of the uncertain and contingent. About these there is more room for argument. Consulting the historical record is illuminating in this regard since it helps to establish the extent of the applicability of Malthusiasn concepts.

Malthus supposed that the assertion that the production of food could not be expanded at more than an arithmetic ratio at best was as unobjectionable as the assertion that man must eat to live. Like the latter it was underpinned by a simple physical fact. The area of land available to be occupied is limited and cannot be greatly expanded once initial settlement is complete. In all societies the best land is taken into cultivation first. As time passes and population grows, less suitable land is taken in. Inevitably, *ceteris paribus*, the return obtained from any unit input of labour or of capital must fall and the quantity of labour or capital needed to produce a unit output of food must rise. At some stage any further extension of the bounds of cultivation or intensification of the use of land already in cultivation must cease to offer a return sufficient to induce additional applications of labour or capital. The

---

[1]Malthus may have been provoked into phrasing his second postulate so firmly by the fact that Godwin had supposed it reasonable to assume that with the advance of civilization sexual passion would progressively decline in vehemence.

expansion of food production then ceases.[2] The notion of a continuous arithmetic gain as an upper limit to growth does not have the same logical or empirical status as the parallel assertion about the capacity of population to rise by geometric progression. By it he intended chiefly to drive home the nature of the contrast in the powers of progression inherent in the two series, though it may also have been a convenient device for acknowledging the possibility of technical advances in agriculture which might successively postpone the arrival of the time when additional inputs of labour and capital would cease to occur and food output would cease to rise.

In making reference to an arithmetic ratio of increase in food production Malthus struck an individual note, but in his general insistence on the central significance of declining marginal returns to unit inputs of labour and capital in agriculture he was conforming to a prevailing opinion. Ricardo shared the same conviction. Both men saw this as the unhappy feature of the economic system that consigned the poor to poverty. Both recognized that many forms of manufacturing were capable of achieving increasing marginal returns but considered that any such effect was sure to be swamped in the long term by the opposite tendency in agriculture. Exponential growth in aggregate output was beyond reach in the long term: an asymptotic growth path might well be the best which could be hoped for. The real wages of the labouring mass of the population were most unlikely to rise in the long run and only too vulnerable to pressures tending to reduce them towards or below some conventional minimum.[3]

---

[2]As Malthus himself put it, after having described the opportunities for both high profits and high wages in lands of new settlement, 'But the accumulation of capital beyond the means of employing it on the land of the greatest natural fertility, and the most advantageously situated, must necessarily lower profits; while the tendency of population to increase beyond the means of subsistence must, after a certain time, lower the wages of labour'; and, a little later, 'In the natural and regular progress of a country towards the accumulation of stock and the increase of population, the rate of profits and the real wages of labour permanently fall together' (1820, pp. 150–1, 162). It is of interest to note that in the second edition of the *Principles* (1836), the last sentence begins, 'In the natural and regular progress of a country towards its full complement of capital and population . . .' (p. 158). This rephrasing indicates how strongly Malthus held firm to the view that there must be limits to economic growth. His views on this issue were given their most complete expression in his classic pamphlet on rent (1815).

[3]Malthus included an extensive examination of the course of corn wages in the *Principles* (1820). It occupied two sections of ch. 4, 'Of the wages of labour' (pp. 267–92).

Ricardo's views on the issues referred to in this paragraph are of great interest and expressed with his customary clarity. 'The natural price of labour is that price which is necessary to enable the labourers, one with another, to subsist and to perpetuate their race without either increase or diminution.' 'It is when the market price of labour exceeds its natural price, that the condition of the labourer is flourishing and happy, that he has it in his power to command a greater proportion of the necessaries and enjoyments of life, and therefore to rear a healthy and numerous family.' When the market price of labour is below its natural price, privation has the opposite effect. In the course of time 'The natural tendency of profits . . . is to fall; for, in the progress of society and wealth, the additional quantity of food required is obtained by the sacrifice of more and more labour', and eventually 'no capital can then yield any profit whatever, and no additional labour can be demanded'. Again, 'There are few commodities which are not more or less affected in their price by the rise of raw produce, because some raw material from the land enters into the composition of most commodities. Cotton goods, linen, and cloth, will all rise in price with the rise of wheat; but they rise on account of the greater quantity of labour expended on the raw material from which they are made, and not because more was paid by the manufacturer to the labourers whom he employed on those commodities' (1951, pp. 93–4, 117–18, 120).

The strength of the general logic concerning declining marginal returns needs no emphasis. It was taken very seriously by economists of the classical period and by most well-informed contemporaries, not simply because of the crucial importance of agriculture within the general economy and of the price of food within the family budgets of the vast majority of households, but because the raw materials of industry were principally vegetable or animal also. The woollen, cotton, linen and silk industries together with all those that were leather-based; brewing and spirit-making; ship construction, cooper's wares, furniture and a host of wood-based industries: these together employed a very large fraction of the non-agricultural labour force. Furthermore, wood remained one of the principal raw materials of the building-industry. Only slowly were industries emerging freed from dependence upon animal or vegetable raw materials, and they employed a limited labour force. Inland transport remained largely horse-based and was also dependent on the agricultural surplus.[4] Malthus and Ricardo therefore naturally supposed that the same pressures on the land which must tend to reduce the productivity of labour and capital would cause the price of most raw materials needed by industry to rise. This was one of the chief immediate reasons why even rising productivity per man engaged in industrial production and hence falling labour costs per unit of output would not necessarily cheapen industrial goods (Malthus 1820, pp. 184–6).

Was the strength of the logic of declining marginal returns in agriculture supported by what Malthus termed 'experience'? In the twentieth century, of course, the evidence is decidedly against the classical economists. Technical change has so massively increased productivity on the land in advanced economies that far more is heard of the problems of disposing of unwanted agricultural surpluses than of food shortage, even though the labour force engaged in agriculture represents only a trivial percentage of the employed population.[5] But were the classical economists right in their own time? Was Malthus's confidence in appealing to the bar of experience justified in this instance? Recently some new evidence has become available bearing on this issue which invites a reconsideration of the matter.

It is pertinent to remark initially that early nineteenth-century England represents a particularly interesting test of the general case. In no other European country for which moderately reliable population estimates exist, with the possible exception of Ireland, had the growth of population been so rapid over the previous three centuries. Between 1550 and 1820, for example, the population of England almost quadrupled while that of the rest of Western Europe rose by only about 80 per cent (Wrigley 1983, p. 122). Even

[4]Malthus noted that, 'it should always be recollected, that land does not produce one commodity alone, but, in addition to that most indispensable of all commodities – food, it produces the materials for clothing, lodging, and firing' (1820, pp. 141–2). On the question of the significance of the distinction between organic and inorganic raw materials, see Wrigley (1962).

[5]In June 1983 there were 11,982,000 males in employment in the United Kingdom. The number of males in agriculture was 240,000 or 2 per cent. The comparable percentage for males and females combined was 1.5 per cent. Yet the country covered the great bulk of its needs in temperate food products. Indeed in some products, notably cereals, exports exceeded imports (*Monthly Digest*, 1984, tables 3.2 and 3.7, pp. 18 and 23).

in 1820 England was largely self-sufficient in food, and therefore, on the assumption that the scale of food consumption per head had not greatly varied, it is clear that agricultural output must have increased four-fold.[6] Throughout the period 1550–1800 there was a strikingly close connection between the secular trend in the rate of population growth and that in the rate of change in the price of a basket of consumables consisting principally of food. When population growth rates rose, there was a parallel and somewhat more pronounced rise in food prices; when they moderated, prices responded immediately; when they were negative, as was the case in much of the later seventeenth century, food prices fell (Wrigley and Schofield 1981, pp. 402–7). There can be no doubt that food-price trends were closely related to population growth rates, but, on the other hand, the relationship did not change over time in spite of the very marked long-term rise in population. Had the effect of declining marginal returns been marked, it would be reasonable to expect the impact of the high population growth rates of the later eighteenth century to be more pronounced than those of the later sixteenth century, since the absolute population total was so much higher at the later date. It would also be reasonable to look for evidence of greater stress in England, striving to cope with comparatively rapid population growth, than on the mainland of Western Europe, where population growth was far less rapid. Yet, if anything, food prices appear to have been under less pressure about 1800 than about 1600, and England was clearly less vulnerable to poor harvests, less close to the edge of the precipice, than any other West European country, with the exception of the Netherlands (Wrigley and Schofield 1981, pp. 320–36 and 368–84).

Another consideration, however, counts even more heavily against the view that the English situation was dominated by declining marginal returns in agriculture. Not only was the volume of food output several times larger in, say, 1800 than in 1500, but the proportion of the labour force engaged in agriculture was far lower. Output per head in agriculture probably roughly doubled between the late sixteenth and the late eighteenth century. Progress in this respect was so notable that it is likely that the labour force engaged in agriculture was only about a quarter larger in 1800 than in 1600, though the population of the country had more than doubled over the period (Wrigley 1985). The same pattern continued throughout the first half of the nineteenth century. The agricultural labour force expanded somewhat down to 1831 but little if at all thereafter, though the volume of food produced continued to rise substantially (Wrigley forthcoming). Pressure on food supplies, indeed, eased so considerably that, after about 1800, although population growth rates were rising to an unprecedented peak, the age-old connection between population growth rates and food-price trends disappeared completely. The price of food, influenced both by agricultural improvements at home and by

---

[6]It seems safe to assume that the increase in agricultural output was greater than the increase in the output of food alone, in view of the importance of the land as a source of raw materials for industry and of the large number of horses employed outside agriculture.

the increase in food imports, stabilized in spite of the huge rise in the number of mouths to be fed.[7]

It would, of course, be doing an injustice to Malthus or Ricardo to suppose that they assumed that the worst problems of declining marginal returns were already apparent. The condition was not immediately observable; it was rather an inescapable constraint upon indefinite expansion which must at some stage produce malign results for both labour and capital. It is also true that there was every reason for lively concern about the future at the time when Malthus wrote the first *Essay*. In 1798, had he been able to consult the price and population data now available, he would have found no sign of decay in the close positive relationship between population growth rates and price trends. For half a century the former had been slowly accelerating and prices had followed suit (Wrigley and Schofield 1981, fig. 10.4, p. 410). Experience certainly provided grounds for alarm and pessimism about the future. There was no hint of the abrupt and historic disappearance in the link between the two, now so readily visible with the benefit of hindsight.

Nevertheless some of the information at Malthus's disposal might well have given him pause in asserting the universal application and strength of the argument to do with the arithmetic ratio, which was so closely linked in turn to the concept of declining marginal returns. In the *Principles*, for example, he noted that in England 'there is a smaller proportion of the people employed in agriculture, and a greater proportion employed in the production of conveniences and luxuries, or living on monied incomes, than in any other agricultural country of the world'. He noted that Süssmilch had asserted that 3 in 10 was the highest proportion anywhere 'who live in towns, and are not employed in agriculture', but that in England non-agricultural employment stood to agricultural as 3:2, and he added in a footnote that 'in foreign states very few persons live in the country who are not engaged in agriculture; but it is not so in England' (1820, pp. 380–1). In common with Adam Smith he had no doubt of the extent of economic growth since the medieval period but, again like Smith, he severely distrusted its long continuance.

Even if Malthus had been more impressed with the weight of the evidence against the supposition that declining marginal returns were a dominant influence on agricultural development in England, however, he might not have felt it necessary to do more than modify slightly the development of his general model of the interlinkage between demographic and economic phenomena, for it was not so much the nature of either of his two postulata taken separately as their joint effect which gave such force to his arguments. As long as the tendency of population to grow in geometric ratio unless constrained holds true, and unless it is demonstrable that food production

[7]For a review of the evidence about the scale of food imports, and the importance of Ireland as a source of both grain and meat, see Thomas (1983). The Phelps-Brown and Hopkins index of the price of a composite unit of consumables consisting principally of food and drink shows the following average annual values for the years in the successive decades 1800–9 to 1840–9: 1474, 1601, 1221, 1146 and 1136, or, re-expressed so that the figure for 1800–9 is 100, the values are 100, 109, 83, 78, 77 (Phelps–Brown and Hopkins 1962, p. 196).

can be expanded in a geometric ratio at least as high as the maximum attainable by a population, there must still be a tension between numbers of people and the resources available to sustain them. This will cause most people to live in comparative penury and rob them of any realistic hope for a permanent improvement in their lot.

On the empirical justification for his views under this head Malthus was especially firm. In 1820, after many years of research and reflection, he wrote, 'I should never have had that steady and unshaken confidence in the theory of population which I have invariably felt, if it had not appeared to me to be confirmed, in the most remarkable manner, by the state of society as it actually exists in every country with which we are acquainted' (p. 11). Experience, he believed, fully supported his initial assumption.

With the second postulate, as with the first, if there is a difficulty it lies less with the postulate itself than with the assumptions which Malthus made in parallel with it. If the passion between the sexes might be taken as a constant, Malthus thought it safe to assume that population would display a tendency to grow exponentially. In his first statement of the case, and in the flush of exuberant youth, he emphasized the near-identity of human and all other forms of life in this respect. 'Through the animal and vegetable kingdoms', he wrote,

nature has scattered the seeds of life abroad with the most profuse and liberal hand. She has been comparatively sparing in the room, and nourishment necessary to rear them. The germs of existence contained in this spot of earth, with ample food, and ample room to expand in, would fill millions of worlds in the course of a few thousand years. Necessity, that imperious, all pervading law of nature, restrains them within the prescribed bounds. The race of plants, and the race of animals shrink under this great restrictive law. And the race of man cannot, by any efforts of reason, escape from it. Among plants and animals its effects are waste of seed, sickness, and premature death. Among mankind, misery and vice. (1798, pp. 14–15)

Later his treatment of the issue was very much refined from his initial formulation, but he never abandoned one of the inferences which flows directly from this postulate. Any increase in the supply of food, disregarding the random fluctuations imposed by the fortunes of the harvest, must produce a proportionate increase in the population. Once more, Malthus was not at all unusual in holding to this belief. Both Adam Smith and Ricardo held the same view and drew the same gloomy inferences from it concerning its implications for the level of real wages.[8] For Malthus the finding was especially important since an increase in the production of food, unlike an increase in the production of any other commodity, ran little or no risk

[8]Adam Smith was particularly forthright on this point. 'Every species of animals naturally multiplies in proportion to the means of their subsistence, and no species can ever multiply beyond it. But in civilised society it is only among the inferior ranks of people that the scantiness of subsistence can set limits to the further multiplication of the human species; and it can do so in no other way than by destroying a great part of the children which their fruitful marriages produce. The liberal reward of labour, by enabling them to provide better for their children, and consequently to bring up a greater number, naturally tends to widen and extend those limits. It deserves to be remarked, too, that it necessarily does this as nearly as possible in the proportion which the demand for labour requires' (1863, p. 36).

of facing inadequate demand, or, as he put it, it was 'a quality peculiar to the necessaries of life of being able, when properly distributed, to create their own demand, or to raise up a number of demanders in proportion to the quantity of necessaries produced' (1820, pp. 139–40).

As in the case of the first postulate, subsequent experience has completely undercut the validity of Malthus's assumptions. From the later nineteenth century onwards, and especially since the Second World War, the connection between the exercise of the passion between the sexes and the scale of procreation has been severed by the practice of contraception. But this was a development far in the future in his day, and, though he had strong objection to the use of contraception in virtue of his position as an Anglican clergyman, he had no need to dwell upon the issue since the practice was so little current at the time. What then of the empirical validity of his second postulate and the inferences which he drew from it? Did 'experience' support him?

The evidence which most strongly impressed Malthus in favour of the view that population would grow rapidly and at a constant rate unless checked by the consequences of a fixed supply of land lay in the history of the North American colonies and the young United States. There for four or five generations the intrinsic growth rate had been sufficiently high to ensure a doubling of population every quarter century, quite apart from the effects of immigration. In race and culture Americans were little different from the stocks from which they sprang, yet intrinsic growth rates in England and other lands of emigration were far lower.[9] The contrast must mean that fertility was higher in the lands of new settlement, or that mortality was lower, or that both differences existed. By comparison evidence from other parts of the world, or about fluctuating growth rates in the past in England, was less clear-cut and unambiguous, but none, in Malthus's view, appeared to contradict expectation.

The historical evidence available to test Malthus's second postulate and the inferences linked to it appears to present fewer difficulties to his position than in the case of the first postulate, especially when the subtlety with which Malthus developed his argument is fully taken into account. In his very first exposition of the case, quoted at length earlier, the passage in which the operation of the geometrical ratio of untrammelled population growth is held to condemn mankind to misery and vice, Malthus struck a somewhat apocalyptic note. But his later discussion of the same central point is calm, delicate, balanced, and distinguished by a remarkably successful blend of what might today be termed sociological, demographic, economic and historical insight. His initial formulation suggests a rather mechanical relationship between food supply and population totals. Later, even within the first *Essay*,

---

[9]The argument, which Malthus based on the evidence of a high intrinsic growth rate in North America, greatly troubled Godwin. As his exchanges with Malthus developed, he appears to have regarded it as peculiarly damaging to his viewpoint if true, and he was consequently at great pains to try to demonstrate that the high rate of growth in North America was due to immigration. He returned obsessively to the issue throughout *Of Population* (1820). Four years later Malthus furnished a crushing rejoinder in his *Encyclopaedia Britannica* article (1824). There he included a sophisticated analysis of the age data in the early censuses of the United States, an exercise the accuracy of which has recently been endorsed by Ansley Coale (1979).

and still more in his subsequent writings, Malthus achieved great sophistication in his discussion of the question.

Among the more important ways in which he modified and developed the first stark statement are the following. First, the distinction between the positive and the preventive check was given greater prominence, and Malthus came to view the latter as the dominant regulator of population growth rates in Western Europe. If the passion between the sexes is solely or chiefly exercised within marriage, then human societies are immediately in a different position from animal or plant communities, and may also differ among themselves. True, in societies where marriage for women universally occurs at or close to menarche, the institution of marriage, though of profound importance in other respects, may have only a limited effect in moderating fertility. But, where marriage is economically and socially regulated rather than governed by a biological trigger, and where therefore women may marry late and many may never marry, marriage, the preventive check, may not merely cause lower general fertility than where early and universal marriage prevails, but enable the level of fertility to adjust to the opportunities of the time.[10]

Malthus was the first social scientist to explore this question and to see its immense significance in distinguishing the countries of Western Europe in the early modern period from other major cultural areas and from the great civilizations of the past. It does not necessarily infringe upon his second postulate but it permits the maximum level of population which may theoretically be associated with a given food base to range within a wide band rather than being fixed close to a single point. It is easy to show that both a lower general level of fertility and a sensitivity on the part of fertility to a worsening economic situation, associated with the West European marriage system, may cause population growth to cease at a lower level than would be attained with high and invariant fertility (Hajnal 1965, Anderson 1980). Intimately linked to this consideration, there is a second point. In common with his predecessor Adam Smith, Malthus was well aware that the minimum standard of living tolerated by the labouring poor may be, and in England then was, well removed from the biological minimum needed to support life. The English labourer would not submit to conditions which were accepted without question in China. Cultural, rather than biological, standards might prevail both in determining the scale and pace of population growth and the cost of reproducing labour.[11]

---

[10]Even in the first *Essay*, and *a fortiori* in his later writings, Malthus laid stress on the effectiveness of the preventive check at all levels in English society (1798, pp. 62–70). There is an excellent survey of the feedback mechanisms which may serve to keep population and production in balance through a responsive system of nuptiality in the West European style in Schofield (1976).

[11]'In some countries', Malthus remarked, 'population appears to have been forced; that is, the people have been habituated by degrees to live upon almost the smallest possible quantity of food. . . . China seems to answer this description. If the accounts we have of it are to be trusted, the lower classes of people are in the habit of living almost upon the smallest possible quantity of food, and are glad to get any putrid offals that European labourers would rather starve than eat' (1798, p. 130). In this he was echoing a passage in *The Wealth of Nations*, in which Adam Smith wrote, 'The poverty of the lower ranks of people in China far surpasses that of the most beggarly

Malthus was also well attuned to the importance of cultural and political structures in influencing population size and growth in other respects. For example, his first, brash formulation of his second postulate in the opening chapter of the first *Essay* might seem to imply that the natural endowment of a country was what chiefly governed its carrying capacity. This would be, of course, a travesty of his views as he went on to develop them. Like Adam Smith, he was strongly conscious that the capacity of a country to achieve economic growth depended as much or more upon its political institutions and legal system as upon its soil, mineral wealth or climate. He knew well that the sociology and psychology of a community might set low limits to its economic potential. For example, his discussion of leisure preference illustrates the point admirably. In the course of examining the way in which gains in agricultural productivity per head might be translated into a release of labour into the production of 'conveniences and luxuries', he wrote, 'But if, after the necessaries of life were obtained, the workman should consider indolence as a greater luxury than those which he was likely to procure by further labour, the proposition would at once cease to be true' (1820, p. 379). The jargon of satisficer strategies and backward-sloping supply curves for labour is absent from the work of economists at this period but such notions were well understood. Elsewhere he wrote,

That an efficient taste for luxuries, that is such a taste as will properly stimulate industry, instead of being ready to appear at the moment it is required, is a plant of slow growth, the history of human society sufficiently shows; and that it is a most important error to take for granted, that mankind will produce and consume all that they have the power to produce and consume, and will never prefer indolence to the rewards of industry, will sufficiently appear from a slight review of some of the nations with which we are acquainted. (1820, p. 359)

Armed with a battery of concepts which lent flexibility to the application of the principle of the geometric ratio, Malthus was well equipped to apply the test of experience to his second postulate. As we have seen, he considered his 'law of population' stood the test well. In recent decades there has been a huge enlargement of the quantity of historical population data and a notable improvement in its quality, so that, as with the first postulate, a reassessment of the validity of his view is possible.

---

nations in Europe. . . . The subsistence which they find . . . is so scanty that they are eager to fish up the nastiest garbage thrown overboard from any European ship. Any carrion, the carcase of a dead dog or cat, for example, half putrid and stinking, is as welcome to them as the most wholesome food to the people of other countries' (1863, pp. 32–3).

Malthus's views on the causes of the variable level of conventional minimum standards of living in different countries may be found in the *Principles* (1820, pp. 248–52). Ricardo expressed the same point cogently. 'It is not to be understood that the natural price of labour, estimated even in food and necessaries, is absolutely fixed and constant. . . . It essentially depends on the habits and customs of the people. An English labourer would consider his wages under their natural rate, and too scanty to support a family, if they enabled him to purchase no other food than potatoes. . . . Many of the conveniences now enjoyed in an English cottage, would have been thought luxurious at an earlier period of our history' (1951, pp. 96–7).

It must be said immediately that an unambiguous conclusion is out of reach. One of the most admirable and, to the historian, gratifying features of Malthus's writings is his keen consciousness of the existence of many different time scales in the progression of historical events. This feature of his thought was early apparent. Already in the second chapter of the first *Essay*, in describing what he termed the 'oscillations' in the welfare of the labouring classes brought about by the homeostatic relationships between the rate of population growth, the trends in real wages, and changes in the level of investment, he showed an awareness of the fact that such relationships worked in a complex fashion and with substantial time lags between changes in the variables in the course of a typical cycle. He wrote,

This sort of oscillation will not be remarked by superficial observers; and it may be difficult even for the most penetrating mind to calculate its periods. Yet that in all old states some such vibration does exist; though from various transverse causes, in a much less marked, and in a much more irregular manner than I have described it, no reflecting man who considers the subject deeply can well doubt. (1798, pp. 31–2)

Malthus was well attuned to the *longue durée* and would have insisted on the vacuousness of analyses confined to contemporaneous events.

However, this makes for great difficulty in assessing evidence concerning population growth rates and their response to changes in the food base. Malthus's argument is about an inevitable tendency towards a position of tension between numbers and resources brought about by the contrast between the powers of arithmetic and geometric ratios to increase any pair of initial quantities. At any given point in time, however, the tension may be latent, temporarily swamped by the play of contingent events, but sure to emerge eventually, though perhaps over centuries rather than decades, or even millennia rather than centuries.

Perhaps the best available test is to review the evidence about the relationship between changes in real wages and population growth rates over as long a continuous period of time as possible. The tension produced by the different attributes of the two ratios found its most serious expression, so far as human welfare was concerned, in the impossibility of real wages rising, other than temporarily, from the minimum level set by the prevailing conventions of the society in question. This was the inference which gave the *Essay* its polemical status and often overshadowed the question of its scientific merit.

On the whole Malthus's views meet with success when put to the test of the experience of England over the preceding 250 years. Changes in the rates of growth of population and of adult male real wages can be plotted over the period from the mid sixteenth century with some confidence, though the latter with less confidence than the former. They reveal both that there was no long-term tendency for real wages either to rise or to fall, and that the rates of change in the two variables were closely and negatively related. In periods when the population was growing rapidly, real wages fell. When population was stationary or falling, real wages rose. The data convey a strong hint that there was sufficient underlying growth in the economy to produce modestly rising real wages with a stationary population, or, consonant with this, that a low rate of population growth, perhaps between 0.25 and 0.5 per cent per annum, could be sustained without provoking a fall in real wages (Wrigley and Schofield 1981, pp. 407–12). Since, however, real wages in 1800 were no higher than they had been in the early sixteenth century, it was open to Malthus to argue that the observed pattern of relationships conformed excellently with his model.[12] The population was reacting to an enlargement in the flow of goods and services produced by increasing its size rather than by securing higher standards of living. The mechanism by which this was secured was predominantly the preventive check in the case of England, but the overall pattern followed expectation (Wrigley and Schofield 1981, chs 10 and 11).

Two other points should be noted. First, even over a period as long as a quarter of a millennium there was time for only just over one full cycle in the real-wage–population-growth relationship. Some of the 'oscillations' to which Malthus referred were indeed likely to be hard to remark by his 'superficial observer'. Testing his model adequately clearly makes severe demands upon historical data series if error is to be avoided. Second, the close link between real wages and population growth rates broke down conclusively just at the time the first Essay was written. For almost the whole of the succeeding two centuries rising real wages and a relatively high rate of population growth went hand in hand. It would be making an unreasonable demand upon anyone's percipience, even a man as sensitive as Malthus, to expect him to have detected the change in the course of the balance of his active life. For reasons which he himself explained so clearly, such changes may be impossible to detect with confidence except ex post facto, and the cycle length of some of the relevant variables was such as to make detection impossible. He was conscious that fundamental change might be in train but did not see any evidence strong enough to warrant abandoning his model.[13]

At present the fairly detailed data available for England from the mid sixteenth century onwards are the only such data. Less detailed data have, however, been assembled for the Netherlands over much the same time span as the English data. In the Dutch case the real-wage data are probably of a quality equal or superior to the English, but the population estimates are very widely spaced in time and more conjectural (De Vries 1985).

Nevertheless the Dutch series are most valuable in that they provide a counter-case while at the same time illustrating the great difficulties involved in testing the Malthusian postulates. The pattern of relationship between real-wage changes and population growth observable in the Netherlands in

[12]In his survey of corn wages in England since the fourteenth century, he found no evidence of a rise or fall over the period as a whole, though very substantial variations sometimes extending over many decades (see note 3 above).

[13]In 1820 he remarked, 'The last twenty or thirty years have besides been marked by a train of events of a most extraordinary kind; and there has hardly yet been time so to arrange and examine them as to see to what extent they confirm or invalidate the received principles of the science to which they relate' (p. 5). He did not, however, elaborate on what he had in mind: he may have meant no more than reference to the war period and its aftermath.

the sixteenth, seventeenth and eighteenth centuries is not consistent with Malthus's model. During most of the seventeenth century population grew rapidly but real wages also advanced strongly, whereas in the eighteenth century, when, exceptionally for the period, there was no population growth, real wages were falling. However, as de Vries stresses, throughout the early modern period the Netherlands was an open economy and met much of its food requirement from import. Therefore, the evidence of the Netherlands is inconclusive. It was neither constrained in the way a more closed economy might have been by pressure on the land as population rose, nor able to escape the effect of rising food prices elsewhere, even though the local demand for food was stagnant.

The available evidence, therefore, scarcely permits Malthus's second postulate to be tested adequately. Whereas the substantial evidence that can be found *against* the validity of his first postulate constitutes a good ground for questioning the universal applicability of the law of diminishing returns to agriculture in long-settled countries, a single case *supporting* the second postulate and another of limited relevance represent a very flimsy basis on which to judge it.

The appeal to experience is therefore inconclusive but nevertheless instructive. There is reason to think that Malthus tended to make too much of the severity of the constraint produced by declining marginal returns in agriculture. As an ultimate bar to growth its influence may have been great in any pre-industrial economy, and in some cases it may have begun to affect economies at an early stage, but the fact that England, a country of ancient settlement, after several centuries of rapid population growth, had greatly reduced the proportion of her labour force in agriculture while remaining largely self-sufficient in food suggests that the range of possibilities remained very wide. Malthus himself drew attention to the fact that about 60 per cent of those at work were not engaged in agriculture, thus demonstrating that a comparatively high level of output per man could be attained even though a high proportion of the potentially cultivable land surface was already in use (1820, pp. 380–1).

On the other hand, the evidence available to Malthus may well be held to justify the views he expressed so forcefully about the tendency of population to increase commensurately with economic opportunity and so to frustrate all possibility of a substantial rise in the living-standards of the mass of the population. The contrast between the powers of production and reproduction must figure prominently in any analysis of the social and economic history of traditional societies.[14]

Since the near-inevitability of poverty was an aspect of Malthus's thinking which attracted much opprobrium to him, and since his views on this subject and on the Poor Laws were so closely linked to his main postulata, it is appropriate to consider it explicitly in this context. The distribution of

---

[14] It is one of the most striking ironies of intellectual history that Malthus should have fashioned his analysis just at the time when it was about to cease to be applicable to the country in which he lived, because of the advent of the changes later generations have learned to call the industrial revolution.

income within society as well as the scale of national wealth and production was a central issue for the economists of the classical period. Malthus, characteristically, not only covered the same main issues as his contemporaries but extended the scope of the debate and increased its complexity by laying emphasis on the importance of transfer payments as an element affecting the well-being of a large fraction of the English population because of the operation of the Poor Laws (R. M. Smith, this volume). The implications of his model of economic–demographic dynamics caused him to dismiss many solutions or palliatives which appealed to others. His consciousness of a time dimension affecting the long-term viability of every scheme and his wish to take account of the secular as well as the short-term, made his sceptical where others were enthusiasts. But he bowed to no one in his desire to find a means to help the poor which should not induce them to behave in ways which must result in their last state being worse than their first.

Malthus devoted a chapter towards the end of the later editions of the *Essay* to this question. It was entitled 'Of the only effectual mode of improving the condition of the poor'. It is quite short, as might be expected from the nature of his analysis of the causes of poverty elsewhere in the work. His conclusion is worth quoting at some length:

In an endeavour to raise the proportion of the quantity of provisions to the number of consumers in any country, our attention would naturally be first directed to the increasing of the absolute quantity of provisions; but finding that, as fast as we did this, the number of consumers more than kept pace with it, and that with all our exertions we were still as far as ever behind, we should be convinced that our efforts directed only in this way would never succeed. It would appear to be setting the tortoise to catch the hare. Finding, therefore, that from the laws of nature we could not proportion food to the population, our next attempt should naturally be to proportion the population to the food. If we can persuade the hare to go to sleep, the tortoise may have some chance of overtaking her. (1826, pp. 290–1)

Malthus then goes on to express a conviction that such an ambition is not beyond reach.

We are not, however, to relax our efforts in increasing the quantity of provisions, but to combine another effort with it; that of keeping the population, when once it has been overtaken, at such a distance behind as to effect the relative proportion which we desire. . . . we must explain to them [the poor] the true nature of their situation, and show them that the withholding of the supplies of labour is the only possible way of really raising its price, and that they themselves, being the possessors of this commodity, have alone the power to do this. I cannot but consider this mode of diminishing poverty as so perfectly clear in theory, and so invariably confirmed by the analogy of every other commodity which is brought to market, that nothing but its being shown to be calculated to produce greater evils than it proposes to remedy can justify us in not making the attempt to put it into execution. (p. 291)

The fact that he held these views was the principal reason why Malthus so firmly advocated the extension of education throughout society, since it was more likely than any other measure to be effectual in persuading a steadily rising proportion of each new generation of young men and women to exercise discretion in deciding when to marry.

In the event, however, poverty was cured in quite another way, which it would have seemed utopian to Malthus to have foreshadowed. The hare did not fall asleep, but the tortoise went against nature by developing a formidable sprinting-power which proved capable of being long sustained. Poverty relaxed its hold over the bulk of the population not because of a sudden exemplary prudence in the contracting of marriage, but because the output of goods and services began to rise more rapidly.[15] The food bottleneck was partly alleviated by the continued rise in domestic output and partly by securing far larger quantities of food from abroad. The contrast between arithmetic and geometric progressions became a concern of the schoolroom rather than of the political economist or the House of Commons. Population could grow geometrically and in fact continued to do so for half a century after Malthus's death, but the economy now also grew in the same manner and at a higher pace. The apparently unattainable goal of achieving both rapid population growth and rising real incomes per head became a commonplace achievement of industrializing countries.

Such developments were not observable as matters of fact by the classical economists, from the accident of the timing of their births. Half a century later, in Marx's day, the question had changed. It was now plain that production could be expanded rapidly and continuously, save for the oscillations produced by the trade cycle, but it was not clear in, say, 1860 whether all would benefit proportionately from these new powers of production or whether the benefits would be confined to those who owned the means of production. History was to prove to Marx, as it had to Malthus, how hazardous attempts to prefigure the future usually prove to be.

Yet Malthus's formulation of the reasons for pessimism suggest clearly what is crucial to any explanation of the transformation of the traditional into the industrialized world. To choose to present the problem in terms of arithmetic and geometric ratios is debatable, but to stress the existence of a tension between the powers of production and reproduction in traditional societies was a just and important insight. Any society whose economic capacity was to be measured principally by the flow of production from its fields, pastures and forests was almost certain to be constrained in greater or less degree in the manner he described. Even though the problems associated with declining marginal returns may have afflicted the English economy less severely than Malthus supposed, finding an alternative resource base for a widening range of industries, substituting mineral for animal and vegetable raw materials, was one of the crucial changes of the industrial revolution. Similarly, if gains in output per head were to be both geometric and sustained at a level higher than prevailing rates of population growth, it is difficult not to regard the substitution of inanimate for animate sources of energy as a *sine qua non*. These could magnify immensely the productive capacity of the individual man or woman, in a way beyond attainment when using conventional sources of power. Because they showed so clearly why a sustained rise in real income

---

[15]The relationship between economic circumstances and nuptiality does not appear to have changed greatly in nature until the period of rapid fall in marital fertility after about 1870 (Wrigley and Schofield 1981, pp. 417–38).

for the labouring poor was so hard to achieve, Malthus's writings can help greatly in identifying the strategic features of the new age which were ultimately to alleviate their condition.

One way of 'placing' anyone who writes about the grand themes of the social or economic functioning of societies is to imagine the existence of a spectrum of possibilities with clarity at one end and comprehensiveness at the other. Those who seek clarity are unlikely to achieve comprehensiveness, and *vice versa*. Malthus had a regard for clarity, for elegance of exposition, to be expected in a mathematician, but a conviction of the complexity of reality and of the danger of oversimplification which locates him closer to the other end of the spectrum. Perhaps he came nearer to achieving both desiderata than lesser men, but where a choice had to be made he gave preference to experience over elegance.

His is a very remarkable case. The concept which Malthus dubbed the principle of population is perhaps the only instance of an idea developed by a social scientist that has had a profound influence on the development of the natural sciences, though the traffic in the other direction has been heavy.[16] He was one of the three greatest of the classical economists. As a subject, demography, or more generally population studies, owes more to him than to any other amongst its intellectual progenitors. His writings on marriage form the starting-point for modern historical demography, even though more than a century elapsed before the profound importance of what he had to say began to be recognized and absorbed into conventional writing on the topic.[17] Yet some of his most important writings are not in print and no complete edition of the full corpus of his work has ever appeared.

It may be that the future will see some of the omissions of the past repaired. There has been a revival of interest in him in recent years which encourages hope in this regard (James 1979, Petersen 1979, Dupâquier et al. 1983, Fauve-Chamoux 1984). But the extent of comparative neglect and misunderstanding remains conspicuous. Part of the answer may lie in the unusual range of his interests; part in his reluctance to divorce his views on morality and natural theology from his observations on economic and demographic issues; part in his willingness to mix scientific inquiry with the discussion of the immediate problems of the day, sometimes in a polemical manner; part in his reluctance to abandon the search for general laws which could be used deductively in favour of purely empirical research, or the reverse. Chiefly, however, he may be regarded as having received less than his due through having fallen foul of history. His view that experience was the surest test of the plausibility of new policy nostrums or of schemes of interpretation is

---

[16]The literature relating to Malthus's influence on Darwin and Wallace is very large. For a recent brief discussion of the relevant literature and some illuminating quotations from the writings of Darwin and Wallace, see Keynes (1983).

[17]It is worth noting that Hajnal, in the conclusion to his widely influential article on European marriage patterns, remarked, 'The main theme of this paper is not new. It is one of the main topics of Malthus' *Essay* and indeed implicit in its very structure (especially in the revised version of the second edition)' (1965, p. 130).

both reasonable in itself and highly typical of English writing on questions of epistemology. His writings do not fall foul of history in the sense that they do violence to what was the past in 1800, but as the nineteenth century developed the contours of the old world changed. The industrial revolution altered the productive capacity of advanced economies in a sensational manner; was followed by a demographic revolution that divorced the exercise of the passion between the sexes and reproduction; and changed fundamentally the nature of the problem of poverty. None of this was foreseen by Malthus; perhaps none of it was foreseeable if experience was to be the touchstone. Certainly no one foresaw it. But Malthus's flank was very exposed. The full title of the first *Essay* is *An Essay on the Principle of Population, as it Affects the Future Improvement of Society, with Remarks on the Speculations of Mr Godwin, M Condorcet, and Other Writers*. Later the title was modified. The second and subsequent editions were entitled, *An Essay on the Principle of Population, or a View of its Past and Present Effects on Human Happiness, with an Inquiry into our Prospects respecting the Future Removal or Mitigation of the Evils which it Occasions* – a title which placed greater emphasis on the past and less on the future. To the extent, however, that Malthus is read as a prophet, he was unlikely to win many plaudits. Only in very recent years, with the expression of worry about the exhaustion of conventional sources of energy and of doubts about the cost and feasibility of replacing them with new, renewable energy sources, have Malthusian modes of thought again begun to appear relevant to the fate of industrialized countries. As an economic, social and demographic historian, on the other hand, he should enjoy the highest standing. No man asked better questions, and very few have framed more incisive or illuminating answers. Both by the tests of elegance and experience he remains largely undiminished by subsequent work.

REFERENCES

Anderson, M. 1980: *Approaches to the History of the Western Family, 1500–1914*. London: Macmillan.
Coale, A. J. 1979: The use of modern analytical demography by T. R. Malthus. *Population Studies*, 33, 329–32.
De Vries, J. 1985: Population and economy of the pre-industrial Netherlands. *Journal of Interdisciplinary History*, 15, 661–82.
Dupâquier, J., Fauve-Chamoux, A., and Grebenik, E. (eds) 1983: *Malthus Past and Present*. London: Academic Press.
Fauve-Chamoux, A. (ed.) 1984: *Malthus hier et aujourd'hui*. Paris: Centre National de la Recherche Scientifique.
Godwin, W. 1820: *Of Population: An Enquiry concerning the Power of Increase in the Numbers of Mankind, being an Answer to Mr Malthus's Essay on that Subject*. London: Longman, Hurst, Rees, Orme and Brown.
Hajnal, H. J. 1965: European marriage patterns in perspective. In D. V. Glass and D. E. C. Eversley (eds), *Population in History*, London: Edward Arnold, pp. 101–43.
James, P. 1979: *Population Malthus, His life and times*. London: Routledge and Kegan Paul.
Keynes, R. 1983: Malthus and biological equilibria. In J. Dupâquier, A. Fauve-Chamoux and E. Grebenik (eds), *Malthus Past and Present*, London: Academic Press, pp. 359–64.

64					E. A. Wrigley

Malthus, T. R. 1798: *An Essay on the Principle of Population, as it Affects the Future Improvement of Society.* London: J. Johnson.

—— 1815: *An Inquiry into the Nature and Progress of Rent and the Principles by which it is Regulated.* London: John Murray.

—— 1820: *Principles of Political Economy Considered with a View to their Practical Application.* London: John Murray.

—— 1824: Population. Supplement to the fourth, fifth and sixth edns of the *Encyclopaedia Britannica,* Edinburgh: Constable, pp. 307–33.

—— 1826: *An Essay on the Principle of Population, or a View of its Past and Present Effects on Human Happiness,* 6th edn, 2 vols. London: J. Johnson.

Monthly Digest of Statistics 1984: London: Her Majesty's Stationery Office.

Petersen, W. 1979: *Malthus.* London: Heinemann.

Phelps-Brown, E. H., and Hopkins, S. V. 1962: Seven centuries of the prices of consumables, compared with builders' wage-rates. In E. M. Carus-Wilson (ed.), *Essays in Economic History,* London: Edward Arnold, vol. II, 179–96.

Ricardo, D. 1951: *On the Principles of Political Economy and Taxation.* In P. Sraffa (ed.) with the collaboration of M. H. Dobb, *The Works and Correspondence of David Ricardo,* Cambridge: Cambridge University Press, vol. I.

Schofield, R. S. 1976: The relationship between demographic structure and environment in pre-industrial Western Europe. In W. Conze (ed.), *Socialgeschichte der Familie in der Neuzeit Europas,* Stuttgart: Ernst Klett, pp. 147–60.

Smith, A. 1863: *An Inquiry into the Nature and Causes of the Wealth of Nations,* new edn by J. R. M'Culloch. Edinburgh: Adam and Charles Black.

Thomas, B. 1985: Escaping from constraints: the industrial revolution in a Malthusian context. *Journal of Interdisciplinary History,* 15, 729–53.

Wrigley, E. A. 1962: The supply of raw materials in the industrial revolution. *Economic History Review,* 2nd ser., 15, 1–16.

—— 1983: The growth of population in eighteenth-century England: a conundrum resolved. *Past and Present,* 98, 121–50.

—— 1985: Urban growth and agricultural change: England and the continent in the early modern period. *Journal of Interdisciplinary History,* 15, 683–728.

—— forthcoming: Men on the land and men in the countryside: employment in agriculture in early nineteenth-century England. In L. Bonfield, R. M. Smith and K. Wrightson (eds), *The World We Have Gained,* Oxford: Blackwell.

—— and Schofield, R. S. 1981: *The Population History of England 1541–1871: a reconstruction.* London: Edward Arnold.

Malthus's 'Total Population System': A Dynamic Reinterpretation

G. N. von Tunzelmann

If people only made prudent marriages, what a stop to population there would be!
W. M. Thackeray, *Vanity Fair*

It is my contention that Malthus's economic–demographic system provides a flexible, powerful and relevant framework for a wide variety of demographic circumstances. The view that it has no empirical foundation, as has been alleged on occasions by eminent demographers (e.g. Davis 1955), rests on serious misunderstandings of the Malthusian model. Though I do not propose to go into empirical applications in this paper, reserving them for another publication[1], I shall attempt to establish the core of Malthus's own theoretical approach. Malthus has frequently been criticized, both by contemporaries and more recent writers, for lack of originality. It is certainly the case that many of the building-blocks of what Spengler (1945) justifiably calls Malthus's 'total population system' were drawn from earlier sources, and I shall note some such components hereafter. But only Malthus had the vision to encompass the system functioning as a whole – in work currently in progress I shall be showing how closely Malthus's approach resembles that of present-day 'system dynamics'.[2] The main thrust of the present paper, however, is to sketch out a very simplified version of the 'total population system' to demonstrate that Malthus was pre-eminently concerned with the behaviour of that system when out of equilibrium, i.e. what happened when its long-run properties were disturbed. As I shall try to imply, the bulk of Malthus's theoretical work was directed to this question. In addition it is the most obvious starting-point for worthwhile empirical tests of the Malthusian model.

---

[1] Some preliminary results were presented in my paper 'Malthus and the standard-of-living debate' (von Tunzelmann, 1984), delivered at the ESRC Quantitative Economic History Workshop at Oxford, September 1984. That paper also included a draft of the present essay, and for comments I am indebted to participants in the Workshop, and to J. Mokyr, R. D. Lee and the editors of this volume.

[2] That some of the models in 'system dynamics' are Malthusian in spirit is widely known, but the extent to which they coincide with Malthus's approach has been much underestimated, not least by the systems-builders themselves. See, for example, Forrester (1971), Meadows et al. (1972), Cole et al. (1973), Nordhaus (1973).

Central to the demonstration of the disequilibrium properties is my view that Malthus's system is quintessentially dynamic. Economists down to the present day have been blinded to the novelty of Malthus's approach, and its powerful relationship to present-day trends in economic theory, because nearly all have come to Malthus via Ricardo, with the result that they (like most of Malthus's contemporaries) have cast his economics and his demography in the practically unrelieved comparative statics of Ricardianism. It is of course always possible to derive the dynamic properties of the 'canonical' classical model (Samuelson 1978) by investigating disturbances to equilibrium, but only Malthus of the British classical economists works from a model that is inherently dynamic in the way it is formulated, and only Malthus explicitly investigates the out-of-equilibrium properties of the classical model. Malthus and Ricardo themselves, despite countless mutual misunderstandings on specific points, appear to have appreciated some of their basic differences:

Ricardo is investigating the theory of the *distribution* of the produce in conditions of equilibrium and Malthus is concerned with what determines the *volume* of output day by day in the real world. . . . In a letter of 24 January 1817, Ricardo wrote: 'It appears to me that one great cause of our difference in opinion on the subjects which we have so often discussed is that you have always in your mind the immediate and temporary effects of particular changes whereas I put these immediate and temporary effects quite aside, and fix my whole attention on the permanent state of things which will result from them. Perhaps you estimate these temporary effects too highly, whilst I am too much disposed to undervalue them. To manage the subject quite right, they should be carefully distinguished and mentioned, and the due effects ascribed to each.'

To which Malthus replied with considerable effect on 26 January 1817:

I agree with you that one cause of our difference in opinion is that which you mention. I certainly am disposed to refer frequently to things as they are, as the only way of making one's writings practically useful to society, and I think also the only way of being secure from falling into the errors of the taylors of Laputa, and by a slight mistake at the outset arrive at conclusions the most distant from the truth. Besides I really think that the progress of society consists of irregular movements, and that to omit the consideration of causes which for eight or ten years will give a great *stimulus* to production and population, or a great *check* to them, is to omit the causes of the wealth and poverty of nations – the grand object of all our enquiries in Political Economy. (Keynes 1933/1972, pp. 97–8)[3]

Even dearer to Keynes's heart, Malthus went on later in that letter to contend that an even greater source of their differences was the better-known one of demand versus supply. These contrasts underlie the discussion of Malthus below.

That Malthus's system exhibits dynamic disequilibrium has been recognized on a number of occasions (e.g. O'Leary 1942, 1943; Dupâquier et al. 1983, ch. 5). Indeed there have been several attempts by economists and a few by demographers to formulate a dynamic version of the Malthusian system in mathematical terms. All of those that I am aware of (e.g. Peacock

---

[3]The relevant letters were subsequently published in Sraffa 1952, VII, pp. 120, 121/2.

1952, Moes, 1958, Lloyd 1969, Lee 1978[4]) depend in part on an explicit formulation of the law of diminishing returns; typically in a form such as $Y/L = F(L/T)$, $F' < 0$ (e.g. Mokyr 1983, p. 43: here Y = output, L = labour force, T = land). Used as it normally has been used, this construction lends itself more readily to comparative-static than to dynamic analysis, and though not entirely absent from Malthus's work is liable to be unhelpful in understanding its essence (Malthus's own role in helping to derive the law of diminishing returns has understandably misled subsequent writers on this point).

Two recent formalizations of Malthus's economics demonstrate this difficulty, though both go a long way further than any of their predecessors in trying to grapple with what Malthus actually said. Eltis (1980; 1984, chs 4–5) is uncommonly alert to the dynamic aspects of Malthus's arguments, which are set out as cobweb theorems. Eltis does not include an equation of exactly the form given above, but still incorporates an expression for Y/L whose derivation from Malthus is obscure and which performs essentially the same role as straight-out diminishing returns.[5] Thus Eltis is led to demand functions for both capital and labour along which the rate of profits moves inversely to the rate of wages – the classic Ricardian result which is explicitly rejected by Malthus on several occasions for both the short run and the long run (on the latter see Malthus 1836/1936, pp. 158–9). Costabile and Rowthorn (1984) derive the same Ricardian inversity from Malthus's acceptance of the tautology that in no-rent situations the share of wages and that of profits are inverse – with the link being the assumption that output is given. As their own work shows, Malthus could not possibly have accepted the latter assumption, nor did he accept the relevance of a no-rent economy in the bulk of his work.

Readers willing to accept the comparative unimportance of diminishing returns to Malthus's results can skim the next section. That Malthus often doubted or rejected diminishing returns was sometimes noticed by his contemporaries (e.g. Hutches Trower in Sraffa 1952, letter 423) and by subsequent writers (e.g. Hickson 1849, p. 138; Cannan 1920, pp. 144–5; Link 1959, pp. 45–6; Sowell 1974, p. 87; cf. also note 4 above). But only his immediate acolyte, Thomas Chalmers, really spotted that diminishing returns were not crucial to the general case of the Malthusian model (e.g. Chalmers 1832, pp. 4–10, 21, 30–2).

It is scarcely possible to read Malthus's *Principles of Political Economy* (1836/1936) without drawing the conclusion that Malthus himself was

---

[4]Several of these authors persevere in diminishing returns despite recognizing their dubious status in Malthus's work: see, for instance, Peacock (1952, p. 116); Lloyd (1969, pp. 24–5), who argues Malthus had a 'fuzzy idea' of diminishing returns; and Minami (1961, pp. 53–4, 60–2). Moes (1958) rejects diminishing returns in his own formulation but believes Malthus to have been the arch-priest of them.

[5]Malthus defined real wages as average annual family earnings, taking into account differences in family size. Eltis (1984, pp. 164–6) notes that profits and family earnings can be low at the same time, though he does not relate this to his formulation of a 'Malthusian' growth model (pp. 167ff.).

prepared to accept diminishing returns only under the greatest sufferance. I would envisage his attitude in that work as being like Keynes' celebrated dictum about the long run – by the time returns diminish we are all dead. There were some political reasons for Malthus taking this stance, most notably his defence of the Corn Laws. However, it can be defended more compellingly from his general theoretical approach, and especially his stress on the short run and on demand as already indicated.

This preoccupation with the short run is expressed in Malthus's overriding emphasis on values rather than on quantities. Malthus's measure of value ('labour-commanded') is generally worked in value terms (though in *The Measure of Value* he does try to present a physical interpretation) because of the incommensurability of different physical units of different factor services (labour, heterogeneous capital); whereas Ricardo's measure of value ('labour-embodied') works first and foremost in terms of quantities – values are presumed to follow suit. For Malthus, on the contrary, values and quantities can and frequently do move in opposite directions (Malthus assumes the demands for products like corn and for factors like labour to be inelastic). Astonishingly little attention has ever been paid to Malthus's theory of value despite its prominent place in his *Principles* and minor later works, though Costabile (1983) and Costabile and Rowthorn (1984) have done something to remedy the deficiency. The reasons for the earlier neglect probably lie in the somewhat convoluted nature of his theory and his way of expressing it, plus an erroneous belief that he was unduly inconsistent in this area. He does effect some changes,[6] but they are modifications rather than wholesale overthrows – I shall use the discussion in the second (posthumously published) edition of the *Principles* here.

Full-scale assessment of Malthus's theory of value would require an article of its own; here I go no further than to make a few points most centrally relevant to the principal issues of this chapter. To begin with, one can envisage 'supply' or 'demand' in purely physical (quantity) terms, whether referring to goods or to productive factors (land, labour and capital).[7] This is demand *ex ante*, as it were (Malthus used the alternative dog-Latinism, demand *in posse*: cf. V. E. Smith 1951, p. 252n.) – i.e. so many units of a commodity (supply) matched against so many hours of work effort a labourer was willing to offer to procure that supply (demand). The level of demand for goods was dictated by considerations of social class, with landlords and large capitalists likely to devote smaller proportions of their expenditure to wealth-creating goods (Costabile 1983, pp. 162–3; Eltis 1984, pp. 151–6). Quantities supplied were predetermined in the short run for goods involving capital or land in their production process; the same was true of the factors

---

[6]In the first edition of the *Principles*, published in 1820, Malthus adopted the mean of corn and labour commanded, rather than pure labour commanded, as the measure. His later reconsideration led him to see the earlier formulation as an attempt to measure working-class wealth rather than value (1836, p. 307 and n.).

[7]Malthus later rejected what he had come to regard as the Ricardian approach of treating heterogeneous capital as a quantity that could be aggregated, anticipating views of the twentieth-century Cambridge school of political economy (1827/1971, p. 38). But his views on fixed capital, etc., were never adequately worked out.

capital and land themselves and to some extent of the labour force. Values would then be determined by the interaction of this quantity supplied and the demand schedule. The correspondence between the values so determined and market prices depended on the 'value of money', which can be most simply thought of as the inverse of the price level in Friedman–Schwartz fashion.[8] The goods market will clear at market prices with relatively little delay, but Malthus was worried about its potential for expansion – growth could depend on technical progress shifting the short-run supply curve leftwards (Malthus 1836/1936, pp. 98–100), though in the short run the dominant difficulty lay on the demand side. 'Satiation of wants' was crucial to early nineteenth-century dissent in political economy (Rashid 1977; contrasting with Ricardo's 'unlimited wants' – e.g. Hollander 1979, p. 505), and Malthus believed that increases of demand to offset such satiation (i.e. upward shifts of the demand schedule) would require labourers and more importantly their social superiors to develop new wants for goods.

The goods market might clear only at prices which failed to cover 'reproductive' costs, i.e. a subsistence wage (below which population size would fall) and a minimal rate of return on capital.[9] In this case there would be unemployment in the factor markets (unemployed labour and/or excess capacity) and a 'general glut' in the goods market (Sowell 1972, 1974; Costabile 1983, p. 157) – there would be what Malthus described as a lack of 'effectual demand'. In *The Measure of Value*, Malthus makes it clearer that he is describing a realization problem of the Marxian kind: values less than effectual demand ruined capitalists, excessive values ruined consumers (1823, pp. 59–68; cf. Chalmers 1832, pp. 115–17). The 'general glut' was maintained partly by sticky money wages, though as Hollander (1979, pp. 532–3) points out, a fall in money wages later in the glut would not necessarily cure unemployment.[10] Values therefore cycled in response to cobweb-type delays but also over a longer period in response to factor–price rigidities and shifts of the supply and demand schedules. I shall come back to cyclical fluctuations presently.

For Malthus there was all the world of difference between high prices set by supply (high costs of production) and those set by demand (powerful

---

[8]Malthus himself rejected any practical possibility of devising an index of general purchasing-power that met all his requirements (1836/1936, pp. 119–20), clearly because he considered that any such would be a consumer-price index rather than a deflator relevant to gross national production or consumption.

[9]The 'subsistence minimum' for Malthus is similar to those for Smith and Ricardo, in being expressly stated as the level at which the rate of population growth falls to zero. It has no necessary connection with minimal physiological needs, being (at least in advanced countries) the reflection of the habits and customs of the country. Ricardo allowed a long-run upward drift of the 'minimum' but Malthus went far further in allowing rapid short-run changes both upwards and downwards. In his view the assumption of constant wages was fatal to classical political economy (1836/1936, pp. 224–5; 1827/1971, pp. 60–2).

[10]Malthus believed that money wages would be maintained at former levels in the early part of a 'general glut' but the quantity of labour hired would fall, less through open unemployment than through underemployment (working shorter daily hours, etc.), lower by-employment for women and children, and 'taskwork' reductions. In consequence, Malthus stated that wages should be assessed as average annual family earnings (Dow 1977; cf. Costabile and Rowthorn 1984, pp. 20–1).

wants), because the latter augmented profits whilst the former squeezed them. Somewhat inconsistently, however, Malthus rejected any policy of cutting costs by way of cutting wages – the objective had to be fair shares for both capital and labour in any technical change, for reasons of aggregate demand as well as equity. The rejection of the Ricardian inversity of the rate of profit and the wage rate made it easier to argue this case.

What role can then be assigned to diminishing returns? They obviously enter into the conditions of production on the supply side, but they are for Malthus a generally distant and very long-run component of costs, of dubious significance for the short-run fluctuations that dominated Malthus's economic interests. Thus in the much-misunderstood example of rents on land, Malthus rejected the textbook Ricardian argument that gradations of soil fertility determined rents, by reversing the path of causation (this is clarified by Chalmers 1832, pp. 316–17, 459–61, 511–12, 527). Malthus's primary objection to the orthodox Ricardian comparative-static approach was that to his mind it left the rise in prices which were supposed in the Ricardian scheme to lead to extensions of cultivation and rising rents quite undetermined (see Malthus 1836/1936, p. 145n.; also Bonar 1885/1966, pp. 235–41, which uses the terms 'static' and 'dynamic' in this context). For Malthus, the expansion of land and agricultural output would in the medium run engender population growth, which would then provide demand and give value to the augmented supply (1836/1936, pp. 141, 150). Malthus did not deny the existence of gradations of fertility – in Britain he saw them as the main source (but not measure) of value – but they were not absolutely necessary for the existence of rents. Moreover, in practice they explained almost nothing of the short- and medium-run movements in rents that he observed – he contended that the last land cultivated in 1813 required no more labour to work it than the last land cultivated in 1790, despite the substantial extension of the external margin of cultivation under wartime influences (1836/1936, p. 165, and 1890, pp. 407–8). As an empirical proposition he had come around as early as the second half of 1815 to the view that the elasticity of supply of corn was fairly flat (see Sraffa 1952, VI, pp. 255–6, and VII, pp. 214–15) – indeed an expansion of output might actually lower costs through its impact on wage costs and thus demand (VI, p. 342).

Much the same was true of diminishing returns in Malthus's theory of profits. Again they operate only in the long run in any consistent way – they constituted what Malthus called the 'limiting principle' for determining the rate of profit. The steady progress towards the Ricardian stationary state implied by the 'limiting principle' would be repeatedly interrupted by the 'regulating principle' of supply and demand, arising especially out of shorter-term discrepancies between the rate of growth of capital and that of labour. Such deflections could last for ten to thirty years, perhaps as much as a hundred years (Malthus 1836/1936, pp. 281–2; also Sraffa 1952, VI, pp. 153–5, 167, 303–4). Thus profits as well as rents rose during the French wars, as a result of labour-saving technical change in agriculture (Malthus 1836/1936, pp. 165–6, 169; 1970) – an outcome rather reluctantly accepted by Ricardo (Sraffa 1952, letters 43, 48; Hollander 1977): the reverse happened in 1720–50 and again after the Napoleonic Wars (cf. Hollander 1979, p. 623). Though

Malthus thought that on average capital was probably deficient in every country relative to land and labour, he believed it could at times be redundant relative to demand (1836/1936, pp. 328, 414n.), and this was what he believed took place after 1815. For Ricardo it was impossible for capital and labour to be redundant at the same time (Sraffa 1952, letters 362, 363; Sowell 1972, pp. 125-7). In the *Principles* (1836/1936, pp. 282-4) Malthus went on to suggest supplementary reasons why in practice diminishing returns might not have the expected outcome for profits: (a) technical progress in agriculture; (b) increasing personal exertion; (c) non-neutral effects of changes in the 'value of money', e.g. through the distortive effects of indirect taxation; (d) technical progress in manufactures.

There is a final and much more straightforward reason for rejecting the centrality of diminishing returns in the Malthusian model – one so simple that I am baffled to find it so repeatedly misunderstood. It is that Malthus hardly ever associated the increase in population induced by higher wages or food supplies with an increase in the labour force – instead he took pains to emphasize the lack of connection. It would take sixteen to eighteen years, he argued, for the additional population to become fully-fledged recruits into the labour force (1836/1936, pp. 257, 280, 319–20, etc.; Paglin 1961, p. 125) – though he admitted in a footnote on p. 257 that if the effect of more abundant food was to reduce mortality the impact could be quite rapid. In the usual case of rising fertility, the lag was quite long enough to ignore the consequences for the size of the workforce, given Malthus's primary focus upon the short run. Population to Malthus is seen predominantly as consumption, rather than as production, as for instance in his metaphor of the reservoir (1798/1926, p. 106n.). It is true that the increment of population in the form of children could store up problems for the labour force in the longer term, and this cohort analysis was employed to help explain Britain's post-war depression – unusually high fertility during the wars gave rise to an excessive labour supply after 1815 when it had reached maturity (see also Malthus 1890, p. 331, for the general case). The basic point about the short run was made by Cannan (1892 and 1920) but has been ignored or rejected ever since:

Malthus himself had never taken the new hands into account at all. He neglected entirely the increment of labour supplied by the increment of population. In comparing the ratios at which population and produce can increase . . . he simply supposed, without any consideration of the proportionate amount of labour, that 'by the best possible policy and great encouragements to agriculture' the produce might be doubled in twenty-five years, and trebled in fifty years, and so on. (1920, p. 180)

It must be admitted that it then becomes difficult to see where the extra labour force required to produce the arithmetic progression of food supplies in the longer run is going to come from, though historical evidence does rather support the argument that for Britain at the time he was writing agricultural output was growing without any increase in the agricultural workforce. The main point I would make, however, is that the famous ratio of geometric to arithmetic progression tells us much more about the short than the long run, and the long-run versions exists mainly for dramatic illustration.

Let me then set out a very simplified form of the 'total population system'. Malthus's term 'population principle' was evidently drawn from Godwin's *Political Justice*, especially the statement that 'there is a principle in human society, by which population is perpetually kept down to the level of the means of subsistence' (Godwin 1793/1946, pp. 466, 516; Malthus 1798/1926, pp. 175–6, 193; Place 1822/1930, pp. 132–4; Bonar 1885/1966, p. 14; Cannan 1920, pp. 134–5). For Godwin the 'principle' was the existence of the equilibrium, but for Malthus it was not only that (though a part of it): even more important was the path by which the equilibrium was approached.[11] This will be called the MV path (Misery and Vice). Its trajectory, the very core of Malthus's 'population principle', represents the 'laws of nature' (that food supply is a necessity – Malthus 1798/1926, pp. 11, 14; and that the passion between the sexes is constant – pp. 11–13 and ch. 11) acting against the positive and preventive checks to population growth through time.

We may trace the MV path using ecological dynamics. As a first approximation to Malthus's scheme one may write out the pair of differential equations:

$$\frac{\dot{P}}{P} = -c + \gamma w \le \left(\frac{\dot{P}}{P} \right)_g \tag{1}$$

$$\frac{\dot{w}}{w} = a - \alpha P \tag{2}$$

where P = population
                                   w = real wage rate

In this pair of equations, c, γ, a and α are all positive coefficients. The left-hand sides represent proportional rates of growth in both cases ($\dot{P} \equiv dP/dt$, etc.).

The derivation of equation (1) requires little justification: if w is thought of as per-capita food supplies it is to be found not only in Malthus's *Essays* but in the work of many of his predecessors (Smith, Steuart, etc.). However, even in the first *Essay* (1798), and increasingly thereafter through subsequent editions and into the *Principles*, the rate of population growth is made to depend upon the 'real funds for the maintenance of labour' (cf. Eltis 1984, pp. 114–15), i.e. on the 'demand for labour' as Malthus interpreted it. Thus strictly interpreted w is a *value* rather than a quantity and will constitute the investible surplus per head subject to 'effectual demand'. At this point all the problems he sought to grapple with in the theory of value raise themselves. For instance, in the return to peace in and after 1815 food prices collapsed – food was abundant but distress prevailed on all sides (e.g. Malthus 1836/1936, pp. 386–7). Thus because of the inelasticity of demand for corn the impact on population growth should have been negative despite the

---

[11]Godwin (1801) explicitly accepted the geometric and arithmetic ratios but rejected the MV path.

abundance of food (cf. also James 1979, pp. 256, 289). Cheap provisions tended to be associated in Malthus's mind with low demand for labour and little or no growth of output or population (1836/1936, pp. 142n., 387). In the *Measure of Value* he saw that it may come down to a question of optimizing between higher quantities and higher unit values for food (1823/1957, pp. 59–60).

The inequality at the end of equation (1) shows that there exists a maximal geometric growth rate (highest attainable geometric progression) for population growth rates; I shall come back to this.

Equation (2) follows from the famous comparison of the geometric progression for population growth with the arithmetic progression for food supplies (Malthus 1798/1926, pp. 14, 16, 90–1). It states that, with a larger total population, food supplies per capita will decline. (It is a matter of regret, as both contemporary and modern critics have often pointed out, that Malthus did not describe food supplies in terms of a slower geometric growth rather than as arithmetic growth, but undoubtedly a good part of his notoriety came from the confrontation between the geometrical and arithmetic progressions. Note that Malthus thought that in the long run British food supplies would not grow even as fast as the arithmetic progression.) A still more fundamental and valid criticism is that the arithmetic progression (or slower geometric progression) is nowhere plausibly justified – it remains an article of faith. Here we do not have even the conventional law of diminishing returns to uphold it, except perhaps in the long run. When John Stuart Mill substituted diminishing returns for the arithmetic progression, the Ricardian comparative–static result came out immediately (cf. McCleary 1952) – this is usually expressed by writing out an equation for w as a function of P rather than for $\dot{w}/w$ as here.

The interpretation placed on Malthus's ratios in the 1820s and 1830s by Whately, Senior and others argued that everything depended on the use of the word 'tendency' by Malthus. It might be granted that $\dot{P}/P$ would tend to exceed $\dot{w}/w$ because the biological maximum $(\dot{P}/P)_g$ was high, but as a matter of historical observation real wages had not been falling (or not much), so the consequences were not found in practice – the checks to population growth constrained $\dot{P}/P$ in practice to equal or even fall short of $\dot{w}/w$. This was sufficient to answer critics who facetiously derived astronomical standards of living in biblical times. But it did not satisfy Malthus, whose unhappiness with this interpretation of his work is revealed in his correspondence with Senior (see Senior 1829/1966). Most subsequent writers have seen in this correspondence Malthus refusing to see common sense and clinging stubbornly to his ratios in the teeth of contradictory evidence. Interpreted, however, as a debate between comparative statics (as developed by Senior and the Ricardians) and Malthus's own dynamics, the intellectual boot looks to be on the other foot: it was Senior who repeatedly failed to grasp what Malthus was driving at. (Later in the correspondence Senior defended his position in terms of the relationship between population and subsistence over a span of 200–300 years – truly a long run to justify Keynes's well-known sarcasm).

It has been rightly asserted that, to Malthus, these two ratios were the least important of his contributions (Bonar 1885/1966; Schumpeter 1954, pp. 251–2) – doubling rates for population growth dated back at least to Petty.

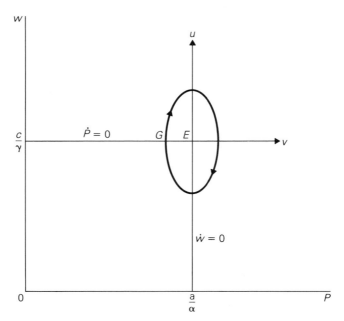

Figure 1   Wages and population growth: the poor-country case

Nor was the existence of checks to population growth by any means original (see Smith 1951, on Hale; also Townsend 1791). What Malthus took far beyond any of his predecessors was the nature of the system as a whole[12] and particularly the way in which the checks returned the system temporarily to equilibrium. Malthus's originality can readily be demonstrated by following out the dynamic consequences of equations (1) and (2), as depicted in figure 1. (The notation here follows that of Boyce and di Prima 1977, pp. 427–34). Pursuing the mathematical development of ecological dynamics by Volterra (1931, 5, 14ff.), one can cross-multiply to get

$$\dot{P} = -cP + \gamma wP \qquad\qquad (1a)$$
$$\dot{w} = aw - \alpha wP \qquad\qquad (2a)$$

Elementary algebraic manipulation then shows that the system has a critical point at $P = a/\alpha$, $w = c/\gamma$, since at that point $\dot{P} = 0$ and also $\dot{w} = 0$. Figure 1 shows this point at the intersection of the straight-line schedules for $\dot{P} = 0$ and $\dot{w} = 0$. Consider small deviations around that critical point $(a/\alpha,\ c/\gamma)$ such that $w = c/\gamma + u$, $P = a/\alpha + v$. Then by substitution in (2a) and (1a):

---

[12]As was pointed out by Boulding (1955), the precise form of the model is only of secondary importance – some different specifications are considered below. The point here is seeing the world operating as a *system*.

$$\dot{u} = -\frac{\alpha c}{\gamma} v - \alpha uv \tag{3}$$

$$\dot{v} = \frac{\gamma c}{\alpha} u + \gamma uv \tag{4}$$

If we ignore the second terms on the right-hand sides of equations (3) and (4) because they are of the second order of smallness (being terms in uv), this system becomes linear. Its roots are pure imaginary $(\pm i\sqrt{ac})$ given the signs of the coefficients, so $(a/\alpha, c/\gamma)$ represents the stable centre of the linear form of the system. The trajectories of the system are ellipses, neither approaching nor receding from the critical point, since

$$\frac{dv}{du} = -\frac{(\gamma a/\alpha)u}{(\alpha c/\gamma)v} \tag{5}$$

Thus

$$\frac{\gamma a}{\alpha} u \cdot du + \frac{\alpha c}{\gamma} v \cdot dv = 0 \tag{6}$$

So that

$$\frac{\gamma a}{\alpha} u^2 + \frac{\alpha c}{\gamma} v^2 = E \tag{7}$$

Equation (7) is of course the equation of an ellipse with centroid E, where E is an arbitrary non-negative constant of integration.

The fact that there are, strictly speaking, terms in uv in equations (3) and (4) can be shown to imply that the trajectories are not true ellipses but are still closed curves, for which the ellipse is a reasonable approximation if the deviations from equilibrium (the us and the vs) are small (see e.g. Sanchez et al. 1983, pp. 100–8).

The model here is of the kind known in ecology as the predator–prey model (e.g. Boulding 1978, app to ch. 4; Hirshleifer 1977), and the fact that Malthus's system should come out this way is hardly surprising in view of his well-known influence on both Charles Darwin and A. R. Wallace (cf. Young 1969). Malthus did not develop the predator–prey concept himself, but a remarkably clear illustration – which as several authors have pointed out manages to encapsulate both Malthus and Darwin within the space of a paragraph – was given by Joseph Townsend (1786/1926, p. 38), whose works profoundly influenced Malthus's second *Essay*. Townsend linked the struggles between greyhounds and goats on Juan Fernandez Island to the human struggle for food. Malthus's own notions of struggle are perhaps most clearly brought out in his 'theodicy' as expressed in the final chapters of the first *Essay* – these discussions have recently been much investigated (e.g. Pullen 1981; Santurri 1982; Dupâquier et al. 1983, ch. 14; Harvey-Phillips 1984). In later editions of the *Essay* the struggle becomes more secularly expressed, especially in the form of 'prudential restraint', to be discussed below; this required a parallel growth of 'mind' to that in his earlier theodicy.

Before examining in greater detail Malthus's rendering of the mathematical results just derived, I shall have to introduce one further complexity. The situation conjectured in figure 1 was, in Malthus's view, most relevant to the most primitive societies. The locus $\dot{P} = 0$ could be rendered a horizontal straight line for Malthus's extreme of a society in which population size was regulated entirely by the positive check, i.e. by unregulated fertility and high mortality. Misery in such forms as famine, war, and debasement of women would be greatest in savage societies (Malthus 1798/1926, pp. 39–44). Many examples are given in the first *Essay* and a great many more in the second *Essay*. Such impoverished societies would be very thinly peopled, he believed – more so than anywhere else apart from new colonies. For example,

In a country [such as New South Wales], the inhabitants of which are driven to such resources [as eating witchetty grubs] for subsistence, where the supply of animal and vegetable food is so extremely scanty, and the labour necessary to procure it is so severe, it is evident that the population must be very thinly scattered in proportion to the territory. (Malthus 1890, p. 17)

The labour-commanded theory is clear enough in that statement, but there is additionally the ratio of man to land. Malthus borrowed from Benjamin Franklin (1751/1907, pp. 63–4, 71–2) the notion that population expanded in proportion to 'room'. Requirements for 'room' would contract as development proceeded. The next notch up the scale from primitive societies, that of hunter societies, needed enough 'room' for the animals that supplied the wants of human beings: nomadic societies searching for food would also be sparsely populated (Malthus 1798/1926, pp. 44–52; 1890, pp. 20–1). At the other end of the scale were advanced countries such as England that had filled up. The lack of 'room' in such countries necessitated a slow rate of population increase. Whereas in a primitive society population size would grow slowly in the long run because of the positive checks, in advanced societies the same would come about as a result of the predominance of preventive checks, i.e. by declines in fertility (Malthus believed that preventive checks had been increasing in Europe for at least a century or two, though they were much greater in some countries, such as Norway, than others). There was a well-established view, which Franklin had been promulgating, that population grew fastest in new colonies because of the abundance of 'room' and food supplies. Thus, for instance, the Revd Ezra Stiles of Rhode Island in 1760:

In new-settled countries, the transplanted colonies, by an established law of nature, in a good climate, do increase to a certain patrial maturity: then they begin to decline. At the beginning of the increase, the period of doubling is very short, and the augmentation rapid. Afterward, the period of doubling is extended, till it gradually ceaseth: and is succeeded with a diminution slow at first but rapid at last. . . . (Short 1767, pp. ii–iii; cf. Godwin 1793/1946, p. 516)

In the long run, this relationship between the density of population and the rate of natural increase should be represented by expanding equation (1) or (1a) to include a term such as $-\delta P$ (or non-linear equivalent) on the right-hand side as in equation (1b):

$$\frac{\dot{P}}{P} = -c + \gamma W - \delta P \qquad (1b)$$

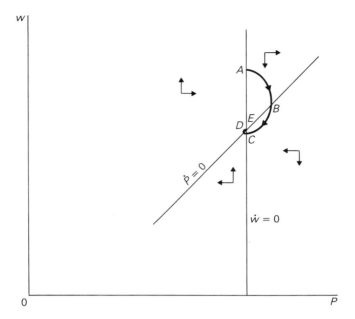

Figure 2   Wages and population growth: the advanced-country case

As Verhulst (1838) discovered, the integration of an equation of this form would yield a long-run logistic pattern of population size (see also Samuelson 1966, pp. 377–8, and Minami 1961, for explicit reference to Malthus).

Malthus is arguing this case, however, not just for the long run, but also in the short run. In the first *Essay* (1798/1926, pp. 120–2) he attempted to show that the amplitude of fluctuations in population in medium-poor countries such as Turkey, Egypt, Russia and Naples was greater than in the advanced countries such as England. The former were not so poor that their spurts of population growth regularly got them into outright famine (unlike say India – p. 131)[13] but they were at somewhat irregular intervals likely to experience a run of 'sickly seasons', with a high incidence of epidemics and so forth that Malthus concluded must be related somehow to poverty. Following the period of crisis the country was left relatively empty, i.e. 'room' was created. Moreover the surviving population was likely to be unusually healthy and industrious. It was in this 'rapid rebound' period that Malthus considered population might grow at the maximal geometric rate, $(\dot{P}/P)_g$ – throughout his work Malthus defines the geometric progression as the rate of growth of population *when unchecked*, i.e. by 'room' and food supplies. Malthus used rough data from North America, exemplified by the quote from Ezra Stiles above, to suggest that the briefest doubling period for population

[13]Malthus includes a rather sophisticated discussion of what more recently has been described as the 'Asiatic marriage pattern' of early marriages but more or less stationary population size (1798/1926, pp. 60–1), e.g. for China.

was about twenty-five years (albeit less in the American hinterland) – this figure was subsequently criticized by Godwin (1820), but recent estimates for the natural increase of the white American population between 1800 and 1830 (McClelland and Zeckhauser 1982, table A-13) indicate Malthus was spot on. In any case, as he often stressed, the precise minimal doubling-time was almost immaterial (see also Trower in Sraffa 1952, letter 423; and Ricardo, ibid., letter 426).

The effect in medium-poor countries is, then, to truncate the ellipse depicted in figure 1. The population principle produces poverty rather than outright famines (Malthus 1890, p. 290), though, in the famous image of the first *Essay*, 'famine stalks in the rear' (Malthus 1798/1926, pp. 139–40). However, in advanced countries exhibiting powerful preventive checks even the poverty will be truncated. The expanded equation (1b) will operate even in the short run. Figure 1 now has to be modified as in figure 2. The phase diagram in (P, w) space will now have a locus for $\dot{P} = 0$ that slopes upward to the right rather than being horizontal. Any disturbance from the temporary equilibrium at E, such as a good harvest shifting a country's location to A, will then be followed by a return towards equilibrium along the path $ABCD$. . . . This is mathematically speaking the consequence of the arrows of motion, which show, first, that for any level of population to the left of the vertical $\dot{w} = 0$ locus, w will tend to rise (hence the vertical arrowheads point upwards) because of equation (2), and conversely to the right of $\dot{w} = 0$. Secondly, for any level of real wages above the zero population growth locus, population will tend to increase (hence the horizontal arrowheads point rightwards) because of equation (1b), and conversely for wages below that locus. The trajectory then follows directly from considering the joint outcome of these arrows of motion in each sector of the phase diagram, coupled with the requirement that the trajectory intersects the $\dot{w} = 0$ locus horizontally and the $\dot{P} = 0$ locus vertically, as in R. D. Lee's similar constructions in the present volume. It is apparent that the proportion of time experiencing Misery and Vice is much less than for the poorer country implied in figure 1, with the ellipse trajectory.

The trajectory charted in figure 2 can be contrasted with that which Malthus describes early in the first *Essay* (and in subsequent editions):

We will suppose the means of subsistence in any country just equal to the easy support of its inhabitants [taken to be point A]. The constant effort towards population, which is found to act even in the most vicious societies, increases the number of people before the means of subsistence are increased. The food therefore which before supported seven millions ['eleven millions' in second *Essay*], must now be divided among seven millions and a half or eight millions ['eleven millions and a half']. The poor consequently must live much worse, and many of them be reduced to severe distress. The number of labourers also being above the proportion of the work in the market, the price of labour must tend toward a decrease;[14] while the price of provisions would at the same time tend to rise [i.e. moving down the AB section with P rising and w falling]. During this season of distress, the discouragements to marriage, and the difficulty of rearing a family are so great, that population is at a stand [in second *Essay*,

[14]In the *Principles* Malthus is more careful to stress that he is talking about a reduction of work rather than a rising number of labourers (1836/1936, p. 312).

'that the progress of population is retarded', i.e. moving below point *B*]. In the mean time the cheapness of labour, the plenty of labourers, and the necessity of an increased industry amongst them, encourage cultivators to employ more labour upon their land; to turn up fresh soil, and to manure and improve more completely what is already in tillage; till ultimately the means of subsistence become ['may become'] in the same proportion to the population as at the period from which we set out. The situation of the labourer being then again tolerably comfortable, the restraints to population are in some degree loosened; and the same retrograde and progressive movements with respect to happiness are repeated. (1798/1926, pp. 29–31; 1890, p. 11)

In the first *Essay* he goes on to state that 'in all old states some such vibration does exist; though from various transverse causes, in a much less marked, and in a much more irregular manner than I have described it' (1798/1926, p. 31) – i.e. more irregularly than in figure 2. The 'various transverse causes' that help bring about this 'vibration' are listed a few pages later as including:

the introduction or failure of certain manufactures: a greater or less prevalent spirit of agricultural enterprize: years of plenty, or years of scarcity: wars and pestilence: poor laws: the invention of processes for shortening labour without the proportional extension of the market for the commodity: and, particularly, the difference between the nominal and real price of labour; a circumstance, which has perhaps more than any other, contributed to conceal this oscillation from common view. (p. 34)

All that is missing from this account is attention to the movement from *E* to *A* – indeed the two points are treated as one. But in the concluding chapter to book III of the second *Essay* Malthus makes it quite clear that 'agriculture may with more propriety be termed the efficient cause of population, than population of agriculture, though they certainly re-act upon each other. . . . there can be no doubt that in the order of precedence food must take the lead . . .' (1890, pp. 433, 434). More explicitly:

What is here said of the order of precedence with respect to agriculture and population, does not invalidate what was said in an earlier part of this work on the tendency to an oscillation or alternation in the increase of population and food in the natural course of their progress. In this progress nothing is more usual than for the population to increase at certain periods faster than food; indeed it is a part of the general principle that it should do so. . . . But then it must be recollected that the greater relative increase of population absolutely implies a previous increase of food at some time or other greater than the lowest wants of the people. Without this, the population could not possibly have gone forward.
  Universally, when the population of a country is for a longer or shorter time stationary, owing to the low corn wages of labour, a case which is not unfrequent, it is obvious that nothing but a previous increase of food, or at least an increase of the portion awarded to the labourer, can enable the population again to proceed forwards. (pp. 433–4)

Ricardo thought this primacy awarded to food output one of the most controversial characteristics of the Malthusian system (Sraffa 1951, pp. 108–11; 1952, letters 233, 335, 380, 387; Chalmers 1832, pp. 107–8; Hollander 1979, ch. 6) – amongst other reasons, because he saw it as admitting the possibility of a 'general glut' (Sraffa 1952, letter 387). In sum, the Malthusian system constructed here consists of an exogenous increase of food, perhaps from a run of good harvests, stimulating population growth, initially at something like the maximal geometric rate and then at declining rates, through the operation of the positive and especially preventive checks. In short, figures 1 and 2 capture two cases of the 'principle of population' as I see Malthus to have understood it. As Charles Hall (1805) pointed out shortly after the publication of the *Essay*, the dynamism of Malthus's approach is shown by the immediacy of the population barriers, rather than the very long-term considerations of his predecessors.

Introducing complexities, as was his wont, Malthus then goes on to ask about the positioning of the $\dot{P}$ and $\dot{w}$ loci, as distinct from their shape – in particular what could lead to shifts in the loci. It is only at this stage of the proceedings that the moral and political ideology so often associated with Malthus's work becomes critical. With the introduction of politics and morals – which as he admits is tacit (1836, p. 309) – the scope for overt disagreement becomes far more manifest. Moreover, Malthus himself gets driven into what look like inconsistencies. Nevertheless I take the argument of Peacock (1952) that the underlying model as discussed above is consistent and politically neutral –it is the elaborations to be discussed hereafter which are vastly more controversial. Malthus's explicit rejection of mathematical language becomes more justified at this stage (1827/1971, p. 2; 1836/1936, p. 1; Sowell 1974, pp. 117–18).

As is well known, his motivation for writing the first *Essay* was to combat schemes of equalizing wealth that ran from the fairly mild pensions scheme put forward by Condorcet (1795) to the advocacy by Godwin (1793) of voluntary redistribution of property (to a basis that better reflected merit rather than inheritance, conquest, etc.). In the 1817 edition of the *Essay* Malthus included an attack on Owenite communities of goods (1890, pp. 319–24, 518–20). The nature of these proposals and of Malthus's response to them is another subject I must defer to a more comprehensive study.[15] In brief, Malthus believed schemes such as Owen's would increase 'indolence', thus diminishing demand per capita and national wealth as implied by his value theory. The supply of food would rise somewhat from the subdivision of property and the lack of need to generate a 'reproductive' rate of profit (Malthus 1798/1926, p. 186; 1890, pp. 210n., 383, 513–14; 1830/1953, p. 147; Bonar 1885/1966, p. 77; Price 1803, II, pp. 138, 146–8; Chalmers 1832, pp. 2, 104, 385, 482, 488, 556). The trouble was that, while total output would rise, output per capita would fall – not so much because of diminishing returns, as in R. D. Lee's very similar conclusion in this volume, as because the population principle would be called into operation with a vengeance since parents no longer needed to take much responsibility for their children's welfare. In *Political Justice* Godwin had already accepted that the preventive check might theoretically be weakened by the redistribution of poverty, but in the wake of the first *Essay* he reiterated his view that the very rationality which gave rise to an egalitarian society would also generate 'prudential restraint'. (Godwin 1801, pp. 72–4; Hazlitt 1807,

---

[15]This will constitute part of a projected study of socialist critiques of the standard-of-living debate, in turn an aspect of my larger studies in that area.

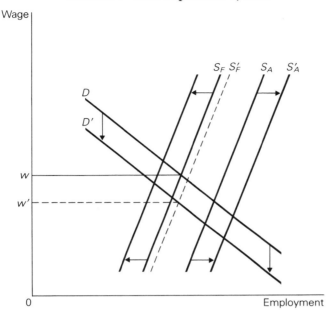

Figure 3 Effects of right to relief on labour supply and demand
Note: Primed curves show net impact of granting legal relief. Graph follows Spindler and Maki (1979).

pp. 287–8). Malthus dated his opposing views back to the ancient debate between Plato and Aristotle (Malthus 1890, pp. 130–2) – the outcome would be a considerably higher rate of population growth for each level of real wages, i.e. a rightward (or downward) shift in the $\dot{P}$ loci.

As is even better known, Malthus also set out to attack on related grounds the whole system of English poor relief, especially post-Speenhamland, to some extent in the first *Essay* but far more in later editions. For Malthus, the Poor Laws had the effect of divorcing population growth from the demand for labour. 'Their first obvious tendency', he argued, 'is to increase population without increasing the food for its support' (1798/1926, p. 83; 1890, p. 342; Chalmers 1832, p. 399) – so with exemplary clarity specifying the displacement of the locus. In general equilibrium the Poor Laws succeeded only in driving up prices (Malthus 1798/1926, pp. 75–6; 1890, p. 343; 1970; Sen 1981, p. 178). Some critics, such as Weyland (1816), stressed the positive effects on aggregate demand of transferring income to those with high propensities to consume. Malthus's views in this respect however, were, monetarist rather than Keynesian. He assumed that aggregate food supply would be highly inelastic in the short run, so that increased demand would drive up prices much more than increase total output. His attitude can readily be understood using an approach made familiar by recent studies in the manner of the 'new classical macroeconomics' of the role of unemployment benefits. In figure 3 there are two labour-supply curves, S_A being the number registered as in the total workforce (employed and unemployed), and S_F being the effective labour actually supplied at each level of real wages.

The adoption of the Poor Laws potentially does three things. First, as Malthus pointed out, it reduces the surplus available for reinvestment to the extent of the additional burden on the parish rates. Hence the demand curve for labour shifts downwards. Secondly, it shifts the effective labour supply leftwards, as indolence increases to take advantage of life on the dole (Malthus 1798/1926, pp. 86–7). Thirdly, it shifts the apparent labour-supply curve rightwards as more notionally register for employment in order to benefit from a generous payout of poor relief. Malthus probably paid least attention to the second of these, though of course it was the greatest complaint of many both before and after him. Most important was the final factor, which he saw as coming about overwhelmingly through the population growth stimulated by the Poor Laws (at this point his 16–18 year lag seems to have been lost again). The net effect of underplaying the shift of S_F and overplaying that of S_A in conjunction with the downward shift of D is to generate a substantial fall in the real wage rate. In terms of food supplies per capita, as in the interpretation he gives in the first *Essay*, this follows even without the lag of workforce behind population, because the number of mouths obviously increases rapidly on Malthus's assumptions. If wages were maintained artificially by trade unions or 'effectual demand' were lacking in the altered situation, there could be unemployment instead of, or as well as, the fall in wages (1890, p. 358; 1823/1957, p. 68) – the latter of course is not a 'new classical' proposition.

In the first *Essay* Malthus called for outright abolition of the old Poor Law; in subsequent editions only for its gradual abolition (1798/1926, p. 98; Chalmers 1832, p. 489; Dupâquier et al. 1983, ch. 7). (His views on the political acceptability of abolition wavered – cf. James 1979, p. 450.) To opponents, Malthus was envisaged as regularizing selfishness (Hazlitt 1807/1930, pp. 181–2; James 1979, pp. 114–15) – Ensor (1818/1967, p. 81) saw him as putting the right to property above the right to life. However, he was defended by Ricardo more stoutly in this area than in any other:

> You [Francis Place] agree with Mr Malthus that his plan if adopted would lower the poor rates, but you say it would reduce the poor to the very lowest state possible. Why? Not if it raised wages, and this is what Mr Malthus expects from it. You are bound to shew, that wages will not be raised, when a portion of the money now paid for labour, under another name, is withdrawn, and transferred to the employers of labour. You say that private benevolence would degrade the poor man more than the aid he receives from the poor rates. I believe otherwise. Mr Malthus be it remembered does not propose the abolition of the poor laws as a measure of relief to the rich, but as one of relief to the poor themselves. (Sraffa 1952, IX, pp. 52–3; cf. letters 197, 201, 249, 363; also Hollander 1979, pp. 559, 567, 573)

Place's view was that Malthus had little understanding of working-class minds (1822/1930, pp. 154–6).

From an early date Malthus was forced to accept that in practice the effect of the Poor Laws on population growth was much less marked than his theorizing allowed. He responded by contending that the most retrograde effects of the Poor Law were offset in actuality by their indirect effect of reducing the supply of cottages, in order to evade an excessive burden of poor-rates; in other words, the effects on 'room' contradicted those on lower-class incomes. He entertained the possibility of a tax on cottages to help solve the problems of Ireland (*Parliamentary Papers* 1826-7, qq. 3361-2). Moreover, he declared in the penultimate chapter of the second *Essay* that 'it is only that kind of *systematic* and *certain* relief, on which the poor can confidently depend, whatever may be their conduct, that violated general principles' (1890, p. 531 – Malthus's emphasis). In modern terms, what he was objecting to was the improvident poor learning the (very simple) 'policy rule' over their 'right to relief'. As we shall see, Malthus saw this logical response as anathema to improving lower-class habits of prudence. His later critic W. P. Alison, however, argued that it was precisely the systematic component of poor relief that would remove the worst evils of degradation and inculcate prudential habits (W. P. Alison 1840, pp. 62, 68-70, 84, 92-8; A. Alison 1840, II, ch. 12). He and many others also criticized the Malthusian remedies on the grounds that reliance on voluntary charity would encourage 'free riders'.

Malthus had a sizable list of other factors shifting the $\dot{P}$ loci. Most emphasized was the substitution of cheap for dear food: especially potatoes for wheat, and also cheap imports for dearer domestically produced supplies. Such substitutions might increase 'indolence' by reducing the total effort supplied to earn a basic subsistence, thus again reducing demand; more importantly they would increase the amplitude of cyclical fluctuations in population because of leaving fewer alternatives in the way of cheap foodstuffs to fall back upon in times of Misery and Vice (Malthus 1890, p. 511; 1836/1936, pp. 233-4; *Parliamentary Papers* 1826-7, q. 3238; Sraffa 1952, letters 225, 228, 515). As with the previous examples, the $\dot{P}$ loci would be shifted rightwards, generating equilibrium at a lower level of wages, and so on. Inversely, Malthus rejected emigration as anything other than a temporary expedient: rather than shifting the $\dot{P}$ loci leftwards as proponents of emigration were implicitly contending, he saw it as shifting the state of things to a point like G in figure 1, following which real wages would rise for a time but by the same token induce population growth that would rapidly fill up the 'room' vacated by the emigrants (1890, pp. 329-32; *Parliamentary Papers* 1826-7, qq. 3421-2; Ghosh 1963; James 1979, pp. 391, 394).

The second paragraph of book II of the *Principles* sets out Malthus's intentions for that work as a whole: 'in a former work [footnote: *Essay on the Principle of Population*] I endeavoured to trace the causes which practically keep down the population of a country to the level of its actual supplies. It is now my object to show what are the causes which chiefly influence these supplies, or call the powers of production forth into the shape of increasing wealth' (1836/1936, p. 309). In my terms, he is using the *Principles* to examine the factors shifting the $\dot{w}$ loci. This is precisely the area surveyed by Spengler (1945, 1971) as composing the 'total population theory', and here I simply recap and apply Spengler's exposition within the framework I am utilizing.

Wage rates (average annual real earnings of the full-employment labour force) shift around rapidly in the short run, tracing out the trajectories observed above, subject to the 'various transverse causes'. In practice disturbances to real wages, unless occasioned by acts of policy such as assisted emigration, were much stronger than disturbances to population, i.e. typically $u > v$ in the mathematical formulation, as drawn in the graphs.

Factors underlying shifts of $\dot{w} = 0$ in the longer term include the following, which, as with the shifts of the $\dot{P}$ loci, Malthus treats as if usually arising in the form of policy issues.

a Shifts in income distribution, especially those arising out of re-distribution of property. Reallocating land from very large estates to the middle classes would, he believed, raise national wealth through increasing demand (Malthus 1798/1926, pp. 287–8n., 344–5; 1836/1936, pp. 350–1, 375); but, as has been seen in the context of egalitarian schemes, excessive subdivision would reverse things and lower wealth (Malthus 1890, p. 510; 1836, p. 377; *Parliamentary Papers* 1826–7, qq. 3201–2; Sraffa 1951, pp. 386–7; Link 1959, pp. 54–5; Paglin 1961, p. 129). Malthus referred explicitly to the possibility of an ideal maximum, and the possibility of using the calculus ('fluxions') to derive it (1836/1936, pp. 7–8).

b An adequate proportion of personal services. This was Malthus putting forward his highly controversial support for a shift from goods to menial services during 'general gluts' – the idea being to maintain the demand for labour at a time of its excess supply, while cutting the supply of goods and therefore the demand for capital while it too was in excess supply (Sraffa 1952, letter 178; Eagly 1974). Malthus asserted that it would theoretically be much better for landlords to spend their wealth on manufactures and imports than to spend it on menial services (1827–1971, pp. 73–4) and equally for capitalists to abate their passion for accumulation at such times (1836/1936, pp. 325–7); but 'satiation of wants', together with the influence of social class and engrained habits of mind, meant that this could not be – indeed the 'general glut' occurred for just such reasons. (By 1827 even Say was accepting Malthus's views on the role of leisure – cf. Hollander 1979, ch. 2.) Malthus's emphasis on the dangers of expanding productive labour relative to unproductive during a 'general glut' gave rise to some sharp jibes by Ricardo (Sraffa 1951, pp. 421, 436), so Malthus clarified his position in 1823 when he compared *advocating* a policy of increasing unproductive employment with *advocating* a bad harvest. 'To wish for such a state of things seems to be something like wishing for a wound in order to see the energy and skill of nature in healing it' (Semmel 1963, p. 169). Note that the stress throughout is on the cyclical fluctuations – in view of Malthus's definition of wealth as excluding services and (over-) emphasizing goods (1836/1936, pp. 37–8) it would be wrong, in my view, to classify him as a long-run underconsumptionist (cf. Black 1967).

c Increases in public expenditure were treated rather similarly by Malthus. He could not share Ricardo's opposition based on complete crowding-out (cf. Sraffa 1955, O'Driscoll 1978), because deficient aggregate demand was important to his own model. But he was rather wary of government spending, partly on political grounds of opposition to bureaucratic interference, partly because of the likelihood that population would grow unless wages in the public sector were kept extremely low. At the same time, he was hesitant to recommend cutting taxation after the Napoleonic wars, unlike the Ricardians, because of the demand-side effects (Petersen 1979, pp. 97–8). He worked with an explicit 'Laffer curve', indicating an optimal level for taxation.

d Rising external commerce, particularly the ability to obtain higher prices overseas for a country's (manufactured) exports relative to import prices. Malthus was rejecting the zero-sum Ricardian view (as he saw it) of foreign trade: trade would stimulate wants and thus demand (Link 1959, p. 56). In practice, foreign trade was seen by Malthus as the most important source of rising British wealth during the French wars (1836/1936, p. 395). In line with his general social views, however, he bitterly rejected the arguments of those pressing for lower wages in order to expand exports (1890, pp. 461, 584n.; *Parliamentary Papers* 1826–7, qq. 3242–3, 3282–91). What of free trade and Malthus's notorious support for the Corn Laws? In part Malthus may have agreed with contemporaries who envisaged him as advocating free trade as a first-best solution for the growth of world incomes but rejecting it for Britain on the second-best grounds of the maintenance of tariffs by other countries, particularly France (Buchanan 1815; cf. Malthus 1970, pp. 123–4, 148–51). This probably overstates Malthus's consistency on the matter, who in any case took a dynamic rather than a static view of comparative advantage; though he did see that, while free trade would on his arguments worsen the position of the labour force in the short run by ruining farmers, it probably would improve it in the long run (Sraffa 1952, letter 336).

e His views on manufacturing and its role in the economy paralleled his views on external trade – not surprisingly since he was presuming Britain would be predominantly an exporter of manufactures. Hence Malthus shifted from blatant hostility in the first *Essay* (because in 1798 he apparently believed labourers would not demand any manufactured goods at all, though he conceded a role for manufacturing in increasing liberty over the previous few centuries) to increasing if restrained support in ensuing editions. There were several reasons for this change of heart. First, he had come to conclude that manufactures were necessary to effect a demand for the agricultural surplus held by landlords and tenant farmers in a world that (desirably for Malthus) fell well short of perfect land equalization. Manufacturing could employ new additions to the work-force without depressing agricultural wages (Malthus 1798/1926, pp. 301–2; 1890, p. 13n.). What was needed was a balance of proportions between agriculture and manufactures (1890, pp. 368–70, 379–80, 409–10; Gilbert 1980). Secondly, he saw manufactures as supporting the existence of a larger middle class (to whom his sympathies most extended), and *vice versa* (Malthus 1836/1936, p. 375; 1970, pp. 118–19). Thirdly, he increasingly appreciated the extent or growth of labourers' demands for manufactured goods; and, the more this could be encouraged, the more likely was 'prudential restraint' whereby labourers would switch tastes from begetting children to consuming conveniences and luxuries (or 'decencies' in Senior's phrase: cf. Senior 1829/1966, pp. 2–5, 26–7, 58).

Malthus disagreed with Senior that rising national wealth would be sufficient to overcome long-run population problems (Senior 1829/1966, pp. 51, 64–5). His view appears to have been that some of the policy proposals just discussed would do no more than damp down the amplitude of the cycles while others would shift the $\dot{P}$ loci leftwards (like reforming the system of poor relief) or the $\dot{w}$ loci rightwards (like rising trade or widespread demand for manufactured goods), in either case allowing higher real wages and a shorter MV duration if the situation was as in figure 2. As stated above, the spiral trajectory of figure 2 in lieu of the ellipse of figure 1 comes about because of the 'preventive check'. The full impact of shortages of room and food thus did not have to be taken out by an extended period of misery. In the first *Essay* the preventive check therefore arises through fear of misery – limiting fertility to minimize further declines of wages (1798/1926, pp. 62–3). Many contemporary critics, such as Godwin (1801) and Perceval (1803), pointed out the richer possibilities of a more sustained preventive check. In the wake of this criticism, Malthus in the second *Essay* formulated the notion of 'prudential restraint'.

'Prudential restraint' is certainly a form of the preventive check, but the latter operates in a wider variety of circumstances. Contrary to some interpretations, such as Hollander's (1984b, p. 260) the behaviour exhibited in figure 2 does not represent the 'prudential check': what is required for the latter is delaying marriage and hence potential offspring for the sake of actually raising the equilibrium wage level. The response to wage changes implied by equation (1) above may be regarded as an example of 'bounded rationality'. The 'passion between the sexes' leads human beings to breed (and thus overbreed) whenever standards of living show a temporary upsurge. Equation (2) would then of course be their undoing. But suppose instead people gave some forethought to equation (2) – suppose, that is, that they were motivated to improve their own living-standards and, seeing that in the end larger families would obstruct this goal, chose to delay marriage and children. Over the relevant horizon the rate of population growth in equation (1) would become negatively rather than positively related to the level of real wages. It is in this sense that 'prudential restraint' in the second *Essay* was offering something analytically new to the population debate.

Significant building-blocks of the argument were present as early as chapter 4 of the first *Essay*. 'The preventive check', Malthus considered, 'appears to operate in some degree through all the ranks of society in England' (1798/1926, p. 63). For the upper classes and most of the lower classes the preventive check was on a scale to bring about the upward-sloping $\dot{P}$ loci already encountered in figure 2. But, for the middle and lower middle classes, plus some of the working class, such as domestic servants, it was conceivable that a rise in wages would on balance lead to a fall in family size. Causation reversed itself and the middle classes restricted their family size partly to 'better their condition' and still more from the fear of losing social status (e.g. Malthus 1798/1926, p. 369). 'Ecological niches', such as for farmers and tradesmen (including the case of Norwegian 'housemen' in Malthus 1890, pp. 144–6), were also part of the argument. Thus, viewed across the whole range of income in society, the relationship between P and w was for Malthus

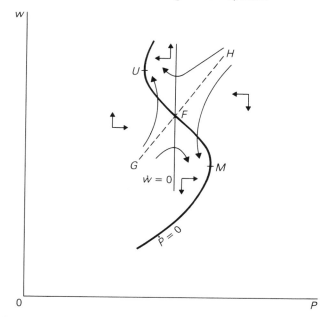

Figure 4   *Wages and population growth: prudential-restraint case*

not monotonic as implied by equation (1) but polynomic[16] – a cubic or higher-order relationship is suggested by his discussion. The curve has a point of inflexion (point *M* in figure 4) where the working class generally gives way to the lower middle class – what Malthus described as that 'round of the ladder, where education ends, and ignorance begins' (1798/1926, p. 65; 1890, pp. 219–21).

The phase diagram in (*P*, *w*) space ought accordingly to be extended upwards from the situation of figure 2, along the lines of figure 4. The intersection of the $\dot{P}=0$ locus with that for $\dot{w}=0$ in the backward-bending part of the former is a saddlepoint. As the arrows of motion show, trajectories evolving from most points of disequilibrium will not cycle around an equilibrium value (as in figure 1) or asymptotically approach it (as in figure 2) but eventually deflect further and further away from it. However, if the location occupied at a particular point of time is along the broken line *GFH*, known as the 'separatrix', then the trajectory will follow straight along the line to the point *F*. Assuming the approach from *G* to be empirically more relevant, the trajectory involves moving further and further away from the MV region.

The derivation of a saddlepoint equilibrium in itself suggests approaching the 'prudential restraint' case using procedures made familiar by the rational-expectations school of macro-economists, since rational-expectations equilibria are generally saddlepoints (see Begg 1982, etc.). The reasons for adopting that framework here, however, go beyond the analytical similarity.

One reason may be unexpected: it is that Malthus used the same phrase. The final chapter of the second *Essay* is entitled, 'On our rational expectations

---

[16]In the empirical work given in von Tunzelmann (1984) the cubic specification is strongly significant in statistical terms.

respecting the future improvement of society', and is devoted to 'prudential restraint' and policies thereto. The phrase 'rational expectations' is used several times in that chapter and elsewhere (e.g. 1890, pp. 456, 460, 524, 543), always in this same connection. Malthus's meaning was of course slightly different in as much as he was referring to the best-grounded forecasts of observers such as himself, rather than the actual participants. These allegedly moderate forecasts for improvement were being contrasted with the 'wilder speculations' of Godwin and others (Godwin had also spoken of 'rational anticipations of human improvement' – 1793/1946, p. 518).

In the next place, the kind of problem being dealt with is strongly analogous to that considered by rational-expectations theorists. The society content to breed mechanistically in response to wage increases as in figures 1 or 2 is doomed to cycle or spiral around the equilibrium point E. But in the 'prudential-restraint' case Malthus is describing 'rational' individuals who look far beyond the bounds of rationality imprisoning their fellows or other societies, to see the virtues of overcoming their reproductive urges in order to benefit their consumption standards. In orthodox rational-expectations models of the monetary system the approach to the saddlepoint F is a hazardous business (cf. Burmeister 1980) because of the 'hit and miss' requirement of having to be located along the separatrix in the first instance. But, as Malthus was well aware, the 'prudential restraint' circumstance was considerably simpler, because, although there were general equilibrium consequences which could be part of the adjustment mechanism via wages and the like (see Chalmers 1841, p. 191), the 'invisible hand' guided the individual in the right direction because he or she would always benefit from such restraint. 'Prudential restraint', he claimed,

> if we ever should make approaches towards it, is to be effected in the way in which we have been in the habit of seeing all the greatest improvements effected, by a direct application to the interest and happiness of each individual. It is not required of us to act from motives to which we are unaccustomed; to pursue a general good which we may not distinctly comprehend, or the effect of which may be weakened by distance and diffusion. The happiness of the whole is to be the result of the happiness of individuals, and to begin first with them. No co-operation is required. Every step tells. He who performs his duty faithfully will reap the full fruits of it, whatever may be the number of others who fail. This duty is intelligible to the humblest capacity. It is merely, that he is not to bring beings into the world for whom he cannot find the means of support. (Malthus 1890, p. 457; Himmelfarb 1984, p. 117)

This of course fitted very conveniently into Malthus's political ideology, as it was the basis of his oft-repeated statement that the remedy for the poor was in their own hands. The role of the government was to provide a context in which such remedies could best flourish – a commitment to civil liberty, especially in regard to security of property. On direct governmental measures Malthus was more hesitant, in the traditional manner of classical economists. The final chapter of the second *Essay*, already alluded to, contained a strong plea for a national system of education – an equally traditional exception to *laissez-faire* in the early nineteenth century – though his later *Summary View* expressed certain doubts (1830/1953, p. 147). Included in Malthus's educational proposals was the idea of drilling the working classes in the principle of population, i.e. instructing individuals in the structure of the model in order to assist them in forming expectations (Chalmers, however, strongly disagreed with the propriety of so doing, preferring instead a general Christian education). There was considerable discussion over the role of savings banks (and thus of state support), and the extent to which they could be agents for promoting foresight among the lower classes. Both Malthus and Ricardo were at one stage managers of savings banks, but appear to have been aware of their lack of popularity among the workers themselves (Malthus 1890, pp. 525–6; Sraffa 1952, letters 156, 161; cf. Fishlow 1961).

On the debit side, Malthus stressed maladministration and misgovernment in discouraging prudence. The Poor Laws were the single greatest obstacle to 'prudential restraint', and Malthus noted the contrast between England and the voluntary Scottish system (1890, pp. 255–6) – later W. P. Alison as a Scot was to reverse the line of attack. Not only would poor-relief condemn the lowest ranks to indolence, unemployment, and so forth, as above; it would also threaten the next ranks above, who were thus unfairly penalized, despite being those amongst whom there was some hope for the spread of greater prudence. Schemes for guaranteeing wages were regarded similarly. Malthus repeatedly affirmed the desirability of higher wages, and there is less reason to doubt that he was being genuine than for some of the other classical economists, in view of his emphasis on aggregate demand and so on, as shown above; but he did not believe that higher wages would necessarily bring about better habits, particularly if the higher wages came about somewhat artificially (*Parliamentary Papers* 1826–7, qq. 3408–11). Instead the system would revert to the cycles or spirals of the bounded-rationality cases.

Yet I think it is valid to see Malthus as quite optimistic about the possibilities for the exercise of rational expectations. As already implied, he assumed from the beginning that the middle classes acted rationally in any case – the point was to induce embourgeoisement of the lower orders (Petersen 1979, pp. 214–15; Himmelfarb 1984, p. 119). Certainly he believed that there were sustained periods of English history for which the preventive check operated sufficiently powerfully to allow wages to rise in trend. But he doubted whether wages at the time he was writing were higher in real terms than they had been at some much earlier epochs, such as the late fifteenth century, and he ventured the opinion in the first *Essay* that European wages would not rise to the level of those in the USA of his day for at least a thousand years (1798/1926, p. 277).

However, I am convinced that a good part of the customary blaming of Malthus for helping give the 'dismal science' its name rests on a confusion. While Malthus did accept the possibilities for generalizing 'prudential restraint', he thought 'moral restraint' quite feeble. 'Moral restraint' meant not just delaying marriage, but refraining from any sexual activity before the delayed marriage. Hopes that it could be relied on to reduce population growth drastically were 'visionary' (1890, pp. 140–1, 538). Thus plumping instead for 'prudential restraint' meant plumping for premarital 'vice', settling for vice as the lesser evil (the confusion here has been pointed out by Levy 1978). Hazlitt (1807/1930, p. 300) sarcastically argued that Malthus was allotting the poor all the misery and the rich as much vice as was necessary for restraint.

At the outset of the *Principles*, Malthus is forthright in his rejection of monocausality (1836/1936, pp. 4–6), determinancy (p. 1) and linearity (pp. 6–8). These have to be built into any model purporting to be Malthusian. He is equally adamant about empirical relevance as a *sine qua non*:

> The first business of philosophy is to account for things as they are; and till our theories will do this, they ought not to be the ground of any practical conclusion. I should never have had that steady and unshaken confidence in the theory of population which I have invariably felt, if it had not appeared to me to be confirmed, in the most remarkable manner, by the state of society as it actually exists in every country with which we are acquainted. (p. 8)

To explain the economic–demographic history of England from the mid eighteenth to the mid nineteenth century, I am showing in other work that it is necessary to invoke both the bounded-rationality and the rational-expectations versions of his model, i.e. figures 2 and 4 above.[17] Nevertheless, in so doing Malthus's boasts in the above quote appear entirely justified.

The present essay examines the logic of Malthus's model, attempting to demonstrate – at least in the skeletal version outlined above – its consistency and generality. I have argued for the relative unimportance of diminishing returns except as a long-run tendency, and the relative importance of short-run disturbances. These cyclical fluctuations occur both in the economic sphere and in the demographic, and their interrelationship is the core of the Malthusian model. My final section shows that the cyclical return to a subsistence equilibrium can be evaded by the exercise of 'prudential restraint', and this is why the latter is such a vital addition to the model when introduced into the second *Essay*. It also gives Malthus an extremely strong claim to be the predecessor of the most important development in modern macroeconomic theory: the school of 'rational expectations'.

From the point of view of 'optimum population' it gives a convincing theoretical backing to Malthus's views on population size. Contrary to his reputation among contemporaries, he had declared in the first *Essay* that, 'there is not a truer criterion of the happiness and innocence of a people, than the rapidity of their increase' (1798/1926, p. 108). He goes on to make it clear that this is because, to obtain such sustained and rapid increase, food output must be growing at least as quickly (p. 137). In the second *Essay* he came to oppose high fertility because it was likely to be associated with the evil of high infant- and child-mortality rates (1890, p. 549), as in the ellipse model of figure 1. At the same time he began an appendix to the third edition by declaring that he was 'no enemy to population' (p. 546), and he was being quite consistent. He came to accept the relationship that many of his eighteenth-century predecessors such as Steuart had drawn between large populations and prosperity, except that he reversed the path of causation (pp. 432–3). What he most wanted was a 'low-pressure' demographic system

---

[17]The former fits well until about 1820, the latter thereafter. It is probably no coincidence that real wages begin to rise in sustained fashion at exactly the same time as the rate of population growth begins to fall (von Tunzelmann 1984).

of the kind that Wrigley and Schofield (1981) argue England was indeed experiencing in his time. The object of 'prudential restraint', brought face to face with the geometric and arithmetic ratios, was to 'unite the two grand *desiderata*, a great actual population and a state of society in which abject poverty and dependence are comparatively but little known; two objects which are far from being incompatible' (Malthus 1890, p. 460).

REFERENCES

Alison, A. 1840: *The Principles of Population and their Connection with Human Happiness*. Edinburgh: William Blackwood and Sons; London: Thomas Cadell.
Alison, W. P. 1840: *Observations on the Management of the Poor in Scotland*. Edinburgh: William Blackwood and Sons.
Begg, D. K. H. 1982: *The Rational Expectations Revolution in Macroeconomics: Theories and Evidence*. Deddington, Oxon: Philip Allan.
Bonar, J. 1885: *Malthus and his Work*. London: Macmillan; repr. London: Frank Cass, 1966.
Black, R. D. Collinson 1967: Parson Malthus, the General and the Captain. *Economic Journal*, 77, 59–74.
Boulding, K. E. 1955: The Malthusian model as a general system. *Social and Economic Studies*, 4, 195–205.
—— 1978: *Ecodynamics: A New Theory of Societal Evolution*. Beverly Hills and London: Sage Publications.
Boyce, W. E., and di Prima, R. C. 1977: *Elementary Differential Equations*, 3rd edn. New York: John Wiley.
[Buchanan, D.] 1815: Malthus on the Corn Laws. *Edinburgh Review*, 48, 491–505.
Burmeister, E. 1980: On some conceptual issues in rational expectations modelling. *Journal of Money, Credit and Banking*, 12, 800–16.
Cannan, E. 1892: The origin of the law of diminishing returns, 1813–15. *Economic Journal*, 2, 53–69.
—— 1920: *A History of the Theories of Production and Distribution in English Political Economy from 1776 to 1848*, 3rd edn. London: P. S. King and Son. (1st edn 1893.).
Chalmers, T. 1832: *On Political Economy, in connexion with the Moral State and Moral Prospects of Society*. Glasgow: William Collins.
—— 1841: *The Sufficiency of a Parochial System without a Poor Rate*, Glasgow: William Collins.
Cole, H. S. D., Freeman, C., Jahoda, M. and Pavitt, K. L. R. (for the Science Policy Research Unit) 1973: *Thinking about the Future: A Critique of 'The Limits to Growth'*. London: Sussex University Press and Chatto and Windus.
Condorcet, A. N. de (M.-J.-A.-N. Caritat, Marquis de Condorcet) 1955: *Sketch for a Historical Picture of the Progress of the Human Mind*, tr. June Barraclough. London: Weidenfeld and Nicolson. (First published in French, 1795.)
Costabile, L. 1983: Natural prices, market prices and effective demand in Malthus. *Australian Economic Papers*, 22, 144–70.
—— and Rowthorn, R. 1984: *Malthus's Theory of Wages and Growth*. University of Cambridge, Faculty of Economics and Politics: Research Paper Series, 31.
Davis, K. 1955: Malthus and the theory of population. In Paul F. Lazarsfeld and Morris Rosenberg (eds), *The Language of Social Research*, New York: The Free Press; London: Collier-Macmillan, pp. 540–53.
Dow, L. A. 1977: Malthus on sticky wages, the upper turning point, and general glut. *History of Political Economy*, 9, 303–21.
Dupâquier, J., Fauve-Chamoux, A., and Grebenik, E. (eds) 1983: *Malthus Past and Present*. London: Academic Press.
Eagly, R. V. 1974: *The Structure of Classical Economic Theory*. New York and London: Oxford University Press.

Eltis, W. A. 1980: Malthus's theory of effective demand and growth. *Oxford Economic Papers*, n.s. 32, 19–56.
—— 1984: *The Classical Theory of Economic Growth*. London: Macmillan.
Ensor, G. 1818: *An Inquiry concerning the Population of Nations*. London: Effingham Wilson; repr. New York: Augutus M. Kelley, 1967.
Fishlow, A. 1961: The Trustee Savings Banks, 1817–1861. *Journal of Economic History*, 21, 26–40.
Forrester, J. W. 1971: *World Dynamics*. Cambridge, Mass.: Wright-Allen Press.
Franklin, B. 1751: *Observations, concerning the Increase of Mankind, Peopling of Countries etc*. In Albert Henry Smyth (ed.), *The Writings of Benjamin Franklin*, vol. III: *1750–9*. New York: Haskell House, 1970. (1st edn 1907.)
Ghosh, R. N. 1963: Malthus on emigration and colonization: letters to Wilmot-Horton. *Economica*, n.s. 30, 45–62.
Gilbert, G. 1980: Economic growth and the poor in Malthus's *Essay on Population*. *History of Political Economy*, 12, 83–96.
Godwin, W. 1793: *Enquiry concerning Political Justice and its Influence on Morals and Happiness*. London: G. G. J. and J. Robinson. 3rd edn (1797), repr. Toronto: University of Toronto Press, ed. F. E. L. Priestley, 1946 (variorum).
—— 1801: *Thoughts, Occasioned by a Perusal of Dr Parr's Spital Sermon*. London: Taylor and Wilks. In Jack W. Marken and Burton R. Pollin (eds), *Uncollected Writings (1785–1822) . . . by William Godwin*. Gainesville, Fla: Scholars' Facsimiles and Reprints, 1968, pp. 281–374.
—— 1820: *Of Population: An Enquiry concerning the Power of Increase in the Numbers of Mankind, being an Answer to Mr Malthus's Essay on that Subject*. London: Longman, Hurst, Rees, Orme and Brown; repr. New York: Augutus M. Kelley, 1964.
Hall, C. 1805: *Observations on the Principal Conclusion of Mr Malthus's 'Essay on Population'*. London: R. Wilks; repr. New York: Augustus M. Kelley, 1965.
Harvey-Phillips, M. B. 1984: Malthus's theodicy; the intellectual background of his contribution to political economy. *History of Political Economy*, 16, 591–608.
Hazlitt, W. 1807: *A Reply to the 'Essay on Population' by the Rev. T. R. Malthus* . . . London: Longman, Hurst, Rees and Orme. In P. P. Howe (ed.), *The Complete Works of William Hazlitt in Twenty-One Volumes*, London and Toronto: J. M. Dent and Sons, 1930, vol. I, 177–364.
Hickson, W. E. 1849: Malthus. *Westminster Review*, 52, 133–201.
Himmelfarb, G. 1984: *The Idea of Poverty: England in the Early Industrial Age*. London and Boston, Mass.: Faber and Faber.
Hirshleifer, J. 1977: Economics from a biological viewpoint. *Journal of Law and Economics*, 20, 1–52.
Hollander, S. 1969: Malthus and the post-Napoleonic depression. *History of Political Economy*, 1, 306–28.
—— 1977: Ricardo and the Corn Laws: a revision, *History of Political Economy*, 9, 1–47.
—— 1979: *The Economics of David Ricardo*. Toronto: University of Toronto Press and Heinemann.
—— 1984a: The wage path in classical growth models: Ricardo, Malthus, and Mill. *Oxford Economic Papers*, n.s. 36, 200–13.
—— 1984b: 'Dynamic equilibrium' with constant wages: J. S. Mill's Malthusian analysis of the secular wage path. *Kyklos*, 37, 247–65.
James, P. 1979: *Population Malthus: His Life and Times*. London: Routledge and Kegan Paul.
Keynes, J. M. 1933: *Essays in Biography*. London: Macmillan. In Donald E. Moggridge and Elizabeth Johnson (eds), *The Collected Writings of John Maynard Keynes*, London: Macmillan and the Royal Economic Society, 1972, vol. X.
Lee, R. D. 1978: Models of preindustrial population dynamics with application to England. In Charles Tilly (ed.), *Historical Studies of Changing Fertility*, Princeton, NJ: Princeton University Press, pp. 155–208.
Levy, D. 1978: Some normative aspects of the Malthusian controversy. *History of Political Economy*, 10, 271–85.

Link, R. G. 1959: *English Theories of Economic Fluctuations, 1815–1848*. New York: Columbia University Press.

Lloyd, P. J. 1969: Elementary geometrical/arithmetical series and early production theory. *Journal of Political Economy*, 77, 21–34.

McCleary, G. F. 1952: *The Malthusian Population Theory*. London: Faber and Faber.

McClelland, P. D., and Zeckhauser, R. J. 1982: *Demographic Dimensions of the New Republic: American Interregional Migration, Vital Statistics, and Manumissions, 1800–1860*. Cambridge: Cambridge University Press.

Malthus, T. R. 1798: *An Essay on the Principle of Population, as it Affects the Future Improvement of Society*. London: Johnson; repr. London: Macmillan and the Royal Economic Society, 1926.

—— 1826: *An Essay on the Principle of Population, or a View of its Past and Present Effects on Human Happiness*. London: John Murray; repr. Ward Lock, 1890.

—— 1823: *The Measure of Value Stated and Illustrated*. London: John Murray; repr. New York: Kelley and Millman, 1957.

—— 1827: *Definitions in Political Economy*. London: John Murray; repr. New York: Augustus M. Kelley, 1971.

—— 1830: *A Summary View of the Principle of Population*. London: John Murray, from *Encyclopaedia Britannica*, 1824. In D. V. Glass (ed.), *Introduction to Malthus*. London: Watts, 1953.

—— 1836: *Principles of Political Economy Considered with a View to their practical application*. London: William Pickering; repr. Tokyo: International Economic Circle and Kyo Bun Kwan, 1936. (1st edn, London: John Murray, 1820.)

—— 1970: *The Pamphlets of Thomas Robert Malthus*. New York: Augustus M. Kelley.

Meadows, D. H., et al. 1972: *The Limits to Growth*. New York: Universe Books; London: Earth Island.

Minami, R. 1961: An analysis of Malthus's population theory. *Journal of Economic Behavior*, 1, 53–63.

Moes, J. E. 1958: A dynamic interpretation of Malthus's principle of population. *Kyklos*, 4, 58–80.

Mokyr, J. 1983: *Why Ireland Starved: A Quantitative and Analytical History of the Irish Economy, 1800–1850*. London: Allen and Unwin.

Nordhaus, W. D. 1973: World dynamics: measurement without data. *Economic Journal*, 83, 1156–83.

O'Driscoll, G. P., Jr 1977: The Ricardian non-equivalence theorem. *Journal of Political Economy*, 85, 207–10.

O'Leary, J. J. 1942: Malthus and Keynes. *Journal of Political Economy*, 50, 901–19.

—— 1943: Malthus's general theory of employment and the post-Napoleonic depression. *Journal of Economic History*, 3, 185–200.

Paglin, M. 1965: *Malthus and Lauderdale: The Anti-Ricardian Tradition*. New York: Augustus M. Kelley.

Parliamentary Papers 1826–7, vol. V: *Reports from the Select Committee on Emigration from the United Kingdom*. Repr. Shannon: Irish University Press, Emigration Series, 2, 1968.

Peacock, A. T. 1952: Theory of population and modern economic analysis: I. *Population Studies*, 6, 114–22.

[Perceval, E.] 1803: *Remarks on Mr Malthus's 'Essay on the Principle of Population'*. London: R. Bickerstaff.

Petersen, W. 1979: *Malthus*. London: Heinemann.

Place, F. 1822: *Illustrations and Proofs of the Principle of Population*. London: Longman, Hurst, Rees, Orme and Brown. In N. E. Himes, *Place on Population*. London: Allen and Unwin, 1930.

Price, R. 1803: *Observations on Reversionary Payments*, 6th edn, ed. W. Morgan. London: T. Cadell and W. Davies. (1st edn, 1771.)

Pullen, J. M. 1981: Malthus's theological ideas and their influence on his principle of population. *History of Political Economy*, 13, 39–54.

Rashid, S. 1977: Malthus's model of general gluts. *History of Political Economy*, 9, 366–83.

Ricardo, D.: *see* Sraffa, P.

Sadler, M. T. 1830: *The Law of Population*. London: John Murray.

Samuelson, P. A. 1966: *The Collected Scientific Papers of Paul A. Samuelson*, ed. Joseph E. Stiglitz, Cambridge, Mass.: MIT Press, vol. I.

—— 1978: The canonical classical model of political economy. *Journal of Economic Literature*, 16, 1415–34.

Sanchez, D. A., et al. 1983: *Differential Equations: An Introduction*. Reading, Mass.: Addison-Wesley.

Santurri, E. N. 1982: Theodicy and social policy in Malthus's thought. *Journal of the History of Ideas*, 43, 315–30.

Schumpeter, J. A. 1954: *A History of Economic Analysis*, ed. E. B. Schumpeter. New York: Oxford University Press.

Semmel, B. 1964–5: Malthus: 'physiocracy' and the commercial system. *Economic History Review*, 2nd ser. 17, 522–35.

—— (ed.) 1963: *Occasional Papers of T. R. Malthus on Ireland, Population, and Political Economy*. New York: Burt Franklin.

Sen, A. K. 1981: *Poverty and Famines: an essay on entitlement and deprivation*. Oxford: Clarendon Press.

Senior, N. W. 1829: *Two Lectures on Population, Delivered before the University of Oxford, 1828*. London: Saunders and Otley. In *Selected Writings on Economics by Nassau W. Senior*, New York: Augustus M. Kelley, 1966.

Short, T. 1767: *A Comparative History of the Increase and Decrease of Mankind*. London: W. Nicoll and C. Etherington; repr. Gregg International, ed. Richard Wall, 1973.

Smith, K. 1951: *The Malthusian Controversy*. London: Routledge and Kegan Paul.

Smith, V. E. 1951: The classicists' use of 'demand'. *Journal of Political Economy*, 59, 242–57.

—— 1956: Malthus's theory of demand and its influence on value theory. *Scottish Journal of Political Economy*, 3, 205–20.

Sowell, T. 1972: *Say's Law: an historical analysis*. Princeton, NJ: Princeton University Press.

—— 1974: *Classical Economics Reconsidered*. Princeton, NJ: Princeton University Press.

Spengler, J. J. 1945: Malthus's total population theory: a restatement and reappraisal. *Canadian Journal of Economics and Political Science*, 11, 83–110, 234–64.

—— 1957: Malthus the Malthusian and Malthus the economist. *Southern Economic Journal*, 24, 1–11.

—— 1965: Today's circumstances and yesterday's theories: Malthus on 'services'. *Kyklos*, 18, 601–14.

—— 1971: Malthus on Godwin's *Of Population*. *Demography*, 8, 1–26.

Spindler, Z. A., and Maki, D. 1979: More on the effects of unemployment compensation on the rate of unemployment in Great Britain. *Oxford Economic Papers*, n.s. 31, 147–64.

Sraffa, P. (with the collaboration of M. H. Dobb) 1951: *The Works and Correspondence of David Ricardo*, vol. II: *Notes on Malthus's 'Principles of Political Economy'*. Cambridge: Cambridge University Press and the Royal Economic Society.

—— 1952: *The Works and Correspondence of David Ricardo*, vol. VI: *Letters 1810–15*; vol. VII: *Letters 1816–18*; vol. VIII: *Letters 1819–June 1821*; vol. IX: *Letters July 1821–1823*. Cambridge: Cambridge University Press and the Royal Economic Society.

—— 1955: Malthus on public works. *Economic Journal*, 65, 513–14.

Townsend, J. 1971: *A Dissertation on the Poor Laws, by a Well-wisher to Mankind*, ed. Ashley Montagu and Mark Neuman. Berkeley, Calif.: University of California Press. (First published 1786.)

—— 1791: *A Journey through Spain in the Years 1786 and 1787*. London: C. Dilly.

Verhulst, P. F. 1838: Notice sur la loi que la population suit dans son accroissement. *Correspondance mathématique et physique*, 10, 113–21.

Volterra, V. 1931: *Leçons sur la théorie mathématique de la lutte pour la vie*, Cahiers Scientifiques, École Polytechnique, 7. Paris: Gauthiers-Villars.

von Tunzelmann, G. N. 1984: Malthus and the standard-of-living debate. Paper for the Economic and Social Research Council Quantitative Economic History Workshop, Oxford.

Weyland, J. 1816: *The Principles of Population and Production*. London: Baldwin, Cradock and Joy; repr. Shannon: Irish University Press, 1971.

Whately, R. 1831: *Introductory Lectures on Political Economy*. London: B. Fellowes.

Wrigley, E. A., and Schofield, R. S. 1981: *The Population History of England, 1541–1871: a reconstruction*. London: Edward Arnold.

Young, R. M. 1969: Malthus and the evolutionists: the common context of biological and social theory. *Past and Present*, 40, 109–41.

Malthus and Boserup:
A Dynamic Synthesis

Ronald Demos Lee

INTRODUCTION

There are two grand themes in macro-demographic theory: the Malthusian one, that population equilibrates with resources at some level mediated by technology and a conventional standard of living; and the Boserupian one, that technological change is itself spurred by increases in population. The striking association between the levels and changes in technology and population over the past million years leaves no doubt in my mind that at least one of these views is correct. But it is also possible that both are, since the two theories are not contradictory, but rather complementary. They share the assumption of diminishing returns to labour for a fixed technological level. To this common ground Malthus adds the assumption that population growth rates are endogenous, while Boserup adds the assumption that technological change is endogenous. This paper examines the behaviour of a system governed by the mechanisms of both theories, and, in particular, considers the broad qualitative features of the dynamics of such a system.

The synthetic theory to be developed here is intended to raise, and to address, some interesting and I believe important questions of the following sort. If larger populations encourage more rapid technological progress, and higher technological states induce more population growth, can stationary or steady-state equilibria exist? If so, what are their properties? Since both theories individually, as well as the two taken together, lead us to expect that population and technology will move together, is there any hope of testing the theories individually using historical data series? Can a synthetic model of this sort explain what neither is able to separately: the accelerating upward spiral of population and technology? Does the nature of Boserupian progress depend on such Malthusian features as the strengths of the positive and preventive checks? Can we explain the relative technological performances of Africa, China and Europe in a framework of this sort? Following a demographic catastrophe, does the system move permanently

I gratefully acknowledge stimulating discussions, suggestions and comments on earlier drafts from Ester Boserup, E. A. Hammel, Kenneth Wachter, Andrew Foster, William Hodges, Daniel Siever, Paul David, John Ermisch, Gary Saxonhouse and David Weir. Research for this chapter was supported by the US National Institute of Child Health and Human Development, grant number H. D. 18107.

to a lower technological level? In short, there appear to be a large number of questions of a sort that have not often been raised before, and that may fruitfully be addressed in this context.

Of course there are great difficulties, perhaps even absurdities, addressing these issues at such a high level of abstraction and in such generality. None the less, I believe the questions are sufficiently interesting to warrant exploration, even if one ends up merely with a useful map of population theory, rather than of reality. Indeed I am not by any means the first to address them. In addition to Boserup's (1965, 1981) seminal work, Simon (1977, 1981), Robinson and Schutjer (1984) and Pryor and Maurer (1982) have also approached these issues, although from a somewhat different perspective.[1] My approach here is closest to that of Pryor and Maurer's; a comparison will be given in footnote 8, below. Also, a number of anthropologists, such as Blanton (1975), have informally discussed the interactions of the Malthusian and Boserupian models.

No model of the highly abstract and simplified kind to be developed here can aspire to realistic interpretation of any actual historical processes, since too much of importance is left out, and among the omitted influences will probably be found the decisive ones for any particular passage of history. But, even if the included influences are relatively weak, their effects will tend to cumulate over the centuries, while others tend to cancel, and therefore they may become centrally important in the very long run.

The approach taken in this essay is simply described. Imagine a blank graph with population size on the horizontal axis and technological level on the vertical axis. Every point on this graph represents a combination of population size and technology, while natural resources, including land, are held constant during this exercise. Malthusian theory tells us that at some of these points, where population is sparse relative to the technology (and resources), welfare will be high and therefore population will be growing. For other combinations population will be declining, and for still others population will be stationary, in Malthusian equilibrium. It is not immediately clear what the shapes and locations of these sets of points will be; that is a subject to be explored in this essay. But the principle is clear enough.

The theory of Boserup suggests that for some points on the graph, where population is dense relative to technology (and resources), technological progress will occur. For others, where population is relatively sparse, technological retrogression will occur, and for still others technology will be stagnant. Once again it is not obvious what the shapes and locations of the regions will be, but the principle is straightforward.

Now note that any point on the graph will fall both in a region described by Malthusian theory and one described by Boserupian theory. Thus for any point, population and technology are both growing, both declining, moving in opposite directions, or one or both is/are stationary. We can therefore qualitatively describe the direction of motion for any point, and we can also

---

[1]For example, Simon (1977, p. 161) asserts that Boserup is concerned not with the cause of original invention, but only with the adoption of existing inventions. My interpretation of Boserup, as sketched above, is quite different.

locate any equilibrium points. Consideration of the shapes and relative positions of the regions turns out to be very suggestive. Furthermore, the diagrams are readily altered to reflect differing strengths of the preventive check, different degrees of returns to scale or diminishing returns to labour and technology in the presence of fixed resources, and so on. This kind of graph, which plots the direction of change against levels, is called a 'phase diagram'.

Before we are able to draw and interpret phase diagrams for the Malthus–Boserup case, a great deal of preliminary analysis must be undertaken to determine the appropriate shapes and locations of the regions. This requires an excursion through a number of branches of population theory beyond those developed by Malthus and Boserup, including elements of the theories of Bowen (1954) and Sauvy (1969) relating to economic surplus, the maximum and minimum population, and so on.

GENERAL DISCUSSION OF THE THEORIES

Malthus

Malthus forcefully expressed the view that the rate of population growth was positively related to the general level of material welfare, which was in turn negatively related to population size, due to diminishing returns to labour inputs on scarce agricultural land. At some level of welfare, population would neither grow nor decline; this level was known as the long-run equilibrium wage. Corresponding to this equilibrium wage there would be an equilibrium population size, depending, of course, on the state of technology and the available resources. Advances in technology or resources would temporarily raise wages, but the resulting population growth would soon force the wage level back to its equilibrium level. This theory provides a simple interpretation of population history: as the equilibrium population size or carrying-capacity of an area expands due to autonomously occurring inventions, actual population size quickly follows. This is what Julian Simon (1977, 1981) has aptly called the 'invention pull' view of population history.

The dependence of the population growth rate on net wages might come about in many ways – through mortality, marriage, fecundity, an implemented decision to alter marital fertility, and so on; the exact mechanism need not concern us, and obviously it would vary by cultural and technological setting. There is a considerable body of evidence to suggest that, in Third World agricultural populations, fertility and mortality do indeed react to material well-being, as measured, for example, by size of landholding, in a manner consistent with the Malthusian propositions (see, for example, literature reviews for fertility by Mueller and Short 1983, and Stokes and Schutjer 1984).

Biological subsistence, technological subsistence and the normative living-standard

The notion of biological subsistence is fairly straightforward: some level of consumption, dependent on climate, work effort, and the general level of morbidity and mortality, is necessary to enable a population to survive and replace itself. Of course, being biologically able to replace itself only means that Malthusian positive checks do not prevent replacement; it does not mean that a population *will* replace itself. Preventive checks, both institutional and individual, may require a much higher level of consumption before replacement takes place. The level of wages behaviourally necessary for replacement is the normative living-standard. The normative living-standard is implicit in the relation between fertility and income levels (in the context of a given level of mortality), and there are many theories about it. Certainly the normative standard eventually rises together with technological level. The 'new home economics' argues that technological advances, particularly as these require human capital, lead to increases in the value of time, and therefore raise the relative price of children, and hence the normative standard of living. At the same time, the increased periods of training and education which are required for children in high-technology regimes also increase the direct costs of children and reduce their economic contributions while in the parental home. This also leads to an increase in the normative standard of living.

The notion of 'technological' subsistence is also helpful. By this I mean the level of income necessary to enable (and induce) parents to make the investments in their children's training (human capital formation) essential for the support of the contemporary level of technology. For technological regimes up to the agricultural, there might be little difference between biological subsistence and technological subsistence, since, although skills may be critical to success, training is largely 'on the job', and it is relatively limited. But, at the industrial stage of technology, considerable investment in human capital is necessary, and, unless the normative standard exceeds the level of technological subsistence, a given level of technology may not be sustainable. In any event, per-capita consumption only rises with technological development in the long run to the extent that the technological and normative standards do. It is only the increase in these that prevents the iron law of wages from dictating a standard of living for Europeans no higher than for the Kalahari Bushmen. Although we cannot read living-standards from the phase diagrams we shall be using, based on the considerations outlined above we can infer that equilibrium living-standards rise with technological level, and do so most sharply during the industrial stage.

It is, of course, peculiar to speak of 'wages' as the indicator of individual welfare, as if labour markets were a universal institution which existed even in hunting-and-gathering regimes. We could instead relate population growth to the average product of labour. However, in this case Malthusian forces would drive population size to the maximum consistent with subsistence, and there would be no surplus at all. In many settings, institutional arrangements of one sort or another will empower an elite to extract a portion of total output – through slavery, competitive labour markets, taxation and so on. Population growth rates for the majority should be related to the per-capita share of the output they retain, which for convenience I shall call the 'wage'. Such institutional arrangements prevent the population equilibrium from occurring at the maximum sustainable level, and ensure the existence of surplus. Surplus may, in turn, play an important role in technological progress. These matters will be discussed in more detail later.

Boserup

Ester Boserup (1965, 1981) has suggested an apparently quite different view of economic–demographic history, stressing that population growth may encourage technological progress in the longer run, although perhaps depressing labour productivity in the short run. This general view has been shared by many economists, among them Kuznets (1960), Clark (1968), Phelps (1966, 1968) and, in most detail, Simon (1977, 1981, n.d.). Boserup observes quite plausibly that the likelihood of technological advance rises in response to increasing population density, which shifts both the supply curve and the demand curve for technological innovation. Higher population density leads to increased intensity of labour use; this raises the pay-off from an innovation. Higher population density leads, *ceteris paribus*, to lower per-capita income, which raises the utility gain from an innovation. Population growth and the resulting urbanization create new problems (that is, opportunities for invention), concerning, for example, organization and food transport. The supply schedule of innovations is also shifted by population growth for many reasons; among these are that transportation and communication become cheaper per capita; the division of labour becomes more specialized; and, in the transition to settled agriculture, the new possibility of accumulating durable goods opens up many areas for innovation, and raises both the supply and the demand for innovations.

Thus as a population grows within a given territory, the rate of technological progress, or better the probability of technological progress, increases. However, these long-run advantages of greater population density are counter-balanced by the short-run disadvantages arising from diminishing returns. It is economically disadvantageous for a small population to become more concentrated, since the productivity of labour in agriculture drops sharply; the most efficient production methods for a small population use vast amounts of land with long periods of fallow, and for this reason are incompatible with population concentration. Therefore population growth, although it initially leads to diminishing returns to labour, in the long run, by forcing population concentration, leads to a higher likelihood of technological advance which may benefit agriculture. Cultivators, in the face of their declining labour productivity, increase their hours of work rather than suffer a proportional decline in their consumption of food. Thus labour inputs grow more rapidly than population, and the supply curve of labour is backward-bending. According to this theory, population grows erratically and autonomously, forcing longer hours and more labour-intensive agricultural techniques, but leading eventually to increasingly sophisticated technology and social organization: population growth is the engine of agricultural progress. There is a small but growing body of statistical empirical literature on the subject, largely cross-sectional, which appears to offer some support to the Boserup hypothesis (in addition to Boserup's own work, see

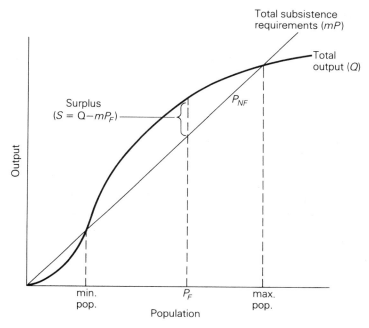

Figure 1 Population size and surplus for given resources and technology

Pingali and Bingswanger 1983, Pryor 1983, and Evenson 1984; and see the literature reviewed by Simon 1977).

Surplus and technical progress

In her more recent book, Boserup (1981) appears to suggest that technological progress depends in part on the quantity of surplus output that is available, measured as the excess of total output over total subsistence requirements. This version of the theory has considerable appeal, provided that technological innovations are expected to come primarily from a non-agricultural sector or an urban population, for these can exist only when the average product of labour exceeds subsistence. This will be true whether the surplus is extracted by a landowning elite through the operation of competitive markets or the coercion of unfree labour, or agricultural production takes place on family farms, and the families choose to consume a portion of their output in the form of non-agricultural goods produced by another sector of the economy. The critical point to emerge from this line of reasoning is that, for a given state of technology, population might not only be too small and sparse to encourage technological progress, but it could also be too large and dense so that no surplus existed at all. These possibilities are illustrated in figure 1. The maximum surplus for a given technology would evidently occur when the marginal product of labour equalled subsistence, as it would in Malthusian equilibrium with competitive labour markets. By a similar argument, for a given population size or density, the state of technology might be either unsustainably high or unsustainably low – this last case arising because at that level of technology and population size the average product equalled subsistence, and thus no surplus was generated.

Figure 1 also shows how the potential population of the non-food-producing sector (P_{NF}) is determined by the size of the food surplus (S), which is in turn determined by the size of the food-producing population relative to its technology and resources (P_F). The larger the population engaged in non-food-producing activities (artisans, intellectuals, service workers, and so on), the greater the possible division of labour, and the greater the possibilities for technological advance.[2] For a *given* P_F, the maximum possible total population is $P_F + P_{NF}$. The overall maximum population, labelled 'max. pop.' in figure 1, consists entirely of food producers, since there is no surplus ($P_{NF} = 0$).

In addition, of course, differences in the way the surplus is used will affect the likelihood of technical progress. If landowners choose to bathe in milk, the surplus will go to support cows, with little or no progress-inducing effect. If they instead invest in social infrastructure, the surplus will go to support labourers and artisans, and should facilitate technological progress, perhaps beyond its immediate effect on the capital stock.

Conceptual units of measure and observation

The question inevitably arises of how one measures technology, or to what geographic area this analysis is to be applied. The geographic area depends on the extent to which information, commodities and people flow between groups. The proper unit now is surely nearly global; not long ago it might have been hemispheres or continents. It has been shown that the neolithic revolution diffused at the rate of about one kilometre per year from Mesopotamia to regions thousands of kilometres away (Ammerman and Cavalli-Sforza 1971), suggesting that even a continental unit is too small for that period. If the relevant unit has been growing geographically larger as transportation and communication improve, then 'population', as defined for present purposes, has been increasing faster than its numerical growth, since growth of the effective unit also occurs through increased contacts and trade.

Technology is usually measured by economists in terms of the amount of output produced from given amounts of inputs. I shall instead understand technology to be measured in some sort of 'natural' unit: numbers of useful ideas, numbers of scientific books or articles published, type of control established over natural processes, and so on. In practice this would probably pose insuperable difficulties. Fortunately the analysis can be carried out in either way, as is explained below (pp. 115–16).

---

[2]Alexander Everett wrote in 1826, 'It is sufficiently notorious, that an increase of population on a given territory is followed immediately by a division of labour; which produces in its turn the invention of new machines, an improvement of methods in all the departments of industry, and a rapid progress in the various branches of art and science (1826/1970, p. 26, as quoted in Simon and Steinmann, n.d.). The Smithian advantages to a finer division of labour are of a static nature, and not to be confused with the present argument that the division of labour encourages technological progress through 'learning-by-doing', and in other indirect ways.

I have so far barely mentioned physical capital, and indeed it appears so closely intertwined with technology in Boserup's analysis as well as in other treatments of induced technological change as to be very difficult to separate clearly: Hahn and Matthews (1964, p. 577) discuss the view that 'capital accumulation and technical progress influence each other in such a way as to make separation of the two impossible or useless'. Not only are capital and gross investment the carriers of technology, but gross investment has also been taken to drive technological progress (Arrow 1962, and Kaldor and Mirlees 1962). Human capital and technology are similarly intertwined. The size of the surplus appears at least as relevant for capital formation as for technological progress. I shall henceforth refer to technology only, while realizing a certain ambiguity.

POPULATION, LABOUR SUPPLY AND OUTPUT

Diminishing returns to labour

Both Malthus and Boserup assert that growing populations encounter diminishing returns to labour in food production, *ceteris paribus*. Let Q represent total output of food. Q is defined to be output net of any activities and inputs necessary to maintain the productivity of the land. Let L be total labour input in food production, measured in hours; let A be the level of relevant technology; and let R be the availability of natural resources, particularly land. Then we may write,

$$Q = Q(A, L, R) \qquad (1)$$

with Q_A, Q_L and Q_R all > 0.

If A and R are held constant, while labour, L, is increased from initially a very low level, then the changes in output, Q, reflect the Boserupian sequence of chosen technique, ranging from hunting and gathering, through progressively shortening fallow, eventually to multicropping. This sequence is implicit in the shape of the function Q; it is accompanied by diminishing returns; and of course it involves no change in technological level, since A is held constant.

It is possible that when total inputs of labour are small, labour will experience increasing returns $(Q_{LL} > 0)$, but eventually decreasing returns will set in $(Q_{LL} < 0)$. The size of the labour force at which diminishing returns set in will increase with both the quantity of available resources, R, and the level of technology, A. At all levels of inputs, however, we should expect there to be diminishing returns to R and to A, for fixed inputs of the other factors. We should also expect that more of any one factor would raise the marginal productivity of the other factors. Thus we should expect, and shall assume, Q_{AA}, $Q_{RR} < 0$; Q_{AL}, Q_{RL} and $Q_{AR} > 0$, where the subscripts indicate partial derivatives. Further conditions on the function will be introduced later.

Surplus extraction, labour supply and leisure

Suppose that the bulk of the food-producing population, which produces an average hourly product of $q = Q/L$, retains a fraction $(1 - e)$ of this product for their own use, where e is the rate of surplus extraction. The proportion e which is not retained will include payment to other factors of production besides labour, taxes, tithes, the share of slave-owners, foreign tribute, or whatever. The quantity $q(1 - e)$ I will call the 'net hourly wage', and for convenience denote w. When there are no taxes on workers, and when workers own no land and work for landowners at rates set by competitive labour markets, then the net wage w will simply be the marginal product of labour, Q_L; however, this is a rather special case.

Workers care both about their leisure and about their consumption of goods, and allocate hours to labour accordingly for any given net hourly wage. Following Boserup, we anticipate that the labour-supply schedule will be backward-bending, so that, in response to a lower net wage, workers will supply additional hours, to prevent their consumption from falling proportionately. If l is the rate at which workers supply hours of labour, then $l = l[q(1 - e)] = l(w)$. Ignoring the population age composition, total labour supply L will be given by $L = lP$, where P is total population. We therefore have equations for Q, L, l, q and w for given P, A, R and e. It will greatly simplify notation to use these equations to eliminate L, l, q and w, and express Q directly as a function of P, A, R and e. Indeed, since both resources and the institutions governing the extraction of surplus are outside the scope of this paper, and resources are in any event expected to remain constant during the application to any area, I shall typically write,

$$Q = f(A, P) \qquad (2)$$

where f_A, $f_P > 0$, $f_{AA} < 0$, $f_{AP} > 0$, and $f_{PP} < 0$ eventually, although initially f_{PP} may be > 0.

It should be borne in mind, however, that this expression reflects processes in addition to production, particularly the changing supply of labour per head as changes in population and technology lead to changes in wages. In order for the conditions given above on $f(A, P)$ to be correct, the supply of labour per head must not respond too sensitively to the wage.[3]

I shall assume that the appropriate conditions on the first and second derivatives of the per-capita labour supply function, $l(w)$, are met.

Surplus and total population

Total subsistence needs are given by mP, where m is the subsistence level. m could be treated as a function of A, to capture some of the costs of training and so on. Total output is given by the production function $f(A, P)$, which treats fixed resources only implicitly. Thus surplus, S, is given by

---

[3] For example, for the first derivatives of f to be positive, the absolute value of the elasticity of the per-head labour supply with respect to the wage must be less than unity. The requirements for the second order conditions to hold are far more complex. I am grateful to John Ermisch for pointing this out to me.

$$S = f(A, P) - mP \qquad (3)$$

where f_A, $f_P > 0$; f_{AA}, $f_{PP} < 0$ (eventually); $f_{AP} > 0$.

The relation of surplus to population size, for given levels of technology and resources, is shown in figure 1.

The surplus could be used to feed a maximum non-food-producing population of S/m, and in this way the size of the food-producing population sets an upper limit on the size of the total population. The non-food-producing population could be servants for the landowning class, soldiers, manufacturers, members of religious orders, government bureaucrats, and so on. To the extent that the surplus was also consumed directly in the form of food, or that agricultural output was an input to other uses, the non-food-producing population would be less than S/m. Also, to the extent that the normative living-standard of the non-food-producing population was above m, its size would be smaller.

It is readily seen by differentiating (3) that the first-order condition for a maximum surplus is $f_P = m$. Let $Z(A)$ denote that population size which maximizes the amount of surplus at any given level of technology. We know that $Z(A)$ must satisfy $f_P(A, Z(A)) = m$. What is the slope of the line $Z(A)$? A little reflection reveals that the conditions listed in (2) imply a positive slope for $Z(A)$. To see this, note that an increase in A will raise the marginal product of labour, and therefore require a larger P to make the marginal product fall back down to m. Thus larger A goes with larger P, which is to say that $Z(A)$ has a positive slope. More formally, it is easily shown by total differentiation that the slope of $Z(A)$ is $-f_{PA}/f_{PP}$, which by the assumptions of (2) is positive. It is also clear that $Z(A)$ must strike the population axis at a positive size, since diminishing returns are not encountered until some minimum size is reached – namely, that size at which the most primitive and most extensive technology (presumably hunting and gathering) first fills up the earth (or area under consideration) and encounters diminishing returns. The population size yielding maximum surplus must occur someplace to the right of this point. The right-hand Malthus line in figure 3 conforms to these conditions.

MALTHUSIAN THEORY IN THE PHASE PLANE

Population growth

The Malthusian assumption is simply represented as

$$\frac{P'}{P} = n(w), \qquad \frac{dn}{dw} > 0 \qquad (4)$$

Here P' is the derivative of population with respect to time; this notation will be used throughout the paper.

Note that this expresses population growth as a function *not* of earnings or per-capita income, but rather of the hourly wage rate. Incomes could be similar in two situations – say close to biological subsistence – but in one hours of work might be higher and the wage lower. The assumption here is that the one with the lower wage would have a lower growth rate.

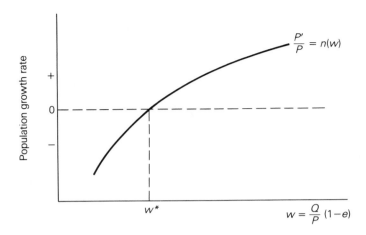

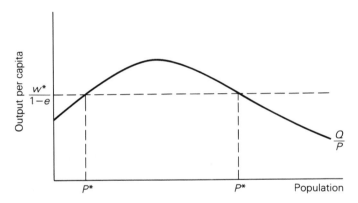

Figure 2   Equilibrium 'wage' and population size for given resources, technology and rate of extraction (e)

There will be some net wage which will correspond to a population growth rate of zero; this is known as the 'equilibrium wage'. The equilibrium wage is given by the solution to $w^* = n^{-1}(0)$, where, here and throughout, the asterisk denotes an equilibrium value. The corresponding equilibrium population size, for a given state of technology, is given by the P^* which satisfies the following equation: $(1-e)f(A,P^*)/P^* = w^*l(w^*)$. Thus the equilibrium population size will depend on the level of technology, the long-run equilibrium wage, the preference for leisure, and the rate of surplus extraction, in addition to the available resources. There may well be two solutions for P^*, one which occurs in the region of increasing returns to labour, and one occurring in the region of diminishing returns to labour. The first of these would evidently be an unstable equilibrium and the second a stable one. These various concepts are illustrated in figure 2, for given levels of technology, resources and rate of extraction.

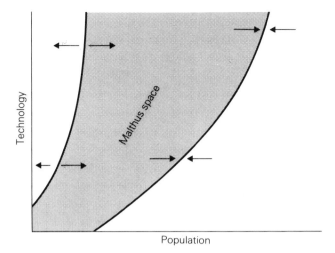

Figure 3 Malthus lines and Malthus space in the phase plane

Since w can be written as a function of A and P alone (for given e and R), and, since the rate of population growth is a function of w alone, we can eliminate w and write,

$$\frac{P'}{P} = h \, (A, \, P) \qquad\qquad (5)$$

$h_A > 0$, h_P may initially be > 0 but eventually is < 0, $h_{AA} < 0$, h_{PP} is initially ambiguous, but eventually < 0, ahd h_{AP} is ambiguous.

This is the form of the Malthusian relationship that describes the regions of population growth, decline and equilibrium on the phase plane.

Earlier, output was defined in *net* terms, such that the productivity of the land was maintained. It follows that the notion of Malthusian equilibrium used here rules out the possibilities of environmental degradation, and is therefore indefinitely sustainable. In reality degradation sometimes occurs, but it falls outside the scope of this analysis. On the other hand, other kinds of situation in which population overshoots its equilibrium and collapses are considered later in this essay.

Figure 3 shows the general shape of the regions in the population–technology plane. The lines trace out the equilibrium population sizes corresponding to each level of technology, and show both a low-level equilibrium where there are increasing returns to labour, and a high-level equilibrium where there are diminishing returns to labour. I shall call these lines the 'Malthus lines' and I shall call the space between them, in which positive population growth occurs, 'Malthus space'. The left-hand Malthus line corresponds to unstable equilibria, since in its neighbourhood an increase in population size raises rather than lowers the wage.

Note that the Malthus lines bend up more and more steeply to the right at higher population sizes. This is the result of two influences. First, I assume that there are diminishing returns to technology (represented in natural units), so that equiproportional increases in population and technology represent decreasing per-capita output. Thus, even at a constant equilibrium wage, the lines would bend up. But as technology increases, the equilibrium wage will also rise, reflecting the increased costs of raising children (due both to the higher direct and time costs of raising them), which will reinforce the first effect.

The benchmark case: Malthusian equilibrium maximizes surplus

Later we shall need to locate the Malthus space in relation to the Boserup space, and for this purpose it is necessary to be more specific about the location of the right-hand Malthus line. This depends on many aspects of the society beyond the scope of this paper, but to get a foothold in the analysis it will help to consider the relatively clear-cut case of a society composed of a numerically small landowning elite, and the landless labourers whom they hire in competitive labour markets. Let us also assume that the cultural standard of living is at the biological subsistence level, m. This particular case is close to the central one that Malthus had in mind, I believe. Under these assumptions, the population of agricultural labourers will grow until the marginal product of labour and the wage are forced down to subsistence level. But this is precisely the condition for maximization of surplus for a given technological level, as was discussed above. In this system, the entire surplus is captured by the landowning class in the form of Ricardian rents. Note that this is *not* the same as the conventionally defined optimum population which maximizes per-capita income (and for which rents would vanish altogether); the maximum surplus population is far larger, and has far lower per-capita incomes. It is what Sauvy (1969) calls the 'power optimum' population. It does represent the optimum population size from the point of view of the landowning class, since it maximizes aggregate rents. The surplus-extracting class will generally have an interest in the reproductive behaviour of the working class, and may seek to manipulate it, a subject discussed in detail by Lesthaeghe (1980). The size of the total population will depend on the way the land owning class spends the surplus; population will be increased by the labour content of goods and services they demand (refer to figure 1).

Deviations from the benchmark case: the extraction and disposition of surplus and the preventive check

This system provides a convenient benchmark, but we should not expect the Malthusian line typically to coincide with the maximum surplus line, $Z(A)$. Among the many influences on the position of the Malthus line, let us single out two for further consideration. The first is the normative standard of living, w^*, which could be higher than, m. But this alone does not necessarily mean that population will equilibrate at a size below $Z(A)$, because equilibrium also depends on the extent to which institutions lead to the extraction of surplus from the population, through rents, taxes, tribute,

Table 1   Equilibrium population size (P^*) in relation to the surplus-maximizing size (Z), as it is affected by the efficiency of extraction and the preventive check

Efficiency of surplus extraction (t)	Strength of preventive check, or normative living-standard (w*)		
	Low	Medium	High
Low	$P^* > Z$	$P^* = Z$	$P^* < Z$
Medium	$P^* = Z^a$	$P^* < Z$	$P^* < Z$
High	$P^* < Z$	$P^* < Z$	$P^* < Z$

aThis corresponds to the benchmark case.

serfdom or slavery, sharecropping arrangements, labour obligations, or whatever. Under a perfectly egalitarian system, with no taxes and a normative standard equal to m, the population would tend to equilibrate at the maximum possible level, with an *average* product of labour equal to subsistence, m; in this situation, there is no surplus at all. The Malthus line falls entirely to the right of the Boserup space (that is, the space within which technological progress tends to occur), and population constantly tends to a density too great to sustain a technology beyond the most primitive.

On the other hand, a perfectly egalitarian population with a high normative standard of living could maximize surplus in equilibrium, even if there were no extraction of surplus whatsoever. The surplus would be retained for the use of the prosperous family-farm households, who might spend it on goods produced by a non-agricultural urban sector, thus stimulating technological advance. Any system with a very high normative standard of living would equilibrate at population levels less than Z (A), to attain the higher average and marginal products of labour. Any system which attempted to extract a very high per-capita quantity of surplus would equilibrate at levels below Z (A) for the same reason. Generally, both higher normative living-standards and higher rates of surplus extraction move the population equilibrium to the left. For some combinations, Malthus lines lying entirely to the left of the Boserup space could occur, owing to a too oppressive regime, or a population too reluctant to reproduce in the face of costs of child rearing. Table 1 shows this schematically.

To express this somewhat more formally, suppose that the equilibrium level of welfare is w^*. If a proportional tax at rate e is extracted, then initially the population will work harder (reduce its leisure) and consume a bit less in order to pay it. But in the longer run they will reproduce less rapidly, since the preventive check is keyed not to gross income, but to after-tax income. The population will decline until per-capita income of workers rises to $w^*/(1-e)$, leaving an after-tax income of w^* as before. Thus we have the iron law of taxes: in the long run the rate of taxation does not affect the after-tax income of the population. We also have a kind of long-run 'Laffer curve': there is an optimal long-run rate of taxation which extracts the maximum surplus (calculated relative to w^*, not m), but attempts to tax at a higher (or lower) rate than this will eventually lead to reduced revenues.

The equilibrium population size will also depend on the way in which the extracted surplus is used by those who control it, and in particular it will depend on the labour demands generated by the expenditure of the surplus. These could be minimal (for example, if it were used for imports of foreign luxury goods, or if it were foreign tribute, or if it were used to bathe in milk) or substantial (if the surplus were used to support military ventures, or to support domestic servants). The more labour-intensive are the uses made of the surplus, the further to the right will fall the Malthus line.

Other influences on the Malthus line

The living-standard at which the population equilibrates, however, is not determined completely by the institutional and cultural setting of the population. It can be displaced independently of these by exogenous changes either in mortality or fertility, and also, of course, by migration.

A secular rise in mortality, occurring as a result of exposure to new diseases or to climatic change, would raise the equilibrium living-standard, since a higher level of fertility would be required to balance mortality in equilibrium and higher fertility is associated with higher living-standards. This sort of change occurred in Europe following the arrival of the Black Death in the middle of the fourteenth century, when life expectancy was depressed substantially for a century and a half, and real wages stabilized at very high levels owing to the low-level equilibrium of population (see Lee 1973, 1978). The introduction of Western health technology to the other regions of the world has an opposite effect, shifting the Malthus curve far to the right, into regions of very high population density. In such circumstances, institutional control of living-standards is derailed, and one can no longer expect the living-standard towards which reproductive behaviour steers the population to be in the neighbourhood of traditional levels.

Similarly, events of the last few decades have shown that it is possible to shift the Malthus curve to the left (that is to lower-density, higher-income equilibria) by the introduction of modern techniques of fertility control, and the active involvement of the government in programmes to disseminate these techniques as well as to create incentives of various kinds for smaller families and delayed childbearing. Additionally, in some areas of the world, notably some West African countries, exposure to fecundity impairing disease has shifted the Malthus curve to the left, and future health programmes may shift it back to the right, as these diseases are controlled.

Thus the location of the Malthus curve is subject to many influences beyond those formally incorporated in the analysis, and is certainly not expected to remain fixed in relation to population and technology, as the diagrams might lead one to infer.

BOSERUPIAN THEORY IN THE PHASE PLANE

In this section I shall discuss the general shape of the locus of pairs of population size and technological level that correspond to technological equilibrium. I shall refer to this locus of points as the Boserup line, since it is completely independent of any assumptions made about reproductive behaviour and the dynamics of population growth. I shall refer to the locus of points for which technology is growing $(A' > 0)$ as the 'Boserup space'. The Boserup space is, of course, bounded by the Boserup line.

Alternative shapes of Boserup space

There is a wide variety of possible shapes for Boserup space, and, before discussing in detail the shape which I will assume for the remainder of the paper, it will be helpful to consider some of the others, as displayed in figure 4. The first possibility is that no equilibrium technological level exists at all. A 'technology' could be viewed as an indestructible set of blueprints and instructions, a set which, once obtained, could be costlessly preserved for ever, and used whenever desired. If this were so, then technology would be expected to improve without limit, since old methods would never be forgotten, and new ones would be thought up from time to time. In this case technological progress would always tend to occur, although more slowly if population were sparse and more rapidly if it were dense. No equilibrium level of technology could exist, and there could be no global equilibrium of population and technology. Boserup space would then occupy the entire phase plane (see figure 4a). While this sort of assumption may be reasonable for a shorter-run analysis, it surely is inappropriate in the context of a model intended to reflect the long-run dynamics of historical change; technology is carried by civilizations, and these rise and fall.

I find it more plausible that technology is forgettable; at least at higher levels, its maintenance requires its utilization, and its utilization requires considerable physical capital and human capital, which therefore involves an important resource cost. If there is 'learning by doing' there is also 'forgetting by not doing'.[4] Imagine, for example, that nuclear war destroyed all the world's population except that of Norway. Unable to engage in international trade in goods or ideas, Norway would have to move to a simpler set of techniques based on a much more limited division of labour. Even if complete descriptions of the higher technology were preserved in libraries, one might well imagine that within a generation or two no one would be able to understand these, and the technology would be lost. The Dark Ages may be an example of such a loss of technology following a decline in population, although surely much else was involved as well. Likewise, one thinks of the collapse of Mayan civilization, the forgotten methods used to erect Stonehenge, and so on.

Figure 4b represents the case in which an equilibrium level of technology does exist, a level which increases with population size. To the left of this line, population is too sparse to support the existing level of technology, so technological retrogression occurs, and the arrows all point down. To the right, induced technological progress occurs.

---

[4]Although Hahn and Matthews (1964, p. 389) in their influential survey explicitly state, 'the knowledge gained from working on a large scale is not forgotten if the scale is later reduced. The economies are therefore irreversible. . . .'

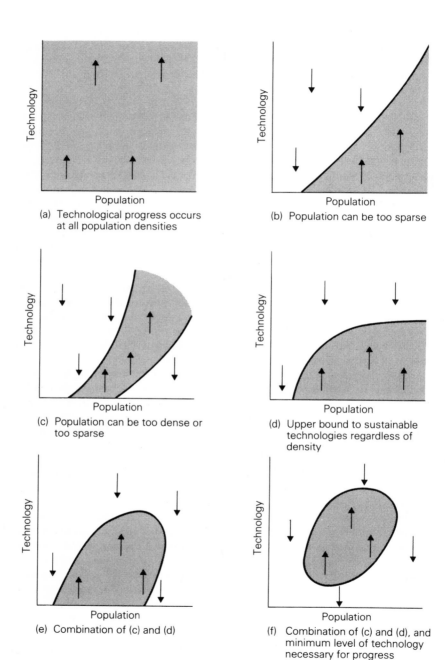

Figure 4   Varieties of Boserup space

The specification shown in figure 4b is consistent with a number of those occurring in the literature, and in particular with the formulation by Darity (1980) and subsequently adopted in modified form by Pryor and Maurer (1982). In their specification retrogression is possible. But this specification does not allow for the possibility that population may become *too* dense, so that the resources available for collective investment decrease. Figure 4c depicts this last possibility. Under the assumption that technological progress is fuelled by the total amount of agricultural surplus, there will be two levels of population at which a given level of technology tends to be stationary, as shown in this figure. For a given population size, the equilibrium line on the left depicts stable equilibrium points, while the one on the right represents unstable ones.

Let us return for the moment to the case of figure 4b, where there is only one equilibrium line, and consider its shape. Since technology is here expressed in natural units, and since resources are held fixed, we should expect diminishing returns to increases in technology. If these are sufficiently sharp, the gains to increased technology will eventually be less than the increased costs of maintenance, and then progress will cease. This argument suggests that Boserup space may be bounded above, as shown in figure 4d. This is not to suggest that technology itself is bounded, but to suggest only that a point is reached when it does not pay to employ more elaborate technologies, no matter how large the population becomes.

If we combine the considerations introduced in cases (c) and (d), we get case (e). This represents a Boserup space which is bounded in every direction. Case (f) is a variant in which at very low levels of technology, technological progress does not occur no matter how large is the population. These last two cases, (d) and (e), will be analysed in more detail in the remainder of this essay. The reader who prefers one of the other cases shown in figure 4 can easily work out the implied dynamic behaviour.

There are, of course, possibilities not considered here. For example, technological change may be very local – that is to say, very specific to particular techniques appropriate at particular densities – and technological change may depend only on the rate of growth of population, and be unaffected by the level of population. The first point must often be correct, but I view it as a qualification of the main argument, not as fundamentally altering it. The second point I dispute. It should be noted that any theory which makes the equilibrium level of technology a function of the level of population will also predict an association of their rates of change, and is therefore quite consistent with such empirical observations as Verdoorn's Law. Boserup herself does not propose a specific functional relationship. Phelps (1966) proposes a function in which progress is driven by the ratio of number of researchers to the level of technology, consistent with the notion that the level of the population drives technological progress. Simon (n.d.) makes the rate of progress depend on the size of the population, per-capita income, and the level of technology.

Surplus and technical change

I shall begin by assuming that technical progress is positively related to the amount of surplus. But further technological progress also depends on the ability of the population to sustain costs of maintaining the currently existing level, which requires certain investments in both human capital (training, appropriate lifestyles and incentive structures) and physical capital (the knowledge of how to build and maintain complicated structures cannot survive the structures themselves for many generations). We are thus led to consider Boserup functions of the following form:

$$\frac{A'}{A} = g(S\ (A,\ P),\ A), \qquad g_s > 0,\ g_A < 0 \qquad\qquad (6)$$

I should warn, however, that the assumption that $g_A < 0$ is critical to my analysis. My results would look different if it were dropped because in that case one could not talk of an equilibrium level of technology for a given population size, since there would be no countervailing force against the tendency of technology to increase.

In the specification of (6), and in later parts of this essay, I state that population affects technological progress only indirectly, through its effect on surplus. But there are many positive influences that are thereby ignored, such as the lower costs per head of social overhead investments with public-good aspects – roads and irrigation systems, for example. In fact, these influences can be incorporated in the present analysis with no real changes, provided the following two conditions are met: first, that the positive effects of population size itself are a linear function of population size or density; and, second, that the positive effect of adding a member of the population is less than mg_S, the effect of the person's subsistence requirements. These assumptions appear acceptable. We should then have a new function g: $g(A, P) = f(A, P) - bP - cA$, where $b > 0$ is the net effect of population size.

In most ways it would be simpler and more straightforward to define 'surplus' to be measured net of both the costs of maintaining population size, mP, and the cost of maintaining technology, say cA. Then g would be a function of surplus alone. I have chosen not to do this in order to preserve consistency with the well-established usage of the surplus concept in the literature. Also note that equation (6) and other specifications of the technological-progress function make the proportional rate of progress the left-hand variable. This has no effect on the qualitative behaviour of the system, since all the equilibrium points are unchanged, and A is always positive, so the direction of change is also unaltered. In the case of the linear form of (6) this specification results in a logistic trajectory of technology as it moves to equilibrium, for a given population size.

The reader less interested in technical details is invited to skip the next three sub-sections, and proceed to the beginning of the next main section ('Dynamic behaviour of the complete system').

The implications of fixed resources

It would be reasonable to assume that, because of ultimately constraining effects of fixed resources, total output is bounded no matter how great are population and technology. For most purposes in this essay, however, a much weaker condition will suffice: that eventually, once labour inputs are great enough to experience diminishing returns, the function $f(A, P)$ is concave. Concavity implies diminishing returns to population and technology, in the sense that, if you increase both of them in any mix, the returns to doing so will diminish (that is, the second total derivative of f in any direction is less than zero). This is *not* because diminishing returns to scale are assumed, but rather because an omitted factor, resources, is held fixed. For a given level of technology, there could well be constant or increasing returns to scale in labour and resources. For example, the Cobb–Douglas production function, $Q = A^{-0.4} P^{-0.5} R^{-0.7}$, would be consistent with the concavity restriction. It should be noted that the latter will hold if, and only if, f_{AA} and $f_{PP} < 0$ and $f_{AA} f_{PP} > f^2{}_{AP}$ (see Chiang 1984, p. 316).

Actually, the concavity assumption is not quite strong enough, since it does not rule out the possibility that the system asymptotically approaches constant returns to scale, although always satisfying the diminishing-returns assumption at any given point. Assuming away this additional possibility appears to be a relatively harmless addition to strict concavity, since we should expect in any case that diminishing returns would grow *stronger*, not weaker, as population and technology increase relative to resources.

Two auxiliary functions

Now let us consider the shape of the Boserup function implied by equations (5) and (6) and the restrictions discussed in the preceding section. To do this, it is convenient first to consider two auxiliary functions. These involve no new behavioural assumptions; they are derived from the f and g functions which have already been introduced. The purpose of these auxiliary functions is merely to facilitate the analysis. The first of these is just $Z(A)$, the surplus-maximizing population size for a given technological level, as discussed above. Note that P affects g, the Boserup function, only in so far as it affects surplus. Along the line $Z(A)$, S_P must be zero (by the first-order condition for population to maximize surplus), so it must also be that g_P is zero along the $Z(A)$ line. Furthermore, to the left of this line, surplus is increasing with population, so g_P is positive, and, to the right of this line, surplus is decreasing with population, so g_P is negative. These facts will be very helpful.

We also need to consider a second auxiliary function, $X(P)$, which, for a given population size, gives the level of technology for which dg/dA is zero. This will correspond to the technology level which maximizes the rate of technological change, but it will *not* do this by maximizing surplus, since $g_A < 0$ must also be taken into account. From (5) and (6) we see that $dg/dA = g_S \times f_A + g_A$. The first term is always positive, but it decreases towards zero as A grows, owing to diminishing returns to technology ($f_{AA} < 0$).[5] The second term is negative, and there is no obvious reason why it should either

---

[5]If we had instead measured A in terms of its ability to shift f multiplicatively, as is done in many econometric applications, then we should say that g_S goes to zero, as it becomes more and more difficult to generate the necessary amount of technical advance, measured by its effect rather than in natural units; this would leave the argument completely unchanged.

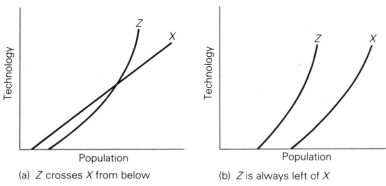

(a) *Z* crosses *X* from below   (b) *Z* is always left of *X*

Figure 5   *Possible configurations of the X and Z lines*

increase or decrease with A. Thus there should be some point (for each P) where these terms just cancel, and $dg/dA = 0$; $X(P)$ is the locus of these points. Above this line, dg/dA is less than zero, and below it, it is above zero.

In order to describe the shape of the $X(P)$ line it will be helpful to make a further simplifying assumption: that g is linear in S and A, so that second derivatives of g (but not of f!) vanish. Then, it is again clear that the $X(P)$ line must be positively sloped: an increase in P will raise f_A, and, in order to keep $g_S \times f_A$ equal to the unchanging g_A, it will be necessary also to raise A, which, through $f_{AA} < 0$, will bring f_A down again. More formally, the slope of $X(P)$ can be shown to be $-f_{AA}/f_{AP}$, which by the conditions on f is positive. Unfortunately, it appears impossible to say anything about the intercept of the $X(P)$ line on the A or P axis.

From the preceding discussions it can be inferred that the ratio of the slopes of the Z to the X line is $f_{PP}f_{AA}/f^2_{AP}$, and by the condition of concavity (see pp. 114–15), once diminishing returns to labour have set in, this will always be greater than unity, and tend to be finitely greater. Relative to the P axis, therefore, the Z line will have a steeper slope than the X line. Global strict concavity and no asymptotic constant returns thus rule out two possible configurations of Z and X. First, they can not be asymptotically parallel, for the Z line will eventually be finitely steeper. Second, if they cross at all, it happens only once, and Z must cut X from below. Thus if the X line intersects the P axis to the left of Z, then Z will cross it from below, and the two lines are configured as in figure 5a. If, on the other hand, the X line intercepts the P axis to the right of Z, then the lines never cross in the positive quadrant, and they will be configured as in figure 5b.

Note also that, if the X and Z lines intersect, with Z cutting X from below, then their intersection corresponds to the global maximum rate of technological progress. If X cuts Z from below (which is ruled out by the concavity assumption) then the intersection would be a saddlepoint, representing a maximum along the horizontal and vertical lines passing through it, but a minimum along the X and Z lines. From the intersection, g increases monotonically for ever along both X and Z; the Boserup space is therefore unbounded in this case.

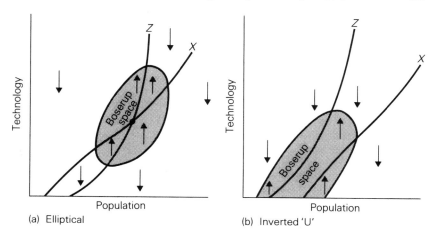

Figure 6   Shapes of Boserup space

The shapes of Boserup space

This completes the discussion of the auxiliary functions $Z(A)$ and $X(P)$, and we are ready to use them to help us locate the Boserup line, along which technology is stationary. First note that this line corresponds to $g = 0$, and therefore along this line A and P must be changing together in such a way as to leave g constant. From this fact we can infer that, when the Boserup line crosses the $Z(A)$ line, it must be horizontal (parallel to the P axis), (since $dg/dP = 0$ along the Z line, and since $g = 0$ is constant on the Boserup line, A must also be locally constant). Similarly, when the Boserup line crosses the X line, it must be vertical. When dg/dA and dg/dP are either both positive or both negative, then the Boserup line must be negatively sloped to reflect a constant g; when the derivatives are of opposite sign, the Boserup line will be positively sloped.[6]

Now note that to the left of its intersection with the Z line, $g(A, P)$ is increasing along the X line (since dg/dA is zero, and to the left of Z dg/dP is greater than zero). To the right of the Z line, g is decreasing along X. Thus, if where X intersects the P line it is less than or equal to zero, there will be *two* points on X where $g = 0$, one on each side of the Z line. (It is also possible in this case that there will be no zero points at all on the X line; in this case the Boserup space will be empty, and technology would never

---

[6]This may all be put more formally as follows. Consider the total derivative of g: $dg = g_S S_P dP + (g_S S_A + g_A)dA$. Along the Boserup line, g is constant at zero, so dg must also be zero. Therefore, along the Boserup line we have: $dA/dP = -g_S S_P dP/(g_S S_A + g_A)$. From this it can be seen that dA/dP will be positive, which is to say that the Boserup line will be positively sloped, when the numerator and denominator of the ratio have opposite signs, and negatively sloped when the numerator and denominator have the same signs. Furthermore, along the line Z the numerator is always zero by construction, so, if the Boserup line crosses the Z line, dA/dP must be zero, and the Boserup line must therefore be horizontal where it crosses. Similarly, where it crosses the X line dA/dP must be infinite, and the Boserup line must be vertical.

grow above its lowest level.) If, on the other hand, g is greater than zero where X intersects the P axis, then g will only have *one* zero point on the X line, and it will occur to the right of Z.

In figure 6 I have sketched the possible shapes of the Boserup line, along with the Z and X lines for reference. The Boserup line could either have the shape of the tilted and inverted 'U', or of the closed 'ellipse'; in fact, as I shall argue below, the two shapes should probably coexist on the same diagram, with an interpretation to be given shortly. In the case of the inverted 'U', the left leg might intersect either the A axis or the P axis in the positive quadrant. If it intersects the A axis, this means that even the tiniest population will tend to experience technical progress; if it intersects the P axis, this means that some critical population density must be reached before progress can occur – for example, that the human population must first expand to fill its habitat at the most primitive technological level. I favour this last assumption, but this is a substantive issue, and the results will not turn out to depend on it in any important way. Experimentation with the position of the Z and X lines appears to establish that, under the assumptions I have made, these are the only possible shapes.

Recall that under the concavity assumptions, an intersection of Z and X corresponds to a global maximum for technological progress. Such a maximum will always occur within an elliptical Boserup space, and is marked in figure 6 by a dot. Within the inverted-'U'-shaped space, there may or may not be an intersection, depending on how the X and Z curves are configured.

I should also point out that, without the assumption of diminishing returns to technology and population (that is, asymptotic strict concavity, as on pp. 114–15), other shapes are possible, and in particular a right-side-up 'U', tilted toward the right, may occur, suggesting the possibility of infinite progress. This would be more in line with the thinking of such scholars as Julian Simon, presumably. To derive this outcome, just consider the case where X intersects the P axis to the left of Z, and the two lines are asymptotically parallel; alternatively, let X cross Z from below.

DYNAMIC BEHAVIOUR OF THE COMPLETE SYSTEM

We have seen in the previous section that, for any state of technology, there are some ranges of population size within which technological progress occurs, and others where it does not. For any given state of technology, Malthusian forces will steer population size towards some equilibrium level. Common sense suggests that the behaviour of the system will depend critically on whether this Malthusian equilibrium population size falls within the range leading to further technological advance, or within the range leading to technological regression, either because population is too small or too large. This depends on the relative locations of the Malthus and Boserup lines and spaces, and is a fundamentally important question for our analysis. In terms of the diagrams we have so far considered, we must determine whether the right-hand Malthus line passes through Boserup space.

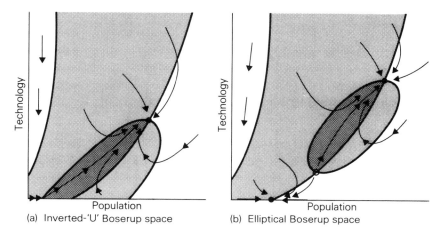

(a) Inverted-'U' Boserup space   (b) Elliptical Boserup space

Figure 7   Dynamic behaviour of the complete system.
Note: Solid circles indicate stable equilibria; hollow circles indicate unstable equilibria.

The benchmark case: Malthusian equilibrium maximizes surplus

Consider the benchmark case in which the right-hand Malthus line, denoting a stable equilibrium, corresponds to the surplus-maximizing population, $Z(A)$. Figure 7a represents this case when the Boserup space is a tipped inverted 'U'. Where the Malthus and Boserup lines cross, neither population nor technology is changing, so that these are equilibrium points of the system, called 'nodes' and indicated by heavy dots. One such node is shown in figure 7a at the top of the Boserup space in the shape of an inverted 'U'. There is also actually a node at the origin (not shown on the graph), since if population is zero the system goes nowhere.

So far, we have been able to identify equilibrium points on the diagram, but the real power of phase-plane analysis is that it enables us to sketch in the paths followed by population and technology starting from any point we choose. Before doing this for the benchmark case, I shall pause to describe how it is done.

We can plot the path starting from any point on the diagram by bearing in mind the following points: when a path crosses the Malthus line it must be vertical, and when it crosses the Boserup line it must be horizontal; a path within the overlap of Malthus and Boserup space will move up and to the right; a path outside both spaces will move down and to the left; a path in Malthus space but not Boserup space will move down and to the right; a path in Boserup space but not Malthus space will move up and to the left.

Let us trace the path of a population in the benchmark case that starts out very small, and with minimal technology. Initially, it will move along the population axis, staying at the lowest technological level, since technology only tends to grow after the Boserup space has been entered. Once this has happened, then population and technology both increase, in a self-reinforcing spiral. If there is a maximum rate of growth of technology in the space, then the rate of technological progress accelerates as it is approached and decelerates after it is passed. At that maximum the growth rate of population would be zero, since it lies on the Z line, so no path will pass through it; rather paths will pass to the left of it, where population is also growing. Presumably per-capita income is highest when the path is in the neighbourhood of the maximum rate of technological growth (g), since high incomes are necessary to maintain high rates of population growth. Then the pace of growth of both technology and population will decelerate gradually as the node is approached, and when it is reached net wages will again drop to the level of the normative standard.

This path is sketched in figure 7a, along with a number of additional representative paths. Note that, if you consider paths originating near to the node in figure 7a, you will find that they all move towards the node; this shows that the node is stable. If population grows beyond this point, diminishing returns to fixed resources and the growing cost of technology outweigh the stimulus to technology, and the population increase cannot be sustained. Thus this stable node is a kind of Malthusian equilibrium, in the sense that Malthusian forces predominate over Boserupian ones.

Although the diagram does not explicitly show income, we can none the less draw inferences about its path. Whenever population is declining, which is to say whenever a path is outside Malthus space, then per-capita income, net of extracted surplus, must be below the equilibrium wage for that level of technology ($w^*(A)$), which in the benchmark case is the level of subsistence ($m = w^*(0)$). Whenever population is growing, it means that net incomes are above $w^*(A)$.

Elliptical and 'U'-shaped Boserup spaces

Now consider the case of an elliptical Boserup space, portrayed in figure 7b. Here there are three nodes, not counting the uninteresting one at the origin. First, there is a stable low-level node at zero technology and low population size. Here we are outside the Boserup space, so there is no tendency for technological progress to occur; this is again a Malthusian equilibrium. Unlike the case of figure 7a, nothing further will happen unless some exogenous shock to the system lifts it up to Boserup space – this might require, for example, a lucky accident, or contact with a more advanced culture.

This node is unstable and has no attractive power. Once it has been passed, or Boserup space has been entered by any other route, self-reinforcing growth will occur, just as it did in the inverted-'U' case. This growth will continue, drawing the system toward the high-level third node, which is again Malthusian, and is again stable. As my colleague David Weir has remarked, this is a story that begins and ends with Malthus, with Boserup in between.

As the reader may have already noted, the cases of the inverted 'U' and the ellipse are closely related; indeed, the inverted 'U' can be viewed as an ellipse that happens to be located partly below the population axis, which therefore cuts it off. Although similar, the two cases differ in an important way: when the P axis cuts the ellipse, this means that Malthusian forces will automatically bring population into the Boserup space, so that self-reinforcing progress is assured and no low-level equilibrium exists. When the ellipse lies entirely above the population axis, then entry into Boserup space is not assured, and indeed requires an exogenous shock. In this case, a low-level equilibrium does exist, a sort of holding-pattern which could last indefinitely. Depending on one's view of the hundreds of thousands of years of human existence in the hunting-and-gathering stage, with relatively stationary population, one might view one or the other of these two cases as more plausible.

Finally, note that if the left arm of the inverted 'U' were to intersect the technology axis, this would imply that technological progress would occur even when population size was infinitesimal.

Technological discontinuities

Deevey (1960), in a provocative article, portrays human history as a Malthusian progression, with population expanding rapidly to new and higher equilibrium levels following a series of technological 'revolutions'. The first technological regime is hunting and gathering, followed by agriculture, and then by industrialization. Deevey calculated each technological revolution to have expanded the earth's carrying capacity by a factor of about 100 – from roughly 5 million under hunting and gathering to about 500 million under settled agriculture to about 50,000 million under industrial production. This sort of interpretation is widely accepted (see, for example, Cipolla 1962) and hardly original to Deevey, but the notion of a technological *revolution* appears antithetical to the basic Boserupian view of gradual population-induced progress, and seems more consistent with the view that inventions occur autonomously. If this view were correct, we should expect to observe millennia of relatively stationary levels of population and technology in broad regions of the world, followed by long periods of rapid change, reflecting the discovery and diffusion of a new technology. On the other hand, if the Boserupian story were correct, we should expect to observe a fairly steady upward trend in both population and technology, without having to wait for a miracle to move on to the next technological regime (although Boserup specifically recognizes the importance of many factors besides population density).

Technological revolutions and Boserup space

It is possible to link the two interpretations, however, using the analytic framework already developed in this paper. We shall suppose that progress *within* each of these regimes obeys the Boserupian dynamic, while transitions between them are largely exogenous, although requiring certain critical preconditions which are necessary, but not sufficient. To be well situated to leap from one regime to another, it is necessary to have reached the highest

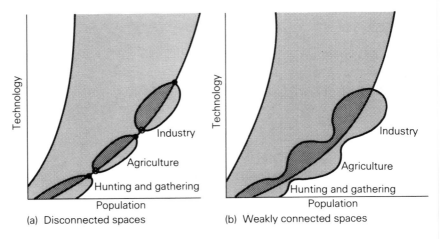

Figure 8   Technological regimes and Boserup spaces

Note: Solid circles indicate stable equilibria; hollow circles 'unstable'. Paths are similar to those in figure 6.

stage of the previous regime, to have 'used up', as it were, all its possibilities for a fruitful interaction of population and technology. Populations such as the Chinese, entrapped in a medium-technology agricultural regime, through prematurely dense population, would not be well situated to make the transition to an industrial economy. Neither would populations in situations such as that of many African countries, entrapped in a medium- or low-technology agricultural regime due to populations too sparse to support the costs of the prerequisite communication and transportation infrastructures.

The notion that the possibilities inherent in a kind of technology could be 'used up' is consistent with either version of the shape of Boserup space, since both are bounded above. The suggestion, then, is that we conceptualize the sequence of technological regimes, each with its own exhaustible possibilities, as a series of disconnected but contiguous ellipses. Entrance to a higher ellipse can be gained only from the population densities and levels of technological attainment characteristic of the highest development of the previous technology. One might think of the several technological regimes as analogous to a row of stepping-stones across a stream; each one can be reached from the previous.

Slightly more generally, we might imagine that the stepping-stones were not completely separated, but rather were joined by very narrow spits. In terms of the familiar model, we might imagine that there was a long ellipse which is, however, pinched to a narrow neck in places, while other portions are wide. Most populations, once entering a wider region, would be assured of making substantial progress, but, as the Boserup space narrowed at higher technologies and densities, many populations would get stuck at relatively low-level equilibria, and thus make no further progress. The more obvious and cheaper technological developments would occur, but those requiring larger collective investments and higher living-standards might not. Only populations blessed with the most advantageous institutions governing reproduction, surplus extraction, and use of surplus, would be able to pass through the neck of the hyperbola and continue to progress into the next-higher technological regime. The sequence of ellipses, then, would correspond to the extreme case when the narrow necks of the hyperbola closed entirely. These possibilities are depicted in figure 8.

CHINA, EUROPE AND THE PREVENTIVE CHECK

The different development paths followed by Europe and China present an interesting application of this framework, since the contrast is discussed at some length by both Malthus and Boserup. The stylized facts are as follows. Four or five centuries ago, China was undisputably the technological leader of the world, and appeared to be perhaps as much as five centuries ahead of Europe in this regard (see Needham 1961, as cited in Boserup 1981, p. 90). At the same time, Europe was much less densely settled than China, and consequently enjoyed a much higher level of living (in the sense of average income, or wage rates, or productivity of labour in agriculture). But, despite its sparser population and relative technological backwardness, it was Europe that surged forward and assumed technological leadership of the world, by experiencing the first industrial revolution.

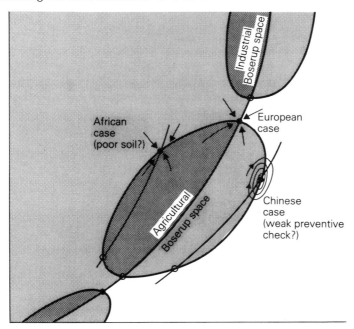

Figure 9   Agricultural equilibria and the preventive check:
China, Europe and Africa

Note: Solid circles indicate stable equilibria; hollow circles indicate unstable equilibria. Oscillations about the Chinese equilibrium could be convergent (as drawn) or explosive.

Malthus, writing before the industrial revolution and European ascendancy, notes merely that China is poor relative to Europe, and attributes this to a cultural difference in reproductive institutions and normative living-standards, which he suggests lead the European population to equilibrate at a higher level of per-capita income and a lower population density. We may translate this to the assertion that the Malthus curve for Europe lies to the left of that for China, after controlling for the difference in quantity and quality of agriculturally usable land.

Boserup, addressing the question of why it was Europe that made the great technological breakthrough, suggests that perhaps the Chinese population was *too* dense, and therefore unable to generate sufficient surplus to support further collective investments (Boserup 1981, pp. 87–90). This interpretation seems consistent with Malthus's. Certainly it appears that the normative standard in China was low; could it also be that the extractive institutions were relatively weak, or that surplus was used in ways not conducive to technological progress? In any event, the Malthus–Boserup interpretation is sketched out in figure 9. This shows how China might have become caught up in a high-population, medium-technology attractive equilibrium on the right arm of the Boserup line. Progress stops early because the too-dense population generates less surplus than it might, with a depressing effect on urban culture and collective investments. Note also that the diagram suggests the possibility that oscillation occurs about this node. Without further information, we cannot tell whether the oscillation is explosive or convergent, but in any event one wouldn't want to take this sort of detailed implication of the model too seriously.

It is worth noting here that the case in which the Malthus stable-equilibrium population line intersects the right-hand Boserup line and thereby leaves Boserup space is perhaps of more general interest. When this happens, the natural progression of the system will be to overshoot the population–technology equilibrium, and then to suffer first a decline in technology, then a decline in population (these are just the first steps in the spiral). Indeed Boserup, speaking of population *increase*, writes, 'Changes in resource-population ratios also played a role in the decay and breakdown of the densely settled urbanized regions. . . . Investments were neglected, the armies grew too small, and the strength of one densely populated empire after another was undermined' (1981, p. 87).

On the other hand, Africa, with its sparse populations, might be stuck at a mid level technological equilibrium on the left side of Boserup space. This could be due to a preventive check or surplus extraction which were too strong, or too-high mortality determined exogenously.[7] Another, perhaps more plausible, explanation is that exogenously given soil–climate conditions did not allow a dense agricultural population to be sustained under any attainable technology.

Europe had a stronger preventive check than China, exogenously lower

---

[7]By a strong preventive check I mean one which leads to a high normative living-standard, *not* the sensitivity of growth rates to the net wage levels.

mortality, a mix of peasant family farms and landless labour, and taxation. This combination of institutions and natural circumstance may have assisted her in avoiding the intermediate stable equilibrium, and increased her chances of getting caught up in the Malthusian–Boserupian spiral of progress and population growth which led her to the top of the agricultural Boserup space, well situated to experience an industrial revolution and leap to the next Boserup space. This interpretation of the Chinese–European contrast appears consistent with that offered by Eric Jones (1981).

THE EFFECTS OF MORTALITY REDUCTION AND
FAMILY-PLANNING PROGRAMMES

I have already noted that the effect of an exogenous decline in mortality would be to shift the Malthus space to the right, while a family-planning programme would shift it to the left. We can now see how the whole system would behave under these circumstances. For this purpose, let us consider the case of China, discussed above, entrapped in a medium-level technology agricultural regime. An exogenous reduction in mortality in this case could shift the Malthus line altogether to the right of the Boserup space, leading initially to population growth combined with technological regression, but ultimately to a reduction in both population and technological level. In a similar counter-intuitive manner, an effective fertility-control programme, by shifting the Malthus line to the left, would initially lead to declining population and rising technology, but eventually the increased technology would sustain a larger population than that in the original equilibrium. Thus, in the long run, fertility control could lead to population increase, while mortality control could lead to population decrease. At the other extreme, consider the African case. Here, fertility control leads to population decline reinforced by technological regression, while mortality declines lead to population growth reinforced by technological progress. Of course, this would be so only if the original low-level equilibrium were due to a strong preventive or positive check; if it were due instead to poor soil or climate, the outcome would be quite different.

HISTORICAL SHOCKS

I have discussed the development path followed by an hypothetical initially small and primitive population as it grows and becomes technologically more advanced, moving gradually from the lower left to the upper right of the diagram. But the diagram also shows the paths that would be followed starting from other initial positions, and the question arises how such initial positions, sometimes very far from the natural path of development, could actually come about. The answer is that historical shocks could well displace the system very powerfully from a mainline development path.

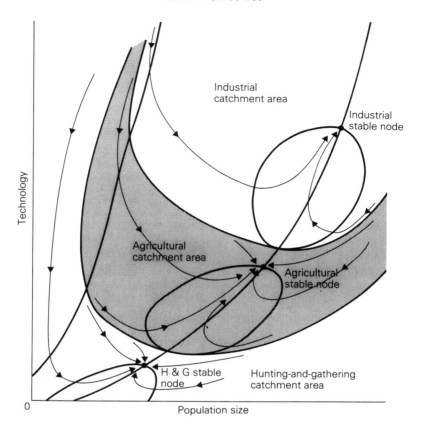

Figure 10   Catchment areas for technological regimes

The most notorious example is the reduction in the Mayan population of Mexico to only about 5 per cent of its previous size in the decades following the Spanish conquest, primarily, it is thought, through disease. Compared to this, Europe's loss of a fourth to a half of its population to the Black Death in the fourteenth century was quite minor. Population series for Egypt (Hollingsworth 1969) and Mesopotamia (McC. Adams 1965) show repeated swings with variations by factors of 5 or 10; most likely such swings would be exogenous in origin. Examples of autonomous increase in population are harder to come by, but might occur through migration, the disappearance of some disease from a region, or an unusual spell of good weather.

Autonomous changes in technology might come about through the immigration of members of a more advanced population, or other forms of cultural contact. Alternatively, they might result from a lucky discovery of some sort, or the work of a genius.

To consider the effect of major shocks of this sort, refer to figure 10, which shows several technological regimes, as in figures 7 and 8. Each of these regimes may be thought of as having a catchment area, from within which all paths lead ultimately to the stable equilibrium, and such catchment areas are also shown on the figure. When a shock occurs, we must first determine whether the population has been displaced into a different catchment area; if so, its position will be fundamentally altered in the long run. Imagine, for example, that an agricultural population is drastically reduced in numbers. If it remains in the same catchment area, but is moved out of Boserup space, then initially population will grow while technology declines, until Boserup space is re-entered, whereupon technology and population will grow together until the stable equilibrium is reached. If, however, it is moved into the catchment area for hunting and gathering, technology will fall much farther before the system enters Boserup space, and when it does it will be a lower Boserup space.

Suppose now that population is autonomously increased, but remains in the same catchment area. Then both population and technology will decline until Boserup space is re-entered, after which technology will increase and population size fall; eventually Malthus space will also be attained, and then population and technology will grow together until the equilibrium is attained. Otherwise, if a new catchment area is entered, the two will decline together until a hunting-and-gathering equilibrium is attained.

From these examples, which could easily be multiplied, it can be seen that it would be difficult to test the theory by examining historical episodes. A wide variety of patterns of behaviour is consistent with it. In many ways this is unfortunate, since it weakens the theory's predictive power.

CONCLUSIONS

A formal synthesis of Malthusian and Boserupian theory is indeed possible, and provides a rich and flexible framework within which to view historical change, as Pryor and Maurer concluded in their excellent article.[8] The

[8]The ideas developed here are closely related to those in Pryor and Maurer's important paper (1982). Some of the differences stem from their emphasis on parameterized functional forms and the solution of differential equations, and mine on phase diagrams; other differences are more substantive. They include the following. First, their technological-change specification makes the rate of progress greater without limit as population becomes denser, holding the initial level of technology fixed; thus the left arm of Boserup space is generated but not the right one. Secondly, their model does not allow for diminishing returns to technology (to 'intensification' in their terminology) or, what would be more appropriate given their model, increasing difficulty in achieving intensification. Therefore their Boserup space is unbounded above as well as to the right. Thirdly, their Boserup and Malthus lines emanate from the origin, and are both multiples of P^a, where $0 < a < 1$. Therefore there can be no initial 'filling-up' of the land at the most extensive technology before intensification begins to occur. Also, if any overlap of Malthus and Boserup space does exist, populations will be in it at the origin and henceforth, unless deflected by accident. Thus no low-level Malthusian equilibrium can occur before Boserup space is entered. Fourthly, the notion of technological regimes, in the sense in which I have used the term, is not developed. The pay-off to Pryor and Maurer's use of the less flexible parametric forms and simpler relationships is that they are able to find explicit solutions for the differential equations, a notable accomplishment, and are able to say far more about the magnitude of the rates of change, rather than being confined to consideration of the signs of rates of change as is the case with a phase diagram.

particular analytic device used in this paper, the phase diagram, is well-suited to express the issues under consideration, and leads to a very simple and intuitive picture which can easily be modified to reflect different assumptions. One important question addressed by the analysis was whether a Malthus–Boserup system would be expected to move onward and upward for ever. I made two key, and perhaps controversial, assumptions: that eventually diminishing returns would set in as both labour and technology increased while resources remained fixed; and that there is a cost associated with maintaining any technological level, due to the need for the maintenance of the human and physical capital stocks without which the technology could not be implemented, and without which it would soon be forgotten. With these assumptions, the system does not move onward and upward for ever, but rather, after first accelerating, then decelerating, it comes to rest at a high-technology–high-population stable equilibrium, beyond which neither increases in population nor technology can be sustained.

The analysis shows how the Boserup space, within which technological progress automatically occurs, may occupy only a limited portion of the phase space, but that Malthusian forces will steer population and technology into that region. The analysis also illustrates how a preventive check that is too weak may lead to a stable equilibrium at a medium level of technology rather than at the high level that would have been attained with a stronger preventive check, possibly at a higher population density. Similarly the effects of too strong a preventive check, too-high exogenous mortality, or too-strong extractive institutions might lead to a medium-technology equilibrium where a higher one might have otherwise been attained. It is also shown how progress to the highest technologies might occur by transition through a sequence of intermediate stable equilibria, at each of which the system might be indefinitely delayed. Premature population growth, or premature restraint, might render the passage from one stable equilibrium to a higher one much less likely.

REFERENCES

Ammerman, A., and Cavalli-Sforza, L. 1971: Measuring the rate of spread of early farming in Europe. *Man*, 6, 674–88.
Arrow, K. 1962: The economic implications of learning by doing. *Review of Economic Studies*, 29 (80), 155–73.
Boserup, E. 1965: *The Conditions of Agricultural Progress*. London: Allen and Unwin.
—— 1981: *Population and Technological Change: a study of long-term trends*. Chicago: University of Chicago Press.
Blanton, R. 1975: The cybernetic analysis of human population growth. In A. Swedlund (ed.), Population Studies in Archeology: a symposium, *Journal of the Society for American Archeology*, 40 (2), part 2, memoir 30.
Bowen, I. 1954: *Population*. Cambridge: Cambridge University Press.
Chiang, A. C. 1984: *Fundamental Methods of Mathematical Economics*. New York: McGraw Hill.
Cipolla, C. 1962: *The Economic History of World Population*. Harmondsworth: Penguin.

Clark, C. 1968: *Population Growth and Land Use*. London: Macmillan.

Darity, W. A., Jr 1980: The Boserup theory of agricultural growth: a model for anthropological economics. *Journal of Development Economics*, 7, 137–57.

David, P. 1975: *Technical Choice, Innovation, and Economic Growth*. Cambridge: Cambridge University Press.

Deevey, E. 1960: The human population. *Scientific American*, 203, (3), 195–204.

Evenson, R. 1984: Population growth and agricultural development in North India. Unpublished manuscript of the Economic Growth Center, Yale University.

Everett, A. H. 1970: *New Ideas on Population*. New York: Augustus M. Kelley. (First published 1826.)

Hahn, F. H., and Matthews, R. C. O. 1964: Growth and technical progress: a survey. *Economic Journal*, 74, 825–50.

Hollingsworth, T. 1969. *Historical Demography*. Ithaca, NY: Cornell University Press.

Jones, E. L. 1981: *The European Miracle*. Cambridge: Cambridge University Press.

Kaldor, N., and Mirrlees, J. A. 1962: A new model of economic growth. *Review of Economic Studies*, 29, 174–92.

Kuznets, S. 1960: Population change and aggregate output. In Universities–National Bureau of Economic Research, *Demographic and Economic Change in Developed Countries*, Princeton, NJ: Princeton University Press.

Lee, R. D. 1973: Population in preindustrial England: an econometric analysis. *Quarterly Journal of Economics*, 87 (4), 581–607.

—— 1978a: *Econometric Studies of Topics in Demographic History*. New York: Arno Press.

—— 1978b: Models of preindustrial population dynamics with applications to England. In Charles Tilly (ed.), *Historical Studies of Changing Fertility*, Princeton, NJ: Princeton University Press.

—— 1980: An historical perspective on economic aspects of the population explosion: the case of preindustrial England. In Richard Easterlin (ed.), *Population and Demographic Change in Developing Countries*, Chicago: University of Chicago Press, pp. 517–66.

Lesthaeghe, R. 1980: On the social control of human reproduction. *Population and Development Review*, 6 (4), 527–48.

McC. Adams, R. 1965: *Land Behind Baghdad: A History of Settlement On the Diyala Plains*. Chicago: University of Chicago Press.

Mueller, E., and Short, K. 1983: Income and wealth as they affect the demand for children in developing countries. In R. Bulatao and R. D. Lee (eds), *Determinants of Fertility in Developing Countries: A Summary of Knowledge*, London: Academic Press.

Needham, H. 1961: *Science and the Civilization in China*. Cambridge: Cambridge University Press.

Phelps, E. S. 1968: Population increase. *Canadian Journal of Economics*, 1 (3), 498–518.

—— 1966: Models of technical progress and the golden rule of research. *Review of Economic Studies*, 133–45.

Pryor, F. L. 1983: The invention of the plow. Unpublished manuscript of the Department of Economics, Swarthmore College, PA.

—— and Maurer, S. B. 1982: On induced economic change in precapitalist societies. *Journal of Development Economics*, 10, 325–53.

Pingali, P. L., and Binswanger, H. P. 1983: Population density, farming intensity, patterns of labor use and mechanization. Unpublished manuscript of the Agriculture and Rural Development Department of the World Bank.

Robinson, W., and Schutjer, A. 1984: Agricultural development and demographic change: a generalization of the Boserup model. *Economic Development and Cultural Change*, 32 (2), 355–66.

Sauvy, A. 1969: *General Theory of Population*. London: Weidenfeld and Nicolson, and New York: Basic Books.

Simon, J. 1977: *The Economics of Population Growth*. Princeton, NJ: Princeton University Press.

—— 1981: *The Ultimate Resource*. Princeton, NJ: Princeton University Press.

—— n.d.: Invention, duplication, and the size of the labor force. Unpublished manuscript.

—— and Gunter Steinmann n.d.: The economic implications of learning-by-doing for population size and growth. Unpublished manuscript.

Stokes, C. and Schutjer, W. A. 1983: Access to land and fertility in developing countries. In W. A. Schutjer and C. S. Stokes (eds) *Rural Development and Human Fertility*, London and New York pp. 195–215.

Stoneman, P. 1983: *The Economic Analysis of Technological Change*. Oxford: Oxford University Press.

Demographic Regimes as Cultural Systems

Philip Kreager

Malthus prefaced his *Essay* with the remark that he wrote it on an impulse and in isolation, having retreated to a country seat where he was without the benefit (or distraction) of libraries full of data or the subtleties of the latest arguments. There, with a clear mental ground before him, he was able to formulate the definite and sweeping formulae which have given a distinctive direction to population theory ever since. Some such removal is probably necessary to making a fresh start on any large and complex problem. Like all contributors to this volume, my topic is large-scale population theory after Malthus, and my special brief is the population and social structures of traditional rural communities. You will, therefore, appreciate my sympathy for Malthus, decamped and undiverted in his curacy at Okewood: mankind has lived in relatively small and simple social organizations for most of recorded history, and the demographic interest of such social forms is in their general and dynamic properties, or, in other words, the comparative study of change in many, and a goodly variety, of them.

Lacking a country vicarage, but still needing to clear the air somehow on this immense topic, I shall begin by reviewing selectively why the study of rural social structures is of especial interest to demography just now. A genuine reorientation of population theory is currently well under way. It may be summarized in three conceptual movements: (1) from 'decision' to 'structure'; (2) from 'demographic transition' to 'demographic regime'; and (3) from 'development' to 'identity'.

The institutions characteristic of many peasant and pastoral societies, such as bridewealth, dowry, lineages, castes, age sets, and so forth, were not anticipated by the idealized family models and contraceptive use surveys exported, with only secondary adjustments, from the West to the Third World in the 1960s and 1970s. Given that rural social organization in these areas has been the object of intensive investigation in other social sciences for over half a century, and that the indirect nature of social and economic determinants of fertility and mortality has been recognized generally for an even longer period, these approaches probably deserved the avalanche of criticism that finally fell on them. Domestic groups, nuptiality, and reproduction are not usually organized with primary reference to maintaining discrete numerical norms of family size. The study of mortality and fertility determinants has made rapid progress since it was freed from this bizarre restriction, and could be applied with due reference to the logic of local institutions and their histories. Familiar examples include studies of lactational infecundability and sexual relations in tropical Africa which reflect economic and ritual relations between groups of kin and affines (Lesthaeghe 1984, pp. 11–17), studies of the relations between birth histories, child mortality and caste hierarchies in the Sahel (Hill et al 1983), and the history of marriage, bastardy and social control in Europe (Laslett et al. 1980).

The old phrase 'calculus of conscious choice' has, in effect, begun to be reinterpreted so that it may better reflect the actual order and contents of peoples' choices. Questions such as the following are now commonplace: How is control over nuptiality used to enhance or consolidate group status and power (Bourdieu 1976, Caldwell 1978)? What advantages and disadvantages do different family and kinship systems have as mechanisms of income distribution (Goody 1976, Liu 1982, Greenhalgh 1982)? What is the relation of the status of women to differentials in infant mortality by sex and birth order (Scrimshaw 1978, Dyson and Moore 1983)? By making the concept of decision a property of particular value and social structures we acquire a hedge against prejudging the nature of reproduction and related vital events as variables in peoples' lives – as to who chooses, what are the actual trade-offs in decision-making, and how or whether decisions are publicly articulated. The interest in the particular ways in which demographic constraints and opportunities are important in different societies thus tends to lead population studies away from fertility declines as the inevitable preoccupation of population theory.

The much greater attention paid in recent years to the social and demographic history of Europe and the Third World means that there is less need for sweeping and speculative notions of development and transition to serve as effective substitutes for history. The convergence of all societies upon a 'European' type having near-replacement fertility no longer seems inevitable, and is not happening with any certainty in most of the world. One legacy of transition and development theory is an unsolved problem of comparative method: namely, how to assess whether a given demographic change is of fundamental, structural significance, or whether it simply indicates the existence of multiple routing, i.e. variation of choice amongst several accepted avenues to established ends. Transition and development theory encouraged the view that radical change was necessary, but social and historical demography in recent years have increasingly shown how traditional family and community structures may be maintained, despite marked changes in vital rates or procreative habits. Thus: in African populations, such as the Yoruba, a large intake of modern contraceptives may be coupled with no change in family size or family-size preferences, since it is related to fertility control before marriage or in traditional periods of sexual abstinence (Caldwell and Caldwell 1976); in Taiwan, reduced fertility and family size coupled with economic growth sustain traditional extended family values and organization, since these developments increase reliance on family networks for alternative sources of security and opportunity (Freedman et al. 1982); further development of extended and complex family arrangements along these lines has been suggested as a measure of lowering fertility rates and improving economic and social conditions in Bangladesh (Cain 1982, p. 173); indeed, in some industrial communities in nineteenth-century England, the elaboration of complex family forms and increased fertility were necessary adaptations to changing demands for labour (Anderson 1971); the adoption of Western family values among Akan elites in Ghana, rather than marking a trend away from tradition, has provided a new medium for the expression of long-standing structural conflicts (Oppong 1974).

With the benefit of hindsight it is clear that to define a transition or course of development we must first clarify the nature of the regime from which behaviour has diverged, and ensure that divergence is in fact what is taking place. Logically, the notion of demographic transition requires the prior concept of demographic regimes. Greater clarity and consistency is therefore needed with respect to the regime concept, for which no agreed formula exists. One purpose of this essay is to suggest two complementary approaches, which suggest a division of labour upon which research and analysis may proceed.

Generally speaking, in a demographic regime population is considered as the recruitment component of social structure. A regime should enable us to see how processes of population composition and decomposition, and peoples' selective understanding of such processes, sustain certain social institutions and groups as opposed to others. Evidently, regimes may be organized to restrict numbers of children in order to secure a certain standard of living in nuclear families; but they may give primary value to other implications of the timing of marriage and child-bearing, or to other sets of demographic variables, as prior considerations in local decision-making. In many Chinese and South Indian communities, control over nuptiality combines with fertility at levels above replacement, to serve multiple purposes: they are means of forging alliances between families: of controlling property transmission via dowry, bridewealth, and inheritance; or preserving continuity and purity of descent lines; and of enforcing social distinctions of age and sex (Ahern 1974, Wolf and Huang 1980, Caldwell et al. 1983, Dumont 1983). The interpretation of changing nuptiality and birth rates – and their possible significance as markers of social structural change – obviously depends on their role in these institutions. Early marriage, high fertility, and a hierarchy of sex and age criteria also figure prominently in Mayan communities in southern Mexico, but there they are adjuncts of an ideology of ethnic boundaries, an economy historically dependent upon labour migration, and competition for political and religious office (Kreager 1984). Delayed marriage, virginity, celibacy, migration, and birth order are the loci of rules preserving family honour and property in many Mediterranean communities (Bourdieu 1976, Campbell 1964, Peristiany 1976). A demographic regime should, in short, model the way peoples are deploying their vital events and relations for their own purposes.

Of course, institutions such as the ones just listed are observed only more or less, as is true of family-size preference in Western societies. The hiatus between knowledge and its imperfect implementation or unintended consequences is no less fundamental to population than to any other social field. It is an objective phenomenon to be explored in each society according to peoples' values and institutions. The suggestion of transition and development theory, however, was that the gap between peoples' knowledge and practice was generally something that ought to be reduced as much as possible by the right combination of education, persuasion, technology and economic improvement. The nature of the hiatus was effectively predetermined by the categories 'underdeveloped', 'transitional' and 'pre-transitional'. Moreover, by confining description and analysis to idealized 'micro-' and 'macro-levels', a kind of leap usually needed to be performed, from consideration of the 'rationalities' of individuals, couples, or small families to those assumed to operate amongst whole communities or even nations.

The idea of demographic regimes, as a species of comparative institutional analysis, makes the jump from 'micro' to 'macro' and the assumption of idealized sequences of development much less compelling, in three closely related respects. First, study of population as a process of insti-tutional recruitment opens to demographic inquiry a broad range of intermediate social structures which guide decisions made at the domestic level. Instances already canvassed include regional variations in inheritance and land use in rural France and other parts of Europe (Berkner and Mendels 1978, Macfarlane 1980), manorial, parish and later extra-familial welfare institutions supporting the nuclear family in English history (Smith, this volume), ideological codes linking school, religious, union, and political allegiances in the Netherlands (Lesthaeghe 1980), the role of kin networks and patron–client relations in sustaining the ethnic identity of contemporary English Pakistani communities (Anwar 1979), and the role of marriage in inter-group politics remarked upon above. Much further work needs to be done on the demography of institutions recruited from members of domestic groups.

Second, since comparative institutional analysis proceeds by examination of differentials amongst alternatives, especial importance attaches to the strategies motivating the several sorts of group in which people live. Vital events and relations are a good starting-point for modelling group strategies, since age, marriage, kinship, death and procreation consistently provide relations which transcend shifting economic and political circumstances, and may be used to adjust to them. Differing but related perspectives may be gained in a single society, depending on which vital processes are selected for analysis. The study of marriage markets – that is, of the several types of marriage recognized in a given society, and their relative advantages, disadvantages and availability – is central to the French, South Asian, Akan and Chinese examples already cited. The logic which builds relations between groups in terms of ties by marriage and kinship is further elaborated in some societies in which adoption, fostering and godparenthood provide institutions of patronage, care for the elderly, apprenticeship and education (Hammel 1968, Goody 1976, Kreager 1980, Wolf and Huang 1980). The 'value of children' in this structural perspective follows from the fact that each child opens up all of the possibilities of a social system, relative to the position of the parents, families or other groups to which a child is affiliated. Some writers emphasize the system of social security inhering in the multiplication of options; more generally, multiplication is described as a feature of competition for socially defined resources (Caldwell 1977, Douglas 1966a, Kreager 1982, Mendels 1972).

In order to translate the aggregate effects of younger age structures, rising unemployment, wage changes or a fall in mortality into something more immediate than an abstract pressure of numbers on resources, it is the range of strategies or alternative routings that people prefer or prescribe for the groups in which they live that is of primary importance, and not the mean tendency or maximal strategy of marriage, family or reproduction. There remains some distance to be covered in the formulation of models in this respect, as will be noted in the following section. Mere plausibility requires a model to tell us how people carry on despite imminent and real imbalances in society. Questions of self- and collective respect, for example, may influence the composition and continuity of groups well in advance of – as well as during and after – the effects of brute material limits.

Hence, the third role of demographic regimes is to lead inquiry into consideration of how vital processes are used by peoples to define not merely sets of personnel and institutional functions, but groups of marked social meaning. Some analyses continue to plump for an application of existing development theories (e.g. the emergence of economic and social strata, 'proto-industrialization', 'proletarianization') which supply the historical meaning of groups as different sorts of human capital. But it may also be recognized that there are local histories in which people use their memory and experience of the vital events and relations of particular groups as a way of distinguishing those units they identify with and live in, and to decide relative social standing. Families, lineages, political factions and other bodies are recognized by successful observance of rules of vital reference: whether group members marry within the right social categories; whether they are able to observe correct patterns of paternal, filial and sexual authority; whether family property is kept intact between generations; and so forth. Individuals and groups that fail to live up to local standards may well find themselves defined out of society by various means: they may, on the one hand, be pushed to migrate by poverty, by the loss of land or face, or by committing crimes (and then fleeing the consequences); on the other hand, they may opt out by marrying into other social groups, or by adopting the marital, sexual or ancestral values of neighbouring populations. Of course, the perceived pattern of marriages, ancestry and so forth may also be used to define down, i.e. to identify groups within a society as more or less permanently lower class, caste or status, and consequently not expected or perhaps allowed to participate in more highly valued social exchanges. Collective memory is a powerful record of social observances, since every individual grows up in a family known to have made certain marriages, suffered certain deaths, and to have deployed its manpower to certain effects.

Just as individuals and groups within a society are differentiated by the value of their vital relations, and make a claim thereby to legitimate social existence, so whole societies (or cultural groups within them) define themselves by their observance of a certain morality with respect to the facts of life, in contrast to the rules and observances of others. Attitudes to sexuality, marriage, and the family are amongst the first and archetypal criteria which peoples insist differentiate them categorically from the behaviour and true nature of other societies.[1] Of course, when we examine the actual relations between groups, then differences may not be so clear-cut. Here there is an opportunity to bring demographic measures and the values of historical and cultural identity into useful relation with respect to the unsolved legacy of comparative method raised earlier. When peoples can be shown to have changed fundamental patterns in the timing, incidence and duration of marriage, reproduction, or group affiliation, do they in fact redefine themselves by adopting new codes of right and wrong conduct with respect to vital processes? To what extent may an apparently 'radical' change in values at one level disguise what are only shifts in practice within extant value structures of greater historical duration?[2]

For the purpose of this paper, a somewhat narrowed definition of 'identity' or 'cultural system' may be used. 'Culture' is defined simply as the sense people make of their material environment; as in ordinary English usage, what is material to a given case need not be physical. In considering systems of culture, I shall emphasize what I take to be their cutting edge: namely, the application of criteria of right and wrong. Cultural or, in this restricted usage, moral systems reflect less the laying-down of absolute codes of conduct than an endless process of negotiation. Such a restriction seems permissible in the case of population theory, since vital processes are the true playground of moral systems: while crucial to the continuity of groups and recognized as such by them, both the relevant facts of life and the values regarded appropriate to them may be juggled by actors and audience alike. In the archetypal case, the social fact of virginity need not depend on an actual copulation. Or, to cite another noted example, for Malthus the enforcement of the preventive check was less important than that the means – 'restraint' and not contraception – were the right ones. Because the identity of groups is bound up inextricably with questions of legitimacy and reputation,

---

[1]This theme is fundamental to the whole way the West has defined itself in history with respect to the non-West (e.g. Said 1978, pp. 311–16), and to groups perceived as 'ethnic' or 'traditional' within Europe (e.g. Chapman 1978). The role of gender differences in defining groups (Ardener 1972) and also of pollution concepts (Douglas 1966b) are aspects of this theme.

[2]For example, Wolf and Huang (1980) describe the near-disappearance of an important marriage strategy in northern Taiwan: namely, marriage with an adopted daughter. This change, while reflecting economic and social changes in generational relations, remains an adjustment within the fundamental ideology and organization of descent which governs family relations. Caldwell et al (1983) demonstrate new adjustments following from the primary importance of affinity as a principle relating groups, a long-standing structural theme in South Asian ethnography (cf. Dumont 1983). Improved mortality, increased education and a wider job market have been experienced locally by adjustments internal to a system which places great emphasis on individual, family and group status as defined by nuptiality and marriage. Shifts have occurred in marriage payments (from bridewealth to dowry), in status criteria (favouring educated sons-in-law) and in the locus of hymeneal purity (from menarche to virginity).

the critical vital events arbitrated by demographic regimes are likely to fall along that precarious line of interpretation by which people separate propriety, misfortune and scandal. What constitutes a good marriage, an untimely death, or too many children? What stigma, if any, attaches to divorce, illegitimacy, celibacy, infanticide, adultery? Which groups in a society are more or less subject to such scruples? An understanding of vital events and relations for their local connotations may thus provide a working model of social structure.

The implications of considering population as a basis of value and social structures are thus not confined to village, community or other local-group studies. The second purpose of this essay is to note than an important reversal has occurred in the way local patterns are interpreted in the formulation of speculative population theories. Time was when the demographic transition as a response to economic development was thought to describe adequately the dynamics of modern population history. The timing and pace of declines, and the selection of proximate mechanisms, however, tend to escape this formula – not to mention causality and cultural difference (Coale 1973). The demographic transition has now probably found its correct niche in the domain of statics: the description of broad levels in population indices with respect to stereotyped stages of development (UN 1980, p. 179).

On the other hand, look what has happened to that supposedly tired, static and encrusted notion 'tradition'. Time was when 'tradition' was a synonym for backwardness and resistance to change. The labels 'pre-transitional', 'pre-industrial' and 'pre-modern' lumped together an amazing variety of social types, and effectively consigned most of history and culture to demographically retrograde periods and conditions. The point to broad classifications such as 'pre-transitional society' was, of course, to serve as a baseline at a time when much less was known about early modern and Third World populations. There was a politics to such classifications too: in so far as societies exist in a self-defeating race of births against deaths, a compelling case could readily be made for inducing development and fertility declines. In the long term, however, the politics of transition and development concepts have tended to work against population being taken seriously as a major basis of social and historical theory. In so far as demographers' energies have been concentrated on showing that the population factor in pre-transitional and transitional societies was a predominantly negative one – an inhibitor of development – there has appeared to be much less interest or importance in exploring how vital processes and values support more general aspects of what is positive or at least characteristic in the history of these societies.[3]

We now know that several population models are necessary to explain natural fertility, and that the self-defeating race of high birth and death rates may be descriptive more, for example, of cities in early states of economic growth (Finlay 1978, 1979), than tribal and hunter–gatherer populations such as described elsewhere in this volume by Lesthaeghe and Howell. The

[3]The notable exception being Boserup (1965).

demographic regimes found in traditional rural societies at varying stages of demographic transitions are not a static backdrop against which externally induced changes work. Population, when considered in its dual capacity as a system of recruitment and an object of cultural identification, provides a fundamental ground for social theory which need not be a mere accessory to notions to development. Here, then, is a common strategy of research and analysis upon which current work appears to be proceeding: measures appropriate to particular social structures, used in light of ethnographic and archival study of values and institutions, reveal changes which, while pointing to some selective aspects of the stereotypes of development and transition, return us to a more fundamental continuity-in-change of a people's way of life.

It is an open question whether the role of population processes in the historical continuity of societies and cultures may prove a better basis for comparative demographic theory than ordained sequences of modernization and development. At least, it is clear that contextually minded approaches do not signal the fragmentation of population theory that some commentators seem to imply (Hawthorn 1978, Freedman 1979, Tilly 1978). Recent proposals tend to adopt a regional and temporal frame of reference rather than a universalistic one (Hajnal 1982, Page and Lesthaeghe 1981, Caldwell 1981). The study of population as an aspect of social structures already provides a challenge to demographers' ingenuity as model-builders, not only by taking on a wider and more complex set of institutions, but by addressing the central problem of 'unconscious rationality' (Wrigley 1978): that is, how societies maintain distinctive population structures suited to certain ends, without having explicit population policies designed to those ends.

PROBLEMS OF SCALE IN REGULATIVE MODELS

Discussion of the ways societies reconcile their numbers and purposes leads, sooner or later, to talk about 'feedbacks', 'homeostasis' and various model 'rationalities'. These discussions are inevitably rather abstract, their language suggesting an idealized social efficiency: 'checks' operate to keep behaviour within certain minimum or maximum bounds; contraception guards 'optimum' levels of materiality by restraining the 'overproduction' of children; the 'demand' for children is carefully balanced between their 'cost' or implied 'risk' and the 'security', 'satisfaction' and 'fringe benefits' they may provide; 'surpluses' generated in one set of 'transactions' are 'cashed in' when some 'vacancy' appears in the system; and so forth. Models described in these terms are intentional tautologies. If societies really were homeostatic mechanisms, they would have to be badly – that is, very approximately – tuned ones. By definition, a finely tuned machine is one highly susceptible of breakdown; although societies have their crises, only exceptionally do they cease to function altogether.

If societies require flexible margins of error, then we could say that, in effect, losers are necessary to their normal operation. This is an important feature of the comparative problem of multiple routing, discussed earlier.

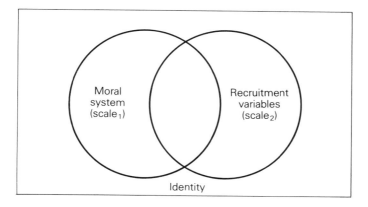

Figure 1

The papers cited provide examples: disinherited sons who become land-less labourers; the early-weaned who die; those forced by the death of a spouse or father to sell or partition land necessary to future well-being; those whose celibacy effectively preserves family honour and property; those killed by rival factions. The continuity of groups in society, and of the identity and composition of a given society as a whole, may be sustained by what are in human terms considerable imbalances or relative diseconomies of scale. The classic case is, of course, the Malthusian population existing at the limits of subsistence. Of course, not all – and, possibly, not most – of the examples just given may be 'objectively' necessary to social continuity; but all are subject to interpretation and definition by the peoples in question, who may be expected to have decided opinions about what is right or wrong about them. Peoples' perception of differences of scale – which, at an extreme, may appear different orders of existence – are therefore inextricable from collective processes of life and death.

Two concepts of scale are consequently at issue in the old problem of selecting units appropriate to modelling a social totality relative to its parts. In one, scale is a property of a moral system, in which the balance of right and wrong establishes dimensions within which any course of action will be interpreted. We are concerned here with moral systems chiefly as they may appear to be attempts to regulate social and economic relations by controlling certain arrangements of the facts of life. The second concept of scale is that of continuous measurement: the aggregate demographic implications of individual and collective action, particularly the calculation of points of diminishing return. Interest naturally centres on the relation of given moral systems (scale$_1$) to the population thresholds (scale$_2$) to which they directly and indirectly give rise, and which variously support and complicate their continuity.

Demographic regimes necessarily incorporate both concepts of scale, since neither processes of recruitment nor processes of identity can be defined exclusively in either aggregate or moral terms. A demographic regime, as a cultural model of population 'feedbacks' into social structure, is concerned with how peoples' perceptions of differences of scale regulate the identity of groups. Two 'feedback loops' are at issue: (1) how moral systems organize recruitment; and (2) how recruitment helps to perpetuate, or underlies the revision of, moral systems. This sort of model can be represented by a Venn diagram (figure 1).

Two sorts of regime, inclusive of both 'loops' may be hypothesized. In the first, which I shall call 'restricted regimes', analysis adheres to the terms and logic of a given moral system, and then traces its aggregate implications. In short, we examine $scale_2$ from the perspective of $scale_1$. The expectation is that aggregate trends may not agree with local convention: in normal situations very probably only a minority are able or interested actually to observe the letter of moral dictates, while the majority make do with some other accepted or less preferred formula, perhaps one actually considered a 'losing' option. Obviously the relation of several courses of action is not static, as new alternatives may always be attempted at the margins of acceptability. The interest, then, is in the several processes of adjustment that are able to coexist with notions of right conduct, and with each other.

Whether or not these adjustments are recognized as overt breaks with tradition, their meaning is adjunct to traditional identity. The significance, for example, of ideas and techniques coming from the West may depend on the history of relations between local groups, as this arbitrates both which parties take them up, and the purposes to which they are addressed. The fact that ideas and techniques are marked 'Western' or 'modern' may be of less significance than the historical role to which they are assimilated (Wallman 1977, Kreager 1984). I shall return to the place of restricted regimes in current theorizing, and how they may be formulated, in the section 'Restricted regimes'.

A second type – or, 'generalized' regime – is one in which the logic guiding local thought and action is supplied by the analyst, in order to demonstrate certain demographic implications of social structures. At the moment there is a growing abundance of generalized regimes, and it is foolish perhaps to attempt a single formula for all of them. None the less, a social structure, when considered as a demographic regime, usually entails the following four components:

1 the main institution under analysis is some form (or set of forms) of domestic group;
2 domestic groups and the individuals that compose them are supposed to be motivated by 'strategies' to improve or maintain material well-being and social position;
3 consequently, the relation of domestic groups to wider social organization is defined in terms of some local application of the laws of supply and demand – although the variables are not entirely economic, the cultural and social factors considered are usually described by economic metaphors (e.g. 'trade-offs', 'marriage markets');

4 differences between groups and the directionality of change may be
expressed by certain thresholds or contrasting formal types, both
preferably subject to measurement.

Well-known approaches, which in some cases overlap each other, include
theories of wealth flows (Caldwell 1978), proto-industrialization and
proletarianization (Mendels 1972), family life-cycles,[4] and the comparative
analysis of systems of inheritance and agriculture (Goody 1976).

A great deal of ink has been spilt usefully in controversy over these
proposals. More doubtless will follow, as local studies fill out the typically
scattered and incomplete data available to support them. It should be
noted that these theories interpret the role of population in social
structure for differing purposes. The study of wealth flows keeps the issue
of fertility declines and values accompanying economic development at
the centre of population theory. Study of the organization of labour makes
population an adjunct of the theory of class formation. The demography
of domestic groups is one basis of social, cultural and economic histories
of the family. Study of the domestic domain under contrasting modes of
production and rules of property devolution is orthodox comparative
sociology.

The problems confronting generalized regimes at this stage are many,
and seem at times to be almost wilfully cultivated by their proponents.
Such an accusation would, however, be unfair. The initial task was to
celebrate the diversity of vital limits and processes as parameters of
domestic and community organization. Work has, however, proceeded
directly to the task of segmenting data so that testable regularities may
be recognized – yet this process has tended thus far to compound diversity
rather than reduce it. Not only are there many more institutions and
differentials under consideration, but our understanding of them is derived
from diverse sources, each having historical peculiarities which often
forbid the identical set of measures being employed from one case to the next.
A generalized regime, therefore, usually consists of a string of inferences
which begins with a number of institutional types and phases derived from
ethnography or local history, and then proceeds by selective measurement
(often using proxy variables, and hypotheses to cover acknowledged gaps in
the data) to build a case for the reality of the 'strategies' said to articulate
the phases or types.

Take, for example, the reconstruction by Berkner and Shaffer (1978) of the
role of the joint family in the Nivernois area of central France in the eighteenth
and nineteenth centuries. The task is to explain the continuity of the joint
family in light of fundamental changes in landownership in this period. The
sequence of their argument may be summarized very briefly as follows. The
authors begin by describing inheritance and marriage practices which social
and legal historians have found in notarial records. They proceed to examine

---

[4]The *Journal of Family History* is a source for many papers taking this approach, as proposed
in their statement of purpose (1976).

a set of such records pertaining to selected villages, during the period 1775 to 1835. The change in rights over property and labour parallels changing proportions of households, as characterized by occupational and marital criteria. Census data for 1820, and a land survey for 1872, are then used to expand the pattern to the province level. The authors conclude that joint family organization helped to keep property intact when peasants were in the position of smallholders, and later permitted labour-force management suited to sharecropping.

These two strategies are implied by the local terms used for servile tenure (*bordelage*) and sharecropping (*métayage*). For various reasons it remains difficult to assess how adequate these types are, given the doubts that have been expressed regarding the aptitude of legal records for capturing the actual conduct of the law (Bourdieu 1976). Indeed, in this case age and kinship data are acknowledged as lacking; the comprehensiveness of the notaries' records has to be taken for granted; the precise relation of households to land over the several periods in question remains unknown; and no case studies of particular families over time are presented. The favourable reviews (Anderson 1980, p. 92; Yanagisako 1979, p. 179) of this study reflect, I suppose, not only the general plausibility and elegance of the formulation, but the intrinsic interest of the problem, given what appear to be inevitable limitations of sources. The possibility of other equally plausible formulations of the same materials cannot be excluded.

Generalized regimes describing contemporary societies are able to reduce some flights of inference inherent in historical reconstructions, but they retain many gaps and ambiguities. Again, a single illustration will have to suffice. Cain, in a series of articles, has presented data and a number of related hypotheses, including the 'erosion of the joint household' and the interaction of economic polarization and household life-cycles in rural Bangladesh (1978, p. 436; Cain et al. 1979, p. 410; other references are cited in Cain 1982). The context is the hierarchical order of 'patriarchy' to which Caldwell (1978) has called attention: a religious and political ideology of male dominance is sustained via the sexual division of labour, rules of marriage and inheritance, kinship obligations, generational authority, and an organization of family life-cycles which not only excludes women from secure independent positions, but may utilize senior women to enforce subservience of their juniors. The case of Bangladesh shows this moral system under conditions of high fertility and rapidly increasing landlessness. Cain uses an extensive set of measures in a single village to take a closer look at household economics and their relation to the composition and decomposition of family groups. He finds, for example, that fertility and infant mortality do not vary substantially by economic class (as defined by landholding), but adult mortality does; the vulnerability of women is underwritten both by the incidence of widowhood and the limited and poorly paid occupations open to them; sale of land to meet medical and food needs is a recurring problem which exacerbates differences between family groups; the landed minority appear to be better able to keep children at home to provide labour and related support; the number of nuclear households, however, is increasing. Nucleation, Cain argues, entails a double strategy: on the one hand, households try to make the best of limited resources by denying assistance to outside kin; on the other, the absence of such assistance puts a premium on the support which their own children can give, especially in the context of floods, droughts and other recurring crises. The fragile position of widows gives particular impetus to high fertility, as does the relation between fertility and economic mobility.

The pattern of nucleation and high fertility Cain describes is evidently not the Western-style emotional and economic nucleation which, according to Caldwell, stimulates fertility declines. Cain follows Caldwell's argument that stronger extended family networks should provide security against risks, but his data suggest, contra Caldwell, that extended family organization, by multiplying options through kin, ought to make high fertility less crucial as a source of insurance. Extended family systems do appear to facilitate declines elsewhere in Asia (Freedman et al. 1982); further study of the relation between 'risk' and multiple options would be of interest, since it might specify the mechanisms underlying the tendency of fertility declines to stabilize above Western levels.

The village described by Cain provides a suggestive example of how the effects of scale$_2$ are expressed through adjustments of scale$_1$; we see how landlessness, disasters and increasing human numbers give a particular direction to local interpretations of a moral system. Norms which link authority to high fertility are supported by the system: those groups which have sufficient numbers of mature male children tend to get through crises, and this gives them an advantage over time. However, norms of responsibility linking one household to another are not underwritten materially in the same way. Kin networks in rural Bangladesh, according to Cain, are at best inconsistent as sources of security. On the one hand, disputes are adjudicated by patrilineal elders, performance of rites of passage remain an important function of wider kin groups, and political and physical threats are met with the support of male kin (1982, p. 174). On the other, kin links at a wider level do not necessarily extend to economic support between domestic groups in times of crisis; at least, a high degree of economic difference exists between brothers, who tend to buy up each other's land and not to support each other's widows. Cain's research suggests a sharpening of the priority of patriarchal position, in which the competition between domestic groups for scarce resources refines differences of power and wealth between them. The deteriorating situation of female-headed households reflects their position at the bottom of both priorities of scale.

Why should kin groups respond to deteriorating local conditions in the way Cain describes? To understand the trade-off between the value of children and the value of assistance from kin outside the immediate domestic group, we need, as Cain remarks, to know more about how kin networks actually function: the way sanctions of authority and responsibility are applied; the kinds of support and the circumstances under which kin do provide for each other; and the implications of sanctions and support supplied or denied for the identity of the groups in question. It seems unlikely that the wider political, legal and ritual bodies to which members of domestic groups are recruited are without implications in the market for land and subsistence.

A standard ethnographic approach would provide a substantial body of longitudinal data of a retrospective kind on these issues, and an internal structure of genealogy, marriage and landholdings necessary to check the consistency of such data. At present, although we obtain a good picture of the limits which $scale_2$ can impose on $scale_1$, the feedback from $scale_1$ – which shapes the way $scale_2$ limits are perceived and, in consequence, guides the selective way they are effected – remains in major respects hypothetical.

Hence, it remains possible that Cain and Caldwell are describing different pieces of the same puzzle. Caldwell is interested in how the power of 'patriarchical' groups is sustained. Cain asks, instead, how vulnerable 'patriarchs' and their widows secure themselves against the power of other 'patriarchs' in cases where there is the added problem of recurring natural disasters. The authors agree that the answer depends on the timing of sufficient numbers of children relative to economic and moral options inherent in kin networks.

To summarize: the analysis of domestic groups, and the use of population measures to articulate types, phases or thresholds that define them appear at present blocked by the need for a better understanding of how wider institutional structures impinge on these groups, and of the characteristic local strategies that arise from peoples' historical experience. In terms of the four-point summary of generalized regimes given earlier in this section, the considerable progress made by population studies addressed to points (1) and (4) awaits a matching improvement in formulations of points (2) and (3). A number of underlying theoretical issues may be noted briefly.

First, the fault lines in our substantive knowledge of the kinds reviewed in the Nivernois and Bangladesh studies are, in many if not most cases, permanent ones. Peoples' motivations usually must be inferred from archival records, and only a partial picture may be gained of the range of alternative courses of action open to them. Studies of contemporary societies that depend for depth on historical research may, therefore, be no different. Field studies do, however, add the considerable advantages of observation and conversation, and their capacity to study actual practices, and to uncover unexpected institutional forms, gains in importance when these forms and practices help us to recognize arrangements in past times.

The danger of the circularity of models, however, grows. Hammel (1978) has remarked that research tends to follow one of two methods in order to identify regularities within a complex range of alternatives. The first is to select data which show how the course of events conforms to a hypothesis. The second is analytical decomposition: a body of data is segmented until its inherent regularities emerge. I would agree with Hammel that the latter technique is to be preferred, since in the former regularities which do not conform to chosen hypotheses may be attributed to chance, or simply dismissed as exceptional. The analytical process of segmentation encourages the analyst to try out a series of alternative combinations, until the best fit is identified. However, the difference between the two approaches may vanish when either the gaps in the historical record, or the strategies which the analyst infers as peoples' motivations, drastically narrow the kinds of alternatives considered.[5] Decomposition in itself is unlikely to provide a check – short of failing altogether to give rise to intelligible regularities – to anachronism, ethnocentrism, or the capacity of codified norms (be they moral, legal, ritual or otherwise) to disguise the actual conduct of affairs.

The real question, therefore, is the substantive basis of the 'strategies' which animate generalized regimes. It is remarkable what a limited range is on offer. A good deal of 'maximizing' still goes on, under the guise of peasants who supposedly strive to keep their property intact, to arrange child-bearing and marriage as security in old age, or to balance the costs of infants and young children against their eventual contributions to family income. These are plausible as short-term models, *ceteris paribus*, but we should scarcely have needed to go to the Nivernois or to Bangladesh either to find or disprove them. They are descendants of a strain in modern culture which insists that, for the purpose of theory, men are everywhere and at all times mentally the same. What began as a tenet of eighteenth-century philosophical rationalism is, by now, a kind of 'folklore of capitalism', used to describe why certain peoples are better at development than others.

The imbalance which this gives to our theorizing is striking. Demographic analysis depends on a concept of population that is eminently structural: it is defined for a given case so that the transformation of an age–sex structure from one state or distribution to another may be traced in the co-variation of its several components. Similarly, an economic model of the household may deploy demographic variables as scale$_2$ parameters in an equation reflecting laws of diminishing returns inherent in a structure of wages, prices, savings and so forth. It is commonplace that institutions are structured by cultural values no less than by their demography and economy. Yet, when we turn to the integration of these value systems with population theories – explanation of a structural kind abruptly goes by the board. The demographic and economic structures are likely to be kept, but beyond this we often get no more than a normative description of a few local institutions, and a 'strategy' which reduces peoples' history and experience to one or two utilitarian pathways linking the institutions. It is as if the order people see in their own tendencies – say, to early marriage as a condition simultaneously of political alliance, family honour and ritual purity – is immaterial. Since peoples regularly use vital events to articulate relations between them, and often see in them means of reconciling aggregate and moral differences of scale, it is curious that we should neglect their own models as sources of structural information.

MALTHUS AND THE DESTRUCTION OF MEANING

As usual, Malthus anticipates the theoretical problems at hand. The *Essay* contains decided answers to both main issues raised thus far: namely, the

---

[5]For example, Berkner and Shaffer (1978, p. 161): 'Throughout this paper it has been assumed that the joint family can be understood only within the context of its legal and economic environment.'

problem of scale and the persistence of differences amongst peoples. The two concepts of scale outlined above are, for Malthus, motive forces in history. His way of dealing with them is, as is well known, to play them off against each other. The 'positive' checks of vice and misery show the effects of $scale_2$ brought to bear on $scale_1$: excessive mortality is characteristic of most of the states and stages of civilization Malthus reviews, and is cast in the role of the revenge of nature upon bad government, unwholesome occupations and inappropriate values, all of which give room for wars, poverty, disease, infanticide and the like. The 'preventive' check shows the effects of $scale_1$ on $scale_2$: the opportunity held out to man in the construction of systems of morals and government of using choice and restraint to hold off the action of the positive checks. Malthus leaves no ambiguity as to which of these alternatives is to be preferred.

According to *The Oxford English Dictionary* (1905), Malthus's concept of moral restraint was a turning-point in the history of our language. With Malthus, it became possible to use the term 'moral' and mean by it chiefly the organization of sexual matters. Since Malthus's time the more general sense of 'moral' – i.e. that societies rest upon rules, customs, and other conventions guiding right conduct – has gone out of fashion as a term of inquiry and explanation. When people speak of 'morality' or 'moral systems' nowadays, what is likely to be understood is 'moralizing', i.e. the use of history to draw prudish lessons. In retrospect, it may be that Malthus's narrowing of the term was an important factor contributing to its eventual unpopularity. His position on the persistence of moral and related differences between societies was, however, equivocal. As his views continue to influence our own attempts to formulate this problem, perhaps we would be wise to consider more fully the moral history contained in the *Essay*.

When Malthus wrote the *Essay on the Principle of Population and its Effects on Human Happiness* (1890),[6] he adopted many of the literary and historical conventions of the Enlightenment and reformist writers he criticized. We could say that he was an internal critic of the development theory of his period. He accepted that history is, on the whole, a record of human progress. For evidence he turned, as had Hume, Smith, Condorcet and Montesquieu before him, to the contemporary 'ethnography' of his day. The reports of the colonists, missionaries and explorers were compared to descriptions of tribes by Tacitus and Caesar, and in turn to evidence about the civilizations of the ancient world. Malthus himself travelled so that he might observe and collect materials on modern Europe. The first two books of the *Essay*, which contain his comparative history of the role of population in the different states and stages of mankind, comprise over half of the volume's considerable bulk.

At issue in the historical tradition within which Malthus wrote was the contest of reason and the passions. This 'problematic', as it might now be called, had the interesting effect of making discussion of the unintended consequences of individual and collective action a principal problem in the meaning of history and the definition of man's true character. Intended and unintended consequences alike had to be reconciled with the order of nature;

---

[6]The edition used here is a reprint of the last edition revised by Malthus.

nature was, in turn, often conceived as evidence of the divine plan. The histories were written as inquiries into the natural and God-given principles underlying right action, in order both to demonstrate and to guide greater conformity with higher purpose. The concepts which coordinate Adam Smith's *Theory of Moral Sentiments* (1767) include, for example, propriety, approbation, sympathy, gratitude and resentment. The morality of savage peoples, according to Smith, is based upon the strict self-discipline necessary to ensure survival; as nations gradually become more 'polished', greater expression of emotions, and a wider range of sentiments, come into play. Smith remarks the persistence of differences in this respect which distinguish the French and Italians as superior to the English (1767, pp. 311–24). A long line of writers including Montesquieu, Turgot, Kames, and Robertson[7] ordered history in more or less explicit stages, and remark the progressive differences which distinguish 'savage' peoples from the ancient civilizations and the differing conditions of contemporary European societies. The progress of society could be followed in the rise of freedom of choice as sanctioned by Christian theology, and supported by political liberalism and *laissez-faire* economics. Condorcet and Godwin, with whom Malthus differed most sharply, held extreme versions of rationalist development theory, in which human progress moved toward the ultimate triumph of reason, in a state of individual and social perfection.

The question of scale or comparative method in these eighteenth- and early-nineteenth-century theories was essentially one of coherence in a moral order: how a system of marriage, mode of production, environment, politics and religion combine to establish and maintain certain basic values. The tight symmetry of Malthus's *Essay*, in which the principle of population serves at once as evidence of divine intention, the dictates of nature, the laws of economics, domestic sexuality and the best critical guide to government policy, is Malthus's own expression of the orthodoxy of his period. However, Malthus expressed too much scepticism of his data, and laid too great a stress on the several qualitative differences between societies, to attempt a schematic ranking of societies into separate stages of development. Nor did he regard progress as inevitable: his history showed that peoples go on being different, and the remarkable fact about these differences is the persistence of forms of social organization and individual behaviour that actually perpetuate suffering. The compelling question, therefore, was to explain the persistence of misery and vice in all levels of civilization, and to derive a formula for its alleviation.

The tightness of Malthus's formulation has often been remarked, of which the compilers of *The Oxford English Dictionary* give example. As in physics, once the right constant is selected, the principles which organize the bewildering complexity of collective, relative motion follow systematically. The passion of the sexes is at once the mathematical and moral constant of Malthus's system. The relation of this constant to the capacities of agricultural production gives rise to a law of diminishing returns. The

[7]I cite here only those writers whose works were present in Malthus's own library, as listed in *The Malthus Library Catalogue* (1983).

demographic operation of this law converts increasing fertility not into an endlessly growing population, but into proportionate increases in mortality. Differentials in mortality are proxy variables for the efficiency of moral systems. Differences in mortality may therefore be read as fundamental differences in history, which describe the implications of living and dying in any one society as opposed to any other. In one fell swoop, Malthus made the 'morals of the sex' the main arbiter of man's action in history. His theorem provided a definitive answer to the problem of unintended consequences which retained developmental theories of rationalism, yet explained the powerful persistence of differences.

Malthus's concept of moral restraint is less accurately described as a method which reduces morality to its sexual reference, than as one which makes the study of population the key to interpreting the meaning of history. The dictionary definition neglects the importance of the avoidance of mortality as a primary motive of restraint. Malthus's comparative moral history is not an inquiry into arrangements of sexual passion, which he for the most part takes as given in his sources. The point of the first two books of the *Essay* is to show that the principle of population separates the sheep from the goats of history. While societies everywhere and at all times confront the same dilemma posed by the principle of population, their moral and political economies give rise to distinctive solutions. The Chinese, for example, are praised for their industrious nature, conscientious government and meticulous agriculture, but damned for their religion, which made freedom of choice impossible with respect to age at marriage, inheritance, and state policies pertaining to them. The Romans and Greeks were also distinguished by their government and their organization of labour, and their philosophers advocated delayed and restricted marriage. The ancients, however, accepted vicious checks such as infanticide, slavery and contraception. Worse, Roman state charity fed thousands of underemployed citizens on imported grain; this policy undermined Italian agriculture, and kept a large population on the edge of subsistence, thus promoting disease, corrupt manners and concubinage. The effects of such policies on production and reproduction were not unlike those produced later in decadent states, such as Turkey and Persia, in which government extortion precluded serious investment in agriculture, poverty and vice assisted the spread of epidemics, and polygamy restricted fertility. And so on and so forth, down through history.

The premise that people go on being different is possibly the most unpopular of Malthus's ideas, since it is difference at a price: to maintain a moral and political economy that varies from the criteria of the *Essay* appears inevitably to embrace one or another form of misery. The differences which Malthus allowed peoples in respect of their values, population and subsistence became nugatory when he identified difference with suffering. Contemporaries did not mind the resulting negative characterization of savage society, or of the Chinese, Persians and so forth. The suggestion that the poorer classes in modern Europe had a right only to levels of assistance that would ensure their need to practise moral restraint was, however, more controversial. The implication was that misery could not be eliminated even from advanced societies.

In sum, although Malthus designed a comparative method to explain the different mechanisms of choice inhering in different societies, he did not escape the prevailing rationalism of his time, and immediately sacrificed the variation of moral and political economies to prove the superiority of a single moral standard. The necessity of differences to his theory is, however, clear from his criticism of Condorcet, and in his responses to critics. Malthus maintained that, because societies have different moral and political economies, they give rise to different patterns of intended and unintended consequences, which either restraint or suffering must resolve. In this light, the problem with utopian theories was less that they were impracticable than that they were absurd: if differences between societies ended, and perfect harmony was achieved, then history and human suffering would no longer have any meaning (1890, p. 301). Similarly, Malthus was happy to agree with Senior, Alison and others that technological and economic developments could greatly improve society, and were to be encouraged (Senior 1829, p. 85). These improvements could not, however, change the principle of population, and, if unaccompanied by improved judgement, only delayed the day of reckoning. For Malthus, the main issue remained the effort to improve upon the inevitably imperfect harmony of reason and morals: economic development, in the last instance, could make no difference.

The imperfection of development, and the inevitability of differences in the meaning of life and death from one society to the next, are themes which provide a strong link between the population research reviewed in earlier sections and Malthus's *Essay*. We do not have to go as far as Malthus in positing a moral last instance to see that giving priority to economic factors in development will not make differences go away. Rationalist development theories either of materialist or moralist persuasion are destructive of differences, since they prejudge them in terms of some trajectory in which the meaning of history is supplied. It so happens that in the latter half of the twentieth century – unlike the latter eighteenth – materialist trajectories are preferred over moralist ones. That is the foible of the present period. The generalized regimes noted in this section have excited interest precisely because they tend to show the limits of explanations couched solely in terms of economic means and ends, and have stressed instead that institutions which unite brothers, control women, ensure deference to parents and underwrite the sanctity of the family and its property have a material import which includes economic factors and yet goes much further.

The kind of exercise in which Malthus was engaged – of reconciling a particular distribution of material wealth with an older set of values about man, nature and the universe – is surely a perennial one. So is his perception that the identity of societies in history may be established by comparing their organization of vital processes. Demographic regimes describe social structures in so far as such structures are attempts to use vital processes as a medium in which to effect just such reconciliations and identifications. The structural properties of peoples' models of vital events and relations – of restricted demographic regimes – may be expected, therefore, to begin from the strategic locus of vital processes in social thought: while the facts of life are everywhere subject to economic and moral rationalization, they cannot be defined completely by either.

RESTRICTED REGIMES

In composing a restricted regime for a given society, a number of questions must be asked. We need to identify the institutions which are the locus of deeply held values, and explore the various ways that vital events and relations are used to define groups in terms of these values. To what extent are observed changes contained within permutations of customary behaviour, or are changes in vital relations a marker of a more profound change in social structure?

Scant space remains for me to illustrate these ideas. I shall take a familiar, indeed celebrated, case which may be related directly to the concentration upon domestic groups in the study of generalized regimes. I refer to the story of the medieval parish of Montaillou, as told by the social historian Le Roy LaDurie (1981). Generally speaking, recruitment in this community, or its 'core reference' as Le Roy LaDurie calls it, was to the *domus* or household in which individuals resided. A *domus* was composed of several adults, usually including one conjugal couple. The remaining members varied – including, according to case, children, unmarried brothers and sisters, widows, cousins, illegitimate children and kin, servants and lodgers. A household, at one or another point in its life-cycle, might adopt an extended or nuclear form, and joint households were possible. Maintenance of family property was a major concern, and to this end control was exercised via a variety of conjugal arrangements, and by inheritance and dowry practices. Family property seems to have passed chiefly to a single heir; sisters would be dowered (if possible: this was expensive and potentially dangerous to the continuity of family property); brothers might in due course be set up on a small portion, or become shepherds, or marry into a suitably propertied family. The expense of marriage made various forms of concubinage desirable for the poor, for men and women belonging to families of markedly different wealth, and for widows and brothers of heirs. A familiar ethnographic pattern emerges from all of this, in which better-off households ally themselves by marriage, and poorer and fragmented groups join the followings or factions of allied families.

Although strata may be observed in the village, Le Roy LaDurie insists that class differences were not recognized in Montaillou, and that the variation in wealth between the better-off and the poor was not great in terms of attitude, diet, dress, dialect, the houses they lived in, and the proximity of people (e.g. intimate affairs of the sexes, or the continuous and scarcely less intimate need for delousing). While economic differences underlie the configuration of households in the village, they do not explain local patterns of recruitment: why certain families were allied or divided; the changing composition of these groups; differences in mobility within and between groups; and the actual course of events in the village. Economic utility – if it may be abstracted from other relations – followed lines of solidarity expressed by kin, marital and other vital relations, on several levels. First, the several paths of recruitment – marriage or concubinage; birth and corporate membership; neighbouring residence; service; and favoured kin links, such as cousinship – comprised a complex interpersonal network of roles, preferences and obligations. Second, just as one married a *domus* and not merely an individual, so almost any individual action contributed to the honour and status of that group relative to others. Third, age, sex and marital authority in the household were supernaturally sanctioned.

A restricted regime for Montaillou may be fitted into a four-point summary such as used earlier to outline generalized regimes, but the nature of each point, and the pattern of inference connecting points have changed. In Montaillou

1 the main value was continuity of the *domus* as a moral, mystical and corporate body;
2 alliance through marriage, subsidiary conjugal forms, kinship, and rules for the devolution of property were usual means of organizing recruitment in a *domus*;
3 factions built up by these means, by patronage and by manipulation of external connexions, provided leverage in competition between one *domus* and others;
4 social mobility, in its downward aspect, was associated with the fragmentation or ill-formation of a *domus*, leading to various client statuses, celibacy and transhumance, and sometimes early death.

A restricted regime provides, instead of one or two continuous and utilitarian strategies, a structure of alternative and discontinuous institutional options, of marked social value. The 'plot' of *Montaillou* follows directly from this regime, for, as Le Roy LaDurie shows, the wider powers of Church and state, in the form of the Inquisition, were cleverly mobilized by one *domus* to serve its interests in opposition to others'. The impact of scale$_1$ (in this case, the value of the *domus*, reinforced by Catholic and heretical ideology) is followed by its historian through a score of scale$_2$ consequences (e.g. increased adult mortality to certain causes, dissolution of households, remarriage, concubinage), in which the power of one *domus* was cemented at the expense of others. The upheaval of the community reflected an intensification of the regime, not divergence from the structural principles inherent in the logic of the *domus*.

To complete this example properly, the restricted regime for Montaillou should be related to generalized hypotheses for the region to which the parish belongs. The Mediterranean, however, is much too big and important to be dealt with briefly here. It will suffice, perhaps, to note a number of fundamental themes connecting the restricted regime for Montaillou to the three trends in population theory with which this essay began. Defined by its cultural, physical and historical continuity, the Mediterranean cuts across the familiar dualities of developed–underdeveloped, Third World–Europe, and traditional–modern, as well as the demographic transition. The study of decision processes in contemporary Mediterranean societies has long been annexed to that of family structures, recent syntheses of which (Davis 1977, Hammel, 1968, Peristiany 1976, Pitt-Rivers 1977) emphasize the persistence of institutional forms in particular regions (e.g. certain marriage and family types, godparenthood, property management, codes of shame and honour).

The continuity of such institutions is further reflected in their capacity to direct recruitment and lend legitimacy to wider frameworks, including political parties, the Church, unions, and an economy characterized by vested family interests, migration networks, tourism, and unequal development.

SUMMARY

The broad outlines of my argument may be summarized as follows. The contextually minded approaches reviewed in the opening section reflect the need for a population theory designed to contribute to current debates over the adaptive capacities of social structures. The role of population in development seems to depend less on outright abandonment of old value structures and institutional arrangements pertaining to vital processes than on their continuity by selective adjustment. Greater appreciation of the actual workings of domestic groups, of their diversity and of the sacrifices they entail have placed a premium on developing a theory that shows the several ways groups deploy vital processes as means of responding to a wider institutional context. Central to such a theory will be some formula describing the several specific 'strategies' that individuals and groups pursue. The problem of 'strategies' is not, however, being solved by the generalized demographic regimes in which the adaptive capacities of domestic organization are being explored. Despite the considerable improvements these approaches represent, the pattern of inference they employ is not really designed to explore strategies as much as to articulate types. The digression on Malthus helps us to see that this is not merely a temporary technical problem in their formulation.

There is a place, therefore, for an approach complementary to generalized regimes, addressed to the systems of meaning peoples build upon their vital events and relations. It is clear that such systems cannot be considered only in ideal or normative terms. As already noted, vital events and relations play a dual role in social organization: first, they are the recruitment component of social structure; and, second, patterns thus traced in human clay become objects of cultural interpretation, by which people identify themselves with particular groups, and contrast their behaviour to others'. Since patterns of marriage, kinship, residence, movement, divorce, and so on, are used by groups to further their interests, their success and failure in these, relative to other groups, become aspects of a working model of social relations. In so far as such patterns are inscribed in collective memory, they coalesce with the history of the society and of particular groups within it. The alternative courses of action which vital processes open or close to particular groups may therefore be followed in their implications for the moral, political and economic jockeying of groups over time. It seems sensible to call such models of population and social structure 'restricted demographic regimes', since their various (and by no means necessarily concordant or fully articulated) purposes are chiefly local ones. Because local purposes are defined with reference to sustaining or adjusting existing arrangements, they are inseparable from traditional values; but it is clear from the active nature of such adjustments that local continuity need not imply simply the perpetuation of a status quo. Restricted regimes give important evidence of the way groups make selective use of vital processes to cope with limited circumstances; and of their capacity to go on making decisions in the face of what appear, at least for their immediate practical purposes, to be effectively permanent imperfections in society.

REFERENCES

Ahern, E. M. 1974: Affines and the rituals of kinship. In A. P. Wolf (ed.), *Religion and Ritual in Chinese society*, Stanford, Calif.: Stanford University Press, pp. 279–307.
Anderson, M. 1971: *Family Structure in Nineteenth-century Lancashire*. Cambridge: Cambridge University Press.
—— 1980: *Approaches to the History of the Western Family, 1500–1914*, London: Macmillan.
Anwar, M. 1979: *The Myth of Return: Pakistanis in Britain*. London: Heinemann.
Ardener, E. W. 1972: Belief and the problem of women. In J. Lafontaine (ed.), *The Interpretation of Ritual*, London: Tavistock, pp. 135–58.
Berkner, L. K., and Mendels, F. F. 1978: Inheritance systems, family structure, and demographic patterns in Western Europe, 1700–1900. In C. Tilly (ed.), *Historical Studies of Changing Fertility*, Princeton, NJ: Princeton University Press, pp. 209–23.
—— and Shaffer, J. W. 1978: The joint family in the Nivernois. *Journal of Family History*, 3 (2), 150–62.
Boserup, E. 1965: *The Conditions of Agricultural Growth*. London: Allen and Unwin.
Bourdieu, P. 1976: Marriage strategies as strategies of social reproduction. In R. Forster, R. and O. Ranum (eds), *Family and Society*, Baltimore: Johns Hopkins University Press, pp. 117–44.
Cain, M. 1978: The household life cycle and economic mobility in rural Bangladesh. *Population and Development Review*, 4 (3), 421–38.
—— 1982: Perspectives on family and fertility in developing countries. *Population Studies*, 36 (3), 159–75.
—— Khanam, S. R. and Nahar, S. 1979: Class, patriarchy, and women's work in Bangladesh. *Population and Development Review*, 5 (3), 405–38.
Caldwell, J. C. 1977: The economic rationality of high fertility: an investigation illustrated with Nigerian survey data. *Population Studies*, 31 (1), 5–27.
—— 1978: A theory of fertility: from high plateau to destabilization. *Population and Development Review*, 4 (4) 553–77.
—— 1981: The mechanisms of demographic change in historical perspective. *Population Studies*, 35 (1) 5–27.
—— and Caldwell, P. 1976: Demographic and contraceptive innovators: a study of transitional African society. *Journal of Biosocial Science*, 8, 347–65.
—— Reddy, P. H., and Caldwell, P. 1983: The causes of marriage change in south India. *Population Studies*, 37 (3), 343–61.
Campbell, J. K. 1964: *Honour, Family and Patronage* Oxford: Oxford University Press.
Chapman, M. 1978: *The Gaelic Vision in Scottish Culture*. London: Croom Helm.
Coale, A. J. 1973: The demographic transition. In *International Population Conference, Liège, 1973*, Liège: International Union for the Scientific Study of Population, vol. I, 53–72.
Davis, J. 1977: *People of the Mediterranean*. London: Routledge and Kegan Paul.
Douglas, M. 1966a: Population control in primitive groups. *British Journal of Sociology*, 17, 263–73.
—— 1966b: *Purity and danger*. London: Praeger.
Dumont, L. 1983: *Affinity as a Value: marriage alliance in south India*. London: University of Chicago Press.
Dyson, T., and Moore, M. 1983: On kinship structure, female autonomy, and demographic behaviour in India. *Population and Development Review*, 9 (1), 35–60.

Finlay, R. A. P. 1978: Gateways to death? London child mortality experience 1570–1653. *Annales de démographie historique 1978*, 105–34.

—— 1979: Population and fertility in London, 1580–1650. *Journal of Family History*, 4 (1) 26–38.

Freedman, R. 1979: Theories of fertility decline: a reappraisal. In P. M. Hauser (ed.), *World Population and Development*, Syracuse, NY: Syracuse University Press, pp. 63–79.

—— Chang, M.-C., Sun, T.-H. 1982: Household composition, extended kinship and reproduction in Taiwan: 1973–1980. *Population Studies*, 36 (3), 395–412.

Goody, J. 1976: *Production and Reproduction*. Cambridge: Cambridge University Press.

Greenhalgh, S. 1982: Income units: the ethnographic alternative to standardization. In Y. Ben-Porath (ed.), *Income Distribution and the Family, Population and Development Review Supplement*, New York: The Population Council, pp. 53–69.

Hajnal, J. 1982: Two kinds of preindustrial household formation systems. *Population and Development Review*, 8 (3), 449–94.

Hammel, E. A. 1968: *Alternative Social Structures and Ritual Relations in the Balkans*. Englewood Cliffs, NJ: Prentice-Hall.

—— 1978: Review essay: family and inheritance. *Journal of Family History*, 3 (2), 203–10.

Hawthorn, G. 1978: Introduction to G. Hawthorn (ed.), *Population and Development*, London: Frank Cass, pp. 1–21.

Hill, A. G., Randall, S. C., and van den Eerenbeemt, M.-L. 1983: *Infant and Child Mortality in Rural Mali*, Centre for Population Studies Research Paper 83–5, London: Centre for Population Studies.

Journal of Family History, 1976: Statement of purpose. 1 (1), 3–5.

Kreager, P. 1980: *Traditional Adoption Practices in Africa, Asia, Europe, and Latin America*. London: International Planned Parenthood Federation.

—— 1982: Demography *in situ*, *Population and Development Review*, 8 (2) 237–66.

—— 1984: Social and supernatural control in a Mayan demographic regime. Paper for a meeting of the International Union for the Scientific Study of Population Working Group on Micro-approaches, Canberra, 3–7 September 1984.

Laslett, P., Oosterveen, K., and Smith, R. M. 1980: *Bastardy and its Comparative History*. London: Edward Arnold.

Le Roy LaDurie, E., 1981: *Montaillou, Cathars and Catholics in a French Village, 1294–1324*. Harmondsworth: Penguin.

Lesthaeghe, R. 1980: On the social control of human reproduction. *Population and Development Review*, 6 (4), 527–48.

—— 1984: *Fertility and its Proximate Determinants in Sub-Saharan Africa: the record of the 1960s and 70s*. Liège: IUSSP.

Liu, P. K. C. 1982: Determinants of income inequality over the family development cycle: the case of Taiwan. In Y. Ben-Porath (ed.), *Income Distribution and the Family, Population and Development Review Supplement*, New York: The Population Council, pp. 53–69.

Macfarlane, A. 1980: Demographic structures and cultural regions in Europe. *Cambridge Anthropology*, 6 (1–2), 1–17.

Malthus, T. R. 1890: *An Essay on the Principle of Population or a View of its Past and Present Effects on Human Happiness*. London: Ward Lock.

Malthus Library Catalogue: 1983. Oxford: Pergamon Press.

Mendels, F. F. 1972: Proto-industrialization: the first phase of the industrialization process. *Journal of Economic History*, 32, 241–61.

Oppong, C. 1974: *Marriage among a Matrilineal Elite*. Cambridge: Cambridge University Press.

Oxford English Dictionary 1905: S. V. Moral. Oxford: Oxford University Press, vol. VI, part 2 (2), 654.

Page, H. J., and Lesthaeghe, R. (eds) 1981: *Child-spacing in Tropical Africa: traditions and change*. London: Academic Press.

Peristiany, J. G. (ed.) 1976: *Mediterranean Family Structures*. Cambridge: Cambridge University Press.

Pitt-Rivers, J. 1977: *The Fate of Shechem or the Politics of Sex*. Cambridge: Cambridge University Press.

Said, E. W. 1978: *Orientalism*. London: Routledge and Kegan Paul.

Scrimshaw, S. C. M. 1978: Infant mortality and behaviour in the regulation of family size. *Population and Development Review*, 4 (3), 383–403.

Senior, N. W. 1829: *Two Lectures on Population, . . . to which is Added a Correspondence between the Author and the Rev. T. R. Malthus* London: Saunders and Otley.

Smith, A. 1767: *Theory of Moral Sentiments*. London and Edinburgh: Millar, Kincaid, and Bell.

Tilly, C. 1978: The historical study of vital processes. In C. Tilly (ed.), *Historical Studies of Changing Fertility*, Princeton, NJ: Princeton University Press, pp. 3–55.

United Nations, Department of International Economic and Social Affairs, 1980: *World Population Trends and Policies, 1979 Monitoring Report vol. I, Population Trends*. New York.

Wallman, S. 1977: Introduction to S. Wallman (ed.), *Perceptions of Development*, Cambridge: Cambridge University Press, pp. 1–16.

Wolf, A. P. and Hjang, C.-S. 1980: *Marriage and Adoption in China 1845–1945*. Stanford, Calif.: Stanford University Press.

Wrigley, E. A. 1978: Fertility strategy for the individual and the group. In C. Tilly (ed.), *Historical Studies of Changing Fertility*, Princeton, NJ: Princeton University Press, pp. 135–54.

Yanagisako, S. J. 1979: Family and household: the analysis of domestic groups. *Annual Review of Anthropology*, 8, Palo Alto: Annual Review, pp. 161–205.

Feedbacks and Buffers in Relation to Scarcity and Abundance: Studies of Hunter–Gatherer Populations

Nancy Howell

It would be of little consequence, according to Mr Godwin, how many children a woman had or to whom they belonged. Provisions and assistance would spontaneously flow from the quarter in which they abounded to the quarter that was deficient. . . .

I cannot conceive a form of society so favourable upon the whole to population. The irremediableness of marriage, as it is at present constituted, undoubtedly deters many from entering into that state. An unshackled intercourse on the contrary would be a most powerful incitement to early attachments, and as we are supposing no anxiety about the future support of children to exist, I do not conceive that there would be one woman in a hundred, of twenty-three, without a family.

With these extraordinary encouragements to population, and every cause of depopulation, as we have supposed, removed, the numbers would necessarily increase faster than any society that has ever yet been known. . . .

Malthus 1798, pp. 183–5

Following Malthus, this essay is concerned with the relationship between the availability of resources and the regulation of population size. Like Malthus, we shall concentrate upon understanding the mechanisms of regulation, whether these are sophisticated contraceptives or unconsciously evoked physiological responses. We want to identify the agents of regulation in each case, whether these are the parents, the offspring, the kin group or other members of the wider society.

Departing from Malthus's perspective, we seek to integrate the models of population regulation in animals (Lack 1954, Wilson 1975) with our understanding of the various kinds of population regulation found in humans. Naturally, there are differences. Since animals cannot explain to us what they are doing, we are forced to concentrate more upon the behaviour and less upon the reasons for the behaviour, ignoring or inferring motives. With humans, we observe a bewildering array of forms of behaviour related to population growth and its regulation, many of which are still rapidly changing in the twentieth-century. When asked what they are doing, people around the world give a wide range of explanations of their behaviour and its goals. The fascination with collecting information about the mental states ('knowledge, attitudes, practices') of vast numbers of individuals selected by random samplying, as in the World Fertility Surveys, for instance, may be coming to an end, as Ryder (1983) questions the value of measuring how individuals reflect a set of attitudes and cultural norms that they do not create and cannot modify.

Even the most sophisticated of human-population regulation models (Caldwell 1982, Easterlin, 1978) hang firmly, in this sense, in mid air, attributing causality to cultural, economic and individual differences without an explicit grounding of the baseline, either human or animal, from which changes are being made.

It is the perspective of this essay that, while both human- and animal-population regulation models have advanced far since the days of Malthus, the failure to integrate these two bodies of literature continues to be an intellectual weakness. The factors and variables that are needed to understand the regulation of population dynamics in a range of species will help us to anchor our understanding of human adaptations in the biological world. And, while no human population group can serve as the 'typical' humans, from which all other groups are merely deviations, we need to construct a model of the human–animal baseline, the unavailable 'facts of life' for humans that underlie the limits to their freedom to control their population size and composition. We need a notion of what the basic human animal is like, in order to understand the consequences of fluctuations in biological conditions, social conditions, and the historical events that impinge upon human groups.

That baseline is to be found among the human hunter–gatherers, the people who lived by collecting plant and animal foods in the wild, before the development of more complex economic bases. Historically, we want to look at the hunter–gatherers who lived prior to the development of food production by the domestication of plants and animals some 10,000–15,000 years ago.

Needless to say, we have severe data problems in studying that baseline (Clark and Brandt 1984). None of the pre-horticultural peoples were literate, so they left us no documents. Some few of them left us rich collections of cave art, paintings and sculptures, which are fascinating but which may tell us nothing, or provide confusing messages, about our greatest concerns. We have the skeletons of members of a few groups, but reconstructing population composition and especially trying to infer population regulation from bones is a shaky exercise (Buikstra 1983, Acsádi and Nemeskéri 1974). However, there are some hunting-and-gathering peoples still living today in the more remote corners of the earth. It is from these people, and especially from the !Kung San of Botswana, that most of the basis for this attempt to clarify the human baseline will be drawn.

POPULATION REGULATION AS AN ADAPTATION,
IN ANIMALS AND IN HUMANS

Economist Kenneth Boulding once summarized all the models of population regulation in animals by saying, 'There are two kinds of creatures in the world, fat things and thin things. Fat things are controlled by some other scarce resource, like nest sites or position in the group, while thin things are controlled by the food supply.'

Boulding's *bon mot* points us toward the prime characteristics of animal species that we have to understand if we are to understand how their population control is achieved. Since we cannot ask them what they think they are doing, a goal of advancing the reproductive success rates of individuals and families is generally assumed for all animals. If some animals do not seem to be motivated by this goal, we simply note that the reproduction success goes to those who act as if they are so motivated.

Although a group-selection model of population regulation that posited a motive to restrict one's own reproduction to avoid crowding for the whole group (Wynne-Edwards 1962) has been enthusiastically entertained and then decisively rejected in recent decades (Wilson 1975), a sophisticated alternative view of animal motivation has been proposed, one that stresses genetic self-interest on the individual and on the kindred levels of selection. Animal-population models view all behaviours by their contributions to genetic self-interest, and place the subject matter squarely in the middle of biology, explained by the Darwinian 'new synthesis'. Human-population models, however, while based upon the analysis of far greater volumes of data and observations, are much further from resolving the difficult questions of motivation, causation and the exercise of choice.

The most striking observation from looking at an overview of the methods and mechanisms used in animal population-growth regulation, such as that provided in Wilson (1975) and summarized in table 1, is not so much the extremely wide variation between species in the methods used to control population growth, but the similarities in the ways in which all species reproduce themselves, and the limited number of ways in which they may interfere with the process and hence control it. Fertility and mortality are the basic processes in all populations that provide the variation upon which selection works. All species, from the shortest-lived to the longest, from the lowest fertility potential to the highest, have variations in the number of offspring in the next and subsequent generations contributed by mated pairs. In all species the average expected number of offspring to survive to become parents in the next generation is two (one in asexual populations). The spider that lays thousands of eggs and the whale that gives birth to an enormous infant rarely can expect the next generation to be approximately the same size as the current one. The deviations from this expectation provide the drama of the biological world, but the expectation is still a strong one, in most populations in most generations.

Each species has a fixed range of reproductive characteristics, such as proportions typically surviving from birth to maturity, typical age at maturity, typical litter size, typical inter-litter intervals, and so on. Within the species-specific range, individuals compete for reproductive advantage, and environmental fluctuations determine whether more or less than the average can succeed in that generation. The differential distribution of that success represents the raw material of both evolution and population regulation. Some of the behaviours used in a range of species to struggle toward reproductive

Table 1   Population control behaviour and level of reference group for behaviours

Stages of survival and reproduction in all species	Self	Intra-family	Intra-group	Intra-species	Inter-species
I The positive checks					
Survival from birth to end of infancy	Appetite Ability to communicate	Lactation Protection Egg-guarding Infanticide	Care of mothers and families Nest-building Infanticide	Infanticide by invaders	Predation on infants and mothers
Survival to lower limit of reproductive age	Competition for food Communication	Incest avoidance Sibling rivalry Parent-offspring crises Weaning	Protected nest Shared food Competition for local resources	Territoriality Trade-co-operation Hostility, war, slavery capture	Food supply Causes of disease
Survival through reproduction	Competition for food and place in hierarchy Suicide	Protection Nursing sickness Emigration	Home-base tasks Provisioning Hygiene Shared information and risks	Rape Killing Warfare	Food supply Avoiding predation Interdependence Symbiosis Parasitic relations
II The preventive checks					
Fecundability	Health and maturity	Spousal sharing	Care of young adults	Migration stresses War Defence of territory	–
Intercourse–mating	Communicating, readiness Competing	Incest avoidance Co-parenting	Permitting mating Competition for mates	Rape Capture	Predation
Conception	Non-coital mating Contraception	Permitted mating	Harrassment of newly mated	–	–
Gestation, including foetal survival	Failure to implant Abortion Miscarriage	Care of eggs and care-takers	Protection of care-takers	Presence of strangers can cause reabsorption of foetus	Predation on eggs or pregnant animals
Measures appropriate to the level of reference Per year or generation. In principle, can be sub-divided by stages above	Individual fitness = no. same-sex offspring that survive to mean age of reproduction	Individual fitness plus fitness of close relatives (times degree of relatedness)	Population growth (r) = births–deaths divided by population size	Population growth (r) = same for a group of living-groups	Biomass = sum of the masses of all species in a defined environment

success, absolute and relative, are subdivided in table 1 into Malthus's categories of 'positive checks' and 'preventive checks'.

The theory of evolution predicts simply that each species will tend to overproduce the number of offspring that can be supported in the environment, and that the species will gradually be transformed in the process of adjusting numbers to resources. Virtually all of the behaviours observed in a species can usefully be understood as part of the total adaptation of that species, including the species-specific biological parameters, the minimization and maximization of the variables that make up those parameters by individuals, and the resulting 'struggle for existence'. Some of the behaviours included in this view of an adaptation are not obviously concerned with their population growth, examples being communication by chemical trails in ants, antler displays in ungulates, and courtship rituals in birds. The general goal of reproductive success is pursued by a wide variety of strategies by members of different species, and by a narrower range of strategies by individuals within species.

An example of widely contrasting strategies can be seen in what is called r and K selection. The r strategy maximizes the number of offspring produced per parent, given some chance of survival, at the cost of body size, length of life, and the investment that parents can make in each offspring. These r-selected animals are generally of the sort that Boulding calls 'thin things', competing with conspecifics to the point where the food supply is exhausted for that species in that environment. Insects that lay thousands of eggs and leave them unprotected may multiply the density of their population many times in one generation if the environmental conditions permit it, whereas animals that follow the extreme of the opposite strategy may require many generations before they can fully invade and occupy a new territory.

K strategists are playing the same evolutionary game as the r-selected species, but they bet upon the effects of increased investment in each offspring to increase their probability of survival and reproduction, rather than maximizing the number of trials. K-selected animals are characterized by large body size, long life, few offspring, and a considerable investment of parents in each offspring. Extreme examples, along with humans, are elephants, whales, dolphins and great apes, along with some birds. K-selected animals are often 'fat things', in Boulding's phrase – in part because they are unable to expand their population fast enough to absorb all available resources quickly. They may live in a situation of superabundance temporarily, until their population has expanded sufficiently to use all the available resources, or permanently, if they have devised a system of scarcity that limits reproduction without approaching the exhaustion of the environment.

It is a bit dizzying to try to increase our understanding of human reproduction by looking at all animal species simultaneously. Wilson (1975) directs our attention to groups of animals that resemble the human animal in interesting ways, such as social animals as opposed to asocial ones, mammals as opposed to egg-layers, carnivores or omnivores as opposed to vegetarian grazers, and so on. But, rather than aiming for systematic comparison along a number of dimensions, we can use our understanding of evolution to focus our comparisons on the species that humans are most closely related to: the living great apes, and our proto-hominid ancestors, the Australopithecine species and *Homo erectus*.

The human adaptation

Based upon observation of our closest primate relatives and upon the archaeological study of our Australopithecine ancestors, we know that there are a number of species-specific features of humans that are not found in the proto-humans. The opposable thumb, fully upright posture, the ability to use language, the loss of oestrus and the establishment of pair-bonding ties between mates, establishment of a home base, and other features could be (and have been) argued to be the crucial evolutionary changes that made the human species what it is. Without denying the importance of any of these biological and social changes, I wish to stress a different list of critical changes, four features that I see as having changed the boundaries of the niche that humans occupied, with permanent and pervasive consequences for the human adaptation.

Two of these features have to do with what the animal ate, and two have to do with providing care for one another. They are all closely related and no doubt co-evolved as a single package. None of these are universal human traits, or equally true of all individuals, but all seem to be found in all human groups to some degree.

The first of these crucial features of the human adaptation is a shift to more calorically rich food items. From a base in browsing and grazing upon leafy vegetation, humans moved to eating meat of both small and large animals, and roots, seeds, fruits, nuts and other more calorically rich foods (Isaac 1978). Without the increase in free time released by this shift in food, the human adaptation could not have developed. Even today, gorillas and chimpanzees in the wild eat during virtually all of the hours of light. They cannot engage in role differentiation or the development of a home base because they cannot afford to stop eating long enough. Higher-calorie foods permitted humans to experiment with variations in their way of life. The shift in diet required evolutionary changes in the digestive tract, in the teeth and, most importantly, in the brain, as the animals came to recognize richer sources as appropriate human food.

A second feature of the human adaptation is provisioning animals other than infants with food. Specifically, humans feed children, who move from dependence upon lactation to dependence upon their parents to bring them the kinds of food that adults eat. Two crucially important demographic consequences of provisioning children result. The first is that children can 'afford' slow growth and many forms of incompetence for a period of time exceeding infancy without death necessarily resulting. The second consequence is that humans were enabled by provisioning children to reverse the trend among the primates to longer and longer birth intervals. Instead of delaying the birth of the next child until the independence of its predecessor, humans overlap the period of dependency of their children. This change dissolved an evolutionary bottleneck. Once parents accepted the need to provision children, there was no longer much of an advantage to parents to hasten the maturity of offspring, and the period of dependence upon parents stretched out to include the birth intervals of two to four subsequent children (Isaac 1978).

The third evolutionary event crucial to the human adaptation is the ability, closely related to provisioning, to provide nursing-services to the sick and injured of any age. Our primate relatives do not, and our hominid ancestors probably did not, have the capacity to recognize what a sick and injured individual needs – above all food, but also warmth, rest, shelter, water, salve, or a splint for a broken leg – and the ability to provide it. Nursing seems to be nothing more than an elaboration of parental care to a dependant, whether that dependency is more or less permanent, as in the case of children and old people, or temporary, in the case of illness or accident. When chimpanzees (Goodall 1972) and gorillas (Fossey 1983) contract infectious and parasitic diseases (and they regularly do so), the probability of death from that cause is much higher for them than it is for humans in even the most 'primitive' society. The difference is the effect of providing nursing-services, which reduces the probability of death from a given cause. Among humans, incapacitating illness occurs routinely to even the strongest adults occasionally. People of all ages suffer from colds, 'flu', dysentery, pneumonia, broken bones, infected wounds, discouragement, depression and grief, and so on. Almost any of these conditions would kill you if your way of life required continual movement at the risk of being abandoned by the group. Instead, it was an early and basic aspect of the distinctively human adaptation that the probability of death was greatly reduced by the development of routine provision of nursing-care for the sick. Humans may be susceptible to more causes of death than our primate relatives, but the probability of death from these causes was so greatly reduced by the provision of nursing-care in a home base where sick individuals could be provided with high-calorie foods during convalescence that the human populations thrived despite a continuation of the low-fertility adaptation of the animal baseline. Effective nursing is a human invention far older than effective doctoring, one which vastly widened the niche within which the population functioned.

The fourth innovation that made the human adaptation a distinctive one is the well-known use of fire to transform food. Fire has an important place in the history of the human adaptation. It not only cooks food, but also provides light and warmth, and frightens animals away from the camp where people may be relaxed or sleeping and hence vulnerable to animal attacks. For primitive peoples everywhere, fire is a characteristic feature of a human place, the sign of home.

It is fire's use as a cooking-device that I want to stress here, along with other food-processing techniques. The point is that early in the human adaptation the niche that humans occupied was vastly widened by the development of techniques to transform species that are inedible into edible species. Skills such as the ability to crack and roast nuts, to bake tubers, to sweeten sour fruits, to leach poisons or bad flavours out of plants, to crush seeds so that they can be digested may make the difference between starvation and plenty. Animals look for, recognize and consume their food species. For humans, the task is far more complicated: they transform raw materials into food sources by applying labour and intelligence, and the extent to which they do this is a determinant of when and whether humans reach the limits of their environment to provide food.

We have to acknowledge the difficulty, at any stage of this analysis, of distinguishing between the evolution of physiological features of the human animal and the evolution of cultural features of the adaptation. It is not possible to say that the evolutionary process depended more or less on culture or physiological change, despite the fact that we can describe any animal adaptation almost entirely in physiological terms and we have to describe any human adaptation, even the most 'primitive', almost entirely in cultural terms. Probably it is most useful to think about the physiological change that permitted or even forced the use of culture as an aspect of all behaviour. Although human cultures differ, among humans culture becomes involved in all behaviour, even something as simple as a sneeze, and it certainly is deeply involved in complex behaviours such as sharing food, providing nursing-care, and food preparation and consumption.

And of course the 'inventions' of shared food at the home base, food preparation, and nursing-care of the sick and disabled also complicated and enriched the human capacity for culture by making it possible to sustain a whole class of post-reproductive males and females who simply do not survive in the wild in animal species (although they are sometimes produced in zoo populations where these same features of human life are routinely provided to animals).

Among hunter–gatherers of the contemporary world, there do not seem to be any societies in which survival to age sixty and beyond is not a relatively common occurrence, and the pace of the human aging-process seems to be quite invariant in all contemporary populations. It is still not clear whether the archaeological record shows the same persistence of at least a minority of the population into old age, as there are so many difficulties in constructing and interpreting life-tables based upon the evidence of skeletons (Acsádi and Nemeskéri 1974, Buikstra 1983). The development of the post-reproductive age group as a regular feature of human populations is another physiological fact tightly intertwined with cultural causes. And the cultural consequences of the development of the old-age population segment are even more profound, as a group which represents a cumulation of learning over five or more decades contributes depth of experience and stability to culture (Biesele and Howell 1981).

POPULATION REGULATION IN A CONTEMPORARY
HUNTING–GATHERING GROUP, THE !KUNG SAN

We now shift focus from the fuzzy outlines of what we imagine to have been true of 'early man', to the sharper outlines of the colourful and attractive !Kung San (or 'Bushmen'), hunting-and-gathering nomads of the Kalahari Desert in Southern Africa. I spent two years (1967–9) living with these people, who have many of the features that Malthus predicted would be associated with 'an extraordinary encouragement to population', and I spent more years disentangling from small numbers an overall understanding of population dynamics in that society (Howell 1979).

In recent years, the !Kung society is changing rapidly, as they cope with new neighbours who herd cattle and goats, and with anthropologists, schools, trucks and stores. Fortunately, the documentation of their way of life started (Marshall 1976) at a stage when they were living almost entirely by hunting and gathering, relatively undisturbed by outside forces. Traditionally, the !Kung have no private property other than the few personal items they wear or carry on their backs during frequent group moves, no landownership, no permanent villages, no fields or flocks or occupational specialities. What they do (or did) has been documented more fully elsewhere (Biesele 1982, Brooks 1981, Draper 1976, Harpending 1976, Howell 1979, Lee 1979 and 1984, Marshall 1976, Konner 1976, Shostak, 1981, Weissner 1977, Wilmsen 1979). Here we shall review their way of life with a focus on the implications for population regulation.

Malthus imagined a society in which there was no marriage (see the epigraph to this essay). !Kung people marry, but are able to dissolve their marriages lightly if they wish, and most people divorce once or a few times in their lifetime. There are no quarrels over property or child custody when a couple marries or divorces, as they own no substantial property. Children are always raised by their mother, if she is alive, but continue to have special ties to their biological father even after their mother marries again. Women have no difficulty remarrying, with or without children, after widowing or divorce.

Food comes into a nuclear family through the gathering-efforts of the woman of the family, supplemented by any small animals caught by her husband, gifts from other gatherers, and a share of the meat from large animals brought in by the hunters of the group (including her husband). Since meat from large animals makes up a substantial and valued part of the diet, and since all members of the living-group receive a share by right, it is almost literally true that, from the point of feeding herself and her children, 'it would be of little consequence . . . how many children a woman had or to whom they belonged' (Malthus 1798/1976). Sharing is such a pervasive feature of !Kung life that there is not much caloric advantage in being married to, or being the child of, a good hunter (or, for a man, being a good hunter rather than a poor or lazy one), since what matters is simply that there should be a good hunter in the group. Economic models of self-interested behaviour, weighing the rewards of activity against the costs to the individual, are not very successful at predicting !Kung behaviour.

Nuclear families (parents and their children) live with three to six other families and closely related unattached adults, who make a camp or a village together. Village sizes cluster in the range of twenty to fifty people. A village with fewer than twenty people is likely to have problems on some occasions when there are not enough able-bodied adults available to provide for all of the members of the group, owing to illness or disability of some of them. And a group larger than about fifty requires such a large volume of food that the group exhausts its nearby resources quickly, and either has to walk long distances from the village to collect food, or has to move the village very frequently. Nuclear families and unattached adults are free to move from one group to another whenever they wish and can find a group where they would be welcome, so that the ratios of providers to dependants and the size of groups are constantly rearranged by the decisions of individuals, without any central co-ordination or planning.

'An unshackled intercourse', in Malthus's delightful phrase, takes the form for the !Kung of universal premarital sexual play, and first marriage (usually monogamous, although polygamy is not forbidden) occurs between the ages of nine and sixteen for girls, and twenty-two and thirty for young men. Divorce and widowing are common events, but remarriage is almost universal for people who are still in the reproductive age group (Howell 1979, pp. 228–52). Young women seem to lose no reproductive opportunities through late marriage: all are married (sometimes for the second or third time!) within a year or so of menarche.

Yet these 'extraordinary encouragements to population' lead to what is one of the lowest fertility rates observed anywhere in the world among non-contracepting peoples, an average of about 4.7 children born per woman over the whole child-bearing span of menarche to menopause, a level of fertility just sufficient to balance the mortality rate observed of an expectation of life of about thirty years (Howell 1979, pp. 122–51).

This low level of fertility is achieved with a reproductive pattern consisting of early and essentially continuous exposure to the risk of pregnancy throughout the reproductive years, ages fifteen to forty-nine for women. There is early marriage, rapid remarriage after termination, and an expressed wish for children. There is a normative pattern of a post-partum sexual taboo, but it is intended to last less than a year, and people sheepishly admit that the taboo is often broken before the child takes its first steps. Certainly the post-partum taboo is not sufficient to account for the long birth intervals observed, which average nearly four years. The long intervals are not caused by sexual aversion or sexual indifference between spouses, although marriages are expected to have periods of celibacy in them. If a couple stop having sexual relations through the disinclination of either party, the marriage is likely to be dissolved and either one or both will marry again. There is very little restriction of fertility caused by failure to engage in sexual relations among the !Kung.

Birth intervals are somewhat shorter for younger than for older women, and are definitely shorter for any woman following the infant death of the first of a pair of children. The range of reproductive success goes from zero (about 5 per cent of women) to a maximum of nine children per woman, with a modal value of four. When the !Kung are asked why women take such a long time to become pregnant again after the birth of a child, they reply that their god is stingy with children.

The Malthusian perspective on the !Kung is that it is a good thing for them that they have low fertility, and little or no population growth, because if their fertility were higher they would be inviting the 'positive checks' to population growth – war, famine, epidemics and misery. But we also note that they apparently do not limit their population growth by adoption of the 'preventive checks' recommended by Malthus – delayed marriage and restraint of the passions – or by resort to the neo-Malthusian devices of deliberate contraception or abortion. From the !Kung point of view, population control does not appear to them to be something they do, but more like something that happens to them. They engage in the behaviours that we all agree maximize fertility, but end up with low fertility and a continuing wish for higher fertility. Like wild animals or colonies of amoebae, the !Kung population seems to grow slowly during good years or series of years, and decline when environmental conditions are poor, but on the average seems just to maintain itself, responding to plenty or scarcity in a minimal way by population regulation, without that population growth or contraction being the cause of the plenty or scarcity.

The causes of the balance that the !Kung achieve between their resources and their population size can be found, I believe, in their diet, in their work load, in the division of labour, and in their physiological response to the thinness that results from these factors. After a consideration of these factors, we shall consider the generality of these observations.

Body size and body composition

Developmentally, the !Kung tend to grow slowly and end their growth at quite small sizes. Although birth weights tend to be on the low end of what we consider the normal range (Howell 1979, pp. 196, 254) few fall below the lower boundary of what are considered to be normal birth weights among other populations. As a ratio of baby's birth weight to mother's weight, the !Kung may actually have somewhat larger babies than Europeans. During childhood, however, !Kung children consistently fall significantly behind European growth standards (but not neurological or behavioural standards) for age (Truswell and Hansen 1976) until by age five or six they are distinctly small and thin for their age. Pediatricians who studied the condition of bush-living children in 1968 were impressed by their good physical condition and the absence of signs of malnutrition in children they considered to be stunted in growth (Truswell and Hansen 1976).

The !Kung are remarkably short (men average about 162 centimetres; women about 148). It is striking that the younger generation of !Kung, those who grew up since the arrival of cattle-keeping neighbours, who sometimes provide substantial amounts of food to !Kung employees and neighbours, are sometimes strikingly taller. And !Kung adults, living under traditional conditions, are all very thin. Adult men weigh, on the average, about 48 kilograms and women weigh about 40. Their weight is not only absolutely little, by European standards, but it is very little as weight per unit of height, for both males and females. As you would expect, low body weight is accompanied by very small fat deposits, as measured by skin-fold thickness. Typical adult men have no subcutaneous fat on their bodies at all, a phenomenon which among European men is usually only observed in athletes in training. !Kung women have more body fat than men, but very little by comparative standards. Women have some tendency to concentrate their fat deposits over the hips and buttocks in the pattern called steatopygia, but most women are so thin that the feature is not very striking. No !Kung woman, living in the bush in the traditional manner, could hope to approach the classic museum display of steatopygia, 'the Venus Hottentot', seen in the Musée d'Homme in Paris. Steatopygia is handy for infants, who ride upon mother's hips and buttocks for hours per day for several years, as it accentuates the flatness of the 'shelf' upon which the baby rides, and pads the area against jolts and bumps as mother walks. The undoubtedly genetic trait of steatopygia does not increase the amount of body fat a woman has, but just concentrates it in one area.

No doubt the !Kung and other Khoisan peoples are genetically distinct from their far taller and more robust Bantu neighbours, in the matter of steatopygia and in other features. Very likely they would not achieve the same height and weight, even if they were matched for diet and activity with Bantus, although we have already seen that the younger generation is growing taller and fatter, in some cases, than their parents. The shortness of the !Kung is likely to have been a genetic adaptation to the desert environment, in the form of a sensitivity of growth to dietary input, rather than a fixed shortness.

Malnutrition and the quality of the diet

Although the !Kung are short and thin, and the physicians Truswell, Hansen and Jenkins considered them to be characterized by stunted growth, they are not starving (at least not very often) and they are not frequently malnourished. Those same physicians remarked on the excellent physical condition of most of the people living on bush foods, noted an absence of signs of malnutrition except in a few people who had debilitating disease, and confirmed the impression of vitality and generally good health.

Some seasonal variation in the adequacy of diet and resulting patterns of growth and physicial condition in the people was observed. During the rainy season and the following period of growth, life is easier and people are better fed than in the hot dry season of September to December. Since the increases in dependence upon cultivated foods during the past decade, Wilmsen (1981) reports that seasonal changes in fatness have increased dramatically, to about a 6 per cent change in body weight. During the earlier period, when people were more dependent upon the traditional foods of the desert, the !Kung adaptation produced a more consistently thin, wiry, vital and healthy people, undernourished but not malnourished on a wide variety of naturally occurring foods that provide abundant vitamins, protein, minerals, fats and complex carbohydrates. By international standards, what is chronically lacking in the !Kung diet is a cheap and readily available source of simple carbohydrates, such as rice, wheat or sugar.

Availability of food in the environment

The !Kung are not so short and thin because they are consuming all of the food in their environment and they cannot get any more. Observers (Lee 1979, Marshall 1976) agree that the food supply of the !Kung is so diversified and so plentiful that it does not seem to be possible that the !Kung should exhaust it. While archaeologists seem to be convinced that humans altered environments wherever they went, especially through the effects of burning the bush in the dry season, human hunter–gatherers do not seem to have overgrazed their environment during the Pleistocene, except possibly by overhunting some of the largest game animals.

It is true that the !Kung exhaust all of the food in their camp before they go out to collect or hunt again, and they do not make any serious effort to store food for the future in their camps. Instead they move camp frequently to minimize the distance between 'home' and the available food sources, and stored food would quite literally be a burden when it came time to move on. The !Kung now have a word for a storehouse, adopted from observing the customs of Bantu and European neighbours, but, as long as they are living off bush foods rather than domesticated foods, they say, 'The bush is our storehouse.'

The !Kung's major food source, the nut *Ricinodendron rautanenii* (also called the mongongo or the mangetti) is superabundant in the forest where it grows, and millions of nuts rot on the ground every year, even after the !Kung have used it as a staff of life for half the year. In addition to the nut, the !Kung have hundreds of species of food plants and animals to select from that are considered edible. The highly polished skill of a hunter or gatherer is not so much the stalking or harvesting of the food, but knowledge of the existence, characteristics and location of the highly diverse food species.

The classification of species as edible or not is, of course, one of the variables in defining what the resource base of a population is. The !Kung reject as sources of food many of the species in their environment, such as rodents, carnivores and most insects. In addition there are many species that are considered edible in a pinch, but which gatherers and hunters as they move through the bush reject as not worth collecting and transporting back to camp, if preferred food sources are available at the time. Sometimes the reasons for rejections are related to the palatability of the food – foods even more sour, or bitter, or fibrous than species the !Kung regularly consume. Sometimes the food is rejected because of the labour involved, as when considerable processing is required to remove edible parts from inedible parts. And sometimes the food may be rejected just because people are tired of it, or owing to a personal preference of the food-collector or family members.

The division of labour and leisure

Neither are the !Kung so short and thin because of a literal shortage of labour, caused by the inability of the people to collect and carry back to camp enough food for everyone. The evidence for this assertion comes from two observations. First, we note that, while the population can be divided into workers and dependants, the workers do not work continuously, or even very hard by some people's standards (Lee 1968, Sahlins 1968). Lee has estimated that hunters and gatherers spend about fifteen to twenty hours per week on the quest for food. Including food-processing, cooking, and collection of non-food items such as water and firewood, adults still only work some thirty to fifty hours per wek. Even the most energetic workers do not go out on a collecting-trip at all on about half the days available, usually staying in the village the other half of the time to visit, rest, make tools, clothing and jewellery, and consume the food obtained on the more rigorous food-collecting days. Some days are spent visiting other camps of !Kung in the vicinity. Even the working-days, while they certainly involve muscular exertion, long walks and, often, carrying heavy burdens, are estimated by Lee to involve an average of only six hours of labour.

The second point that leads us to conclude that limiting factor in the economy is not a shortage of labour is the observation that large proportions of the population are dependants, collecting little or no food, even though they seem to be able-bodied.

Children do not help much in the food quest, although they occasionally go to fetch drinking-water or run errands for adults. And children are not systematically trained or taught the skills of hunting and gathering. Instead, they spend their days in the village, playing from morning to night, with all the other children who are there, under the casual supervision of whichever adults have stayed in the village that day. Older children might take their games outside the village, but they are usually within shouting-distance of the village. It is not until children reach adolescence that they are allowed to move through the bush, from one village to another, without adult supervision, and even then they usually go in groups.

Babies and very small children are carried by their mothers as the mothers work, as long as the child is being weaned, which may extend to age four. Increasingly, as the child gets older and able to eat a wider variety of foods, the mother prefers to leave the child in the village while she collects food, and the child comes to prefer to spend the day playing with other children. This 'weaning from the back' may be even more important than 'weaning from the breast' in allowing the mothers to achieve the return of efficiency in the food quest which eventually leads to the next pregnancy.

Girls start taking an interest in the food quest around the time of their adolescence, after a childhood remarkably free from demands by adults that they help or even learn how to do the work of gathering. The teenage girls seem sometimes to be motivated by the extra hunger of the adolescent growth spurt to volunteer to accompany the women out into the bush, thereby having the opportunity to eat hours sooner than they otherwise could, and increasing the amount of food brought back for the family. Such behaviour attracts the approval of the whole group, and the girl is likely to be thought of as a candidate for marriage to some young man by approving relatives, if she has not already been promised to someone. Food-collecting, as much as breast development, is felt to be a signal that a girl is ready for marriage. By the time they have their first baby, some three or four years after menarche, the girls are usually competent gatherers, even though no one has systematically taught them their business.

The young men continue their adolescent pattern of visiting other groups, planning their future, dancing and singing, and generally fooling around for another six to ten years after their female contemporaries have married. Indulgent adults refer to the young men, past adolescence but not yet married, as 'the owners of the shade'. As in the case of the girls, the young men are not taken seriously as candidates for marriage and adulthood until they voluntarily start participating in the food quest, a process which seems to be accomplished by trial and error over a few intense months of hunting, alone and with other hunters. Young hunters, showing off for a potential bride or for the potential parents-in-law, are often energetic hunters, and the culture encourages this development. When the young man succeeds in killing his first large antelope (kudu, wildebeest, gemsbuck or eland) there is an important ceremony performed. The hunter is tattooed on his face with soot and eland fat in a distinctive pattern. People say that applying the eland fat to the skin causes 'his heart to burn hot toward meat. He will desire meat. He becomes a real hunter, and he will spend the whole day out, and not come back to camp. When he is in the village, he will say to himself, "Why am I sitting here when I could be out hunting?"' (Lewis-Williams 1981). When they have started hunting and have the face marks of a hunter, the young men are much more likely to be accepted by young women as lovers or as husbands.

Adults, from the age of marriage to about the age of fifty, are the primary workers of the society. Women go out gathering three or four times a week, on the average, depending upon the needs of their immediate family. A woman who is pregnant or lactating goes out nevertheless, as these conditions are present during much of a woman's adult life. Women who have no infants currently may ease up on the workload, but they may choose instead to help out a sister who is heavily burdened, or may have equally heavy responsibilities for older children or old people.

A gathering-day consists of walking out from camp in the direction of known food resources, stopping to collect attractive foods along the way for immediate consumption. There will likely be a group of three to six women keeping within voice contact, each carrying water for the day (if needed, and for most of the year it is needed) and very likely a baby. When the furthest point of the planned trip is reached, which may be anything from a few kilometres to about 25 kilometres distant, the women put down their loads, build a fire, and have a rest. Next comes gathering of the major food source, and sometimes this is followed by some quick processing of the food to reduce its bulk and lighten the load. The women will eat as much of the gathered food as appeals to them on the spot, sometimes making this their major meal of the day. Eventually the food is packed into the woman's leather cape, the last of the water carried out is drunk, the baby is loaded on top of the food, and the walk home begins, each woman typically carrying 30–35 kilograms. The women may stop once or a few times on the way back to add some food to the supply or to rest, and if they are not too heavily loaded they may stop again near camp to add bulky sticks of firewood to the top of the load. Typically the women re-enter the camp around sunset, swinging the baby down to a friendly pair of hands before dumping the load at the fireside.

The caloric and food value of the produce gathered in a day varies from one species to another. Nuts and roots provide relatively dense food values, and leaves and fruits typically provide far less. Generally speaking, the woman has probably brought in one to three species of food, containing sufficient caloric value to provide her family with their vegetable foods for several days. A woman has the right to donate some of the food to anyone for whom she wishes to provide, such as an aged parent, a sick person or a special friend, and she has the right to keep it all for her immediate family if she wishes. Women typically prepare some of the food for eating in a minimal way, cooking or pounding the foods for immediate consumption, and distribute pieces or servings to family members as quickly as possible.

Men also work on the average three or four days a week, usually by hunting but sometimes trapping, collecting arrow poison, or collecting vegetable foods. All !Kung work tends to be unco-ordinated and under the control of whoever does it, with few rules. Success at hunting, however, is less secure than the results of gathering, and there is more drama and interest in the results of hunting. Small animals and vegetables collected by men are dumped by the family fire to be cooked by either mother or father, and consumed by the immediate family with perhaps a chunk or two given to others. But large catches are distributed by rather elaborate rules for dividing and sharing the meat, and the whole process is carried out with considerable interest and close observation from others, who will be assessing the fairness and generosity of the division.

After the food has been collected, the whole group generally spends some sociable hours 'debriefing' each other on what was seen in the bush that day, including the state of ripeness of plants, and animal prints and signs seen, even if not followed. The talk will be mixed with accounts of things that happened in the village that day, along with old stories and sometimes bawdy joking. People may play musical instruments, compose and perform songs, dance for entertainment or for ritual reasons. Gradually the village settles down, each family by its fire, to continue talking within the family group and, by simply raising the voice a little, to others at more distant fires.

From age fifty, and increasingly thereafter, hunters complain that their eyes 'refuse' them, and they cannot hunt large and swift animals. The contribution shifts to small animals, to digging out sleeping animals from underground dens, to trapping and snaring; and finally hunting is up entirely. Gatherers may continue to make a contribution somewhat longer, and give up their work more gradually as the needs of their dependants decrease, and the gifts from adult children and close relatives increase. When sickness or disability intervenes so that older people cannot provide for their own needs, their fate will depend heavily upon the ability of their close relatives to provide for them in addition to dependants. When food is scarce for everyone and when able adults are heavily burdened taking care of themselves and their children, old people may be seriously short of food. Typically old people end their life in a bout of infectious disease, most often pneumonia, which may be aggravated by food shortage. As the old person becomes ill, typically the efforts of surrounding kin and especially adult children increase in an effort to save him or her. Killing and outright starvation of the old never seem to occur within the group.

While the !Kung way of life is far from one of uniform drudgery – there is a great deal of leisure in a !Kung camp, even in the worst time of year – it is also true that the !Kung are very thin and complain often of hunger, at all times of the year. It is likely that hunger is a contributing cause to many deaths which are immediately caused by infectious and parasitic diseases, even though it is rare for anyone simply to starve to death. The mortality rate of the population is only slightly related to the food supply, increasing when food is scarce and expensive in terms of labour, and decreasing when the living is relatively easy, the weather good, and the food supply plentiful.

It is perhaps less obvious that the fertility rate of the society is also related to the food supply, with both long-run and short-run consequences to plenty and scarcity. Scarcity produces small children who need fewer calories per day to support their body size, so that there is a reward to parents for slow and steady growth. Scarcity also produces children who mature at a later age, hence restricting the number of children they can produce. Scarcity produces thin mothers, who find that the extra work of lactation plus the usual tasks of food-collecting and housekeeping make them slow to return to ovulatory cycling after a birth. And scarcity produces a thin mother who finds it impossible to put on much weight while continually providing for the needs of her husband and herself and three or four children, so that she ceases ovulation, and so ceases to be able to bear children, at an early age. The result is a low-fertility adaptation well suited to the environment in which the !Kung find themselves, and very stable under hunting-and-gathering conditions, but very unstable when the central features of the hunting-and-gathering way of life are abandoned.

FEEDBACKS AND BUFFERS THAT MAINTAIN THE !KUNG LOW-FERTILITY ADAPTATION: PHYSIOLOGY, CULTURE AND MOTIVES

Conscientious mothers and highly motivated fathers cease hunting and gathering after some fifteen to thirty hours per week of effort, in the belief that they have enough resources to take care of their families and to meet their obligations in the wider group, even though their children are stunted in growth, old people may be dying prematurely, fertility is restricted, and everyone is thin and hungry. We believe that more food could be obtained from the bush, and that there are the labour resources with which to obtain it, yet people following their cultural dictates and their own free choice do not take advantage of the opportunities. Despite having a type of society identified by Malthus as conducive to high fertility, and despite an expressed preference for both fatness and higher fertility, the !Kung are thin and have low fertility. In order to understand this dilemma, we need to look more closely at the points in the adaptation where the restrictions on fertility impinge, and consider whether the behaviour related to the fertility restriction is conscious or unconscious, deliberate or accidental, and whether it stems from the individuals most closely concerned, the potential parents, or from the nuclear- or extended-family members, or from a wider group.

Table 2 shows a modification of a commonly used typology developed by Davis and Blake (1956), modified to include the actors who engage in fertility limitation as well as the types of mechanisms invoked. We cross-tabulate the stage of the normal fertility process in which the intervention takes place – at ovulation and spermatogenesis, at pregnancy, at childbirth, or later – with three levels of intervention mechanism: physiological, cultural,

Table 2   Population-growth restriction methods: a classification

Stage of intervention	Locus of control		
	Physiological	*Cultural*	*Individual*

Fecundability	Late maturation
	Early senescence
	Anovulatory episodes
	Lactation anovulation
		Caloric scarcity
		Division of labour
		  that stresses
		  parents
			Hormonal contra-
			  ception
			Sterilizing-operations

Intercourse	Celibacy or
	  impotence from
	  illness or
	  malnutrition
		Late marriage
		Celibate roles
		Post-partum sex
		  taboos
		Prohibitions of widow
		  remarriage, etc.
			Celibacy by choice
			Homosexuality

Conception	Venereal diseases	Contraception	Contraception, mechanical methods

Gestation	Spontaneous
	  abortion and
	  miscarriage
		Deliberate abortion	Deliberate abortion

Infant survival	Stillbirth and neo- natal mortality	Infanticide	Infanticide

Adapted from Howell (1980).

and individual–rational. These three levels are often difficult to distinguish in a particular behaviour, and more than one of them may be involved in any particular behaviour. Indeed, the value of table 2 is primarily in directing our attention to the way the categories overlap and the difficulty of placing in any particular cell a particular behaviour such as abortion or failure to ovulate.

Clearly populations differ in the types of solution they adopt to the fertility-limitation problem, and clearly there are great differences among individuals and groups in their use of these methods. Advanced industrial societies tend to depend upon mechanical and chemical interference with conception, under individual and couple control, whereas peasant societies tend to rely upon methods which restrict intercourse, by late marriage and permanent celibacy of portions of the population. Peasant methods tend to be under the control of extended families rather than the individual or the couple.

Animal-population growth tends to be controlled primarily by the probability of survival at various stages of the life-cycle. Fertility methods tend to affect the probability of ovulation rather than intercourse. All the mechanisms used by animals can be classified as physiological, as it does not make sense to talk about cultural or individual motive controls in animals, despite evidence for the existence of some forms of animal culture.

Among the !Kung, the mechanisms that seem to be working to restrict population growth seem largely to be physiological, as with animals, but unlike the case with animals each mechanism involves a strong component of cultural legitimation and regulation, and a grounding in the individual motives for reproductive success, prosperity and personal comfort. In humans, we never see a purely physiological method of population control, just as the cultural and individual methods must have a physiological mechanism. The difference lies in the occasions on which the physiological mechanisms are invoked, and whether this is under voluntary control. The distinction is problematical but sometimes rewarding: an example might be fertility limitation which occurs because the woman is too thin to ovulate, under conditions such as those that the !Kung experience, as contrasted with a similar suppression of ovulation during a culturally set period of fasting such as Ramadan, which might well have the same effect temporarily, and as contrasted again with the individually imposed dieting of a fashion model so extreme that her ovulation is suppressed. All three types of fertility limitation depend upon the suppression of ovulation by the depletion of fat deposits (Frisch 1978).

The !Kung fertility pattern depends very heavily upon the first division in table 2: the physiological control of fecundability through late maturation, early senescence, anovulatory episodes and lactational anovulation. All of these, I have argued, inpinge upon the !Kung more than people in other societies owing to the chronic thinness that they, especially the women, experience. In addition, the !Kung restriction of fecundability is reinforced by a cultural pattern which makes it difficult or impossible to break out of the physiological consequences of thinness, for oneself or for spouse and family members. The !Kung culture contains both positive and negative instructions that tend to make it impossible for individuals to avoid the mechanisms, and tends to buffer and minimize the effects of environmental fluctuations on individuals.

The management of scarcity

The !Kung pattern of thinness and low fertility is a buffering-system in the sense that the physical condition of the people fluctuates less than the environment. The low-fertility adaptation responds to environmental fluctuations: that is the sense in which it is a mechanism for relating population and resources. But, when the system works well, fertility fluctuates less than rainfall and harvests. The mediating variable between the environment and fertility is the physical condition and specifically the fatness of the adults of the group.

When times are difficult the adults, already thin, work harder and tend to bring in less per unit of labour. As a result, they become thinner, even if they are bringing in as much food for their dependants back in the village as before. Hard-pressed adults can work harder if they wish, going out on more days and perhaps temporarily giving up some of the pleasurable luxuries of !Kung life, such as visiting and jewellery-making, but that is likely to reduce their own fat deposits even further. They may be prepared to do this if it is necessary to preserve the chances of survival, again as measured by fat deposits, of their children and other dependants. But generally adults tend instead to vary their demands on the environment. During periods of scarcity people use several strategies. If the scarcity is thought to be local, the whole group may move. If the scarcity is related to the composition of the group, having too many dependants for the number of able-bodied workers, the group may split up and nuclear families seek a better arrangement by joining other villages in the area. But, if the problem is merely that none of the favourite plant foods is ripe, or the hunters are unsuccessful with favourite animal species, the group must move down their rank-order list of preferred food species, accepting as food plants and animals that might otherwise be scorned. Some of these food sources can be converted into more attractive foods by processing; hence we tend to see more human energy being invested in the transformation of plants and animals into food during times of scarcity, which is another way of increasing the labour investment of adults in the food quest. In the average year, !Kung adults lose only a small amount of weight in the dry season, when food is scarce, and children's growth may be slowed but they do not actually lose weight (Truswell and Hansen 1976). In recent years, as the !Kung have come to supplement their diet with milk, meat and grains from domesticated plants and animals, living in association with Bantu immigrants to the area, seasonal weight losses have been increased to approximately 6 per cent (Wilmsen 1979), but people are fatter at all times of the year.

The management of plenty

In some ways, what is even more interesting about !Kung living on traditional foods obtained by hunting and gathering is the behaviour of adults in the presence of plenty. When the rains arrive plentifully and on time, both adults and dependants are pleased to see the bush full of rich, ripe, lush food sources, plants and animals (Shostak 1981). Under these circumstances, people eat more, gather in large groups, enjoy leisure activities, and say they get fat. Children's growth tends to be concentrated during the rainy season (Truswell and Hansen 1976) and especially short and thin children may 'catch up' with contemporaries during the rainy season of a good year. But what is particularly fascinating is the standard way the !Kung have of damping down the peaks of the cycle, behaviours that *minimize* rather than maximize seasonal weight gains and variations in consumption.

Just as in times of scarcity, during plenty the adult hunters and gatherers collect as much as they can carry back to camp. Their day may be shorter during a time of plenty and the walk may be shorter, but the amount of food brought back will be basically the same per person. There may be some tendency for more adults to go out when the food to be collected is conveniently nearby and particularly attractive, but this tends to average out over a week or so until about the same proportion of adults are going out each day as in times of scarcity.

The food will be served to the family and shared across the group with the same degree of care or lack of care that was displayed during the worst time of the year. If there is a difference, less care will be taken and less effort put into food-processing during times of plenty, when the foods are inherently more attractive. In time of plenty as in time of scarcity, there will be little or no choice between available foods, there will be little or no investment made by the 'cook' in spices, in sauces, in attractive combinations or attractive presentations of food. To compare our own diet with that of the !Kung, it is as if we came back from the supermarket with 20 to 30 kilograms of celery and walnuts, offering our families all they could eat of these foods, along with the meat that the hunters brought in, until it was all eaten in three or four days. The supermarket gatherers might then bring back generous amounts of pumpkin and raspberries, to be offered to their families. Even very hungry people, offered no choice, will limit their consumption of such foods to amounts which will not produce rapid weight gain or florid obesity. When 'hunger is the only spice' the amounts of food consumed are likely to be modest.

Much of the restriction of rapid weight gain during times of plenty is embedded in the !Kung culture. The culture prescribes that parents must collect food to feed their families, but it is not prescribed by their culture (as it is with ours) that parents are responsible for getting their children to eat their food. The omnipresence of hunger is taken for granted in !Kung notions of motivation: no one is told to eat, or to clean up his or her plate, or to try some of this nice food. The culture is more negative than positive in these messages, but the !Kung attitudes toward eating and food are just as much a part of their culture, their adaptive system, as French *haute cuisine* is a part of another culture. Because I found the !Kung lovely, hospitable people, friends as well as study subjects, it was difficult for me to notice overtly that they are poor cooks and habitually serve unattractive and unpalatable meals to their families and friends, unpalatable by their standards as well as mine. To be less judgemental and culture-bound, we can accurately observe that the food offered has been subjected to a minimum of processing: fruits may have had outer husks removed; nuts are roasted, cracked and shelled; meat is either boiled or roasted in the coals of the fire. There are no recipes, no seasonings or spices, and no planned meals or meal times. People scoop some cooked food out of a pot, or roast and crack their own nuts from a pile near the fire when they are hungry. Most of the food becomes liberally sprinkled with sand in the process of cooking, and most people make no serious effort to brush it off before eating. People eat until the edge is taken off their hunger, and then stop.

Despite more than twenty five years of ethnographic observation of the !Kung, I believe that their attitude toward food has not yet been thoroughly understood by any of the anthropologists. Shostak (1981) comes closest, with her translations of the actual words of an articulate !Kung woman. What we observers have trouble understanding is what chronic hunger feels like, and how human appetite responds to the availability of a kilo or so of rather tart berries, or somewhat fibrous roots. Food is eaten eagerly, and it seems mad to these people to fuss about preparing it attractively. My own style of cooking, observed by !Kung during two years of fieldwork as a kind of spectator sport, probably translates into !Kung as something like 'gilding the lily'. Certainly !Kung offered samples of my cooking seemed to be as puzzled at the appeal of the bland smoothness of my dishes as I was puzzled at the strong flavours and abrasiveness of theirs. Cultural standards differ, but I think

Table 3   Types of human-population control

Malthusian population growth	Access to rich food supplies	
	'Thin things'	'Fat things'
Positive checks Starvation Epidemic disease War Misery	Hobbesian model of 'life in a state of nature' – 'nasty, brutish, and short'. Peasants, when times are bad	Rare among humans. Model of a domesticated species 'harvested' by others. Warriors?
Preventive checks Delayed marriage Prolonged birth intervals Contraception Celibacy	The !Kung and other hunter–gatherers whose culture is geared to chronic restriction of intake	Advanced industrial people; peasants, when times are good

there is no doubt that one can more easily and quickly make oneself obese on my kind of cooking and food preparation than on theirs.

The result of their cultural dictates, applied to the traditionally available bush foods, is a population of well nourished, very thin people with low fertility, even in the midst of an abundance of food sources. The peaks as well as the valleys of resource availability are avoided by the !Kung adaptation, at a cost to the people of constant hunger but not malnutrition. The !Kung culture permits them to maintain individual freedom from the control and direction of others, a lot of leisure, and an impressively secure economic base for themselves and their families.

The restriction of fertility, which is so much a part of this adaptation, is achieved by a physiological response rather than a consciously adopted policy, but it is just as much a product of culture as delayed marriage or contraception would be. Table 3 contrasts dependence upon thinness as a fertility-restriction method for those such as the !Kung who engineer it through their cultures, with the fertility restriction that occurs when the density of people pressing directly upon resources leads to starvation.

HOW GENERAL IS THE !KUNG ADAPTIVE PATTERN AMONG HUNTER-GATHERERS?

Hunter–gatherers have been found on all the continents of the world during the twentieth century, and additional groups are known from travellers' accounts in earlier centuries. While the groups in question are by no means all genetically related to one another, and their cultures have distinctive roots, there are a number of features widely shared by hunter–gatherers. These features, found in widely separated groups living in a range of environments, provide the basis for the hypothesis that there is a human baseline population-regulation system from which other arrangements have been derived.

Some of the most colourful and distinctive peoples to be found in the world are among the group of hunter–gatherers: the pygmies of the Central African rain forest, the Eskimos of the Arctic, and the Australian aborigines. While many of the accounts of hunter–gatherers are not useful for our purposes, made up as much of fantasy as observation, reliable observational studies of reproductive behaviour have been made of at least a few of these groups. The available data allow us to refine the hypothesis somewhat.

Many hunter–gatherers share the !Kung trait of a free and unco-ordinated life, with an absence of hierarchy in human relations and the ability of the individual to control his or her own work and leisure. The picture is not entirely consistent: some of the north-coast Australian aborigines have a system of gerontocracy (Hart and Pilling 1960, Rose 1960) that allows the oldest men to tyrannize all the women and the men younger than themselves, who suffer resentfully until they get the chance to take their place at the top. Most hunter–gatherers, however, are like the !Kung in that they live lightly on the land, move frequently, share widely, own little, and make little attempt to exercise control over one another.

Another hunter–gatherer general trait, probably related to the first, is early and universal marriage for women, with easy availability of remarriage when a woman is widowed or divorced. Hunter–gatherers all seem to recognize that women are the scarce resource in reproduction, and arrange marriage to minimize the occurrence of non-marriage for reproductive-age women. The Tiwi of Australia are again an extreme case, insisting that women be continually married from birth to death (Hart and Pilling 1965). The martial success of men is more highly variable: whereas some groups concentrate a large proportion of the wives with a small proportion of polygamous husbands (while other men still hunt and, it is widely acknowledged, have sexual access to the women) other groups resemble the !Kung in being more egalitarian. Adult !Kung men can be unmarried for substantial periods of time, although they generally do not like to be. Adult !Kung women never stay unmarried very long if there is any chance of having more children.

Most (but not all) of the hunter–gatherers are like the !Kung in having relatively small body sizes, and typically have a body composition with low deposits of subcutaneous fat. All of the 'pygmoid' peoples of the earth are hunter–gatherers, or recent converts to horticulture from a hunting–and-gathering base. And many of the hunter–gatherers who are not classified as pygmy, such as the Hadza of Tanzania (Woodburn 1968), turn out to be remark-ably short and light. It is striking that most observers note that children grow taller after the settling-down process that typically ends the hunting-and-gathering economy by wage labour or mission stations. It is not at all clear whether the increases in body size are owing primarily to changes in diet, changes in activity patterns, or reduction of infections with settlement, but it is clear that the initial cause of the shortness cannot have been genes alone.

Another distinctive feature of hunting–gathering life around the world has been the extremely heavy reliance upon lactation to feed infants. Typically, hunter–gatherer babies are carried by their mothers next to a naked breast all day and night, and babies take milk very frequently throughout the day (Konner 1976), take a large amount of calories and a high proportion of total calories in the form of mother's milk, and continue the lactation for a very long period of time by the standards of other peoples. The pattern of lactation is distinctive to hunter–gatherers and almost universal among them, so much so that some observers have hypothesized that lactation may be the only or the prime component of hunter–gatherers' reproductive-control strategies (Lee 1979, Konner 1976).

The reasons for the heavy reliance upon lactation to feed infants and young children seem to be based in the scarcity of appropriate 'baby foods' in a hunter–gatherer diet. The lean meat, nuts, fibrous roots and sour berries of the diet of tropical hunter–gatherers is not well suited to the requirements of infants. The breast, to a hunter–gatherer baby, is food and drink, warmth and comfort, the source of the necessities of life. !Kung say that the baby cannot live if the mother dies in childbirth, and people around the world who have no domesticated animals, no permanent home sites, agree.

Konner and Worthman (1980), who have done the only detailed studies of lactation in hunter–gatherers to date, stress the bursts of the prolactin hormone that are released by suckling and speculate that lactation may suppress ovulation and hence lengthen the birth interval far more in hunter–gatherers than in other people, because the hunter–gatherer mother typically carries her baby and keeps it very close to her all the time, for safety and for convenience in feeding. Among tropical hunter–gatherers, the breast is not likely to be covered, and babies are able to determine the frequency and duration of lactation, rather than mothers. Under these circumstances babies feed very often (several times an hour) during waking-hours, and briefly. Konner and Worthman therefore conclude that lactation alone could be causing the long birth intervals.

Certainly it is true that frequent lactation is a common feature of hunter–gatherer populations, and there can be little doubt that the lactation forms an important part of the population–regulation adaptation, through the physiological mechanisms which lead to ovulation or the suppression of ovulation. We can see its centrality in the shortening of birth intervals that almost invariably occurs after the death of a child in infancy (Howell 1979, p. 133). Few babies in hunter–gatherer societies are weaned before their mother becomes pregnant again: instead the typical pattern is that the mother feeds her baby until she becomes pregnant again, and then weans the child early in the next pregnancy. Clearly, then, lactation does not suppress ovulation completely, or permanently. What is distinctive for the hunter–gatherers is how long the birth intervals are, and how long the lactation goes on. !Kung children are commonly weaned at age four; children still taking breast milk at age six are not unknown.

Lactation, however, is a constant for the various populations and for the babies that survive, and hence is not an entirely satisfactory explanation for the variable aspect of population growth in response to environmental fluctuations. There is some latitude for population regulation in lactation mechanisms: when times are good, perhaps the baby grows more quickly and becomes burdensome to the mother at an earlier age, so that she will leave the baby behind in the village while she goes collecting and hence returns to ovulation somewhat faster than she otherwise would. Or perhaps a well-fed baby is energetic and secure at a younger age than a more hungry baby, and wants to stay behind in the village at a younger age. In either case it is unlikely that this kind of mechanism would shorten the birth interval by more than a few months, and there is no observational support for even that kind of effect.

Lactation does, of course, represents a considerable caloric drain on the mother, a major contribution to the problem of thinness that mothers have among hunter–gatherers. And the thinness of the mother is, clearly, responsive to environmental fluctuations of scarcity and plenty through the intersecting variables of the mother's workload (including lactation), her diet, and her load of infectious and parasitic diseases.

The effects of thinness and fatness on reproductive states have been hypothesized by Rose Frisch (1981, 1983) and Frisch et al. (1971, 1974), based upon studies of age of menarche and characteristic of menstrual cycles in a wide range of women, none of them hunter–gatherers. Frisch and her colleagues suggest possible physiological mechanisms for the 'critical-fatness' hypothesis, which posits that there is a given amount of fatness needed for onset of menstrual cycling and a higher level needed for ovulation within those cycles. The basic physiological studies needed to test the hypothesis are difficult to carry out, but seem not to be under way. Instead there have been a number of studies attempting to apply the critical-fatness hypothesis to a range of natural-fertility populations around the world (Chowdhury 1978, Huffman 1980, Bongaarts and Delgado 1979). In addition there have been several critical evaluations of the critical-fatness hypothesis (Menken et al., 1981).

The critical responses to Frisch's work are odd in several respects. Most of them start by conceding that Frisch must be correct that there is some level of undernutrition that interferes with menstrual cycles and ovulation, but go on to review the systematic studies that have examined the question, concluding that there is little evidence for the proposition. Studies cited show variations in age at menarche or length of post-partum amenorrhoea that seem to be accounted for by other variables (such as age, health, separations from husband, stress, and so on) rather than fatness. The evidence suggests that differential levels of fatness in women do not account for the differential fertility in these populations, but does not address the question of whether there is a feedback between fatness and fertility if the other variables could be controlled.

Unfortunately, the question of the mechanism of fatness in reproduction necessarily becomes embroiled in the complex questions of what governmental and ethical policy ought to be in the face of population growth in poor and underdeveloped countries. Demographers have widely adopted the liberal position that neo-Malthusian birth control programmes should be provided, as opposed to a leftist position advocating a redistribution of wealth or a rightist position advancing what is sometimes called (unfairly, biologists would agree) a neo-Darwinist rule of 'Let the poor starve until the "natural" level of population size is obtained' (presumably by positive checks). Frisch's hypothesis has been interpreted as a pseudo-scientific formulation of the right-wing position on this political question.

At the same time, Frisch's position seems heartless on empirical grounds to those who have seen malnourished and unhealthy families victimized by high fertility. If thinness 'automatically' protects against excessively high fertility and threatening population growth, why, one wonders, is it not working for poor and malnourished peasants and rural workers in the world today?

This is not the place to try to answer this question, or to try to resolve the basic question of exactly what the physiological mechanism of this hypothesized relation between fatness and fertility must be. We can, however, make several observations while the basic research work that will eventually resolve the question is under way. First, the political implications, pleasant or unpleasant, have no bearing on whether there is a physiological mechanism which suppresses reproduction in the absence of a critical amount of body fat in women. Second, the political questions fade away when we distinguish the hunter–gatherers from the peasants of the world, owing to the (in part erroneous) conviction that hunter–gatherer societies are independent social forms, not influenced by modern nation states. Third, on biological grounds it would be astonishing if there were no such mechanism, and it is not surprising that the mechanism should be adjusted to the body type and composition that results from living by hunting and gathering rather than to that which results from living on domesticated foods, when you consider the respective periods of time that the evolutionary process had to adjust to the way of life. Hunting-and-gathering, as a basis for human life, is far older, has lasted much longer, than any other economic base.

The fatness mechanism, which allows humans to relate the condition of the environment to the size of the population, is universal not just to hunter–gatherers but to all humans, though only operative when people are on the margin of thinness and undernutrition so common to hunter–gatherers but, so rare among food-producers.

Assuming that the fatness mechanism is important in suppressing the fertility of hunter–gatherers, knowing about their diet is not enough to predict its effects. We also need to know about their state of health, particularly the 'load' of parasites and infections that adults commonly carry in that environment. And we need to know about the division of labour in the society, specifically to what extent it is the women of reproductive age who are expected to do the calorically expensive work of the society. Most hunter–gatherers seem to be like the !Kung in expecting women to do a full share of the heavy work (Dahlberg 1981), along with pregnancy, lactation and household chores, while old people and children do little or no work. While women, among the tropical hunter–gatherers, work long and hard, there are particular kinds of tasks, involving bursts of energy and physical exhaustion, that women do not do in most societies, such as hunting large animals and dancing (as opposed to singing and clapping). No doubt the frequency of pregnancy and the presence of a nursing baby play a large role in this allocation of tasks, but protection of existing fat deposits in non-lactating, non-pregnant women may also be a factor.

The exceptional societies among hunter–gatherers on the division of labour between the sexes are the far-northern and Arctic peoples. Among Eskimos, for example, women rarely leave the village space during the long winter, depending entirely upon the men to hunt and bring back food from caches

(Balikci 1968) for them and the children. There are of course no vegetable foods available in the winter in the Arctic, and the women could not work alongside the men and take proper care of themselves and the children at the same time. It is only the richness of the Arctic animal foods and the high productivity of the hunters that allows humans to occupy that niche.

Finally, we shall look at one more factor in the hunter–gatherer population-regulation strategy, and that is the unlovely custom of infanticide. Some analysts stress the necessity and the frequency of infanticide (Birdsell 1968), while others (Howell 1979, p. 120) see it as playing a smaller role. But all observers agree that infanticide is a universal or near-universal trait in hunter-gatherer societies. The implication is clear that individuals judge the value of each birth as it occurs, and decide that some infants should not survive.

Typically the agent of infanticide in human society (unlike many animal species (Hausfater 1984)) is the mother, sometimes acting upon the advice and perhaps instructions of the father or other close relatives. The advantage of infanticide as a method of population control as opposed to methods that prevent pregnancy is that the infant can be examined before the decision is made, so that the sex and physical condition and appearance of the baby can enter into the decision. A number of hunter–gatherer societies, particularly those in the Arctic, practice female infanticide differentially, presumably because the male contribution to the parents is far greater than that of females. Some groups use infanticide only upon malformed, unhealthy-looking or particularly small infants, presumably on the assumption that these babies will either die in any case or grow up to be a burden to their families. Some groups practice infanticide when the circumstances of a particular birth are considered unfortunate: perhaps the father died during pregnancy, the mother was pregnant by a man other than her husband, or the baby is born at a time of hardship and scarcity for the group. And finally infanticide may be used as a device to reduce the number of babies being raised in the environment, whether the judgement is based upon the supply of infants in the group as a whole, or (more likely) upon the supply of infants in the particular family. Only the last category of infanticide is density dependent, although all eliminate babies.

The demographic consequences of infanticide depend upon the extent to which babies are killed who would die in any case. 'Normal' infant mortality is relatively high in all hunter–gatherer societies (15–25 per cent infant mortality can be expected). To the extent to which the babies deliberately killed at birth are drawn from that proportion, infanticide does not reduce the size of the population. On the contrary, infanticide would lead to shorter birth intervals and hence higher fertility than would result from a prolonged death. From this point of view, infanticide is rational and eugenic: the investment of parents and especially mothers in the infant is stopped just at the point when the most 'expensive' portion of the investment, lactation, is about to start. The sunk cost of the pregnancy and the childbirth has been paid, and the mother has the advantage of being able to see and judge the viability of the infant before making a decision.

The widespread existence of infanticide tells us plainly that the 'preventive checks' on population, the low-fat adaptation or others, do not always work for hunter-gatherers. Schrire and Steiger (1974) have shown that even relatively moderate estimates of the frequency of infanticide cannot be applied mechanically as a constant probability to every female birth in the small populations with the relatively high birth and death rates that characterize hunter–gatherers, or the populations will decline to extinction. But of course hunter–gatherers do not apply infanticide in that way. Infanticide is used situationally, as one of the rights of mothers (as with the !Kung) or as a deviant act, in many societies, raising normal infant mortality slightly. And it is used to eliminate weak and sickly babies in many societies, which probably has no effect on mortality at all. And finally infanticide is used to space babies more widely or to limit the total number of babies to be raised by particular families when other methods of spacing or limiting fertility, including the critical-fatness adaptation, have not worked for the group or the individual.

Among hunter–gatherers, then, we might expect to see clusters of traits related to their primary form of population-growth limitation. The !Kung may serve as a model of one type: small, skinny people with low natural fertility and a cherishing attitude toward those 'scarce' children. Another polar type might be the Groote Eylandt aborigines, a relatively tall and husky people, described (Rose 1960) as having high fertility, high rates of infanticide, and considerable hierarchy and 'power politics' in human relations. Most hunter–gatherer groups would fall somewhere between, and probably all societies have the capacity to shift from one mechanism to another as the environment fluctuates.

CONCLUSION: THE FOOD-COLLECTING VERSUS FOOD-PRODUCING STRATEGIES

This essay started by arguing that, while there were many changes between our animal ancestors and our proto-human ancestors, four of these were crucial for defining the distinctively human organization of population. These were provisioning of children and other dependants, provision of nursing-services to reduce the probability of mortality associated with sickness or accidents, a shift to more calorically rich food sources, and the adoption of food-processing techniques that made it possible for humans to eat a wider range of plants and animals.

When we consider the shift from hunting and gathering to horticulture and herding, we can see further changes in these four features. There are only minor changes in the ability of humans to provide food and nursing-care to temporary or long-term dependants, changes dependent upon storage of food and the construction of shelters permitting somewhat better protection from an equally serious threat to life. Unfortunately, at the same time the larger living-groups and higher densities probably produced somewhat greater threats to health from epidemic diseases.

The more substantial changes come in the shift to a yet more calorically rich group of food sources, and the adoption of another magnitude of food-processing technology. The foods domesticated tend to be those with high density food parts, and once domesticated they tend to be selected for an enlargement of that trend. Hence early domesticated plants are emmer wheat and barley, for instance, and later generations of the plants have enlarged grains compared to the early forms. Similarly the cattle, sheep and goats chosen for domestication start as relatively docile and meaty animals, and develop a higher capacity for fat deposition as they are selected. Nowhere do hunter–gatherers domesticate the fibrous roots and sour berries of the traditional diet, partly because of the characteristics of the plant and partly owing to the characteristics of the people.

Food-processing is also increased, along with the inherent caloric values of the foods produced. Some of this is necessary as a product or by-product of the storage of food. The grains cultivated, for instance, have to be dried before they can be stored without spoilage. After drying the grains require either pounding or at least long slow cooking before they become edible again. Similarly meat may have to be smoked or dried in order to be kept more than a few days, a fact that hunter–gatherers know and practise on a small scale. Outside the Arctic (where freezing solves the storage problem over much of the year), animals have to be either kept on the hoof (the usual way) or the meat has to be preserved. To the problems of preservation, we add the problems of the control of appetite and the problem of boredom. The result tends to be a population of considerably fatter people, with a far more elaborate set of customs surrounding food preparation, than hunter–gatherers, even if you would not consider the diet of the Yanamamo (Chagnon 1968) or New Guinea Highlanders (Rappaport 1974) *haute cuisine*.

Horticulturalists tend to be fatter than hunter–gatherers in part because, when appetite drives them to eat, it is easier to do so. To resist eating stored food when it is readily available takes real self-restraint, so horticulturalists do not aim to produce the same amount of food they would harvest under hunting-gathering, plus an allowance for the seed for the next year, but rather enough to reduce their hunger drive to lower levels than hunter–gatherers habitually endure. The higher level of food intake produces larger children and larger adults, who demand a yet-higher level of food production. Add to this the inevitable losses from rodents, insects and storage, and you realize that food-producers require quite considerably higher amounts of food than hunter–gatherers, even without taking into account the likelihood of population growth and increased density.

Table 3 summarizes the argument of this paper in comparative perspective. By Malthusian standards, the hunter–gatherer adaptation is based upon a balance between preventive checks and positive checks (as all adaptations are balanced) which leans to an unexpected degree in the direction of the preventive checks. We can refine our understanding of this achievement by recognizing that hunger-gatherers tend to be thin not because they have exhausted the food in their environment, but because they have evolved a culture which gives them security, leisure and egalitarianism at a price of chronic hunger and undernutrition. When they avoid the hunger and thinness, by environmental plenty or by harvesting more of their potential food supply, they experience higher fertility and either experience population growth or resort to infanticide. All three occasions are commonly known among hunter–gatherers, and the character of the hunting-gathering societies we observe are probably in large part a result of the historical sequence of such changes.

While it lasted, and it is by far the longest-surviving form of human social organization, the hunter–gatherer way of life produced a solution to the continual problem of population growth outstripping resources. No doubt many features of contemporary human life are long-term survivals or adjustments to problems of life under hunting–gathering conditions, and our difficulties with population growth, before and after Malthus, arise in the context of institutions, norms and values, opinions and intentions very different from those of the conditions under which we all became human.

REFERENCES

Acsádi, G., and Nemeskéri, J. 1974: *History of Human Life Span and Mortality*. Budapest: Académiai Kaidó.
Aries, P. 1980: Two successive motivations for a declining birth rate in the West. *Population and Development Review*, 6, 645–50.
Balikci, A. 1968: Netsilik Eskimos: adaptive processes. In R. B. Lee and I. De Vore (eds), *Man the Hunter*, Chicago: Aldine.
Becker, G. 1981: *A Treatise on the Family*. Cambridge, Mass.: Harvard University Press.
Bicchieri, M. G. 1972: *Hunters and Gatherers Today*. New York: Holt, Rinehart and Winston.
Biesele, M., and Howell, N. 1982: The old people give you life. In P. Amoss and S. Harrell (eds), *Other Ways of Growing Old*, Stanford, Calif: Stanford University Press.
Birdsell, J. B. 1968: Predictions for the Pleistocene based on equilibrium systems among hunter–gatherers. In R. B. Lee and I. DeVore, *Man the Hunter*, Chicago: Aldine.
Bongaarts, J. 1982: The fertility inhibiting effects of the intermediate fertility variables. *Studies in Family Planning*, 13, 179–89.
—— and Delgado, H. 1979: Effects of nutritional status on fertility in rural Guatemala. In H. Leridon and J. Menken (eds), *Natural Fertility*, Liège: Ordina.
Boulding, K. 1978: *Ecodynamics: a new theory of society evolution*. Beverly Hills, Calif.: Sage.
Brooks, A., Gelburd, D. E.., and Yellen, J. E. 1984: Food production and culture change among the !Kung San. In J. D. Clark and S. Brandt, *From Hunters to Farmers: causes and consequences of food production in Africa*, Berkeley, Calif.: University of California Press.
Buikstra, J. 1983: Persistent problems in paleodemography. Paper presented at the annual meetings of the American Anthropological Association, Chicago.
Caldwell, J. C. 1982: *Theory of Fertility Decline*. New York: Academic Press.
—— and Campbell, D. P., Caldwell, P., Ruzickor, L., Cosford, W., Packer, R., Grocolt, J., and Neill, M. 1976: *Toward an Understanding of Contemporary Demographic Change*, Australian Family Formation project, monograph no. 4. Canberra: Australian National University.
Chagnon, N. A. 1968: *Yanamamo: the fierce people*. New York: Holt, Rinehart and Winston.
Chowdbury, A. K. 1978: Effects of maternal nutrition on fertility in rural Bangladesh. In W. H. Mosley (ed.), *Nutrition and Human Reproduction*, New York and London: Macmillan, pp. 401–10.
Clark, J. D., and Brandt, S. (eds) (1984): *From Hunters to Farmers: causes and consequences of food production in Africa*. Berkeley, Calif.: University of California Press.
Dahlberg, F. 1981: *Woman the Gatherer*. New Haven, Conn.: Yale University Press.
Darwin, C. 1871: *The Descent of Man*. London: John Murray.
Davis, K., and Blake, J. 1956: Social structure and fertility: an analytic framework. *Economic Development and Cultural Change*, 4, 211–35.
Draper, P. 1976: Social and economic constraints on child life among the !Kung. In R. B. Lee and I. DeVore, *Kalahari Hunter-gatherers*, Cambridge, Mass.: Harvard University Press.

Easterlin, R. 1978: The economics and sociology of fertility: a synthesis. In C. Tilly (ed.), *Historical Studies of Changing Fertility*, Princeton, NJ: Princeton University Press.

Fossey, D. 1983: *The Mountain Gorilla*. New York: Houghton Mifflin.

Frisch, R. E. 1975: Demographic implications of the biological determinants of female fecundity. *Social Biology*, 22, 17–22.

—— 1978: Nutrition, fatness and fertility: the effect of food intake on reproductive ability. In W. H. Mosley (ed.), *Nutrition and Human Reproduction*, New York and London: Macmillan.

—— and McArthur, J. W. 1974: Menstrual cycles: fatness as a determinant of minimum weight for height necessary for their maintenance or onset. *Science*, 185, 949–51.

—— Revelle, R., and Cook, S. 1971: Height, weight and age of menarche and the 'critical weight' hypothesis. *Science*, 194, 1148.

Goodall, J. 1968: The behavior of free-ranging chimpanzees in the Gombe Stream Reserve. *Animal Behavior Monographs*, 1, 161–311.

Harpending, H. 1976: Regional variation in !Kung populations. In R. B. Lee and I. DeVore (eds), *Kalahari Hunter-gatherers*, Cambridge, Mass.: Harvard University Press.

Harris, M. 1980: *Culture, People and Nature*, 3rd edn. New York: Harper and Row.

Hart, C. W., and Pilling, A. R. 1960: *The Tiwi of Northern Australia*. New York: Holt, Rinehart and Winston.

Hausfater, G., and Hrdy, S. B. 1984: *Infanticide: comparative and evolutionary perspectives*. New York: Aldine.

Henry, L. 1961: *Some data on natural fertility*. Eugenics Quarterly, 8, 81–91.

Howell, N. 1976: Toward a uniformitarian theory of human paleodemography. *Journal of Human Evolution*, 5, 25–40.

—— 1979: *Demography of the Dobe !Kung*. New York: Academic Press.

—— 1980: Demographic behavior of hunter–gatherers: evidence for density dependent population control. In T. K. Burch (ed.), *Demographic Behavior: interdisciplinary perspectives on decision-making*, AAAS Symposium 45. Boulder, Col.: Westview Press.

—— 1985: Components of microevolution in the !Kung. In K. C. Malhotra and A. Basu (eds), *Human Genetics and Adaptation*, V, I, *Proceedings of the Indian Statistical Institute Golden Jubilee International Conference*, 1–5 February, 1982, ISI, Calcutta.

Huffman, S. et al. 1980: Lactation and fertility in rural Bangladesh. *Population Studies*, 33, 337–47.

Isaac, G. 1978: The food-sharing behavior of protohuman hominids. *Scientific American*, 238, 90–108.

Konner, M., and Worthman, C. 1980: Nursing frequency, gonadal functioning, and birth spacing among !Kung hunter–gatherers. *Science*, 207, 768–70.

Lack, D. 1954: *The Natural Regulation of Animal Numbers*. Oxford: Clarendon Press.

Lancaster, J. B. 1978: Carrying and sharing in human evolution. *Human Nature*, 1, 83–9.

Leakey, R. 1976: *Origins*. New York: Dutton.

Lee, R. B. 1968: What hunters do for a living: how to make out on scarce resources. In R. B. Lee and I. DeVore (eds), *Man the Hunter*, Chicago: Aldine.

—— 1979: *The !Kung San: men, women and work in a foraging society*. Cambridge: Cambridge University Press.

—— 1984: *The Dobe !Kung*. New York: Holt, Rinehart and Winston.

—— and DeVore, I. (eds) 1968: *Man the Hunter*. Chicago: Aldine.

—— 1976: *Kalahari Hunter-Gatherers*. Cambridge, Mass.: Harvard University Press.

Leridon, H., and Menken, J. (eds) 1979: *Natural Fertility*. Liège: Ordina.

Lewis-Williams, J. D. 1981: *Believing and Seeing*. New York, Academic Press.

MacArthur, R. H. 1962: Some generalized theorems of natural selection. *Proceedings of the National Academy of Sciences, USA*, 48, 1893–7.

Malthus, T. R. 1976: *An Essay on the Principle of Population, as it affects the Future Improvement of Society*. London: J. Johnson.

Marshall, T. 1976: *The !Kung of Nyae Nyae*. Cambridge, Mass.: Harvard University Press.

Menken, J., Trussell, J., and Watkins, S. 1981: The nutrition-fertility link: an evaluation of the evidence. *Journal of Interdisciplinary History*, 16, 425–41.

Rappaport, R. 1975: *Pigs for the Ancestors.* New Haven and London: Yale University Press.

Rose, F. G. G. 1960: *Classification of Kin, Age Structure and Marriage amongst the Groote Eylandt Aborigines.* Berlin: Akademie-Verlag; London: Pergamon.

Sahlins, M. 1968: Notes on the original affluent society. In R. B. Lee and I. De Vore (eds), *Man the Hunter*, Chicago: Aldine.

Schrire, C., and Steiger, W. L. 1974: A matter of life and death: an investigation into the practice of female infanticide in the Arctic. *Man*, 9, 161–84.

Shostak, M. 1981. *Nisa: the life and words of a !Kung woman.* Cambridge, Mass.: Harvard University Press.

Trussell, J. 1978: Menarche and fatness: reexamination of the critical body composition hypothesis. *Science*, 200, 1506–9. (Reply: 1509–13.)

Truswell, A. S., and Hansen, J. D. L. 1976. Medical research among the !Kung. In R. B. Lee and I. De Vore (eds), *Kalahari Hunter-gatherers*, Cambridge, Mass.: Harvard University Press.

Weissner, P. 1977: Hxaro, a regional system of reciprocity for the !Kung San. PhD thesis, University of Michigan, Ann Arbor.

—— 1982: Risk, reciprocity and social influences in !Kung San economics. In E. Leacock and R. Lee (eds), *Politics and History in Band Society*. Cambridge: Cambridge University Press.

Wilmsen, E. 1979a: Dietary intake and sex hormone patterns among desert dwelling hunter–gatherers. Manuscript, African Studies Center, Boston University, Boston, Mass.

—— 1979b: *Diet and Fertility among Kalahari Bushmen*, Working Paper no. 14, African Studies Center, Boston University, Boston, Mass.

Wilson, E. O. 1975: *Sociobiology: the new synthesis.* Cambridge, Mass. Belknap Press.

Woodburn, J. 1968: An introduction to Hadza ecology. In R. B. Lee and I. De Vore (eds), *Man the Hunter*, Chicago: Aldine.

Wrigley, E. A. 1978: Fertility strategy for the individual and the group. In C. Tilly (ed.), *Historical Studies of Changing Fertility*, Princeton, NJ: Princeton University Press.

Wynne-Edwards, V. C. 1962: *Animal Dispersion in Relation to Social Behaviour.* Edinburgh: Oliver and Boyd.

Transfer Incomes, Risk and Security: The Roles of the Family and the Collectivity in Recent Theories of Fertility Change

R. M. Smith

INTRODUCTION

It is interesting to observe how certain elements in Malthus's writing in the fields of population and economics have maintained a central place in demographic theory and method while others have been infrequently debated or almost wholly ignored. It is Malthus the economist, the archetypal nineteenth-century methodological and political individualist who almost invariably emerges as a focus of discussion and apparently able to withstand the test of time. Those parts of his writings that display an eclectic empiricism and an interest in cultural relativism and specificity are, even allowing for some recent notable attempts to reintroduce them to the centre-stage of demographic debate (Wrigley and Schofield 1981, Wrigley 1983, Schofield 1985a), largely ignored.

Some would regard it as undeniable that the extension during the 1960s of 'household demand theory' with its concern for the allocation of market goods and time to the analysis of fertility provided a micro-economic context for the analysis of secular fertility decline as the relative price of children increased (Becker 1960) that finally overturned Malthus's notion of an income–marriage–fertility relationship so appropriate for the understanding of certain pre-industrial and pre-transitional societies (Schofield 1976, Lee 1973). However, Malthusian 'economic demography' and present-day 'household economics' could also be viewed as interlinked by numerous fundamental common denominators. We can appreciate these links most readily if we think of Malthus primarily in terms of his break with a kind of political economy within which there was a significant place for moral philosophy, in the process becoming more directly associated with a science organized around understanding individualism, *laissez-faire* and a reverence for the market mechanism as the equilibrating force in society (Blaug 1980, Collini et al. 1983). Of course, such preoccupations in Malthus's work have encouraged generations of writers from Marx onwards to see his writing as the embodiment of a kind of political individualism in which the purpose of the government is confined to enabling individuals' wants to be satisfied and against the idea that it might legitimately influence or alter the populace's needs. The subsequent mathematical formalization of both this classic liberal approach and its offspring, utilitarianism, by such economists as Jevons and Marshall provides one lifeline extending directly to those present-day economic demographers who treat individuals or households (regarded as if they are quasi-individuals) as reacting to a wide range of 'goods' which include children and wives that can be substituted for these goods and *vice versa*. Hence individual households are perceived as islands trading with the outside world and displaying preferences 'imbibed by some unspoken process independent of society's interests' (Arthur 1982, p. 394) and suffering no social manipulation of their activities (Sen 1983).

In drawing these connections it is easy to allocate to Malthus the responsibility for the fact that demography has developed in the twentieth century very largely as a science concerned with the study of population, based on observations about individual members and, in particular, events occurring to those members so as to change the size of populations. But Malthus should in no sense be regarded as a fully fledged methodological individualist, appealing to fixed and ubiquitous psychological elements whether they be the 'passion between the sexes' or the desire to 'maximize'.[1] Indeed, there are significant parts of Malthus's writing suggesting that he sits rather uncomfortably alongside the arch-exponents of political and economic individualism. We have already noted recent attempts such as those of Wrigley and Schofield to portray Malthus as a theorist who, especially in his later writings, was not inclined to present his ideas as the, or indeed *the only*, demographic model. They depict him as specifying a highly distinctive version of the 'preventive check' which in its operation formed an integral part of a culturally specific family system. It is this little-understood and rarely perceived aspect of Malthus's thinking that suggests he has no ancestral place among household economists of the likes of Gary Becker who blatantly treat family organization as a given rather than as something that has itself to be explained.

MALTHUS ON THE DEMOGRAPHIC EFFECTS OF TRANSFER INCOMES

Whether our inclination is to treat Malthus as if he were the archetypal political and economic individualist who would have no truck with earlier ideas of moral economy, as is believed by many commentators, or whether we see him as a theorist with a more complex and indeed compassionate view

---

[1]In using the term 'methodological individualism' in relation to demography, I am referring to the discipline's implicit rejection of explanations of the phenomena studied by its practitioners unless couched wholly in terms of facts about individuals, conforming thereby to Hobbe's dictum that 'everything is best understood by its constitutive causes' (Hobbes, ed. Molesworth 1839–45, II, xiv). This is essentially the same as Popper's argument (1949, II, 98) that 'all social phenomena and especially the functioning of all social institutions should always be understood as resulting from the decisions, actions, attitudes, etc. of human individuals, and . . . we should never be satisfied by an explanation in terms of so-called "collectivities".'

of society, we have to recognize that he did in his writings confront the demographic influences of collectivist institutions in no uncertain terms. Indeed his consideration of the demographic implications of the Poor Laws forms a backcloth to his 'principles of population' and one to which they are related.

His views had an apparent clarity as presented in the first *Essay* when he wrote,

If men are induced to marry from a prospect of parish provisions with little or no chance of maintaining their families in independence, they are not only unjustly tempted to bring unhappiness and dependence upon themselves and children, but they are tempted, without knowing it, to injure all the same class with themselves. A labourer who marries without being able to support a family may in some respects be considered as an enemy to all his fellow labourers. (Malthus, ed. Flew 1970, p. 98)

A consistency in his ideas on this matter might be assumed from the views he expressed in the article on population for the 1824 Supplement to the *Encyclopaedia Britannica* (issued separately in 1830 as *A Summary View on the Principle of Population*). In this latter work he forcefully argues that, if

the discredit of receiving relief is so diminished as to be practically disregarded, so that many marry with the almost certain prospect of becoming paupers, and the proportion of their numbers to the whole population is in consequence, continually increasing, it is certain that, the partial good attained must be much more than counterbalanced by the general deterioration in the condition of the great mass of the society, and the prospect of its daily growing worse. (Malthus, ed. Flew 1970, p. 270)

On the basis of these remarks, Malthus clearly showed an awareness of fertility as having social consequences that extended beyond the confines of the immediate reproductive unit – the conjugal family; in other words, he is drawing attention to the fact that the reproductive behaviour of individuals in one way or another affects the welfare of other people of a similar social status. In fact, he was addressing issues that in recent years have been reintroduced to demographic discussions through the writings of that currently small band of demographers who are involved with defining the so-called 'institutional' determinants of fertility.

McNicoll (1975, 1980, 1983), to date the leading theorist in this field, has been notable for his attempts to identify the characteristics of local organizational forms likely to induce social incentives and sanctions that would work to encourage demographic restraint. He suggests that, when communities are modest in size, are able to monitor and influence their relations with the outside world and have considerable autonomy in controlling their own affairs, and their inhabitants can at least partially identify their own interests with those of other co-residents, they present characteristics likely to reduce the need for high fertility. For instance, communities able to regulate in-migration can benefit from restrained fertility without fear that their success will be offset by an influx of new entrants; similarly, a community that can transfer unemployment problems to other parts of the society through out-migration will have little incentive to invest in local fertility control. In particular, he argues that the felt need for co-operative effort in addressing mutual problems is likely to be greatest where 'all members have a stake in the village economy' (1980, p. 452). As examples of communities in which social and administrative pressures have been mobilized to advance the collective demographic interest over and above that of family or wider kin-based groups, he has taken up the cases of Tokugawa Japan, China in the 1950s, contemporary Kwantung province, and Bali since the late 1960s. He also presents Bangladesh as a case where dysfunctional social organization marked by the almost total absence of an administrative or political role for hamlets and villages gives an overwhelmingly dominant place for kin and patronage groups that are advantaged by recruitment through high fertility and do not at the same time bear the costs of such behaviour.

Although Malthus apparently viewed social-security systems in which the costs were born by politically constituted groups beyond the confines of the family and household as likely to prove pro-natalist in their effects, his argument holds tenaciously to an age-old belief that the poor possess 'a right to support'. He seems never to have deviated fundamentally from that principle. A young Malthus in 1796 in an unpublished essay, 'The crisis, a view of the present interesting state of Great Britain', took the position that both population and happiness could be augmented by those parts of Pitt's bill which provided for outdoor relief, especially the family-allowance provision. He wrote, 'it is the duty of society to maintain such of its members as are absolutely unable to maintain themselves' (Malthus 1836/1951, p. xxxvi). Indeed, he can be seen displaying an adherence to the classic canonist doctrine, incorporated in the Tudor Poor Law and embodied in that strong sense of reciprocal obligation between the individual and the society of which he or she was a part, which is widely held to be a hallmark of the concept of 'moral economy' that, so a certain school of historians believe, had conditioned the relations between English rulers and those over whom they ruled (Thompson 1971, Hont and Ignatieff 1983). For, in objecting to the suggestion that the elderly should be cared for in the institutionalized environment of the workhouse he argued that 'it seems peculiarly hard upon old people who perhaps have been useful and respectable members of society, and in their day "have done the state some service", that as soon as they are past their work, they should be obliged to quit the village where they have always lived' (Malthus 1836/1951, p. xxxvi).

Almost three decades later similar sentiments remained prominent when he claimed that 'nothing seems to be thought so absolutely intolerable to reasonable beings as the prevalence in the same society of the right of the strongest' (Malthus, ed. Flew 1970, p. 268). However, there is also an ever-present tension in his ideas as they assessed the relative dangers of seeking the appropriate balance between measures likely to instil a sense of independence and those that were needed to insure against unacceptable levels of hardship in the population at large. He believed that 'the best mode of relieving the poor was in assisting them at their own homes and placing out their children as soon as possible in different employments, apprenticeships etc.' but feared the dangers that might flow from such 'interventionist' measures in so far as if 'the poor saw all their children would be thus

provided . . . every employment would presently be overstocked with hands'
(Malthus, ed. Fogarty 1958, II, p. 248).

Where Malthus does differ from many who wrote within the traditional
perspectives on welfare was in the way he identified what he thought was
a threat to the whole welfare system from an 'inappropriate' response by the
recipients of welfare. That is, the form welfare assumed must not destroy
the very possibility of welfare at all. The extent to which this will occur,
Malthus suggests 'depends mainly upon the feelings and habits of the
labouring classes of society and can only be determined by experience'
(Malthus, ed. Flew 1970, p. 269). Whether there is a problem or not will
depend therefore on the specific mental and behavioural characteristics of
the recipient groups – that 'certain morality with respect to the facts of life'
to which Kreager refers in his contribution to the present volume.

As is well known, Malthus's worst fears were reserved for the effects of
subsidizing the wages of the labourer, who he believed as a consequence of
the supplements to his earnings could be seduced into earlier marriage. Of
course, such behaviour would depend greatly on whether it was 'discreditable
to receive parochial relief' and whether 'few or none marry with a certain
prospect of being obliged to have recourse to it' (p. 268). If many did, then
'the partial good attained must be much more than counterbalanced by the
general deterioration in the condition of the great mass of the society' (ibid.).

One should not therefore expect to find in Malthus's writings any
generalizable principle concerning the likely effect of community-organized
wealth transfer on fertility levels in a society in which the age and incidence
of marriage very largely determined the intensity and tempo of child-bearing.
Indeed, it should be noted that most modern scholars interested in the
institutional determinants of fertility have discussed welfare and its likely
anti-natal effects with reference to cultural contexts in which marriage for
women has traditionally been early and very largely universal (McNicoll 1980,
Cain 1982, 1983).

We proceed now to consider the political structures within which transfer
incomes are provided and managed, and the relationship between Malthus's
views on these matters and certain present-day arguments. On the question
of the political units within which people live and the extent to which their
members are able to control their own affairs in ways that might prove
inimical to high fertility, we can detect much that is common to McNicoll
and Malthus. For instance, Malthus expressed the view that the
encouragement of colonial emigration was likely to be a stimulus to fertility
unless it was accompanied by the demolition of the emigrant's houses, so
that they were not available to be occupied by those left behind who might
be encouraged to marry earlier and set up residence in them (*Parliamentary
Papers* 1826–7, qq. 3252–3). Although as a young man he had seen the
settlement laws of the Poor Law as inhibiting the freedom of movement of
individuals who might migrate in their search to be economically self-
sufficient (Malthus, ed. Flew 1970, p. 101) he thought that by discouraging
indiscriminate migration they acted overall to limit the incidence of marriage
in society (James 1979, p. 450). Such a position is not dissimilar to that
advanced by McNicoll and referred to above, on the incentives to high fertility

stemming from the freedom to transfer unemployments to other parts of society. Malthus anticipated further sentiments detectable in McNicoll's recent writing when he suggested that the Poor Laws appeared to 'counteract with one what they encourage with the other', since 'each parish is obliged to maintain *its own poor* it is naturally fearful of increasing their number' (Malthus, ed. Fogarty 1958, II, 58; emphasis added). Of course, much of this concern for controls over labour mobility and the creation or the removal of residential facilities and their supposed impact on the operation of the preventive check to population growth stemmed from the form taken by their local revenue-generating procedures, which gave to local ratepayers the right to be vigilant in administering the system and interfering in the lives of the poor – so much so that Malthus saw the limited scale of the relief to the 'peasantry of England' and the begrudging manner of its distribution by the overseers as a means of deterring 'the more thinking and virtuous part of them from venturing on marriage without some better prospect of maintaining their families than mere parish assistance' (p. 53). Malthus's cautious and indeed rather tentative views on this matter are highly pertinent given the unresolved debate that has been pursued for many years by economic and demographic historians of late-eighteenth- and early-nineteenth-century England on the supposed effects of subsidizing wages upon the marriage behaviour of agricultural labourers (Huzel 1969, 1980, 1984, Levine 1984, Schofield 1985b).

Much, therefore, can be found in parts of Malthus's writing to suggest that he was most definitely not painting an image of society in which human devices of any kind were seen as helpless in the face of a biological necessity that constantly determined social and political arrangements. As Wrigley in his contribution to this volume notes, Malthus constantly found it necessary to call on comparative and historical evidence to support his diagnosis of contemporary problems, potential or actual, and unlike Ricardo was reluctant to proceed to clear-cut theoretical and policy results on the basis of simplified 'strong cases' and deductive reasoning (see von Tunzelmann, this volume). Indeed, he does, contrary to Winch's recent indictment, appear to be a 'sensitive relativist concerned to point out the limitation of general laws' (Collini et al. 1983, p. 70). However, Winch is correct to suggest that Malthus should be seen as the proponent of a view which is eminently 'political' in so far as, at base, his arguments depend upon the virtues of the unique British Constitution, and a view of what developments are likely to threaten the mixture and of how such threats can be best avoided (p. 72). His allegiance to an 'institutional framework' for the analysis of demographic processes and their broader social consequences and determinants would seem to be readily identifiable in his famous rebuke of Ricardo in declaring that 'the science of political economy bears a nearer resemblance to the science of morals and politics than to that of mathematics' (Malthus 1820, p. 1).

ON THE FAMILY AS A GOD-GIVEN STRUCTURE IN MALTHUS'S WRITINGS

In citing Malthus's remarks in the previous sections of this essay we have highlighted his preoccupation with subsidies to family or household economies that took place at a particular phase in the life-cycle – namely, at, or in the months immediately following, the household's formation. His views about other phases in the household's history are less readily detectable and are perhaps less consistently maintained. We have already noted his position on society's obligations to the old as presented in the essay on the 'crisis' and the benefits derived from relieving the poor and removing their un- and under-employed offspring into gainful employment as parish apprentices residing in the households of others. But do we find in Malthus's writings so coherent an understanding of the family over the course of its complete development cycle as we do in his masterful writing on marriage? My view is that as a student of the family Malthus leaves a great deal to be desired.

Where Malthus failed, and one must not underestimate the extent of this shortcoming, was not in his demographic investigations *per se*, which, given the information at his disposal, were exemplary, but in his reluctance to incorporate a large mass of comparable inductive and historical material into his arguments concerning the day-to-day management of the Poor Laws and in the relationship they had historically with the kinship system of his own society.

In many respects, just as in the 'household-economics' approach to fertility behaviour, Malthus's arguments are developed with reference to a family system that is perceived as a God-given structure in no need of explanation. For, in the end, the key question of how family structure and especially intra-familial relations and obligations are determined floats free from his *Essay* in all of its various editions. Such an interpretation would, of course, have been disputed by Malthus and many of his contemporaries, whose conceptions of family structure depended on an appeal to 'laws of nature' depicted as part of God's purpose in designing a universe in which men as individuals would be obliged to exercise their creative energies. Family or kinship rules seem to be equated with God's laws in an effort to deliver the quietus to any prospect of beneficial change in social and political circumstances. As Kreager in his essay in this volume writes, 'nature was . . . often conceived as evidence of the divine plan'.

Malthus says very little about the wider kinship system and confines the bulk of his comments to the 'laws of nature' as they relate to obligatons of men to their wives and children – the conjugal family unit: 'By the laws of nature a child is confided directly and exclusively to the protection of its parents. By the laws of nature, the mother of a child is confided almost as strongly and exclusively to the man who is the father of it' (Malthus, ed. Fogarty 1958, II, 204). As a consequence of these 'laws', which appear, interestingly, to confine the wealth flows of intra-familial support to those between husband and wife and from father to children, it follows, in Malthus's reasoning, 'that if any man chose to marry, without a prospect of being able to support a family, he should have the most perfect liberty to do so' (ibid.). However, it follows too that the hardships and privations flowing from such acts (i.e. marriage without the capacity to support the household so created) fall 'directly and most severely upon the individual who commits the act, and through him, only more remotely and freely, on the society', with the unfortunate but for him inevitable consequences, given his view of the 'moral government of the world', that 'the sins of the fathers should be visited upon the children' (p. 206).

Malthus appears, then, to describe a family system and ideology based fundamentally upon the capacity of the family's individual members ideally to be self-sufficient or on the capacity of its numerically limited household membership to sustain one another. Extra-familial institutions capable of subsidizing the economic well-being of these nucleated family 'cells' are therefore presented as being incompatible with the 'natural' tendencies in these populations. In no sense, therefore, is Malthus inclined to regard the family and the collectivity as integrally related in any positive sense, for both are seen in categorical terms with either entity a potential threat to the well-being or equilibrium of the other.

Such a theoretical stance is not basically dissimilar to that frequently employed by some demographers in their discussions of family patterns and their implications for fertility levels and trends. Change, when it occurs, is seen, for the most part, as deriving from exogenous influences, whether demographic, social or economic in character, that penetrate into the family confine, dissolving its structure while its members assume new postures as, to use Ryder's term (1983, p. 25), 'the inter-generational contract' is renegotiated with changed implications for reproductive behaviour. Such a conceptualization tends, therefore, to treat the kinship system essentially as if it were a dependent variable determined by developments in institutions beyond its own sphere of influence. As such, kinship systems would appear to have no autonomy or only limited capacity to determine, rather than to be determined by, the societies of which they are part.

Conventionally the relationship between nuclear family systems and collectivist arrangements concerning social welfare, a relationship that so exercised Malthus's thinking, is treated in one of two ways. On the one hand, privatized means of wealth accumulation are regarded as a developing feature of the transition to a capitalist mode of economic organization, with the effect of undermining the extended family or the lineage as an integrated unit of consumption, production and social welfare. Such developments are believed to necessitate the emergence of communally organized means of risk devolution which function through the efforts of their managers as a form of social control over highly vulnerable individuals (Lesthaeghe 1980). On the other hand, emerging nation states are portrayed as beginning to offer, through their governmental agencies, services that undermine the functions of the extended family as a provider of such assistance to its members while at the same time promoting new ideologies and allegiances that are at odds with those that individuals might hold with respect to their families and to those institutions that uphold 'family' values (Caldwell 1980). Many arguments contain an amalgam of both these interpretations, and this is especially evident in interpretations of the social functions of institutions sustaining the capitalist welfare state.

In his attempt to establish the social structures that support what he termed the 'starting pattern of reproduction', i.e. a late age and low incidence of female marriage, found to be characteristic of pre-industrial Western Europe,

Ron Lesthaeghe (1980, pp. 531–2) allotted an important role to systems of communally organized welfare and charity, which, in addition to helping to insure individuals and simple or nuclear families against risk, acted as a force for their social control. Lesthaeghe argues that the ruling groups who managed the welfare schemes and charities wished to prevent demographic growth not primarily because of the strains it placed upon the funds but because of the threat a large destitute population might constitute to the legitimacy of the ruling group's hold upon the resources it had appropriated. Prudential and moral restraint would therefore be values inculcated into the society through the promotion (by lay and Church elites) of ideologies that advanced 'individual responsibility', and through the allocation of charitable assistance only to those who deferred to the elite's wishes. Lesthaeghe's arguments would seem to imply that, contrary to the doubts that plagued Malthus throughout his career, systems of social control exercised through institutions such as the English Poor Laws would be an effective means of reducing total fertility, both through brainwashing the populace into accepting a late age of marriage as socially responsible, and through selectively victimizing or punishing those who failed to abide by the moral regulations. Indeed, there are historians who would see the origins of the so-called 'European marriage pattern' in North-western Europe as the direct product of an era in which welfare increasingly was organized on a secular basis in politically constituted communities rather than on an *ad hoc* basis through individual benefactions and random acts on the part of the medieval Church (Stone 1975, Hill 1964). Others view the Christian Church as instilling an ideal of marriage that emphasized both the freedom of choice of the bride and groom on the one hand, and the public scrutiny and approval of their nuptial celebrations on the other, although there are differences of opinion concerning the supposed chronology of these developments (Sheehan 1978, Flandrin 1979).

Lesthaeghe (1980, pp. 532–3) is, however, careful to note that the emphasis on the 'starting'-pattern of fertility cannot itself be explained by the attempts of the wealthy to cause the poor to desist in proliferating. Instead he prefers to regard it as intimately linked with the 'early emergence of the predominantly nuclear family as an independent unit of production'. In fact, the proximate source of control over marriage, Lesthaeghe suggests, is the parental generation which forbids the formation of new households by its children until these new units can be economically self-sufficient but benefits from its children's labour until that point is reached. One is led to suppose that the parents in this approach are agents of the village elite, socializing their children into an acceptance of behaviour that conforms to the desire of that elite.

None the less, despite the possible disclaimer from Lesthaeghe, one might interpret his argument to mean that the depression of marital incidence was indeed an induced phenomenon. Such an argument, through a variant of methodological individualism, seeks the logic of the institution of late marriage as deriving, to use a phrase employed by McNicoll (1983, p. 10), from 'a logic of individual transactions' – in this case, the actions of individuals who had appropriated resources and were the managers of the communal welfare funds.

But McNicoll warns us (ibid.), I believe correctly, that there are dangers in such an approach of over rationalizing the observed patterns to the extent that the institutions are seen simply as induced phenomena possessing no autonomy whatsoever. There is much to recommend his view that 'the belief that institutions are merely the instruments of their leading participants is a sort of conspiracy theory of the world . . . every bit as naïve as the opposite extreme'.

It should be recalled, however, that Lesthaeghe adopted this approach through a dissatisfaction with interpretations of demographic homeostasis that revolved around interpreting behaviour that was concerned with population growth regulation as a target, without exploring the extent to which such feedback systems could be the result of 'short-run goal-setting (conscious rationality) by individuals with respect to the other facts of social life' (1980, p. 530). There is much to be said for this position, although few demographers of pre-industrial West European societies have gone so far as to suggest that late marriage was a strategy adopted by populations with a specific fertility effect in mind. The view is commonly held that late marriage has much to do with a system of nuclear household formation that emphasizes a considerable degree of economic independence for the newly married couple, who reside neo-locally and whose later age at marriage gives them a sort of demographic 'bonus' through the fertility that is consequently lost (Hajnal 1982, pp. 476–81).

THE NUCLEAR FAMILY AND ITS HARDSHIPS

Nuclear families in a regime of late marriage, while creating considerable demographic advantages at the aggregate level in society, do impose very considerable 'hardships' on individuals and individual households (Laslett 1979). For, as Ryder (1983, p. 20) notes, although the nuclear family may be seen as a type of regularized arrangement by which productive adults are committed to caring for young and old dependants, in that task they 'do not suffice'. They fail to balance the resources available with the resources required over time, for in their early stages they have a disproportionate burden of pre-mature dependants, and later a disproportionate burden of post-mature adults.

One can show, for instance, in very approximate terms, by reference to a notional set of age-specific consumption and production profiles, that a nuptiality regime with marriage of both sexes in the middle to late twenties is not an optimal means of dealing with the problem of *direct* support of older generations by their own offspring (especially if these offspring are intent upon forming neo-local and economically 'self-sufficient' households), because the married children will frequently find themselves entering their first family 'deficit' phase between approximately the ages of 35 and 45, reaching their peak family deficits just as their parents were entering their own second 'deficit' period in their late sixties (Smith 1984a).

Likewise it can be seen why such a household formation pattern might lead to the shedding of labour from the natal hearth rather than its retention.

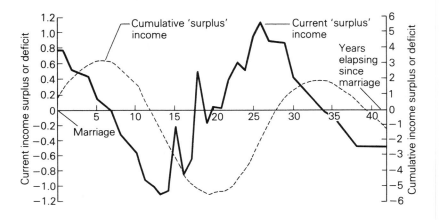

Figure 1   Hypothetical family economy based on its labour production and
consumption (age at marriage 27 and age at leaving home 19)

Note: In the calculation of the family's production–consumption surpluses and deficits over
its life-cycle an individual's production and consumption at any given time is determined as a
function of age and sex and (in the case of women) marital status. An adult male has a surplus
of production to consumption equivalent to +0.97 units until age 54, but not going into deficit
until age 65 years. Married women are assumed never to be in surplus, consuming more than
they produce (−21 units until 55 years and thereafter worsening), in so far as their economic
role is assumed to be largely 'supportive' rather than 'productive' within the family economy.
Children of either sex remain in deficit until age 15, when they begin rapidly to produce more
than they consume. These examples represent only two of a number of 'family economies'
that have been modelled along these relatively simple deterministic lines at the ESRC Cambridge
Group for the History of Population and Social Structure using different marriage ages and
ages of leaving home by Dr R. S. Schofield with the aid of a computer program. The
models rely heavily on age-specific production and consumption profiles originally presented by
Mueller (1976).

For example, in the hypothetical situation in which husband and wife are
both assumed to be 27 at marriage and in which children are born at three
yearly intervals, with no infant and child mortality, and do not begin to leave
home until 19, the household will display an annual excess of consumption
over production at its most severe level in the fourteenth year of existence,
although beginning to produce a surplus of production over consumption
requirements from the fifteenth year (see figure 1). However, if children leave
home at age 10, the household's deficit phase is reduced both in length and
in depth (see figure 2). In fact in such a situation there would only be one
year of cumulative deficiency before the household head reached 69 years
of age, compared with seventeen such years if children stayed with their
parents until their nineteenth year. Of course, such a comparison and the
conclusions we have drawn only have validity if children do not return
earnings to their natal households after departure, and if the accumulated
assets, when eventually liquidated, can be regarded as secure and predictable
for subsequent use in the medium to long term.

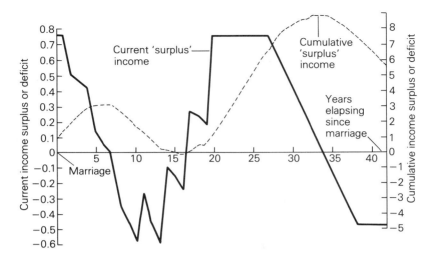

Figure 2 Hypothetical family economy based on its labour production and consumption (age at marriage 27 and age at leaving home 10). For assumptions see note to figure 1

What such patterns possibly suggest is that nuclear-family household-formation patterns cannot adequately be treated in isolation from the society in which they are implanted, for, contrary to Malthus's assumptions, such households will continually encounter difficulties in achieving economic self-sufficiency, even though their formation rules insist that the married couples forming them should be self-sufficient.

As we have seen, Malthus showed some awareness of the problems likely to be faced by the elderly and widows left with young children but reserved his venom for the subsidies utilized to sustain families through their 'first-deficit' phase, most severe among couples in their late thirties and forties, for these were what Malthus saw uncompromisingly as the 'able-bodied poor'.

Furthermore, Malthus concentrated attention on the individual family or household and not on the aggregate patterns of family households and deficits. His adherence to a variant of classical liberalism with all the economic and political liberalism that this entailed made him unwilling to countenance taxation systems that involved redistribution of wealth from families in their surplus phases to those in deficit (Malthus, ed. Fogarty 1958, II, ch. 11; Digby 1983, p. 101). In practice, however, this was to a very considerable extent what the English Poor Law did through its rating-system, in so far as a ratepayer's family situation was very frequently taken into account when rates were exacted; many potential ratepayers, if their property assets alone are considered, were excused payments when their family circumstances were unfavourable to their economic well-being, returning as contributors to the fund when those circumstances improved (Newman Brown 1984). Malthus, as is well known, advocated voluntary personal, rather than institutionalized, savings (taxation) as a means of dealing with the question of individual hardships and periods when incomes failed to meet expenditures. Again we see in this view a desire to confine asset generation and management within self-contained household units.

In practice, many, indeed the majority of, families depended on wealth flows in which those with few family dependants who were economically active gave to those with costly dependants or those who were economically inactive. Such a system was in its operation, therefore, highly susceptible to changes in age structure and associated real incomes within society as a whole rather than in families or households. Indeed, it implies potential competition between the generations for funds raised by the transfers, not so much at the familial but at the broader, aggregate societal level. One might therefore be justified in giving greater attention to the impact of demographic change on the inter-generational competition for communally organized welfare than to the family *per se* (with no intention, it must be emphasized, to treat population as an exogenous variable). In considering this issue historically we should expect there to have been considerable variations both in the practice and in ideologies concerning the roles of individuals, families and extra-familial institutions in the provision of risk insurance and welfare. What is so notable when we do this in an English context (which I shall consider as if it were a representative *par excellence* of the North–west European pattern) is the remarkable consistency in the *extra-familial* locus of welfare institutions, although particular institutional arrangements have varied over time with the source of relief – for example, shifting from manors, guilds and charitable benefactions to parishes, the Poor Law Union and eventually the state itself. Also interesting is the notable constancy in those identified as 'deserving' recipients of community-financed support. The new Poor Law after 1834, in its attempts to distinguish between an able- and non-able-bodied poor, was not fundamentally different from local medieval manorial ordinances that have survived: for example, those relating to rights to glean the fields after harvest, where reeves on royal manors in 1282 were informed 'that the young, the old and those who are decrepit and unable to work shall glean in autumn after the sheaves have been taken away, but those who are able, if they wish to work for wages will not be allowed to glean' (Ault 1972, pp. 29–32). Investigators of social conditions in the nineteenth century have shown a life-cycle of poverty beginning with below-subsistence destitution in childhood, returning in the period after marriage when children had been born but none were working, and finally reappearing in old age (Rowntree 1901, p. 171; see figure 3); these categories of the poor are the same as those identified by pamphleteers and commentators involved in the debate surrounding the legislation for the Tudor Poor Laws (Wales, 1984). Indeed people in these categories loom large as the principal recipients of regular out-door relief in the evidence that survives relating to the administration of the poor throughout the period extending from the sixteenth to the nineteenth centuries.

The limited scholarly discussions of the writings of medieval canonists and decretists in Western Europe concerning the poor shows them to reflect on the part of their authors, an awareness of the potential conflict between the different generations (or demographically distinctive categories of

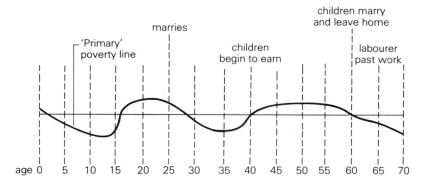

Figure 3 Seebohm-Rowntree's graph (1901, p. 171) portraying the life-cycle of poverty of the British labourer at the beginning of the twentieth century

'deserving' poor) in their claims to the relief funds (Tierney 1958–9). The most perennially relevant of all the canonists' considerations is surely the distinction which they so often draw between the situation that existed when funds were sufficient and that which obtained when the resources available were insufficient to provide for all the needy.

It is worth noting that in England, for instance, the more 'individualistic' or family-oriented solutions for the care of the older generations were proposed (embodied as they were in the 1601 Act, which stated that 'the children of every poor old, blind, lame and impotent person . . . shall at their own charge relieve and maintain such poor person') during the late sixteenth and again in the nineteenth century when the welfare claims on the communal funds were very pressing.[2] Both these periods experienced what by the longer-term standards of English demographic history were high levels of demographic growth (intrinsic growth rates of 0.75–1.5 per cent) with obvious repercussions for age structures. For instance, in the decade prior to the passing of the 1601 Poor Act there were between 850 and 900 children under 14 years of age for every 1000 persons aged 25–59 (see Slack 1984, p. 232, where the increasing attention devoted in late-sixteenth-century poverty surveys or censuses to married couples and their children is noted), while

---

[2]The limited extent to which this legislation was accepted as a basis for popular practice (or perhaps even appreciated) is suggested by Malthus's failure, when writing the first edition of the *Essay*, even to recall that such a statutory obligation remained part of English law, for he remarked that 'In China . . . sons are obliged by law to support their aged and helpless parents' and went on to muse that 'whether such a law would be advisable in this country I will not pretend to determine' (Malthus, ed. Flew 1970, p. 99). Of course this might be interpreted as indicating just how deeply Malthus was imbued with the values of the 'moral economy', which assumed that these were matters for the collectivity rather than the family. In fact the discrepancy between legal theory and customary practice is brought out admirably by evidence relating to the Ampthill Poor Law Union in Bedfordshire, covering an area with about 15,000 inhabitants in 1830. In 1836 over 500 elderly persons were in receipt of a regular weekly pension, but the legal records show only three cases of overseers attempting to enforce maintenance orders on sons for the support of their elderly parents. Indeed, in the 15 years from 1843 no such orders at all are recorded in the court records (see Thomson 1984).

in 1831, close in time to the enactment of the new Poor Law, there were 1086 children for every 1001 such adults. However, the welfare needs in the second half of the seventeenth and the first half of the eighteenth century were much diminished, with generally fewer than 700 children under 14 needing the support of every 1000 adults between 25 and 59 years of age (Wrigley and Schofield 1981, pp. 528–9).

Research into the Poor Law records of communities in Norfolk and Hertfordshire in the late seventeenth century suggests that the bulk of relief was devoted at that date and in an era of very modest 'youthful dependency' to elderly couples and widows on particularly favourable terms and relatively little was devoted to young married couples and their children (Newman Brown 1984, Wales 1984). That this can in no sense be regarded as a 'traditional' pattern of poor-relief is evident from recent research on the Essex village of Ardleigh in the very last years of the eighteenth century, which exemplifies the changed character of requirements by that date.[3] In 1796 the village had a very youthful age structure by the standards of the later seventeenth and early eighteenth centuries; 38 per cent of the population was under 15 years of age. The Ardleigh village listing was drawn up following the severe winter of 1795–6 and the attendant disruption of the agricultural economy and farm workers' wages. When it is realized that this disruption was taking place in the context of relative agricultural underemployment with burgeoning rural labour supplies, it is not surprising to find that married couples with children loomed very large as recipients of relief. In these circumstances the situation of the elderly and especially elderly widows changed compared with the earlier part of the century, since it appears that they had to compete with many others for welfare. It is a striking feature that almost 50 per cent of the Ardleigh paupers listed were children under 15 and that there were no pauper widows whatsoever living alone in that community, for they were to be found in the households of their married children. Of course, we do not know whether residentially independent elderly paupers were discriminated against or forced by the authorities to seek their children's hospitality.

Ardleigh's particular conditions may have been rather extreme but they broadly reflect conditions found more widely in parts of southern and eastern England at the turn of the eighteenth century and with which Malthus was probably reasonably familiar (Williams 1981, pp. 149–50). However, as we have already noted, his usual sensitivity to a need for historical detail failed him, so that he showed an inability to come to terms with the complex, detailed relationship between collectivism and individualism (or perhaps what might be termed a reluctant 'familism') that characterized the social responses to welfare and to insurance against the risks of those in 'hardships' specific to the household-formation system that accompanied the preventive check. What in effect varied over time was the proportional significance of persons at various family life-cycle stages of risk. Such

---

[3]These references to the situation in Ardleigh are based on research in progress by T. Sokoll, Clare Hall, Cambridge, for his Cambridge PhD. Details were presented to a seminar at the ESRC Cambridge Group for the History of Population and Social Structure, 1983.

categories were very sensitive to the demographic growth rates and associated age structures.

These patterns of dependency on communal support were an integral part of the principles of household formation to be found in North-western Europe. Such an interpretation is implicit in the comments of a nineteenth-century correspondent cited by Booth in his report on the aged poor (Anderson 1977, p. 56). The individual concerned noted that the basic problem concerning the feasibility of support for the elderly by their children was 'that the children's own families are costing most just at the time of [greatest parental] need'. There is little reason to suppose similar life-course 'crises' afflicted societies where marriage for females was early and involved their departure from the natal hearth while their brothers married later in their twenties but continued as married men to reside patri-virilocally rather than creating a new co-resident domestic group. Overall savings potential in such systems would be lower than in those possessing a North–west European pattern of household formation, but within individual households parents would be greatly helped in their current income requirements in their fifties and sixties if the marriage of their sons were postponed until 25 or 27, thereby delaying the deficit-forming effects upon the joint family's income of an early arrival of grandchildren from the sons' marriages (Mueller 1976, p. 143).

What much of this discussion suggests is that in certain historic West European contexts the kin group or household is an inadequate unit within which to conduct an investigation of behavioural practices bearing upon fertility. Of course, some of the more widely discussed ideas relating to such behaviour in pretransitional situations have been developed with regard to inter-generational relations and in particular to the directional bias in intra-familial wealth flows that are believed responsible for the absence of family limitation of a parity-dependent kind when it is claimed that the benefits of fertility accrue disproportionately to those who make the reproductive decisions, while the costs are displaced onto those without decision-making power – the women and children. Consequently, it is argued by Caldwell (1982), the leading advocate of this view, that a shift in the balance of inter-generational exchanges, switching the direction of the net transfer of resources away from the old and towards the young, accounts for marital-fertility decline. A connected, but very distinct, argument elaborated by Cain (1979, 1981, 1982, 1983), maintains that fertility remains high where parents, and especially mothers (who have a very high probability of being widowed), are obliged to look to their children to furnish them support and security in old age. Cain, in particular, has addressed the question of the availability of alternatives to children in differing South Asian contexts and has argued impressively for the rationality of high fertility as an insurance against risks when few, if any, attractive alternatives are available in the form of privately or governmentally provided disability and old-age insurance. Moreover, he has argued that the underdeveloped state of financial institutions has in certain contexts militated against the accumulation of assets as a dependable store of value that might be converted into income streams for use in emergencies and especially in old age. The thinness of rural land markets or the insecurity of property rights among petty landholders can also be shown to undermine strategies that might lead to the accumulation of land such as would permit retirement on a rentier's income. Likewise, limited wage-work opportunities outside the ambit of the family tend to limit the risks that children will default on their commitment to their natal household, where the allocation of earnings is not directed towards the satisfaction or remuneration of workers on an individualistic basis.

Such features, whether present wholly or partially in societies, provide their investigators with considerable justification for conducting their inquiries in terms of the negotiation of outcomes between family members that are beneficial either to them as individuals within that kin-based environment or for the group as a whole (Ryder 1983, David and Sundstrom 1984). Many features of pre-industrial North–west European societies, the isolated nature of conjugal family units (within the kin system), the well-developed character of land and labour markets, the existence of reasonably strong state institutions that created a reliable sense of security in the tenure and transmission of property and in particular communally organized and financed systems of welfare provision can be interpreted as generating conditions unlikely to yield what Caldwell has termed 'stable high fertility'.

For instance, when inter-generational transfers from the young to the older generations take place via transfer systems such as those based on communal rating or taxation systems of the kind that sustained the English Poor Law funds, or through the accumulation of financial assets during the 'surplus' phases of the life-cycle and their dissipation during old age, there might be thought to be a divergence between the private and social rate of return to investments in children. In effect, parents pay the costs of rearing their children, but they receive the economic returns from other people's children (a principle that might also apply in part at least to the institution of life-cycle service that was to be found in large parts of North–west Europe until the end of the nineteenth century). In such circumstances it might be supposed that parents' private incentive to invest in the human capital of their own children would be reduced (Willis 1982, p. 277).

ON THE COMMUNAL MANAGEMENT OF RISK AND THE APPARENT LATENESS
OF THE DEMOGRAPHIC TRANSITION IN WESTERN EUROPE

The absence of parity-dependent fertility control in those West European societies which did have well-developed, communally organized security systems which superficially appear to have downgraded the need for children as a source of risk insurance and old-age support has attracted some recent comment. Potter (1983), for instance, expresses the view that such systems took the weight off the nuclear family and served to spread the cost of fertility over the wider community, thereby acting to diminish the economic incentives for couples to control marital fertility. Influenced by Lesthaeghe, Potter argues that, in return for securing resources that they had appropriated, village elites were prepared to maintain pauper households at an acceptable economic standard through a kind of *quid pro quo* which depended greatly on economic, social and especially geographical immobility. Potter argues too (p. 652) that elites, although motivated to control the rate and the pattern of household formation, were concerned to ensure that fertility, once marriages were created, did not fall in such a way as to endanger the adequacy of future local labour supplies.

Potter is therefore drawn to argue that a necessary step in the movement towards marital-fertility control was the dismantling of locally financed welfare systems and the removal of restrictions on the physical mobility of labour in such a way that married couples came to bear a larger share of the costs of their own fertility – something, he believes, that coincided with an increase in the range of economic opportunities. In effect, the simultaneous growth in the perceived cost of children and the relative reduction in the prices of alternatives to them initiated an era in which the incentive to invest in one's children made for a situation in which individual freedom of choice at least allowed an extension of the domain of economic rationality to the phenomenon of reproduction. Such an interpretation Potter would see as compatible with Lesthaeghe's view (1980, p. 537) that the localized system of relief provided a moral code that was remarkably successful in withstanding the potentially disruptive effects of industrialization and urbanization on the authority vested in the elites who paternalistically managed the basic welfare requirements of an increasingly proletarianized society, whose marriage practices were constrained but whose fertility within marriage remained inviolate.

Of course, there are many striking similarities between Potter's position and that of Malthus concerning the pro-natalist effects of the Poor Laws. The same holds for Malthus's later view, already noted, of the beneficial effect of the Settlement Laws in helping to generate wider resort to the preventive check. However, the evidence concerning the marital fertility of those in receipt of relief does not as yet exist in a form that can be said to support Potter's general position (Huzel 1984, Levine 1984). Likewise, the view that the Poor Laws depended for their operation on very low levels of physical mobility fundamentally misunderstands the extent of geographical mobility in early-modern English society. If anything, a very plausible case could be made to suggest that the Settlement Laws acted to reduce the risks associated with labour mobility, as did other aspects of the institutional organization and government management of labour practices and markets (Souden 1981). The coexistence of a mobile labour force with institutions that might be thought to have restrained the geographical movement of labour warns us against too categorical a treatment of individualism and collectivism as principles governing behaviour patterns in pre-industrial West European demographic regimes. Furthermore, Potter's position inclines one to view economic developments as happenings that must be seen separately from welfare facilities, or as processes that might have been adversely affected by their operation.

It could again be argued that such a categorical treatment of these issues is frequently to be found in Malthus's writings. In general Malthus always prefers to interpret England's economic success as occurring in spite of the Poor Laws, or as having provided the economic means to 'bear up so long against this pernicious system' (Malthus, ed. Fogarty 1958, II, 207). Similar sentiments are to be encountered in his remarks concerning Holland's undoubted economic success in the seventeenth and early eighteenth centuries, which Malthus believed allowed her to 'employ and support all who applied for relief' (p. 208). Never is the evidence viewed with an eye to the possibility that causation runs from the poor-relief and the minimization of risk and uncertainty that it entailed to economic success, as well as (or instead of) from economic success to poor-relief.

The relationship between changes in welfare policy and practice in the second half of the nineteenth century and the way it might have related to changing practices likely to have influenced marital-fertility levels is, of course, far more complex than is suggested by Potter's interpretation. Certainly after 1834 the parish-based system of poor-relief was changed to one based on larger units, although it continued to provide out-relief for the non-able-bodied poor. The Settlement Laws remained on the statute books until the mid twentieth century, removed eventually by legislation enacted by the post-war Labour government, although the laws are not widely believed to have had much effect on migration in the nineteenth century (Rose 1976, p. 25). Nor is it clear that the level of migration (although this would require very careful definition) necessarily increased in the course of the nineteenth century. It is, however, true that in the 1870s and 1880s out-relief to the elderly in their own homes was severely reduced; this was combined with attempts on the part of Poor Law authorities to cajole the children of elderly persons into caring for them, and the situation was not alleviated in any fundamental way until 1908, when a state-financed scheme of old-age pensions was introduced (Thomson 1980). The interlude of the 1870s and 1880s might look to some like a shift in welfare policy which would promote higher fertility in so far as it theoretically increased the dependence of parents on children (although it could admittedly have had the opposite effect on the marriage cohorts of those decades).

However, what evidence there is concerning changes in marital fertility by occupational category, especially that available in the 1911 census, would caution us against too ready an acceptance of Potter's views; there would appear to have been no great changes by that date in marital-fertility levels among the principal beneficiaries of welfare institutions, those who by that date might have been bearing the costs of their own fertility decisions more heavily than had their counterparts in the early nineteenth century (Szreter 1983). Such an argument in its cruder form is too ready to assume that children had in the earlier period been produced because of the wealth their parents would receive from the Poor Law funds, rather than that the wealth flow itself was the response to poverty specific to life-cycle stages, requiring community assistance for its alleviation.

CONCLUSION

Lesthaeghe (1980, p. 532) seems to have been on very firm ground when he drew attention to the considerable differences in the way village charity and welfare funds were managed, and their likely demographic repercussions where fertility was very largely determined by what he terms the 'starting'-mechanism of fertility (i.e. nuptiality). Historical demographers have perhaps not given sufficient attention to his important suggestion that the extent of risk-sharing across social-class boundaries might be regarded as a good measure of social integration and that in the more integrated societies the prime role would be performed by the starting-variant of the preventive rather than the positive check. Although historical demographers have dampened their enthusiasm for harvest-induced mortality crises as the equilibrating force in pre-industrial West European populations, there do seem to have been considerable differences in the extent to which they were a factor, and ample evidence survives to suggest that this owed much to differences in the degree of governmental and institutional intervention in the economy during periods of dearth, determining both the stock and the distribution of resources in the event of major deficiencies (Schofield 1983, Appleby 1979, Weir 1984, Lebrun 1980).

Furthermore, institutional structures that facilitated inter-community and regional flows of goods and people varied a great deal and in some cases may well have done much to reduce the virulence of epidemic disease and in the longer term determine the pace at which mortality 'stabilized' over time (Smith 1986). Likewise welfare given on a regular basis in people's homes may have proved a more effective way of maintaining low levels of infant and child mortality than the practice of irregular, sometimes spectacular, shows of gift-making to relatively few people (primarily in the towns or through institutions such as hospitals and foundling-homes, where mortality levels were often, indeed almost invariably, high). Regularized out-relief to mothers and their young children may have indirectly increased the fertility-reducing effects of breast-feeding, by improving infant-survival prospects and by lengthening the non-susceptible period, comparatively much longer in England than in many parts of Western Europe (Wilson 1986, Weir 1982).

In turn this may have been a major factor creating a sluggish tempo in marital fertility in pre-industrial England, which together with the restrained but economically responsive marriage regime produced a modest level of total fertility. Finally, the overall, moderately high level of life expectancy created conditions in which the preventive check became the principal determinant of the intrinsic growth rate. The institutional influences responsible for very considerable differences in pretransitional West European demographic regimes and their relationship to subsequent marital fertility decline would repay far greater attention than they have received to date (Smith 1985a).

Clearly, explanations of much of this demographic variation in the European past will be helped by considering the way in which territorial-based systems of social control functioned to sustain the *status quo* in local resource distributions, although it will not always be a useful, or the only, paradigm within which to consider the dynamics of such regimes. Implicit within the work of two writers, Potter and Lesthaeghe, who have made important contributions to the debate that has dominated this discussion, is the view that the fertility transition in Western Europe is bound up with the passage between two worlds. Individuals somehow escape from a 'sociology world' in which they find themselves entangled within social groups or in the clutches of elite-managed social controls which imposed norms serving to regulate fertility by creating supply constraints in the form of marriage taboos and customs, rather than by influencing practices within marriage. Via 'modernization' these individuals enter an 'economics world' where voluntary, individual goal-seeking behaviour causes fertility to fall, constrained by rational choices between children and other goods (David and Sundstrom 1984). As Ryder (1983, p. 20) has recently remarked,

> there is something at least incomplete if not wrong with a model which denies free will (sociology) just as there is with a model in which free will is the guiding principle (economics). A major element in the complexity of the problem of devising a satisfactory theory of social change consists of finding complementary roles to be played by these contrasting orientations.

Risk, and transfer incomes that provide security against it, can be studied in relation to both present and past West European fertility patterns only with due attention to the area's very distinctive pattern of household formation. One hopes that the recent important growth of interest in such issues and their implications for fertility behaviour in non-European areas will not make scholars too ready to create general theories that fail to take account of similar specificities in other geographical contexts (Smith 1984c). Mead Cain (1985) is one scholar who shows himself to be fully aware of these matters and has written recently that the security value of children in societies where the joint-household system is in place is likely to create considerable resistance to fertility decline until suitable substitutes for children as a source of security emerge.

It would be more instructive to view demographic developments in West European societies, past and present, in terms of the effects they have on the generation of income and expenditure surpluses and deficits specific to individuals at different stages of their own and their family life-cycles than to view them as phenomena themselves caused directly by the way these life-cycle specific risks are managed, although it would be naïve to assume that no causal relationships whatsoever exist in the opposite direction. The current concern with pension funds and their adequacy in an era of unprecedented low fertility is perhaps the converse of some of the worries that Malthus himself reflected in the late eighteenth and early nineteenth centuries in an era of unprecedented high fertility. The debate about the respective roles of kin and collectivity in dealing with these demographically induced social problems proceeds unperturbed as a long-standing feature of English, and indeed West European, political discourse (Smith 1984b).

REFERENCES

Appleby, A. 1979: Grain prices and subsistence crises in England and France 1590–1740. *Journal of Economic History*, 39, 865–87.
Anderson, M. 1977: The impact on the family relationships of the elderly of changes since Victorian times in governmental income-maintenance. In E. Shanas and M. Sussman (eds), *Family, Bureaucracy and the Elderly*, Durham, NC: Duke University Press, pp. 36–59.

Arthur, W. B. 1982: review of G. Becker, *A Treatise on the Family. Population and Development Review*, 8, 393–7.

Ault, W. O. 1972: *Open-field Farming in Medieval England*. London: George Allen and Unwin.

Becker, G. S. 1960: An economic analysis of fertility. In *Demographic and Economic Change in Developed Countries*, Princeton, NJ: National Bureau of Economic Research.

Blaug, M. 1980: *The Methodology of Economics*. Cambridge: Cambridge University Press.

Cain, M. 1979: Class, patriarchy and women's work in Bangladesh. *Population and Development Review*, 5, 405–38.

—— 1981: Risk and insurance: perspectives on fertility and agrarian change in India and Bangladesh. *Population and Development Review*, 7, 435–74.

—— 1982: Perspectives on family and fertility in developing countries. *Population Studies*, 36, 159–75.

—— 1983: Fertility as an adjustment to risk. *Population and Development Review*, 9, 688–702.

—— 1985: The fate of the elderly in South Asia: implications for fertility. Paper prepared for Session F23, the Twentieth General Conference of the International Union for the Scientific Study of Population, 5–12 June, Florence.

Caldwell, J. C. 1980: Mass education as a determinant of the timing of fertility decline. *Population and Development Review*, 6, 225–55.

—— 1982: *Theory of Fertility Decline*. London: Academic Press.

Collini, S., Winch, D., and Burrow, J. 1983: *The Noble Science of Politics: a study in nineteenth-century intellectual history*. Cambridge: Cambridge University Press.

David, P., and Sundstrom, W. A. 1984: *Bargains, Bequests and Births: an essay on intergenerational conflict, reciprocity, and the demand for children in agricultural societies*, Stanford Project on the History of Fertility Control, Working Paper no. 12. Stanford, Calif.: Stanford University.

Digby, A. 1983: Malthus and reform of the Poor Law. In J. Dupâquier, A. Fauve-Chamoux and E. Grebenik (eds), *Malthus Past and Present*, London: Academic Press, pp. 97–110.

Flandrin, J. L. 1979: *Families in Former Times*. Cambridge: Cambridge University Press.

Hajnal, J. 1982: Two kinds of pre-industrial household formation system. *Population and Development Review*, 8, 449–94.

Hill, C. 1964: *Society and Puritanism in Pre-revolutionary England*. London: Secker and Warburg.

Hobbes, T. 1839–45: *The English Works of Thomas Hobbes*, collected and ed. Sir W. Molesworth. London: John Bohn.

Hont, I., and Ignatieff, M. 1983: Needs and justice in the *Wealth of Nations*: an introductory essay. In I. Hont and M. Ignatieff (eds), *Wealth and Virtue: the shaping of political economy in the Scottish Enlightenment*, Cambridge: Cambridge University Press, pp. 1–44.

Huzel, J. P. 1969: Malthus, the Poor Law, and population in early nineteenth-century England. *Economic History Review*, 22, 430–52.

—— 1980: The demographic impact of the old Poor Law: more reflections on Malthus. *Economic History Review*, 33, 367–81.

—— 1984: Reply to David Levine. *Historical Methods*, 17, 21–7.

James, P. 1979: *Population Malthus: his life and times*, London: Routledge and Kegan Paul.

Laslett, P. 1979: Family and collectivity. *Sociology and Social Research*, 63, 432–42.

Lebrun, F. 1980: Les crises démographiques en France aux XVIIe et XVIIIe siècles. *Annales: économies, sociétés, civilisations*, 35, 205–34.

Lee, R. D. 1973: Population of pre-industrial England: an econometric analysis. *Quarterly Journal of Economics*, 87, 581–607.

Lesthaeghe, R. 1980: On the social control of human reproduction. *Population and Development Review*, 6, 527–48.

Levine, D. 1984: Parson Malthus and the Pelican Inn Protocol. *Historical Methods*, 17, 21–7.

McNicoll, G. 1975: Community level population policy: an exploration. *Population and Development Review*, 1, 1–21.

—— 1980: Institutional determinants of fertility change. *Population and Development Review*, 6, 441–62.

—— 1983: *The Nature of Institutional and Community Effects on Demographic Behaviour: an overview.* Centre for Policy Study Working Papers, no. 101. New York: Population Council.

Malthus, T. R. 1820: *Principles of Political Economy Considered with a View to their Practical Application.* London: John Murray.

—— 1836: *Principles of Political Economy Considered with a View to their Practical Application.* London: William Pickering; repr. New York: Augustus M. Kelley, 1951.

—— 1958: *Essay on the Principle of Population*, 2 vols, ed. and intro. M. Fogarty. London: J. M. Dent.

—— 1970: *An Essay on the Principle of Population* and *A Summary View of the Principle of Population*, ed. and intro. A. Flew. Harmondsworth: Penguin.

Mueller, E. 1976: The economic value of children in peasant agriculture. In R. Ridker (ed.), *Population and Development: the search for selective interventions*, Baltimore: Johns Hopkins University Press, pp. 98–153.

Newman Brown, W. 1984: The receipt of poor relief and family situation: Aldenham, Hertfordshire 1630–90. In R. M. Smith (ed.), *Land, Kinship and Life-cycle*, Cambridge: Cambridge University Press, pp. 405–23.

Outhwaite, R. B. 1978: Food crisis in early modern England: patterns of public response. In M. W. Flinn (ed.), *Proceedings of the Seventh International Economic History Conference*, Edinburgh: Edinburgh University Press, pp. 367–74.

Parliamentary Papers 1826–7: *Select Committee on Emigration.*

Popper, K. 1949: *The Open Society and its Enemies*, 2 vols. London: Routledge and Kegan Paul.

Potter, J. E. 1983: Effects of societal and community institutions on fertility. In R. A. Bulatao and R. D. Lee (eds), *Determinants of Fertility in Developing Countries*, vol. II: *Fertility Regulation and Institutional Influences*, London: Academic Press, pp. 648–54.

Rowntree, B. S. 1901: *Poverty: a study of town life.* London: Longman.

Rose, M. E. 1976: Settlement, removal and the new Poor Law. In D. Fraser (ed.), *The New Poor Law in the Nineteenth Century*, London: Macmillan, pp. 25–44.

Ryder, N. B. 1983: Fertility and family structure. In *Fertility and Family*, Proceedings of the UN Expert Meeting, New Delhi: United Nations, pp. 15–33.

Schofield, R. S. 1976: The relationship between demographic structure and environment in pre-industrial Western Europe. In W. Conze (ed.), *Die Sozialgeschichte der Familie in der Neuzeit Europas*, Stuttgart: Ernst Klett, pp. 146–60.

—— 1983: The impact of scarcity and plenty on population change in England, 1541–1871. *Journal of Interdisciplinary History*, 16, 265–91.

—— 1985a: Through a glass darkly: *The Population History of England* as an experiment in history. *Journal of Interdisciplinary History*, 15, 571–93.

—— 1985b: English marriage patterns revisited. *Journal of Family History* 11, 10, 2–20.

Sen, A. 1983: Economics and the family. *Asian Development Review*, 1, 14–26.

Sheehan, M. M. 1978: Choice of marriage partner in the middle ages; development and mode of application of a theory of marriage. *Studies in Medieval and Renaissance History*, 1, 1–34.

Slack, P. 1984: Poverty and social regulation in Elizabeth's England. In C. Haigh (ed.), *The Reign of Elizabeth I*, London: Macmillan.

Smith, R. M. 1984a: Some issues in the family cycle of the propertyless or property-deficient. In R. M. Smith (ed.), *Land, Kinship and Life-cycle*, Cambridge: Cambridge University Press, pp. 68–85.

—— 1984b: The structured dependency of the elderly as a recent development: some sceptical historical thoughts. *Ageing and Society*, 4, 409–28.

—— 1984c: Transactional analysis and the measurement of institutional determinants of fertility: a comparison of communities in present-day Bangladesh and pre-industrial England. Paper presented at the International Union for the Scientific Study of

Population Seminar on Micro-approaches to Demographic Research, Australian National University, Canberra, 3–7 September 1984.

—— 1985a: Variety in the demographic Regimes of pre-industrial Western Europe. In S. Feld and R. Lesthaeghe (eds), *Pre-industrial European Demographic Regimes*, Brussels: Uitgeverij Lannoo for the King Baudouin Foundation, pp. 31–49.

—— 1986: *The Demography of England and her European Neighbours 1500–1750*. London: Macmillan.

Souden, D. C. 1981: Pre-industrial English local migration fields. Unpublished University of Cambridge PhD thesis.

Stone, L. 1975: The rise of the nuclear family in early modern England. In C. Rosenberg (ed.), *The Family in History*, Philadelphia: University of Pennsylvania Press, pp. 13–58.

Szreter, S. 1983: The decline of marital fertility in England and Wales, c. 1870–1914: a critique of the theory of social class differentials through an investigation of its historical origins and an examination of data for the constituent male occupations. Unpublished University of Cambridge PhD thesis.

Thompson, E. P. 1971: The moral economy of the English crowd in the eighteenth century. *Past and Present*, 50, 76–136.

Thomson, D. 1980: Provision for the elderly in England 1831–1908. Unpublished University of Cambridge PhD thesis.

—— 1984: 'I am not my father's keeper': families and the elderly in nineteenth century England. *Law and History Review*, 2, 265–86.

Tierney, B. 1958–9: The decretists and the 'deserving poor'. *Comparative Studies in Society and History*, 1, 360–76.

Wales, T. C. 1984: Poverty, poor relief and the life-cycle; some evidence from seventeenth century Norfolk. In R. M. Smith (ed.), *Land, Kinship and Life-cycle*, Cambridge: Cambridge University Press, pp. 351–422.

Weir, D. R. 1982: *Contraception, infant mortality and breast feeding in rural France 1740–1830*, Stanford Project on the History of Fertility Control, Working Paper no. 9. Stanford, Calif.: Stanford University.

—— 1984: Life under pressure: France and England 1670–1870. *Journal of Economic History*, 44, 27–47.

Williams, K. 1981: *From Pauperism to Poverty*. London: Routledge and Kegan Paul.

Willis, R. J. 1982: The direction of intergenerational transfers and demographic transition: the Caldwell hypothesis reexamined. In Y. Ben-Porath (ed.), *Income Distribution and the Family*, New York: The Population Council, pp. 207–34.

Wilson, C. 1986: The proximate determinants of marital fertility in England, 1600–1799. In L. Bonfield, R. M. Smith, and K. Wrightson (eds), *The World We have Gained*. Oxford: Blackwell.

Wrigley, E. A. 1983: Malthus's model of a pre-industrial economy. In J. Dupâquier, A. Fauve-Chamoux and E. Grebenik (eds), *Malthus Past and Present*, London: Academic Press, pp. 111–24.

—— and Schofield, R. S. 1981: *The Population History of England 1541–1871: a reconstruction*. London: Edward Arnold.

On the Adaptation of Sub-Saharan Systems of Reproduction

R. Lesthaeghe

INTRODUCTION

Ever since Malthus defined the notions of preventive and positive checks, thereby firmly integrating population dynamics in the context of a complex social system, natural and social scientists alike have continued to be fascinated by findings supportive of his views. During the two centuries that followed, historical and cross-cultural comparisons have confirmed that Malthus had indeed defined the core mechanisms that govern the 'moral economies' of agrarian societies: cultural adaptation operating via a normative check on the reproductive capacity creates *simultaneously* a reproductive reserve that can be used if a population is decimated, while it reduces the likelihood of this occurring by bringing population growth well below the level that would prevail if the biological capacity to reproduce were fully released. In other words, Malthus not only provided an explanation of how populations achieved some equilibrium with respect to resources, but he also provided the mechanisms through which the homeostatic feedbacks would operate.

Contemporaneous models need to include many more variables and mechanisms if they are to account for two additional centuries of history. Obviously, the factor of technological innovation has to be introduced, since it makes it possible to break through any older subsistence equilibrium. Then, one has to determine whether technological innovation is a result of a cultural development, an import or the consequence of population growth itself. If the technology factor is attached to the Malthusian subsistence model as such, bridging the gap between the previously linear growth of resources and exponential growth of population, the chances are that the positive checks will weaken while population growth will be continuously sustained. This did not happen in the West: around the time of maximal economic growth during the nineteenth century, virtually all West European populations followed the French example (or, for that matter, the example of their own property-owning classes) and curbed fertility again. This time Condorcet was proved to be right, as this control was achieved with respect to marital fertility itself. Moreover, the marital-fertility transitions often occurred when the older preventive check, namely the late-marriage pattern, was still intact, and when life expectancies had not risen much above fifty years. The net outcome was

212

that these populations discovered that the optimal solution was exactly the opposite of Malthus's doom scenario: everyone would be well off indeed if it is income that rises exponentially while population reverts to slow growth or no growth at all. As a result, the feasible response was a population curve that followed the logistic 'S' shape, as defined by Verhulst only fifty years after Malthus.

From this summary it is clear that demographers have essentially two models to draw from: that of dynamic homeostasis with feedbacks and that of a subsequent demographic transition leading to a new regime. These two models are historically and conceptually connected: one can indeed envisage a scenario whereby the older preventive checks become obsolete as a result of structural changes and are gradually replaced by the new check of contraception. The earlier preventive checks are predominantly enforced through communal controls and are strongly linked to the maintenance of a particular organizational pattern; the new control would rather seem to be a matter of more personal choice and increased calculation of individual advantage.

The move from one system to the other is a complex affair and there is no unique transition pattern. In fact, some may have doubts about the universality of the transition. So far, the record is heavily in favour of the optimists: large Asian and Latin American populations have started the transition, sometimes in a rather spectacular way. Yet, one could hardly claim that the political and moral issues faced by Malthus have become irrelevant. Such a claim would be particularly inappropriate for sub-Saharan Africa, where population growth is currently setting new historical records and where food production has taken a turn for the worse.

In this essay, we shall concentrate on the fertility aspect of the sub-Saharan problem. More specifically, we shall present a summary of the findings that establish a link between the particular nature of sub-Saharan preventive checks on reproduction and various aspects of the ecosystem and forms of social organization. Here, we shall draw heavily on cross-cultural analyses of associations between organizational variables. The aim of this section is to establish the organizational basis from which a transition is supposed to take off. The following sections deal with changes in this system produced by exogenous factors, such as the introduction of cash crops, agricultural and industrial wage labour and migration, the growth of the urban sectors, the expansion of formal education and the cultural influences of Christianity and Islam. More specifically, we shall argue that the reproductive system of black Africa is adapting in an *uneven* way, with some ingredients changing at a rapid pace, while others show a high degree of resistance. The picture is heavily diversified: the original system of reproduction shows cultural–geographic heterogeneity and so does the influence of exogenous factors of economic, social and cultural change. To achieve some clarity, we shall use casuistic and typological methods. The data for this exercise stem largely from the series of censuses and demographic surveys. A more detailed presentation of this material is given elsewhere (Lesthaeghe 1984), but we shall recall the most important features of it.

The last part of the essay contains some speculation about the possible future developments in sub-Saharan reproductive regimes. Then, I shall try to start a broader discussion concerning the inhibiting versus the permissive effects of cultural, organizational and economic developments on the emergence of new forms of adaptive behaviour with respect to fertility.

PRODUCTION, SOCIAL ORGANIZATION AND PROCREATION IN SUB-SAHARAN AGRARIAN SOCIETIES

As the preventive checks are located at the level of the 'intermediate fertility variables', it is essential to understand why some societies rely predominantly on controls on the starting-pattern of fertility (postponement of first sexual unions, celibacy), while others have depended on spacing- or stopping-patterns (e.g. through long post-partum non-susceptible periods, reduced remarriage or early 'terminal' abstinence). An exploration of this differentiation leads inevitably to patterns of kinship organization and further to systems of production and control over resources. At this point, the link can be made between 'production' and 'reproduction'.

Several attempts have been made to establish a list of variables through which the connections operate, and to measure the strength of these associations. In this respect, the Murdock 'Ethnographic Atlas' (Murdock 1967), which gives a relatively detailed (but sometimes questionable) coding of many organizational variables in over 800 societies, has often been used. The comparisons drawn from Murdock's 'atlas' are highly illuminating for understanding the basics of African reproductive regimes. A brief account of the findings is offered here. Note that for the time being we are only dealing with the broad outline and that more detail will be added later.

At the 'production' end of the spectrum, all authors start from the degree of sophistication of agriculture (essentially 'slash and burn' versus intensive cultivation). Yet, already at this point, a major bifurcation occurs, depending on whether the stress is placed on the nutritional and health-related factors or on the social and demographic implications, such as the division of labour between the sexes, simpler forms of social stratification and control, and population density.

The nutrition theory is most clearly followed by J. W. Whiting (1964) and by G. P. Murdock (1967): in tropical climates and most notably in the forest belt, primitive agriculture produces essentially low-protein tubers and fruits, while the presence of the tsetse fly inhibits cattle-raising. A low-protein diet for infants in such societies enhances the need for mothers to breast-feed their children intensively and for a prolonged period, i.e. for many months after the introduction of solid food. As the survival of the infant is dependent on pronounced child-spacing and the maintenance of high prolactin levels in mothers, a post-partum taboo on sexual intercourse during the lactation period is essential. This taboo creates a large social and psychological distance between the spouses. Forms of social organization which enhance such segregation between the sexes are therefore favoured and selected as cultural adaptations to a given ecosystem.

The 'social organization' theory leads into a different causal chain. The starting point for E. Boserup (1970) is the marked association between shifting cultivation and the high input of female agricultural labour, which exceeds that of males by a substantial amount. In such settings, women have only a limited right of support from their husbands, but may sometimes enjoy greater freedom of movement and economic independence. The crucial variable in J.-F. Saucier's hypothesis (1972) is the existence of male gerontocracy and the dominance of unilineal kinship organization. The package of indicators between which Saucier seeks to establish associations on a worldwide scale is expanded to twenty-four propositions. They involve positive relationships between the existence of a long post-partum taboo and factors such as polygny, localized kinship groups, bridewealth and sister exchange, primogeniture, segregation of adolescent boys, duolateral cross-cousin marriage, hereditary headmanship, isolation of wife, genital mutilations, endemic tribal warfare and the existence of a lazy god. In this set, the four best indicators of the taboo were bridewealth (phi = 0.38), swidden agriculture (phi = 0.36), polygyny (phi = 0.35) and physical or psychological separation of spouses (phi = 0.31).

Jack Goody's chain (1976) provides a variant which pivots on what he calls 'diverging devolution' or the diffusion of a person's property *outside* the clan or lineage through bilateral inheritance at death (i.e. also leaving property to wife and daughters) and/or through a dowry at marriage (i.e. leaving property to a son-in-law's household via a daughter). Goody's explanation obviously joins Saucier's in the sense that unilineal kinship organization and the *lack* of 'diverging devolution' of property are strongly connected. In addition, both variables correlate positively with Boserup's female dominance in agricultural production (phi = 0.40).

The relative advantage of Goody's addition, i.e. the tendency to maintain property within a clan, and, for that matter, the lack of *individual* appropriation of land, is that it accounts in a plausible way for a particular feature of the sub-Saharan reproductive regimes. If property belongs to lineages and stays there, there is less need to control partner selection and to engage in a scouting-expedition for a 'good match', and hence also less need for in-marriage, i.e. both endogamy and homogamy. Moreover, if the identification of a good match is not essential, there will be *less control over premarital sex* and *no major distinction between children born in and outside wedlock*. Incidentally, the same factor also explains the lack of prearranged child marriages.

On the other hand, Saucier's factor of gerontocratic control and Boserup's factor of higher female productivity in swidden agriculture account more readily for the high incidence of polygyny ('many wives, many powers' – Clignet 1970) and for fast remarriage following both widowhood and divorce. In other words, gerontocrats control both production factors, i.e. land and female labour, and fend off competition from younger males, who have to 'sit out their time'. This feature accounts furthermore for the fact that *age at marriage for women is fairly early* (shortly after menarche, which, however, can be retarded in some instances, possibly as a result of protein deficiency), while *that of men is much later*. The net result of these patterns of social organization is that sub-Saharan agrarian populations very nearly make an integral use of the overall reproductive age span and *lose little time as a result of celibacy, widowhood or divorce.*

There are, however, two major qualifications. First, polygyny enhances the spread of venereal disease and hence the *incidence of sterility.* This in its turn leads to higher divorce rates and to more polygyny as sub-fecund or sterile women are drawn into polygynous unions as higher-order wives. Second, a very substantial amount of the reproductive age span is not used as a result of *lactational amenorrhoea* and possibly a net bonus of non-susceptibility stemming from *post-partum abstinence.* Among the Yoruba of south-west Nigeria for instance, the total number of person-years lived in the post-partum non-susceptible state very nearly amounts to the total number of person years lived in celibacy under the traditional North-west European regime (Caldwell and Caldwell 1977).

The social organization and nutrition theories most clearly converge when it comes to accounting for the child-spacing feature. Not only is such spacing beneficial for infant and maternal health, but the existence of a sexual taboo during all or part of the lactation period also sustains the organizational pattern in the sense that it prevents 'emotional nuclearization' between the spouses (Caldwell and Caldwell 1977) and strengthens the bond between a woman and her kinship group. It is not uncommon, then, for a woman to depend on her own kin for support, food or shelter during the later months of pregnancy and part of the breast-feeding period.

There is no continent where the prevalence of the social-organizational props of the fertility regime just outlined is as strong as in sub-Saharan Africa. For instance, Goody (1976, p. 12) counts as many as 178 societies in the Murdock file out of the 193 sub-Saharan entries, or 92 per cent, where diverging devolution is lacking. Very much the same holds for polygyny, with 81 per cent (own count for 299 entries). Higher female than male input in farming, with 54 per cent of entries (p. 131) and the long post-partum taboo of twelve months or more, with 55 per cent (Schoenmaeckers et al. 1981, p. 30), have lower scores, partly because of the inclusion of non-agrarian ethnic groups, but their incidence is still far higher in sub-Saharan African than in any other major region of the world (see Saucier 1972, p. 242; or Goody 1976, pp. 12 and 131).

Despite the high significance of the associations, it would be a mistake to consider them as 'monolithic'. On the world wide scale, the highest phi-coefficient between any two variables on the ecological, production, organizational or reproductive checklist discovered by either Saucier or Goody does not exceed 0.42, even after optimalization of the cutting-points used in establishing the contrasting dichotomies. Inspection of the tables, furthermore, hints at the fact that the relationships between X and Y are often asymmetric. For instance, highly polygynous societies often have a sterility problem, but there are also many highly polygynous groups which do not. On the other hand, if sterility is high, there is likely to be a high level of polygyny. This points in the direction of the existence of superseding conditions. Hence, the analysis of a matrix of bivariate asssociations is not adequate and what is needed is a scouting-expedition for interaction variables

Z whose presence or absence strengthens or weakens the association between X and Y.

The second set of problems emerges when dealing with sub-Saharan populations alone, rather than with a worldwide comparison. As already indicated, several variables become so common (e.g. the lack of diverging devolution of property, polygyny, or higher female agricultural productivity) that they lose any discriminating power. Aside from a loss of contrast with respect to crucial predictors, the story becomes much more complex because these societies did not live in a state of isolation. The example of the post-partum taboo documents this point.

If a set of characteristics typical for the patterns of social organization is taken, incorporating those that still show adequate variation, one notices that the varying combinations of such characteristics produce relatively little predictive power. Schoenmaeckers et al. (1981), for instance, used eleven societal features identified by Saucier which ought to lead to the long taboo. They found that the 131 sub-Saharan societies had mostly six to nine of these characteristics, and, more importantly, that the particular combination leading to such a total score had no additional predictive power. Furthermore, the few societies that fell short of a total of six features were about equally divided between societies with a long and those with a shorter taboo. Part of the problem was that the coding of the length of the taboo, both in Murdock's list and in the one used by Schoenmaeckers et al., was often debatable and that the date of the reference was associated with the reported length of the taboo. This points in the direction of a major complicating factor: most African populations have had a long history of symbiosis with other groups (e.g. through migration or military conquest), so that cultural and organizational patterns have always been in a state of flux. Mutual penetration and the emergence of new cultural syntheses presumably produce a substantial number of effects that are not readily sorted out by a simple statistical scanning. The uneven penetration of exogeneous factors during the nineteenth and twentieth centuries has added still more complexity. As a result, it may be useful to leave the smaller ethnic group as a unit of analysis, admit that idiosyncrasies occur at this level which require casuistic explanation, and move on to broader regional variation within the continent. At this point, more extensive statistical information, mostly gathered subsequent to the Second World War, provides additional information.

In the following sections we shall try to kill two birds with one stone. First, the information from demographic sources (censuses and surveys) provides contrast between relatively large regions with respect to their reproductive regimes, and, second, it also provides a first idea of the variation of responses to social, economic and cultural agents of modernization. Four main areas of study are set up, depending on the intermediate fertility variables concerned: (1) the length of the overall exposure period as determined by the formation and dissolution of sexual unions; (2) the child-spacing pattern; (3) the sterility and fecundity problem; and (4) the adoption of contraception.

REGIONAL VARIATIONS IN SUB-SAHARAN REPRODUCTIVE REGIMES

A contrast between traditional sub-Saharan reproductive regimes and those found elsewhere yields some basic insights into the general pattern, but the description of the various sub-patterns within the region and the explanation of this variation are quite different matters. First, there is no convenient demographic counterpart to Murdock's anthropological list: most post-partum variables, for instance, which provide insights on the strength of the preventive checks, can only be obtained from the recent round of surveys by the World Fertility Survey (WFS) or from a few smaller and scattered samples. Second, classic demographic definitions, such as those of 'marriage' or 'marital fertility', are not always easy to apply. Third, measurement error, even after cross-checking via indirect techniques, is considerable, so that, at most, only orders of magnitude are available. Fourth, basic information is missing for large areas (e.g. Ethiopia, southern Sudan, Zambia, Malawi, Mozambique, Zimbabwe, Angola), thereby restricting the detection of further revealing variations. At the time of writing, the WFS information for large populations such as those of Nigeria or the Ivory Coast had not been released, which further hampers the enterprise. Fifth, non-African cultural influences (Christianity, Islam) have changed some older patterns, thereby breaking the links between the organizational variables used in the previous section and the pattern of reproduction. Last but not least, the highly different forms of colonial and post-colonial developments have left additional traces. Hence, all we can do here is to untangle a tiny portion of the variation.

A starting-point can be provided by juxtaposing changes with respect to (1) union formation and dissolution, or, in other terms, with respect to the overall exposure time (starting and stopping; loss of exposure owing to union disruption); and (2) the pattern of child-spacing mainly operating via lactational amenorrhoea and post-partum abstinence. This duality is essential for several reasons. First, as already indicated, the sub-Saharan organizational systems generally favour a maximum exposure span, but correct this via the child-spacing obligation: the two sets of variables act in opposite directions on fertility. Second, the variables delimiting *overall exposure* and those producing *child-spacing may have highly different elasticities with respect to cultural or economic influences*. In other words, differential degrees of resistance or erosion of the overall exposure variables and of the child-spacing ones results in synthesizing new 'uneven' forms of demographic transition. Obviously, if the overall exposure pattern is retained while the spacing ones are weakening, overall fertility must go up, unless a new check is adopted in the form of contraception. To sum up, the following three issues are likely to dominate the discussion on the future patterns of the sub-Saharan fertility transition. (1) Which cultural and organizational factors account for a change or lack of change in the variables of overall exposure? (2) Which factors produce resistance or erosion of the child-spacing tradition? (3) Which factors inhibit or favour the adoption of the new controls via contraception? The current variation with respect to these three clusters of 'dependent variables' will now be described for the major regions of sub-Saharan Africa.

Western and central Sahelian agrarian populations

A first major reproductive pattern (see table 1) is the one found among the western and central Sahelian settled populations (roughly from Senegal to northern Cameroon). This regime is characterized by the highest levels of polygyny encountered on the continent, very early marriage for women, a high incidence of marriage disruption but equally high and rapid remarriage. Among currently married women aged 15–49, 40 per cent or more are commonly found to be living in a polygynous union; 60–80 percent of women aged 15–19 are already married, thereby implying singulate mean ages at marriage (SMAM) of the order of 15.5–17.5 years. Pre-marital fertility, however, is low to moderate, partly because of marriage following so soon after puberty. The percentage of marriages ending in a divorce by age 50 is of the order of 20–30 per cent, but 80 to 90 per cent of all disruptions have already been followed by remarriage prior to that age. Widowhood is also a major factor of union disruption, not only because of high mortality in these least-favoured regions of the continent, but also because of large age gaps between the spouses. Polygyny retards the age at first marriage for men and high union disruption through either divorce or widowhood fuels polygyny. To judge from the WFS data on this record, it seems that these mutually supporting mechanisms are very much intact to date. The lack of any drop in polygyny or of a rise in average age at marriage (see Lesthaeghe 1984, p. 30, for quartiles and median ages at marriage by cohort) is undoubtedly linked with the very high illiteracy levels among females of these Islamized societies (85–100 per cent). But, in addition, the factor of male out-migration to richer areas further south contributes heavily to the maintenance of the system as well (Capron and Kohler 1975). Among the Voltaic groups, for instance, the necessary wealth to acquire a first wife can mainly be obtained from employment in the wage sectors of the Ivory Coast. The sex ratios in the home regions are permanently skewed, which directly favours the gerontocrats who continue to 'monopolize' the younger women. The net results are increasing transaction costs, longer periods of absence of younger single males and no weakening of polygyny. Probably, it would be an exaggeration to claim that male-labour out-migration has considerably exacerbated the situation, but it is not an exaggeration to attribute a supportive function to it.

In contrast to this fairly uniform situation with respect to the overall-exposure variables, much greater variation can be found with respect to the child-spacing ones. This does not apply so much to the average durations of breast-feeding, which seldom fall below 18 months (the average of 17 months in West Senegal is owing to the inclusion of Dakar in the region), as to the average length of the post-partum abstinence period. At the western end of the region, post-partum abstinence has eroded away to less than three months, probably because a majority of women now follow the Quranic prescription of 40 days only, while, further east, abstinence durations of three years are encountered, setting the average to about 20–4 months. In short, the local variation covers the entire width of the sub-Saharan variation.

Table 1 Indicators of marriage, child-spacing and fertility for selected settled populations of the western and central Sahel, 1978 and 1979

	% of single women (15–19)	% of currently married women (15–49) in polygynous households	% of union disruption by age 50	% remarried by age 50	Mean post-partum abstinence (months)	Mean non-susceptible period (months)	% of women with ≥ 10 years exposure having ≤ 2 live births	% of married women (15–49) currently using contraception	Total fertility rate
Senegal 1978									
West (incl. Dakar)	64	45	31	88	±3	12	12	3	7.3
Central	30	50	27	90	±3	14	15	3	7.1
North-east	27	45	31	88	±4	14	16	3	7.2
South	28	54	27	93	±5	15	16	9	6.9
Ghana 1979									
Northern	21	40	14	82	20	21	14	1	6.7
Upper	44	56	13	81	25	26	19	2	5.7
Cameroon 1978									
North	19	44	25	87	11	16	39	0	5.4
Median value	28	45	27	88	too hetero-geneous	15	16	3	6.9

Source: World Fertility Survey.

The fertility impact of this large variation in post-partum abstinence should be properly understood. If breast-feeding is intensive and long – which it is in the Sahelian region – lactational amenorrhoea will be of the order of 11 to 18 months on average. Any period of abstinence, even if only for two months, will lengthen the average duration of non-susceptibility beyond the average duration of lactational amenorrhoea. The magnitude of this 'abstinence bonus' is small (less than 2.5 months) for as long as the mean duration of abstinence is shorter than that of amenorrhoea. In a population with an amenorrhoea average of 14 months, for instance, the abstinence bonus remains small irrespective of whether the mean duration of abstinence is two months or ten months (see Lesthaeghe 1984, pp. 18–19). However, once the mean of abstinence starts exceeding that of lactational amenorrhoea, an accelerated increase of the abstinence bonus occurs. It becomes four months extra non-susceptibility if the excess is two months, and six months bonus if the excess is four months. This feature explains why the non-susceptible periods in Senegalese populations are still of the order of 14–17 months despite the heavy erosion of post-partum abstinence, and why those of Ghana's Northern region are close to the African maximum. In other words, the fall in abstinence durations in Senegal are not accompanied by a comparable fall in non-susceptibility because of the long breast-feeding and amenorrhoea, while, at the other extreme, the intact long post-partum taboo considerably extends the non-susceptible period beyond that of lactational amenorrhoea. Incidentally, male-labour out-migration is again a factor associated with the preservation of the long taboo, if *married* men also spend considerable periods away from home. The case of the Northern Ghanaian populations is well known in this respect.

The outcome at this point is that the populations of the Sahelian region have essentially maintained their marriage regime, which contributes forcefully to maximizing time spent in a sexual union. By African standards, they have also maintained clear patterns of child-spacing, despite the huge variation in abstinence practice. The maintenance of the breast-feeding pattern is essential, given the combination with the early marriage pattern and the virtually complete absence of contraception. Given medium-level sterility and sub-fecundity, implying total fecundity rates (TFRs) of about 13 live births (15–16 is indicative of low prevalence of fertility impairments), the child-spacing effect results in TFR levels of 6.0 to 7.5, which is moderate to high by present African standards. High sterility and sub-fecundity (e.g. in North Cameroon) in combination with this pattern of marriage and spacing lead to TFRs of 5.0 to 6.0, whereas low levels of sub-fecundity and primary sterility can push the TFR to 8.0 (see table 1 for indicators for selected regional populations).

Western and Central Africa

The pattern most closely resembling the western Sahelian one is found among a large number of populations living in Western and Central Africa (probably from Liberia to Angola and stretching inland to the Central African Republic or central Zaire). Many of them are located in the wet savannah or forest

Table 2 Indicators of marriage, child-spacing and fertility for selected West and Central African populations, 1976–9

	% of single women (15–19)	% of currently married women (15–49) in polygynous households	% of union disruption by age 50	% remarried by age 50	Mean post-partum abstinence (months)	Mean non-susceptible period (months)	% of women with ≥ 10 years exposure having ≤ 2 live births	% of married women (15–49) currently using contraception	Total fertility rate
Ghana									
Western	58	34	39	76	8	13	7	7	6.9
Central	64	30	42	67	8	13	15	4	7.1
Greater Accra	78	27	27	78	6	10	20	20	5.2
Eastern	78	27	30	76	10	14	10	16	6.5
Volta	79	43	36	75	17	19	14	15	6.6
Ashanti	71	31	27	61	9	15	12	8	6.1
Brong-Ahafo	64	28	22	68	9	15	8	8	6.6
Cameroon 1978									
Central–South	65	29	26	61	13	14	28	5	6.4
East	45	39	27	76	9	12	30	6	6.5
Littoral	60	28	23	38	13	16	20	2	6.2
North-west	39	45	15	41	19	21	13	1	6.2
West	53	58	18	53	19	22	13	1	7.0
South-west	49	27	22	40	15	16	9	2	6.9
Yaounde	66	23	16	21	10	11	9	9	5.2
Douala	71	23	20	33	10	12	23	10	4.9
Zaire 1976									
rural Bas Zaire	83	17	–	–	+11	15	11	–	7.2
rural Bandundu	76	36	–	–	+8	13	13	–	6.1
rural W. Kasai	63	35	–	–	+8	11	21	–	6.0
Kinshasa (1980)	77	7	–	–	9	14	8	16	7.5
Nigeria 1979									
rural Calabar	51	13	–	–	11	13	9	2	8.7
Togo 1976									
Sud-Est (SE) and Plateau de Dayes (D)	75(D)	28(D)	–	–	8(SE)	17(SE)	12(D)	–	7.1–7.4 (SE) (D)
Median value	66	31	26	61	10	15	13	–	6.6

Sources: World Fertility Survey, Enquête Demographique de l'Ouest de Zaire, Tambashe, Locoh and Adaba, Weiss, Vimard.

belt, have been at least partially Christianized, have levels of female education higher than in the western Sahel, and often benefit to a larger extent from economic modernization. A sizeable portion of them are already living in large cities or participating in urban economies. Long-term and long-distance migration is often converted into a shorter-distance shuttle movement between town and 'home'. Moreover, both sexes participate in such movements – unlike in the western Sahel, where migration mostly involves men. As a result, there is generally much less spousal separation for long periods of time. Last, but not least, these populations are also characterized by a relatively high level of economic independence of women from their husbands, although one should not extend the proverbial example of West African market women, who hold considerable political and economic power, to all women in the region.

As Boserup's factor of high female agrarian and commercial activity, Goody's factor of a lack of diverging devolution of property and Saucier's factor of strong lineage control are all strongly represented in the area, it comes as no surprise to find the classic ingredients of the reproductive regime as well. The previously used indicators are presented in table 2 for this group.

The general pattern is that the West and Central regime is a 'softened' version of the regime encountered further north. Polygyny is still widespread, but often in the range of 25–35 per cent of women aged 15–49. This is 5–15 percentage points short of the Sahelian levels. The classic correlates of less polygyny also emerge. The proportion of single females aged 15–19 is between 50 and 80 per cent, as compared to 20–40 per cent for the western and central Sahel. This defines values of SMAM between 17.5 and 21 years. The pattern continues with respect to union disruption and remarriage: the frequencies of disruption are similar, but the pace of remarriage is slower.

Within the group, there are obviously variations. Some areas come very close to the Sahelian pattern (North-west and West Cameroon). Furthest removed are the province of Bas Zaire and all the major cities (Kinshasa, Greater Accra, Lagos, Douala, Yaounde). The impact of Dakar on later marriage in West Senegal was similarly noticed in table 1.

Although there is little doubt that urbanization and education beyond the primary level for women lead to later marriage, it is not directly evident that rural marriage patterns have changed to a significant degree. We should in fact take account of the fact that there is an improvement in the quality of age-reporting, leading to less age over- or under-reporting in function of marital status. As such, a modest increase in the proportion of single women aged 15–19 may well reflect the reduction of erroneous transfers across age 20 for married and single women respectively. On the whole, genuine rises in SMAM by more than one year are probably rare on a national level and even more rare for rural areas of these countries. Moreover, there are no traces of weakening polygyny either (van de Walle and Kekovole 1984). The overall result is that the nuptiality variables linked with overall exposure are either unaltered (mostly rural areas) or altering as a result of modernization factors such as urbanization and high female education. Given the fact that the bulk of the population is still rural and has not proceeded beyond primary education, the overall changes are modest indeed.

The traditional child-spacing pattern is, generally speaking, best preserved in Western and Central Africa. The post-partum non-susceptible period is about 15 months for the region as a whole and seldom drops below one year (except in some major cities such as Accra or Yaounde). Within the region, abstinence durations vary again. A portion of this variation is of long standing: the Akan groups of Ghana – even in rural areas – are reported as far back as the 1950s to have had abstinence durations of seven to eight months only and they are still at this level. By contrast, the Yoruba of Nigeria and the ethnic groups in the Western Highlands of Cameroon (Bamileke, Bamoun, Banen, Bali) still had abstinence durations in rural areas in excess of 20 months in the late 1970s.

The combinations of nuptiality and child-spacing patterns commonly produce TFRs of between 6.0 and 7.5 children. These values may again be exceded if infertility is low (i.e. with TFRs of 15.0 rather than 12.0–13.5) or marriage on the early side of the distribution (e.g. rural Calabar). Moreover, use of contraception has to be taken into account in several larger urban areas. In this instance the combination of later marriage and contraception may neutralize the effect of less spacing, and TFRs of less than six children can be found (e.g. Accra, Yaounde, Douala, but not Kinshasa).

On the whole, the West and Central region contains numerous examples of populations with only slowly changing reproductive regimes but also cases of much more marked alteration. In the latter instance, urbanization and high female education are the dominant co-variates of such changes in overall exposure and child-spacing. The problem, however, is that these 'internal' changes have opposite effects on overall fertility, and in the balance all three outcomes are possible: no change in overall fertility, a modest decline, or a detectable increase. In other words, from the evidence so far it seems that all three response variables of the reproductive regime (overall exposure and nuptiality, child-spacing, contraception) are indeed reacting to education and urbanization, but that the elasticities are such that the overall impact on the TFRs is nil or very small. Infecundity differentials are thereby allowed to surface.

The Central African sterility regime

The region comprising north-west Zaire, south-west Sudan, the Central African Republic, Congo, Gabon, Equational Guinea, parts of Cameroon and southern Chad stands out on the African fertility map of the 1950s as having TFR levels that fall below five live births. The major reason for this was the very high proportion of childlessness (25–50 per cent after ten years of exposure) and the high proportion of women with low parities. A detailed description of the medical pathology and the dramatic social consequences can be found in Retel-Laurentin (1974, 1975) and Frank (1983). The gist of the problem was the positive feedback between polygyny, the spread of venereal disease, infertility or sub-fecundity, divorce and a further increase in polygyny through which such large proportions of the population were inflicted with the curse of primary or early secondary sterility.

Since the 1950s, however, substantial improvements have taken place at least among the Zairean regions. Cohorts born between 1900 and 1925 in Tshuapa and Equateur (Cuvette Centrale, mainly Mongo) had childnessness levels (no live births) of 35–45 per cent. This was gradually reduced, from the cohorts of 1925–35 onward, to 10 per cent among women born between 1942 and 1947. The problem also existed in the Kinshasa region, with 35 per cent childlessness for the cohorts born prior to 1915, but the decline set in much earlier and reached the 10 per cent level for the cohorts of 1927–32. In Cameroon as a whole, the cohorts who are presently 50–4 years old (born 1918–23) had 27 per cent childnessness, and the figure drops to 10 per cent ten years later. In the regions with high infertility, however (North and Central–South), the change starts from a slightly higher level of 30 per cent (women married 30 + years in 1978) and occurs more slowly: in Central–South, the 10 per cent mark is crossed for those married 10–14 years in 1978, but in the North the most recent cohort figure is still 18 per cent (see Lesthaeghe 1984, pp. 75–7). For the other countries involved, we have no figures pertaining to the amplitude of the decline. In terms of cross-sections, rather than cohorts, these figures still imply that TFRs in the 1960s and 1970s did not exceed ten live births (ten in Congo Brazzaville 1974; nine in North Cameroon 1978, Equateur 1976 and central Chad 1964; and eight in Tshuapa 1976 and southern Chad 1964). However, the fact that women currently below age 30 are considerably less affected also means that fertility levels are increasing markedly. The TFRs for Equateur and Tshuapa, for instance, have risen from about four to six live births between 1956 and 1976. Moreover, post-partum abstinence had probably declined in these regions during the high infertility period and is not currently being restored. Also early ages at first marriage are maintained. This implies that increases in TFR that go well beyond six live births are very likely to be occurring in the 1980s. These populations are hence catching up with the remainder of the Central African pattern, but with an early-marriage–reduced-spacing variant.

The eastern Sahel

Data for the eastern Sahel are limited to the provinces of northern Sudan and the region around the Somalian capital. However, from the indicators reported in table 3, striking contrasts with the western Sahel emerge. First, the age at marriage in the east is much higher. Proportions of women still single in the age group 15–19 are all above 70 per cent, thereby defining SMAM values of 19.5 or more. The difference in SMAM from the western Sahel, then, amounts to 2.5–4.0 years. Second, at similar levels of marital disruption, remarriage is much slower in the eastern than in the western Sahel. Third, at durations of post-partum abstinence which are slightly longer than those in Senegal, northern Sudanese populations have shorter durations of breast-feeding and, in the absence of any abstinence bonus, shorter durations of overall non-susceptibility. In fact, the non-susceptible period already falls short of one year.

The most remarkable finding of the Sudanese fertility survey of 1979 was undoubtedly the recent rise in age at marriage. The first quartile value is

Table 3 Indicators of marriage, child-spacing and fertility for selected populations of the eastern Sahel, 1979–80

	% of single women (15–19)	% of currently married women (15–49) in polygynous households	% of union disruption by age 50	% remarried by age 50	Mean post-partum abstinence (months)	Mean non-susceptible period (months)	% of women with ≥ 10 years exposure having ≤ 2 live births	% of married women (15–49) currently using contraception	Total fertility rate
Sudan									
Khartoum	84	0	13	62	5	9	16	20	4.9
North and Nile	83	32	24	45	5	11	15	3	5.4
Kassala and Red Sea	75	4	14	45	6	10	13	3	6.0
Gezira, Black and White Nile	79	27	17	51	6	10	13	8	6.6
Kordofan	79	28	19	68	6	11	13	3	5.9
Darfur	70	43	20	78	7	12	22	2	6.3
Somalia 1980									
Benadir, Bay and Lower Shebelle (settled population)	72	–	–	–	–	9	20	1	7.1

Sources: World Fertility Survey, and Central Statistical Department, Mogadishu.

currently 17.9 for women aged 15–19; it was 13.4–14.3 for women currently aged 25 +. The pattern also holds with respect to the median, which rose from 16.0 among women aged 30 + to 18.6 among those in the age group 20–4. No other WFS data set for sub-Saharan Africa shows shifts of such magnitude. The responsiveness of the nuptiality pattern in the northern Sudan is all the more remarkable given the low levels of literacy of the female population and the high degree of Islamization.

East African regimes

The variable that most clearly discriminates between Eastern Africa and Western or Central Africa is the low duration of post-partum abstinence. In Kenya, it is reduced below six months in virtually every single region and ethnic group (see table 4), and from the Tanzanian national demographic survey of 1973, in which qualitative appreciations were collected from informants, it also appeared that post-partum abstinence had been greatly reduced, probably also to durations below six months. This information agrees with the findings of Molnos (1973), who interviewed anthropologists living with a large variety of East African ethnic groups, including those of Uganda. Further checking by Schoenmaeckers et al. (1981) on the basis of older anthropological records revealed that the duration of the post-partum taboo may have varied considerably at the outset, but also that the current levels could only have been reached as a result of a *universal* decline. The lack of a long post-partum taboo stretches further west to the lacustrine populations of the Kivu (Zaire), Rwanda and Burundi (Schoenmaeckers et al., 1981). Occasional references are, however, made to coitus interruptus during the lactation period (Molnos 1973).

The net outcome of the abstinence decline is that child-spacing rests exclusively on lactational amenorrhoea. East African values recorded so far (Kenya and lacustrine populations) show that the non-susceptible periods fall short of the Central and West African ones by about four to five months on average.

All other indicators for East African populations, by contrast, show a high degree of internal heterogeneity. This is particularly true for age at first marriage for women and for the incidence of sterility and sub-fecundity. Furthermore, variations in these two variables account for striking regional differences with respect to fertility levels: TFR values range from a low of about five live births in several Tanzanian areas to the African maximum of 8.8 in Kenya's Rift Valley.

The proportion of single women aged 15–19 ranges from just over 40 to nearly 90 per cent, thereby defining SMAM values between 17.5 and 22 years. A pattern of very late marriage is found in densely settled agrarian zones such as those of Rwanda and Burundi, the Kenyan Central Highlands and the Kilimanjaro district of Tanzania (proportions single at least 80 per cent). High percentages are also found in several other areas, such as Kenya's Eastern, Rift Valley and Western provinces (proportions single at least 70 per cent). At the other end of the distribution, early-marriage patterns are found in Tanzania (14 districts out of 19) and among the Mijikenda of the Kenyan

Table 4 Indicators of marriage, child-spacing and fertility for selected East African populations, 1970–8

	% of single women (15–49)	% of currently married women (15–49) in polygynous households	% of union disruption by age 50	% remarried by age 50	Mean post-partum abstinence (months)	Mean non-susceptible period (months)	% of women with ≥ 10 years exposure having ≤ 2 live births	% of married women (15–49) currently using contraception	Total fertility rate
Rwanda 1970	82	15	–	–	–	11	15	2	7.7
Burundi 1970–1	88	–	–	–	5	11	13	2	5.9
Kenya 1977–8									
Nairobi	67	22	13	29	4	9	9	6	6.1
Central	88	13	15	31	3	11	7	5	8.6
Coast	53	33	26	64	3	12	18	3	6.5
Nyanza	65	42	13	61	3	12	11	1	8.0
Rift Valley	72	25	11	20	6	13	7	1	8.8
Western	72	38	21	69	3	11	10	2	8.3
Eastern	89	24	20	56	4	12	8	6	8.2
Tanzania 1973									
Tanga	68	27	–	–	–	–	18	–	7.0
Coast	61	21	–	–	–	–	36	–	5.1
Dar Es Salaam	47	13	–	–	–	–	43	–	4.7
Morogoro	56	21	–	–	–	–	33	–	6.0
Lindi	50	29	–	–	–	–	42	–	5.1
Mtwara	47	32	–	–	–	–	29	–	5.2
Ruvuma	51	37	–	–	–	–	18	–	6.4
Arusha	59	24	–	–	–	–	22	–	6.5
Kilimanjaro	80	14	–	–	–	–	15	–	7.0
Singida	53	34	–	–	–	–	37	–	5.5
Dodoma	53	24	–	–	–	–	20	–	6.7
Mara	42	30	–	–	–	–	30	–	6.9
Shinyanga	52	16	–	–	–	–	35	–	6.4
Mwanza	53	21	–	–	–	–	31	–	6.6
West Lake	55	28	–	–	–	–	31	–	6.8
Tabora	55	25	–	–	–	–	36	–	5.4
Kigoma	61	42	–	–	–	–	27	–	5.9
Iringa	64	45	–	–	–	–	15	–	6.9
Mbeya	51	37	–	–	–	–	19	–	7.1
Median values	61	25	(15)	(43)	(4)	(11)	19	(2)	6.6

Sources: World Fertility Survey; Bureau of Statistics and Bureau of Resource Assessment and Land Use Planning (Dar Es Salaam); Enquête Démographique (Bujumbura); Bureau National de Recensement (Kigali).

Coast province (proportions single less than 60 per cent). Polygyny levels vary considerably as well, partially along the lines already indicated by the variation in age at first marriage: the areas with high population density tend to have polygyny levels below 20 per cent (Rwanda/Hutu, 15; Central province Kenya/Kikuyu, 13; Kilimanjaro/Chagga, 14). At the other extreme, some areas have polygyny levels reminiscent of the western Sahel (Nyanza, 42; Kigoma, 42, Iringa, 45). Between these two tails of the distribution, the classic inverse relationship between polygyny levels and age at first marriage is not so obvious. Judging from the limited information for Kenya, the expected positive correlation between polygyny and the intensity of remarriage is present: the highly polygynous societies of Lake Bassin (Western and Nyanza) and of the Coast province all have remarriage intensities of 60 per cent or more by age 50. By comparison, this remarriage percentage drops to 31 per cent in the Central Highlands (Kikuyu) and to as low as 20 per cent in the ethnically mixed Rift Valley.

The regional and ethnic contrasts with respect to nuptiality patterns are obviously of long standing and a substantial portion of the current variation is not attributable to recent socio-economic change. Yet, modernization variables such as increased female education have affected regions and ethnic groups in a highly differential way. In Kenya at least, it seems that older contrasts have been strengthened rather than weakened by educational development. The groups who benefited most from female education, such as the Kikuyu, Meru-Embu and Kamba, were the ones that probably had the latest marriage pattern anyway, while those who benefited least, such as the Muslim Mijikenda in the Coast province, presumably had the earlier marriage pattern at the outset.

Taking Kenya as a whole, the tendency is toward later marriage: the data from three censuses (1962, 1969 and 1979) show a steady increase in SMAM from 18.5 to just over 20 years. This trend is essentially confirmed by the Kenyan fertility survey of 1977–8: the retrospectively reported ages at first marriage by the successive cohorts show a noticeable increase in the median age for women aged 20–4 (18.7 versus ± 17.5 for older women).

Aside from this rather recent development in age at first union, the most remarkable feature is probably the resistance of polygyny. Here, the three Kenyan censuses show hardly any change at all (van de Walle and Kekovole 1984) with polygyny ratios (number of married women per 100 married men) of 120–130. Converted to our measure of currently married women aged 15–49 in polygynous households (for empirical conversion table, see Lesthaeghe 1984, p. 146) these ratios imply polygyny percentages of 30–9, which agrees with the findings of the Kenyan fertility survey (30 per cent of currently married women 15–49 in polygynous households).

The sterility and sub-fecundity levels in Eastern Africa show impressive variation. From the information available in table 4, it seems that in general there is a contrast between Kenya and Tanzania, with higher sterility along the coasts of the two countries a long-standing feature. Compared with Central Africa, sterility levels in East Africa in the 1950s and 1960s were generally more modest (± 20 per cent childlessness as against 35–45 per cent), but plots of childlessness by cohort indicate that there was no systematic fall

Table 5 Indicators of marriage, child-spacing and fertility for selected Southern African labour-exporting populations, 1971–7

	% of single women (15–19)	% of currently married women (15–49) in polygynous households	% of union disruption by age 50	% remarried by age 50	Mean post-partum abstinence (months)	Mean non-susceptible period (months)	% of women with ≥ 10 years exposure having ≤ 2 live births	% of married women (15–49) currently using contraception	Total fertility rate
Lesotho 1977									
Lowlands	74	8	15	20	15	17	20	8	5.3
Foothills	64	8	14	19	15	17	20	4	5.9
Orange River Valley	63	8	14	14	17	18	17	1	6.3
Mountains	63	8	17	20	16	17	20	3	6.0
Botswana 1971	87	–	–	–	–	–	–	–	6.5
Swaziland 1976	–	–	–	–	–	–	17	–	6.9

Sources: World Fertility Survey; Central Statistical Office (Gaberone); Central Statistical Office (Mbabane).

prior to 1973 (Lesthaeghe 1984, p. 75). By that time, the trend for sterility levels in Central Africa was already firmly downward. The latest census of Tanzania, however, indicates an improvement in the situation (Ewbank, personal communication). Whether such a decline in fertility impairment is currently producing a net fertility increase depends of course on the recent path of the other intermediate variables, but, judging from the low TFR values in many regions of Tanzania in 1978, and from the relatively early starting-pattern of procreation in these areas, there seems to be ample room for such an overall fertility increase during the 1980s.

Southern African labour-exporting regimes

Roughly a third of the total labour force of Botswana, nearly a quarter of that of Lesotho and a tenth of that of Swaziland are employed in the Republic of South Africa (Cobbe 1983). The percentages for the *homelands* are probably higher still. As male labour exports far exceed female, very skewed sex ratios are produced. In Lesotho, for instance, this ratio is about 170 women per 100 men in the age group 15–49.

Unlike the labour-exporting populations of the western Sahel, those of Southern Africa do not fall back on polygyny as an adaptive mechanism. For, as far as is known from older anthropological references, polygyny was never widespread in these populations, and at present less than 10 per cent of married women aged 15–49 are found in polygynous households. Instead, Southern African labour-exporting areas have large numbers of female-headed households. Aside from the lack of polygyny, another institutional factor intervenes: inheritance tends to follow the rule of male primogeniture, implying that males with few productive assets are heavily selected for out-migration (in Lesotho, soil erosion contributes to the scarcity of productive assets as well). This implies that female-headed households are strongly concentrated at the lower end of the income distribution and, in addition, that the lack of capital diminishes the productivity of labour of women and children in such households (Kossoudji and Mueller 1981).

The lack of polygyny and the skewed sex ratio combine to produce a relatively late age at first marriage: SMAM values in Lesotho are not below 18.5 and in Botswana around 21.0. The overall reproductive span is shortened further as a result of high widowhood and relatively high divorce which is not rapidly followed by remarriage. In Lesotho, the percentage remarried by age 50 following a union disruption is only 20 per cent or less, as compared to 80–95 per cent in the western Sahelian labour-exporting populations (see tables 5 and 1). Furthermore, in Lesotho about 12 per cent of the reproductive span following first marriage is lost as a result of time spent in widowhood and divorce. This is the highest percentage of all those produced by African WFS data.

The absence of males and polygyny has a major impact on child-spacing as well. Under 'normal' circumstances, the populations of these areas do not have a long post-partum taboo, but the Lesotho fertility survey of 1977 produces a mean duration of post-partum abstinence of 15–17 months and a very large average abstinence bonus between six and eight extra months of non-susceptibility (mean of abstinence less mean of lactational amenorrhoea, four to seven months). Obviously, such a feature is produced by the 'facilitating' circumstance of husbands being absent. The outcome is that the overall non-susceptible period increases to levels of 17–18 months, which is well above the East African values and even above those of many Western and Central African populations.

Relatively late marriage, a high proportion of time lost due to widowhood and divorce not directly followed by remarriage, and a long post-partum non-susceptible period coupled to fairly low proportions of childlessness (± 5 per cent) produce overall fertility levels that are on the low side by African standards. The TFR values for Lesotho are between 5.3 and 6.3, while the estimate for Botswana is about 6.5. Swaziland is believed to have a slightly higher TFR of nearly 7.0 live births and this could be owing to less male-labour out-migration and hence to less loss of exposure.

THE FIRST PHASE IN THE MODERNIZATION OF REPRODUCTIVE REGIMES

Older descriptions of the fertility transition relied rather heavily on trends with respect to marital or overall fertility and missed earlier adaptations of the various components of the reproductive regime, for as long as these produced no net fertility decline. The more recent upsurge of interest in the proximate determinants has corrected this view by illustrating that several populations pass through a first phase during which the onset of the transition is visible through the components of overall exposure and child-spacing.

The information collected in recent demographic surveys in sub-Saharan Africa has further substantiated the existence of such a first phase. In Lagos in 1976, for example, there was no apparent difference in TFRs between illiterate women and those with secondary or higher education, but there were very striking contrasts in the combinations of intermediate variables that produced identical TFRs (Lesthaeghe et al. 1981, p. 174). The comparisons were repeated with WFS data. In Ghana, Lesotho, Kenya and Cameroon, a drop in the TFR only occurs for women with at least some secondary education. Much of this reduction is owing to a rise in age at first marriage for such (atypical) women (Lesthaeghe 1984, p. 116). For all other women, differences in intermediate variables kept each other in check.

Also regional data of African WFS countries were considered. Here, the elasticities of age at first marriage, length of the post-partum non-susceptible period and current use of contraception with respect to provincial levels of female literacy were such that compensation took place up to a literacy level of no less than 70 per cent (Ghana, Kenya, Cameroon). In other words, there was no reduction in the TFR unless literacy levels were reached typical for these nations' capitals. If regional differences in total fertility were introduced as well, the pattern became even more striking: TFR values *rose* as provincial literacy increased from a low of 10–30 per cent among women aged 15–49 to intermediate levels of 35–55 per cent. Clearly, the pattern of reduced spacing coupled with less infertility was no longer compensated by more contraception and later marriage (Lesthaeghe 1984, p. 114).

The last example pertains to the combined effects of *individual* and *contextual* levels of education in the provinces of Kenya. Here, it was noted that five years extra individual schooling produced a *rise* in lifetime fertility in virtually all settings, controlling for individual marriage duration and age. Moreover, this individual impact of schooling produced more of an increase in lifetime fertility in the lower-educated zones of each province than in the more highly educated zones. It was solely in the better-educated sample clusters of Nairobi that the impact of personal education on lifetime fertility was negative. This pattern of interaction between individual and contextual levels of education with respect to overall fertility was checked against the pattern for non-susceptibility and contraception. The interaction emerged again: in the sample clusters with low average education in each of the Kenyan provinces (excluding Nairobi), five years of personal education led to a drop in the length of the non-susceptible period which was not matched by a sufficient increase in contraception. In the better-educated areas and in Nairobi, there was sufficient compensation (Lesthaeghe 1984, pp. 131–5). Closer inspection of the composition of the population in the various educational strata revealed, furthermore, that a rise in contextual education was often accompanied by an increase in ethnic heterogeneity, and that there already existed a possibility of a net overall fertility decline in typically urban melting-pot situations. The striking finding by Gaisie, who repeated the exercise for Ghana, was precisely that increasing education produces a net fertility-lowering effect *only* in better-educated zones of regions *with* such ethnic mixes (Greater Accra and Eastern province), and not in regions with similar aggregate levels of education, but with ethnically homogeneous populations (e.g. better-educated clusters located in Ashanti, Brong-Ahafo, Volta, Western and Central provinces) (see Lesthaeghe 1984, p. 131).

The first phase corresponds essentially with a weakening of the old preventive checks (here, child-spacing) which is not fully matched by new checks. These new checks would ideally take the form of later marriage and greater use of contraception. The only places so far where these new checks have risen to greater prominence are some of the large urban concentrations with ethnically mixed populations. The rest of sub-Saharan Africa still firmly exhibits the features typical of the first phase only, leading to horizontal or upward trends in overall fertility.

PROSPECTS FOR THE SECOND PHASE OF THE FERTILITY TRANSITION

There are several indications of a delay in the emergence of the second phase of the transition, i.e. the phase characterized by falling marital and overall fertility. These indications pertain to possible changes with respect to fertility components themselves, such as child-spacing and infertility, and to aspects of social organization and modernization.

First, there is still ample room for a more substantial drop in the length of the non-susceptible period. As shown earlier, many populations have already lost the benefit of the abstinence bonus and are currently relying solely on lactational amenorrhoea to achieve the spacing-pattern. If lactation intensities and durations continue to decline, thereby reducing the non-susceptible period from 16 months to only eight, the prevalence of contraception would have to increase from 5 per cent to 29 per cent among currently married women by the year 2000 in order to prevent a net marital-fertility increase. The highest figure for use of contraception so far encountered in the WFS data set is 20 per cent in Greater Accra and Khartoum. If a modest reduction of marital fertility of 10 per cent is to be achieved by the year 2000, the prevalence of contraception would have to rise to 15 per cent if the non-susceptible period is to remain at 16 months, but to 37 per cent if it is to decline to eight months (Bongaarts et al. 1984). A 20 per cent decline in total marital fertility by 2000 would require a rise in use of contraception to 26 and 45 per cent respectively. These calculations clearly show that the start of the second phase of the transition requires a revolution in the use of contraception if the length of the non-susceptible period is to fall. Hence, speculations about the future course of fertility in Africa hinge not only on prospective levels of contraception, but equally on the prospects for a further weakening of the old props of child-spacing.

The second element that leads to a prolonged period of stable or increasing fertility is a reduction in sterility and sub-fecundity. This reduction is essential, as it is difficult to imagine how a fertility transition could start in highly pathological situations. For the 1970s and 1980s, however, the likely outcome of a decline in the prevalence of fertility impairment in Central and Eastern Africa is a net fertility increase from TFR levels of about five to six live births to seven or eight.

Aside from these two considerations, there are also numerous features in the domains of culture, social organization and patterns of economic change that may act as brakes on the onset of the second phase.

As already indicated, there is, for instance, no evidence of a weakening of the custom of polygyny, contrary to what was expected by several Western sociologists. This implies not only that patterns of kinship organization and of partner exchange are robust, but also that a forceful prop of early marriage and of maximized exposure continues to operate in most parts of the continent. Considerable rises of age at first marriage are, then, more difficult to envisage. This argument is strengthened for as long as female schooling-levels are still far short of the point of incompatibility between early marriage and secondary education. This does not imply that rises in the mean age at marriage are excluded, but means only that there is at present little scope for the sort of rises in rural areas that would decisively contribute to an overall lowering of the TFR. Instead, rises in mean age at marriage are more likely simply to contain a fertility increase produced by less child-spacing or reduced infecundity.

Powerful impeding factors exist with respect to contraception. First, short- and long-term utilities of children are still considerable and are likely to continue to tip the balance in favour of a high demand for children, even when child costs are increasing. Second, the cultural barrier to forms of contraception which are conceived as 'tampering with nature' is not likely to be lifted in areas where female schooling-levels are low or where there has been a sub-fecundity problem. Third, family-planning programme effort is extremely low even in African countries with relatively high national income. Maternal and child health family-planning clinics are often swamped by more urgent medical interventions, and the geographical distribution of such facilities is heavily skewed in favour of urban areas. Moreover, a system based on national family-planning councils suffers from the inadequacies generally applicable to state intervention in Africa.

A legitimate question is whether there are *local* institutional frameworks which could fulfil a function in this respect. Christian churches, for instance, which are already running schools and health facilities and often have a good record in community mobilization, would seem to be a prime candidate. Moreover, non-appliance methods of contraception have been neglected. 'Natural' methods have advantages in situations where the next *child* is welcome, almost by definition, but where the next *pregnancy* is felt to be a burden if it occurs too soon. Such methods, furthermore, do not interfere with lactation as do the presently available forms of hormonal contraception, they have no alarming side effects, and greater use of them could, despite lower effectiveness, still boost *overall use effectiveness*. Last but not least, even Catholic organizations can be motivated to pay attention to such methods, which is of major importance in regions such as Rwanda where the Catholic Church controls virtually every community service and where population pressure is undeniable.

Other impediments stem from the unequal demand of the different sexes for children, and in many African situations that gap is very substantial, especially when it comes to stopping. Finally, the feature of male-labour migration is continuing to produce traditional responses. Both the western and central Sahel and the labour-exporting economies around South Africa provide examples of this: very long abstinence combined with spousal separation, enhanced polygyny, women heavily relying on children as their major productive assets, and hence low levels of contraception.

The existence of such powerful impediments does not imply that much of Africa will not make it to the second phase of the transition. There are, I think, also important mechanisms acting to facilitate contraception.

First, the effect of female schooling is cumulative: the positive effect of personal education (say, five years of primary education) on current use of contraception is amplified in regions with higher contextual levels of education, i.e. in regions which for historical reasons have already built a tradition of female schooling. This effect is clearly noticeable not only in the WFS data for Kenya and Ghana (see Lesthaeghe 1984, pp. 125–7), but also in those for Senegal, which has much lower levels of female education (Sarr, personal communication). There is a subsequent amplifier: slightly higher use of contraception within the community weakens the adverse effect of older social control mechanisms, so that the growth of contraception can accelerate. In short, high dams too can burst.

Second, migration to urban areas generally favours the adoption of contraception. This, combined with the pattern of close contacts between kin residing in urban areas and those in rural districts, may produce a geographic diffusion pattern, especially if the sending areas have better-than-average educational levels. Third, costs of child-rearing are rapidly increasing, partially as a result of price increases in basic goods such as food, clothing and school materials, and partially because of increased aspirations. If, in addition, child survival is slowly increasing, large numbers of women will be facing family sizes exceeding seven children, especially if they have had a record of poor spacing. The balance between marginal costs and utilities for such *high parity* children may therefore decisively change in favour of earlier stopping, in which case *also* the appropriate stopping-types of contraceptives should be more widely available.

Finally, governmental views on the issue of family limitation are currently changing in the appropriate direction, as younger elites realize that the older prop of child-spacing is weakening and that it is going to be exceedingly difficult to keep up with a population growth rate of 2.5–4.0 per cent. Whether this is likely to be translated into an increase in official programme effort and efficiency is, however, another matter. But a major advantage of the new climate may be that other organizations and the private sector will no longer be stigmatized for activities in this field.

At this point, it is clearly impossible to predict when the overall fertility decline will begin, but it would be very surprising if it should happen without considerable regional differentiation. Personally, I should not be surprised if the surveys scheduled for the late 1980s revealed the first drop in fertility and an increase in current use of contraception above the 20 per cent level in certain rural areas with good access to major urban centres. Candidates would be the southern regions of the Ivory Coast and Ghana, south-west Nigeria, Bas Zaire, the Gezira or the three central provinces of Kenya (Central, Rift Valley and Eastern). However, whether changes in such areas would produce a point of inflexion in the fertility trend for sub-Saharan Africa as a whole by the end of the 1980s is highly questionable.

CONCLUSIONS

Two issues that figured prominently on Malthus's agenda were the abandonment of 'moral restraint' and the possibility of a widening gap between population growth and food production. Nobody today can deny that Malthus's formulation of the problem constitutes an adequate description of the present challenges for sub-Saharan Africa: the weakening of the traditional props of child-spacing, the spurt in population growth and the decline in agricultural output for reasons other than climatic ones are all fully documented. Although we have replaced Malthusian doom by the optimism of the demographic transition model, we must still temper this optimism: sub-Saharan Africa does not *currently* exemplify the Boserup–Simon types of technological adaptation generated by population pressure, nor is it a region where one can safely assume that 'positive checks' will not emerge. Droughts, or conflicts with an ethnic–economic undercurrent, serve to remind us of the fact that the two positive checks, out-migration and mortality, are slumbering just beneath the surface. For them to remain there, a variety of conditions must be fulfilled, *one of which*, in my view, is indeed the need for greater fertility control.

This, however, implies that a new strategy is required with respect to family planning: methods have to be more supportive of spacing *without* interfering with lactation: non-appliance methods need to be propagated as viable complements to 'medication'; and local institutional bases must play a far greater role, in collaboration with governmental intervention. Moreover, one must recognize that the chances of fertility limitation succeeding are highly diversified by region: those with most assets have a much higher likelihood of being receptive than those that are trailing with respect to socio-economic development. The contrast between regions that make the transition to greater reliance on the new preventive checks (contraception, later marriage) and those that do not is therefore expected to sharpen.

REFERENCES

References to the numerous statistical sources are given in Lesthaeghe (1984).

Bongaarts, J., and Potter, R. 1983: *Fertility, Biology and Behaviour*. London: Academic Press.
—— Frank, O., and Lesthaeghe, R. 1984: The proximate determinants of fertility in sub-Saharan Africa. *Population and Development Review*, 10, 511–37.
Boserup, E. 1970: *Women's Role in Economic Development*. London: Allen and Unwin.
—— 1981: *Population and Technology*. Oxford: Basil Blackwell.
Caldwell, J. C., and Caldwell, P. 1977: The role of marital sexual abstinence in determining fertility: a study of the Yoruba in Nigeria. *Population Studies*, 31 (2), 193–217.
Capron, J., and Kohler, J. M. 1975: *Migrations de travail et pratique matrimoniale – migrations à partir du pays Mossi*. Ouagadougou: Organisation de Recherches Scientifiques et Techniques d'Outre Mer, mimeo.
Caraël, M. 1981: Child-spacing, ecology and nutrition in the Kivu province of Zaire. In H. J. Page and R. Lesthaeghe (eds), *Child-spacing in Tropical Africa: traditions and change*, London: Academic Press, pp. 275–86.
Clignet, R. 1975: *Many Wives, Many Powers*. Evanston: University of Illinois Press.
Cobbe, J. 1983: Emigration and development in Southern Africa, with special reference to Lesotho. *International Migration Review*, 17, 837–68.
Frank, O. 1983: *Infertility in Sub-Saharan Africa*, Center for Policy Studies, Working Paper no. 97. New York: The Population Council.
Goody, J. 1976: *Production and Reproduction: a comparative study of the domestic domain*. Cambridge: Cambridge University Press.
Kossoudji, S., and Mueller, E. 1981: *The Economic and Demographic Status of Female Headed Households in Rural Botswana*, Population Studies Center. Working Paper no. 81-10. Ann Arbor: University of Michigan.
Lesthaeghe, R. 1984: *Fertility and its Proximate Determinants in Sub-Saharan Africa: the record of the 1960s and 70s*. Paper presented to International Union for the Scientific Study of Population Committee on Comparative Analysis of Fertility and Family Planning, Seminar on Integrating Proximate Determinants into the Analysis of Fertility Levels and Trends, Brussels: Vrije Universiteit, IPD Working Paper 1984-2.
—— Page, H., Adegbola, O. 1981: Child-spacing and fertility in Lagos. In H. J. Page and R. Lesthaeghe (eds), *Child-spacing in Tropical Africa: traditions and change*, London: Academic Press. pp. 151–72.
Molnos, A. 1973: *Cultural Source Materials for Population Planning in East Africa*. Nairobi: Institute of African Studies, University of Nairobi.
Murdock, G. P. 1967: Postpartum sex taboos. *Paideuma*, 13, 143–7.
—— 1967: Ethnographic atlas: a summary. *Ethnology*, 6 (2), 109–234.

238 R. Lesthaeghe

Retel-Laurentin, A. 1974: *Infécondité en Afrique Noire: maladies et conséquences sociales*. Paris: Editions Masson.
—— 1975: *Infécondité et maladies: les Nzakara*. Paris: Institut National de la Statistique et des Études Économiques.
Saucier, J. F. 1972: Correlates of the long taboo: a cross-cultural study. *Current Anthropology*, 13 (2), 238–49.
Schoenmaeckers, R., Shah, I. H., Lesthaeghe, R., Tambashe, O. 1981: The child-spacing tradition and the postpartum taboo in tropical Africa: anthropological evidence. In H. J. Page and R. Lesthaeghe (eds), *Child-spacing in Tropical Africa: traditions and change*, London: Academic Press, pp. 25–71.
Van de Walle, E., and Kekovole, J. 1984: *The Recent Evolution of African Marriage and Polygyny*. Paper presented at the Annual Meeting of the Population Association of America, Minneapolis, mimeo.
Verhulst, P. F. 1844: *Recherches mathématiques sur l'accroissement de la population*. Brussels: Académie Royale des Sciences, des Lettres et des Beaux-arts de Belgique.
Whiting, J. W. M. 1964: Effects of climate on certain cultural practices. In W. H. Goodenough (ed.), *Explorations in Cultural Anthropology*, New York: McGraw-Hill, pp. 511–44.

Shifts in the Determinants of Fertility in the Developing World: Environmental, Technical, Economic and Cultural Factors

Ester Boserup

In all societies in which they were strongly motivated to do so, parents and rulers have attempted to influence fertility. Because child mortality was high until recently, the desire was often to obtain higher fertility by prayers and sacrifices, social pressure, early and universal marriage, tax advantages for large families, and so on. But in many societies there were periods in which large population groups attempted to limit family size or space births by folk methods of fertility control or infanticide. The idea that parents in pre-industrial societies always aimed at maximum family size is unrealistic. In the developing countries, in which fertility has been declining rapidly, family control by folk methods seems to have been widely applied before modern contraceptive means and family-planning services became available. Although some parents with relatively weak motivation for control may first have begun to restrict fertility when better methods came within their reach, experience shows that the operation of family-planning services has mainly led to replacement of one method by another and better one (UN 1983). Therefore, a focal point in fertility theory is to determine the factors which may induce parents and governments to restrict fertility.

Throughout history the desire to seek security in numbers seems to have been the predominant motive for large family size. Rulers were preoccupied with defence and with the number of subjects who could be taxed, and parents wanted large families for physical protection and economic survival. At early stages of development, individual families or kin groups are left to provide their own physical security and economic support, and the parent generation depends upon the strength of the new generation for support in old age. The techniques of production and organization of work allow children to make a significant contribution from a young age. Such conditions do still exist in peripheral regions of some developing countries. In such regions rural families are largely subsistence producers with small sales of agricultural products or labour, and with little or no protection and support from government services. Child mortality is high and average family size smaller than desired, except for rich men in polygamous marriages. However, in most parts

239

of the developing world subsistence production and labour investments in kind have been replaced by production for sale and monetized private and public investment, either as an indigenous process or as a result of colonization and neo-colonization.

This process of specialization of agricultural and non-agricultural production is accompanied by the appearance and growth of occupations such as transport, trade, urban construction, and educational services designed to train the specialized labour force. As specialization proceeds, the share of subsistence producers in the population declines, and some family members or whole families take up new informal sector activities or become members of the modern-sector labour force (Boserup 1970). These changes have important effects on family organization and desired family size, especially in cases when women as well as men replace or supplement subsistence production with money-earning activities.

The process of specialization does not only move production of consumption and investment goods from the family to specialized enterprises: many services previously performed by family members for each other also become specialized, and are taken over by private enterprises or public institutions and services. Among these are educational, health and other social services, which gradually replace family training and family care, and police, courts, army and other areas of government administration, which replace family discipline and tribal defence. Also these changes strip the family of functions and create and expand specialized occupations, of which many employ a highly trained labour force of men and women, who have motivations for keeping their families smaller than those of other occupational groups. By these changes, the family loses not only functions but also power. When the government provides protection against physical and economic risks, family members become less dependent upon help from each other, and the government acquires more and more power over the family. By means of economic regulations, criminal law, compulsory education, marriage regulations, and in many other ways, the government becomes able either to reinforce the power of the family head over other family members, or to limit this power, giving women and youth more liberty or more security. Such changes have important effects on duration of marriage, age of marriage and fertility in marriage.

OCCUPATIONAL DISTRIBUTION AND FERTILITY

Motivation for family restriction is much stronger for people working in the modern sector than for those in the informal sector. The labour force in the modern sector consists of government staff, members of the professions, and salary- and wage-earners in large industries and large construction, trade, transport and service enterprises, while the labour force in the informal sector mainly consists of self-employed workers and workers in small family enterprises, which produce goods and services for the market. Usually some of the personnel in the modern sector benefit from some limited social security, even in those developing countries at low stages of economic development. This means that they are less dependent upon family help than are people in the informal sector, who rarely have access to any sort of social security, except perhaps some health services. Moreover, enterprises in the modern sector do not use child labour, while children perform many jobs in the informal sector, working with their parents, or for wages, or on their own. Thus, in the modern sector, dependence upon adult children for security in emergencies and old age, and help also from smaller children provide little, if any, motivation for large family size. In the informal sector, there is more motivation for having a large family, but, even when children are active in the urban informal sector, there is often more motivation for limitation of family size in this sector than among people in rural areas, because in towns at least a part of the childrens' food must be purchased. Families who live in metropolitan areas or other large cities must buy all food for their children, while many inhabitants of smaller towns produce most of their own food, often with help from the children.

In some developing countries wives and children of men who work in the modern sector may add to the family income by self-employment or by operating small family enterprises in the informal sector, so the inducement to reduction in family size is smaller. But often men in the modern sector prefer to have non-working wives, and children who qualify for modern-sector employment by school attendance. Families in which the male head works in the modern sector are also likely to live in rented flats, which with a large family would be either very crowded or extremely expensive, while families in which the family head works in the informal sector often live in self-built slum housing and pay little or no rent (Loza 1981).

The World Fertility Survey produced some information about differences in total marital fertility by husband's occupation, which is reproduced in table 1 (Alam 1984). The fertility differences by occupation are large. In twenty out of twenty-eight countries there is a difference of 1.0–4.5 children between the group with lowest and the group with highest fertility. The exceptions with small fertility differentials are African or Moslem countries. The persons in the lowest-fertility group (group 1) belong to the modern sector, are educated and largely urban, usually have their children educated and non-working, often have some social-security or property income, and rarely live in subsistence housing. These living-conditions explain why their fertility is lower than that of the other groups.

Some of the families in groups 2 and 3 share some of these conditions with group 1, but they usually have somewhat higher marital fertility than group 1, because of different age composition, lower marriage age or less fertility restriction. The highest fertility levels are usually in the agricultural group, in which the statistics unfortunately fail to distinguish between landless workers and members of cultivator families.

Decline of fertility may occur either because the families within a particular occupational group get more extra-familial security or reduce their dependence upon child labour, or because development is accompanied by shifts of population from occupational groups with little to groups with more motivation for fertility control. In many developing countries, a large share of the population is on the move from higher- to lower-fertility occupations

Table 1   Total marital fertility rates by occupation of husband, for women aged 15–49

Technology group	Country	Professional, managerial technical and clerical (1)	Sales and service (2)	Manual work (3)	Agricultural work (4)
		Husband's occupation			
1	Nepal	5.6	6.7	7.3	7.3
1	Bangladesh	7.0	7.1	6.7	7.0
1	Haiti	5.4	6.9	7.1	8.5
1	Senegal	8.6	7.9	8.5	8.2
2	Pakistan	7.6	7.9	8.2	7.8
2	Indonesia	6.9	6.9	7.0	5.9
2	Sudan	7.0	8.1	8.4	8.7
2	Kenya	10.1	10.1	9.9	9.8
2	Ghana	7.2	8.0	8.5	8.2
2	Lesotho	8.8	8.0	7.4	7.5
3	Malaysia	7.3	7.7	8.3	8.6
3	Thailand	5.8	6.7	7.1	8.0
3	Sri Lanka	6.7	7.4	7.1	7.2
3	Philippines	7.7	7.9	8.9	9.5
3	Paraguay	5.5	6.2	6.8	9.5
3	Peru	7.8	8.3	9.1	10.2
3	Dominican R.	5.4	7.2	7.2	9.8
3	Jordan	9.4	10.7	11.0	11.8
3	Syria	10.0	9.6	10.7	11.6
4	Korea R.	7.5	6.4	6.9	8.3
4	Guyana	5.5	6.6	7.1	8.2
4	Venezuela	6.2	10.4	7.6	7.5
4	Jamaica	4.9	5.6	6.7	7.8
4	Trinidad T.	3.8	4.4	5.2	6.5
4	Columbia	5.7	6.5	7.0	9.8
4	Mexico	7.6	8.7	9.4	10.1
4	Panama	4.1	4.5	4.4	6.1
4	Costa Rica	3.7	4.4	4.1	5.1

Source: Alam and Casterline (1984).

with more motivation for family restriction than their parents' occupations provided. A dynamic process of fertility decline is set in motion when economic development both increases family size by reducing child mortality and promotes major changes in the occupational distribution of the population. Some groups with motivation for relatively small family size will begin to use folk methods of contraception when their family size becomes larger than expected, or when they move to an occupation with more motivation for restriction, or from rural to urban areas without change of occupation.

Table 2 gives an impression of the differences in occupational distribution of the adult male population in countries at different stages of development.

Table 2   Occupational distribution of adult male population in 39 countries around 1960

Occupation	Technology group (% of adult men aged 15+)				
	1	2	3	4	5
Professional, administrative and clerical staff	–	4	6	11	16
Employees in production, trade, transport	–	9	13	24	38
Owners and family labour in production, trade, transport	–	10	8	9	6
Services and casual labour	–	6	8	9	6
Total non-agricultural labour force	–	29	35	53	65
Agricultural workers	–	8	17	14	4
Owners, tenants, family labour in agriculture	–	54	40	24	10
Outside the labour force (including students, army personnel, old people)	–	9	8	9	21
Total adult men	–	100	100	100	100
Number of countries included	0	5	15	10	9
Number of countries in group	26	26	26	26	26

Source: Boserup (1970, tables 31–64), and national statistics.

The stage of development is measured by indicators and not by per-capita gross national product, in order to avoid distortions due to changes in terms of trade and exchange-rate problems. The indicators are energy consumption, representing technological levels in production, construction and transport; number of telephones, representing levels of communication; life expectancy at birth, representing health technology and quality of food supply; and adult literacy, representing levels of skills and know-how. These indicators are given equal weights. For details of classification, and the countries belonging to each group, see Boserup (1981). The first two occupational groups in the table include mainly male modern-sector personnel, the next two mainly the male labour force in the informal sector. In the countries at the lowest level of economic development, white-collar workers accounted only for 4 per cent and the whole of the modern sector for only 13 per cent of adult men, while, in the developing countries at the most advanced level, i.e. in technology group 4, white-collar workers accounted for 11 per cent and the modern sector for more than one third of adult men. Quite obviously, many more people were motivated to restrict family size in the more advanced developing countries. But these still fall far short of the industrialized countries, which had 16 per cent of adult men in the white-collar group and 54 per cent in the modern sector, to which should be added a much larger group of adult students than in developing countries. Moreover, even in the most advanced developing countries, families benefited less from social-security systems than families in the same occupational group in

Table 3 Total fertility rates 1975 and 1981 by region and technological level

Region	Years	Technology group (unweighted averages)						Technology group (no. of countries)					
		1	2	3	4	5	Total	1	2	3	4	5	Total
Africa south of Sahara	1975	6.3	6.3	6.6	5.6	–	6.3	18	14	1	1	–	34
	1981	6.5	6.7	8.0	5.1	–	6.6						
South and East Asia and Oceania	1975	6.5	6.0	5.7	3.3	2.7	5.1	4	5	5	3	3	20
	1981	6.5	5.2	4.2	2.3	1.9	4.3						
Arab Region	1975	7.2	7.2	6.7	5.7	–	6.6	1	1	11	3	–	16
	1981	6.6	7.0	6.5	4.4	–	6.1						
America	1975	4.9	6.2	6.5	4.6	2.3	5.1	1	1	8	12	2	24
	1981	4.7	6.0	5.4	3.5	1.9	4.1						
Europe	1975	–	–	–	3.0	2.3	2.4	–	–	–	5	20	25
	1981	–	–	–	2.6	1.9	2.0						
World	1975	6.3	6.3	6.4	4.3	2.3	5.1	24	21	25	24	25	119
	1981	6.5	6.3	5.8	3.3	1.9	4.7						

Source: World Bank, *World Development Report 1978*, table 15, and *1983*, table 20. For classification of countries by technology group, see Boserup (1981, appendix table, pp. 214–15).

industrialized countries, and so were more dependent upon family support, or property.

Most occupational shifts are from occupations with lower to occupations with higher income, but it is important to note that it is the occupational shift and not the increase of income which motivates a reduction of fertility. Income increases unaccompanied by occupational changes are unlikely to lead to reduced fertility, and occupational shifts to a lower income group are unlikely to lead to higher fertility even if the new occupation is one which normally motivates higher family size than the previous occupation does.

Information about marital-fertility differences by occupation are only available for a limited number of countries, but inter-country and regional differences in total fertility rates are published annually by the World Bank. Since fertility levels and changes are dependent upon the stage of development reached by the country, comparisons are only meaningful for countries at similar stages of development. It can be seen from table 3 that fertility differences between industrialized countries are insignificant, but there are large regional fertility differences among the developing countries. The African and Arab regions have the highest fertility levels, with two to three more children than Asian and Latin American countries at similar levels of development. Fertility decline is also smaller between 1975 and 1981 in the Arab region, and fertility in Africa seems to be increasing (Tabutin 1984; Lesthaeghe this volume). Some of the changes reflected in table 3 are probably owing to revisions of earlier estimates for 1975, rather than estimated changes between 1975 and 1981 (World Bank 1978, 1983). The higher fertility levels in the Arab world are related to the lack of security for women in this region. In nearly all countries married women have less security than men, because, in addition to the risks of life which they must share with their male provider, they are less economically self-reliant than men and are therefore in a more difficult position if their spouse dies or abandons them. Women in the Arab world are even more dependent upon the male members of their families – husbands, fathers, brothers and sons – than women elsewhere. Both legislation and custom discriminate against women, and prejudice against their participation in the labour market is stronger than elsewhere. Divorce is easily obtained by men, or repudiation and abandonment are legal (Allman 1978). Dissolution of marriage and widowhood are far worse for women in societies in which there is no room for women in the labour market except as beggars and prostitutes than it is in societies where large numbers of women, illiterates as well as educated, are part of the labour force. The more secluded the labour market, the more women are limited to domestic work in their own home, and the larger the insecurity of married, and also of unmarried, women (Cain et al. 1979).

Risk of divorce, repudiation and abandonment is largest for sterile women, and women without sons. Therefore, in societies where they have no option in the labour market, women have a very strong motivation to have as many children as possible and to discriminate in favour of their sons with care and food (Chen et al. 1981, Miller 1981). They are motivated to avoid spacing of children in order to increase the chance that their sons will survive to support them when they are old, widowed or deserted. The extremely low

Table 4 Adult female non-agricultural labour force in 39 countries around 1960

Region and sector	Technology group (% of adult women)					Technology group (women as % of occupation)					Number of countries included
	1	2	3	4	5	1	2	3	4	5	
Africa south of Sahara											
modern sector	–	1	–	–	–	–	9	–	–	–	3
informal sector	–	9	–	–	–	–	29	–	–	–	
South and East Asia and Oceania											
modern sector	–	1	4	12	21	–	6	20	23	28	11
informal sector	–	4	7	7	9	–	18	31	30	44	
Arab region											
modern sector	–	–	2	–	–	–	–	10	–	–	6
informal sector	–	–	2	–	–	–	–	11	–	–	
America											
modern sector	–	–	5	8	22	–	–	23	28	30	14
informal sector	–	–	11	13	7	–	–	50	43	44	
Europe											
modern sector	–	–	–	–	18	–	–	–	–	28	5
informal sector	–	–	–	–	10	–	–	–	–	46	
Number of countries included	0	5	15	10	9	0	5	15	10	9	39
Number of countries in group	26	26	26	26	26	26	26	26	26	26	130

Source: Boserup (1970, table 28), and national statistics.

level of labour-force participation of Arab women around 1960 is shown in table 4. In the group with middle-level technology, in which comparison with other regions is possible, only 2 per cent of adult Arab women were employed in the modern sector, against 4–6 per cent of Asian and Latin American women. Most of these women were probably young unmarried girls, so the employment of married women was lower still. Even worse from the point of view of economic security for women, the share of Arab women in the informal sector was equally low, while three to six times more Asian and Latin American women worked in the informal sector, which is the one sector open to women with little or no education or professional qualifications. It is also the sector where women with responsibility for children have a chance to support their family, or earn an income, which makes them less dependent upon male family members (Boserup 1970). In some Moslem countries outside the Arab region, for instance in Pakistan and Bangladesh, women's status is also low and their access to the labour market very low (Cain et al 1979, Miller 1981). Also in such countries fertility is high, and in northern India, more influenced by Arab culture than southern India, fertility is higher than in the south (Dyson and Moore 1983), although the level of development is higher.

AGRICULTURAL SYSTEMS AND FERTILITY

Property-owners are less dependent upon help from family members than people without property, and this is important in regions in which a large share of the population is of small and middle-sized landowners. If child labour is little used in such regions, there is little economic motivation for the landowners to have a large family. In emergencies, they can obtain credit by giving security in land; in old age, they can cultivate their land with hired labour, or rent it out. A generation effect may also operate in favour of smaller families if sons who inherit a small share of the family land want to avoid further sub-division in the next generation (Poffenberger 1983). Many dry regions of India, which afford little motivation for large family size, (Vlassoff and Vlassoff 1980, Cain 1982), provide examples of landowning families with lower fertility than landless families in the same area, and studies of other countries have found the same (Stokes et al. 1984).

In order to understand the often complicated relations between land-ownership and fertility, it is necessary to distinguish between different agricultural systems, which provide different motivations for family size. The agricultural system which is used in an area is related to the population density. Areas with high rural densities use systems which yield high outputs per unit of land, while areas with low rural densities use systems with low output per unit of land. Both the suitability of child labour and the system of landownership vary according to the agricultural system (Boserup 1965).

Long-fallow systems, which are used in sparsely populated areas at low levels of development, for instance in Africa, encourage high fertility (Boserup 1984). The land is tribally owned, and the user cannot mortgage or sell it. A large family can dispose of more land than a small one, and child labour is widely used for herding, for gathering food, fuel and water, for scaring birds and animals away from crops, for weeding crops, and for carrying them home. So parents are dependent upon children both for work when they are small, and for support when they have grown up. Since child mortality is high in such regions, parents often have fewer surviving children than they would have liked to have.

In other sparsely populated areas with extensive land use – for instance, in many parts of Latin America – large-scale private landownership predominates, and most of the rural population are hired workers in large farms and ranches. These workers are either landless or have small plots for some subsistence production. Children help their parents both in the subsistence plot, by gathering, and by working for wages, either with their parents or on their own (Collins 1983). Many plantations engage the whole family, and in tea plantations in Sri Lanka and Indonesia fertility is often higher than elsewhere in the region (Wijemanne and Wijeysekara 1981, Saefulla 1979).

In regions of Asia with high population densities and intensive agricultural systems, cultivator holdings are usually small or middle-sized and are either owned by the cultivators or rented from small or large landowners. Cultivators with large families and small holdings either cultivate the land very intensively, or rent additional land from non-cultivating owners or from families with small numbers in relation to the land they own. However, if holdings are small and the rural population is increasing, crop shares and other rents for additional land are extremely high, and this may provide motivation to restrict family size instead of renting additional land. Parents with many children often make distress sales of land in order to provide marriage payments, while landowners with small families become rich by renting out land. The difficulties which parents may have in finding suitable marriage partners and sufficient marriage payments for their children lead to delay of marriage and thus to reduced fertility. In other words, parents have more motivation for limitation of family size if they have land enough to support themselves in old age and emergencies, but not so much land that they can supply a large number of children with sufficient land or dowry. By contrast, landless labourers and people in areas with tribally owned land are more likely to be motivated to raise large families, because they are much more dependent upon help from children.

THE IMPACT OF DEVELOPMENT STRATEGIES ON FERTILITY

Governments in developing countries influence fertility partly by actions designed to reduce – or increase – fertility, and partly by their choice of development strategy. The encouragement to industrialization provided by nearly all governments in developing countries tends to promote occupational changes, which reduce fertility, but in the least-developed countries, especially in Africa, industrialization efforts are often unsuccessful. Moreover, there are large differences between countries in agricultural policies, which in some cases promote, but in others tend to delay, fertility decline.

In contrast to countries in Africa and Latin America, which often neglect agricultural development, it is characteristic for most countries in the South and East Asian region to promote both industrialization and agricultural development. As a result they have experienced large structural changes in both the urban and the rural labour markets. Most Asian countries promote not only import-replacing industrialization for the home market, but also exports of manufactures. The increasing population provides an expanding labour supply at low wages, and increasing labour productivity in the modern sector keeps wage costs at levels which make Asian countries highly competitive in the markets of the industrialized countries, where the labour force has increased more slowly and there is strong upward pressure on wages (Boserup 1981).

Except for the most industrially advanced of the Asian countries, married women work mainly in the informal sector, if they take part in non-domestic work. This is partly because work in this sector is more compatible with child care, partly because employers in the modern sector prefer young single women, and, in some countries, because men do not want to have working wives but have less objection to working daughters (Boserup 1970). The rapidly increasing employment of young unmarried girls in both national and multinational industries and services has had important effects on fertility, and on the status of women, because it has helped to make young women more independent. The marriage age has increased either because parents have agreed to late marriage, because they can benefit from the girl's wages as long as she stays under parental authority, or because the girl herself has delayed marriage until she has saved enough money to finance a marriage of her own choice. In some Asian countries, including Malaysia and Thailand, economic change, increase of marriage age, other improvements in female status, and fertility declines have been large (Jones 1981).

Agricultural policies in Asian countries have responded to their high population densities and high pressure of population on land. When population growth accelerated in the period after the Second World War, governments were concerned about how to achieve a sufficient increase in food supply. Therefore, nearly all of them promoted rural development and technological change in agriculture by means of credits, subsidies and direct investment. The resulting Green Revolution led to increases in food production greater than the increase in population, and in nearly all Asian countries the dependency on food imports declined, with the notable exception of Bangladesh. Moreover, a number of Asian governments, including India, transformed tenants into owners, or organized settlement schemes in areas of relatively low population density. These types of land reform had different effects on fertility: tenants who became owners got a new motivation for fertility control, but the effect of settlement schemes was pro-natalist, if land distribution gave priority to large families for social reasons, or if a family's new holding was substantially larger than its previous one.

Because the emphasis in the Asian type of agricultural development is on irrigation, multicropping and labour-intensive methods such as transporting of paddy, output per hectare increased and so did the demand for labour.

Therefore it became possible for larger families to live better on smaller landholdings than before. There was some replacement of female and child labour by chemical and mechanical inputs, but there is still a demand for these types of labour in small-scale agriculture. In some cases, the first effect of the Green Revolution seems to have been an increase of family size, but this was temporary, and on the whole the development strategies of most Asian governments have helped both to reduce fertility and to ameliorate the effects of increasing population pressure on resources. The main exception is the Moslem countries of Pakistan and Bangladesh, which have had very little fertility decline in spite of official birth-control policies. In some of the Asian countries, coercive government policies have played a major part in the reduction of fertility. This is true of China and Vietnam, which have tried to improve the food–population ratio not only by efforts at intensifying agriculture, but also by introducing rationing of births (Jones 1982). China, moreover, has tried to reduce family size by a marriage law which makes parents responsible for large numbers of relatives in addition to their own children ('China's new marriage law', 1981).

In Latin America, development strategies have been very different from those in most Asian countries. Some Latin American countries have had settlement schemes, but very few have transformed tenants into owners or redistributed land to agricultural workers. Thus a large share of the rural population continues to be landless or nearly landless labour, with no security except that provided by family members. Because of the abundant land resources in most of the continent, governments seem usually to have assumed that market forces would assure that food production expanded in step with demand, so they have done little to encourage expansion of food production. In many cases they have directly discouraged food production, by promoting imports of food from the industrialized countries in order to supply urban consumers with food at favourable prices, thus reducing urban wage costs and promoting industrialization. Because of the better opportunities for financing development with primary exports, the pattern of industrialization is more home-market and regionally oriented than in Asian countries, and less focused on exports to the industrialized countries. The result of the encouragement to industry and discouragement to agriculture has been an increasing gap between urban and rural employment opportunities and incomes. Rural-to-urban migration has become very large with most migrants moving to metropolitan areas and other large cities. The abundant labour supply in these areas has encouraged the creation of industries and ancillary informal-sector activities.

This Latin American pattern of development contains elements which have promoted fertility decline and elements which have delayed it. The occupational changes in the urban labour market, and the rapid increase in the proportion of population living in large cities have helped reduce fertility, but the lack of rural development has kept rural fertility at high levels. It is true that migration from rural areas has tended to reduce fertility, if spouses are separated, but, if migrant youth of both sexes transfer part of their earnings to parents left behind, rural fertility decline will be delayed by good employment opportunities for migrants in urban areas and in the United States.

Table 5 Differences in total marital-fertility rates between educational, occupational and locational groups (by husband's occupation and wife's education, ages 15–49)

Technology group	Country	Low-fertility groups			High-fertility groups			Fertility differences by		
		Secondary education	Professional, managerial	Urban population	Illiterate	Agricultural	Rural population	Education	Occupation	Location
	Asia									
1	Nepal	4.8	5.6	6.2	7.1	7.3	7.2	2.3	1.8	1.0
1	Bangladesh	7.2	7.0	7.2	6.8	7.0	6.9	1.3	0.3	-0.2
2	Pakistan	6.7	7.6	7.8	7.9	7.8	7.8	1.2	0.6	0.0
2	Indonesia	7.3	6.9	7.4	6.0	5.9	6.2	-1.3	-1.1	-1.3
3	Malaysia	7.3	7.3	7.4	8.1	8.6	8.0	0.7	1.0	0.6
3	Thailand	6.0	5.8	6.5	7.5	8.0	7.7	1.5	2.2	1.3
3	Sri Lanka	7.3	6.7	6.8	7.1	7.2	7.2	-0.2	0.7	0.4
3	Philippines	8.1	7.7	7.5	8.8	9.5	9.4	0.7	1.8	1.9
4	South Korea	6.4	7.5	6.6	7.8	8.3	8.1	1.4	0.8	1.5
	Latin America									
1	Haiti	5.6	5.4	6.3	8.3	8.5	8.3	2.7	3.1	2.0
3	Paraguay	5.9	5.5	5.8	10.4	9.5	9.0	4.6	3.9	3.1
3	Peru	7.7	7.8	7.8	10.3	10.2	10.4	2.6	2.4	2.6
3	Dominican Rep.	6.2	5.4	6.7	8.9	9.8	9.5	2.7	4.4	1.8
4	Guyana	6.9	5.5	5.6	8.2	8.2	7.5	1.4	2.7	1.9
4	Venezuela	6.1	6.2	6.2	9.2	7.5	10.3	3.1	4.2	4.1
4	Jamaica	6.3	4.9	5.2	7.4	7.5	7.3	1.1	2.9	2.1
4	Trinidad	4.8	3.8	4.3	6.0	6.5	5.4	1.3	2.7	1.1
4	Columbia	5.9	5.7	6.1	9.4	9.8	9.9	3.4	4.1	3.6
4	Mexico	7.2	7.6	8.4	10.0	10.1	10.2	2.3	2.5	1.8
4	Panama	3.9	4.1	4.0	6.6	6.1	5.9	2.7	2.1	1.9
4	Costa Rica	4.0	3.7	3.7	5.8	5.1	5.1	1.9	1.4	1.4

Source: Alam and Casterline (1984).

Table 5, which, like table 1, is derived from the World Fertility Survey, shows differences in marital fertility in twelve Latin American and nine Asian countries. The differences between rural and agricultural families on the one hand, and urban population and white-collar workers on the other, were much larger in Latin America than in Asia. There were usually differences of 2.0–4.0 children in Latin America, against 1.0–1.5, or less, in Asia. The large fertility differences in Latin America reflect a very high fertility in the groups of rural, agricultural and illiterate women in Latin American countries, even some at high levels of economic development (technology group 4 in the table). These high agricultural and rural fertilities in Latin America, compared with Asia, seem to reflect the density-related differences in occupational structure. In Asia, population pressure on the predominant system of small-scale peasant farming induced governments to promote both rural development and fertility control, and many peasants were motivated to make use of family-planning services, or they used folk methods of control, including late marriage. In Latin America, both rural development and rural fertility control have suffered from lack of government encouragement, and the landless rural population have had less motivation for control than the Asian peasants.

Although fertility has declined much in urban Latin America, even the most developed Latin American countries have considerably higher fertility than the highly industrialized countries. Not only are public social-security systems less widespread and comprehensive, so the dependence of both sexes on their family is larger, but female access to employment in the modern sector is lower. Therefore married women have more fear of divorce and abandonment, and more are willing to accept the burden of many pregnancies and a life devoted to child care and domestic duties.

In most African countries, the burden on rural women is heavy. The nutritional strain of many pregnancies, long periods of breast-feeding and heavy agricultural and domestic work often undermines their health (Harrington 1983). In many areas women still produce the subsistence food for the family with little or no male help, and the assignment of food production to women is a major reason for the lack of interest in conditions of food production by African male farmers and African governments. In many African countries, the growing towns are supplied mainly by food imported from industrialized countries, which is supplied at low prices owing to the support policies in industrialized countries and transportation by sea, which is cheaper than local African transport, because of the poor infrastructure in the sparsely populated continent. (Boserup 1981).

The long-fallow system, which encourages high fertility, is still predominant in many regions of Africa; also child mortality is high compared with most other developing areas, and widespread use of child labour continues to encourage high fertility (Dow and Warner 1983). In African regions, in which the long-fallow system with tribal tenure has been replaced by private property in land, either by legal reforms or by takeover by direct action, women have usually lost their cultivation rights in land without getting ownership rights, which have been granted or usurped by the men as family heads but preserved by the men even if they abandon or divorce their wife (Pala Okeyo 1984). Thus in many cases women have become more dependent upon male members of their family, because they are less able to support themselves and children by agricultural work. Also, increasing monetization and the declining importance of subsistence production make it less feasible for women to be self-supporting, since the cash crops are usually produced by the men, who cash the income even when the women have helped to produce the crops.

In many areas of Africa, there has been considerable expansion of export crops, which has benefited from increasing labour imports. However, expansion of production of traditional export crops with the traditional methods has not provided motivation to reduce fertility, and in many parts of Africa fertility has increased, owing to improvements in health, and to abandonment of traditional fertility-reducing measures, without replacement by contraceptive means (Lesthaeghe 1980). Owing to the low level of development in most of Africa, African men have little inducement to change their pro-natalist attitude: sub-fecundity of the wife is usually a cause of polygamy or divorce, and even the small elite of educated women often have large families under pressure from husbands and older family members (Oppong and Abu 1984).

African governments, like those elsewhere, are in favour of industrialization, but because of the small and scattered population in most of the continent and the extremely poor infrastructure, efforts at industrial development are often frustrated. Therefore, the growing towns are usually service towns. They have little, if any, modern industries: the population consists of administrators, educational and health personnel, persons handling foreign and internal trade and transport, and large numbers of informal-sector workers, serving the above-mentioned occupational groups. As already noted, the informal sector provides little motivation for fertility reduction, and even the small elite groups often have high fertility, because their high incomes allow them to satisfy their desire for large families.

Prices for most African exports have fluctuated wildly. When export prices have collapsed, there has been large-scale emigration from the country with unfavourable prices to one with more favourable conditions, or to Europe. When export prices have fluctuated upwards, a large share of the income increase has been used to raise consumption of imported manufactures and imported food. It is often assumed that increase of per-capita income has a negative impact on fertility, at least when the families are not among the very poorest. But the factor which reduces fertility is the structural change in the labour market, which may be the cause also of the income increase. If income increase occurs not because of structural change but because of windfall profits in terms of trade, and are used for imports of ready-made goods, the effects on fertility are more likely to be positive than negative. Improvements in prices of primary exports are only likely to reduce fertility if and when they induce national economic development, which causes structural changes in the labour market and in family organization. The large declines in fertility in recent years have occurred not in Arab and African countries, which have had improved terms of trade, but in Asian and Latin American countries, in which the governments have pursued policies leading to changes of the occupational structure.

When declining child mortality results in increasing family size, a family can either adapt income to family size or adapt family size to income. The husband, or the wife, or some of the children can take a job, or an extra job, in the modern sector, or they can engage in an informal-sector activity, or some family members can migrate for seasonal or more permanent employment elsewhere. All these options are alternatives to fertility control. Because of the economic expansion in both developed and developing countries in most of the period of rapid population growth, many families have had the opportunity to increase income by one or more of these options, and so avoid reducing family size. However, because of increasing protectionism and unwillingness to receive migrants in both developing and industrialized countries, and because the debt crisis forces economic contraction in many countries, migrants return, it becomes difficult to find employment and extra jobs, and markets for products and services in the informal sector become less expansive.

In those developing countries, which have become heavily dependent upon exports of manufactures, or remittances by migrants, or capital imports, the choice between options is narrowing. This situation is likely to force many families to choose fertility control as the means of restraining their expenditure. Some African countries, including Ghana, have for a long time suffered from a severe economic crisis, while in others, including Kenya, economic growth has been strong until recently. This may help to explain why use of family-planning services is more widespread in Ghana than in Kenya, although in Kenya the services are available in a larger part of the country than in Ghana, and more people are aware of their existence (Lesthaeghe 1984).

In an economic crisis, parents have more need for help from their children, but at times of crisis this is likely to be more than outbalanced by the reduced possibility of getting any help from children, either young ones or adults. In other words, while fertility will decline further, or begin to decline, in countries with continued economic development and occupational change, there are countries in Latin America in which the economic crisis may accelerate the existing downward trend in fertility, and the economic crises in large parts of Africa will probably make family-planning acceptable to many more African families, especially in urban areas.

REFERENCES

Alam, I., and Casterline, J. B. 1984: *Social and Economic Differentials in Recent Fertility*. World Fertility Survey, *Comparative Studies*, 33. Voorburg, Netherlands: International Statistical Institute.
Allman, J. (ed.) 1978: *Women's Status and Fertility in the Muslim World*. New York: Praeger.
Boserup, E. 1970: *Woman's Role in Economic Development*. London: Allen and Unwin and New York: St Martin.
—— 1965: *The Conditions of Agricultural Growth*. London: Allen and Unwin and Chicago: Aldine.
—— 1981: *Population and Technology*. Oxford: Blackwell and Chicago: University of Chicago Press.

—— 1984: Technical change and human fertility in rural areas of developing nations. In W. A. Schutjer and C. S. Stokes (eds), *Rural Development and Human Fertility*, London and New York: Macmillan, pp. 23–33.

Cain, M. 1982: Perspectives on family and fertility in developing countries. *Population Studies*, 36, 159–75.

—— Khanam, S. R., Nahar, S. 1979: Class, patriarchy, and women's work in Bangladesh. *Population and Development Review*, 5, 405–38.

Chen, L. C., Huq, E., D'Souza, S. 1981: Sex bias in the family allocation of food and health care in rural Bangladesh. *Population and Development Review*, 7, 55–70.

China's new marriage law, 1981: *Population and Development Review*, 7 369–72.

Collins, J. L. 1983: Fertility determinants in a high Andes community. *Population and Development Review*, 9, 61–75.

Dow, T. E., Werner, L. H. 1983: Prospects for fertility decline in rural Kenya. *Population and Development Review*, 1, 77–97.

Dyson, T., and Moore, M. 1983: On kinship structure, female autonomy, and demographic behaviour in India. *Population and Development Review*, 9, 35–60.

Harrington, J. A. 1983: Nutritional stress and economic responsibility: a study of Nigerian women. In M. Buvinic, M. A. Lycette and W. P. McGreevy (eds), *Women and Poverty in the Third World*, Baltimore and London: Johns Hopkins University Press, pp. 130–56.

Jones, G. W. 1981: Malay marriage and divorce in Peninsular Malaysia: three decades of change. *Population and Development Review*, 7, 255–78.

—— 1982: Population trends and policies in Vietnam. *Population and Development Review*, 4, 788–810.

Lesthaeghe, R. 1980: On the social control of human reproduction. *Population and Development Review*, 6, 527–48.

—— 1984: *Fertility and its Proximate Determinants in Sub-Saharan Africa*. Liège: International Union for the Scientific Study of Population.

Loza, S. F. 1981: *Egypt, studies on determinants of fertility behaviour II*. Liège: International Union for the Scientific Study of Population.

Miller, B. D. 1981: *The Endangered Sex: neglect of female children in rural North India*. Ithaca, New York and London: Cornell University Press.

Oppong, C., Abu, K. 1984: *The Changing Maternal Role of Ghanaian Women*. Geneva: World Employment Research Working Party, International Labour Office.

Pala Okeyo, A. 1984: *Towards Strategies for Strengthening the Position of Women in Food Production: an overview and proposals on Africa*. Nairobi: Institute for Development Studies.

Poffenberger, M. 1983: Toward a new understanding of population change in Bali. *Population Studies*, 37, 43–59.

Stokes, C. and Schutjer, W. A. 1984: Access to land and fertility in developing countries. In W. A. Schutjer and C. S. Stokes (eds), *Rural Development and Human Fertility*, London and New York: Macmillan, pp. 195–215.

Saefulla, A. D., 1979: The value of children among tea estate workers. Review by V. J. Hull in *Population Studies*, 35, 147–8.

Tabutin, D. 1984: La fécondité et la mortalité dans les recensements africains des 25 dernières années. *Population*, 39, 295–312.

United Nations Secretariat 1983: Recent trends and conditions of fertility. *Population Bulletin of the United Nations*, 15, 1–4.

Vlassoff, M., and Vlassoff, C. 1980: Old age security and the utility of children in rural India. *Population Studies*, 34, 487–99.

Wijemanne, E. L., and Wijeysekara, M. 1981: *Sri Lanka: studies in determinants of fertility behaviour*. Liège: International Union for the Scientific Study of Population.

World Bank 1978, 1983: *World Development Review*.

Culture, Economy and Reproduction in Contemporary Europe

John Simons

In the two centuries that have passed since Malthus wrote the first version of his *Essay*, its relevance to Western societies has been extinguished by their success in increasing production and decreasing reproduction. It is now their restraint in child-bearing which gives these societies their distinctive demographic character, a restraint evident in the persistence of period fertility rates lower than any previously achieved.

From an analysis of recent fertility movements in fifteen industrialized countries, Calot and Blayo (1982) report a rapid decline of total fertility rate from the mid 1960s until around 1975 in North, West and Central Europe. Modest upward movements occurred subsequently in some of the countries in these regions. In Italy, Portugal and Spain, the decline from the mid 1960s has been continuous; it was more moderate than elsewhere in Europe for the first ten years but became much steeper after 1974. An analysis of cohort fertility for six countries showed that, owing to a trend towards later child-bearing in recent years, the decline in total fertility has given an exaggerated impression of the fall in completed fertility. Nevertheless completed families will be small.

Inevitably there has been much speculation about the reasons for the decline of fertility, just as there was about its rise in the mid 1950s. In neither case have any of the speculations led to a widely accepted explanation, which is not surprising given the limited development of theory in this field. Research on the fertility behaviour of industrial society has produced a considerable collection of empirical generalizations, relating fertility to other phenomena such as social class, religion, and the employment status of married women. What is not available is a well-established general theory, if by this is meant 'the explicit formulation of determinate relations between a set of variables in terms of which a fairly extensive class of empirically

This study was funded by a grant from the Economic and Social Research Council. I am grateful to the European Value Systems Study Group for allowing me to use the data, to Gordon Heald of Social Surveys (Gallup Poll) for his encouragement and his help in obtaining the data, to Patrick Slater for advice on the application of his computer program, and to Ian Timaeus for computing-services and perceptive criticism during the development of the study. I am grateful to the editors of this volume and to the following for helpful comments on earlier drafts: Heather Joshi, Kath Kiernan, Colin Newell, John Osborn, Maire Ni Bhrolchain, Bruce Penhale, Veronika Simons and David Watson.

ascertainable regularities can be explained'. The quotation is from Schutz (1962), who was himself quoting, and endorsing as equally relevant to social and natural science, a definition of theory proposed by Ernest Nagel. Sociology's most famous example is probably the attempt to explain empirical generalizations about suicide rates in terms of cultural variation in the dimensions egoism–altruism and anomie–fatalism (Durkheim 1897). It is also a relevant example, since Durkheim thought there was a relationship between suicide rates and birth rates, arguing that excessive decline in birth rate reflected a degree of social pathology that led to an increase in suicides.

While short of general theory, fertility research has adopted hypotheses specific to industrial society in partial explanation of some aspects of their fertility trends and patterns. The best known class of these hypotheses may be summarized in a broad generalization that, when deciding whether or when to produce a child, people take into account the likely effects of doing so on other aspects of their projected lifestyle. In fact the generalization serves as a criterion by which modern industrial societies and those adopting their values are distinguished from other societies. Implicit in the generalization are the independent variables that may feature in particular models of fertility variation: lifestyle variables such as the quality of acceptable housing; the cost of maintaining projected lifestyle; income; and the expected effects of a birth on both costs and (if the earning-capacity of a parent would be affected) income. Not included in the list, though also implied by the generalization, are those factors which determine the importance of a birth itself to projected lifestyle, and therefore the extent to which people may be willing to forgo, say, a better car, or any car, in order to have a child or another child. Clearly these factors would be strategic in any general theory of fertility variation, though it may of course be possible to infer something about them from observations of the effects of other variables on fertility. For example, it may be possible to infer something about the importance of additional children by determining, as Ermisch (1983) and others have tried to do, the extent to which the prospects of additional income and higher living-standards affect fertility. But an explanation of the effects would require reference to dimensions which, among other things, could explain variation in the propensity to forgo additional children for additional income.

What kind of dimensions should be sought? What is the nature of the phenomena represented by intentional child-bearing? Whatever may be the case in other kinds of society, it is clear that people in industrial society do not have children as a means of increasing their wealth or their power in the community, nor because they do not know how to avoid having children. Why then do they have children, any children? Current fertility rates and estimates of increasing childlessness may give this last question a new salience. The usual starting-point for research on motives for fertility behaviour has been not why people have any children but why some have more or fewer than others; voluntary childlessness has become a research issue, voluntary child-bearing has not.

It is probably a common assumption that the fundamental reasons are to be found in human biology, that the organism has mechanisms that create an urge to reproduce. Whatever the role of such mechanisms, they are clearly under tight control. Remaining childless by choice is not a rare phenomenon, and according to some estimates the proportion in this category is rising. Moreover, an explanation drawn from biology would need to be supplemented by one that explained how stimuli with a non-mental origin came to be converted into relevant attitudes and intentions, and by another that explained social and temporal variation in these.

Another type of explanation offered is that children are a unique source of gratification, a means perhaps of establishing a haven of intimacy and commitment in an impersonal world. Again, some cheerfully dispense with these gratifications and many more seem willing to postpone them until a relatively late age. Here too there is the problem of explaining variation, over time and among social strata.

A third category of explanation refers to normative influences. Such interpretations range from those which see the family as a pawn of the economy or the Church to those which see the 'maternal instinct' as a cultural invention of male-dominated society. In general such interpretations have in common the view that, for the individual, the idea of reproduction is experienced as a moral obligation. It is explanations of this type which will be pursued here. They do not exclude, and may be complementary to, some other types of explanation.

FERTILITY AND RELIGION

The idea of reproduction being a matter of moral obligation is usually treated as an aspect of the effect of religion on fertility, usually in discussions of the decline of this effect. Thus Notestein (1945) refers to the importance of religious doctrines and moral codes in keeping fertility high before the demographic transition, and to the freeing of populations from 'older taboos' during the transition itself.

Typically analysts interested in the effects of secularization on fertility have in mind the effects of specific religious doctrines on reproductive behaviour. However, in order to consider more generally the idea of reproduction as a moral obligation, it is necessary to abandon the common practice of equating religion with the beliefs and practices enjoined by a particular religious institution such as the Christian Church. In fact the foundation of the theory to be described here is the concept of human society itself as a universal form of religion, a concept proposed by Durkheim (1912) in his classic work on the sociology of religion. According to Durkheim, religion is 'a system of ideas by means of which individuals represent to themselves the society of which they are members, and the obscure but intimate relations which they have with it'. For society is to its members 'what God is to his worshippers . . . the empire which it holds over conscience is due much less to the physical supremacy of which it has the privilege than to the moral authority with which it is invested . . . it is the object of a venerable respect'. In Durkheim's view this venerable respect is symbolized and sustained by the idea of God as a metaphor for society itself, or by alternative sacred metaphors.

Durkheim's views on the nature of religion in general, together with the views of another classical theorist, Max Weber, on the development of a pervasive rationality in the economic, religious and other institutions of modern society, have been elaborated in a way pertinent to the subject of this paper by Luckmann (1967). In a book entitled *Invisible Religion*, he attempts to elucidate the character of religion in modern society, a subject that was of major concern to the two theorists on whose work he draws. In the summary of his analysis that follows, the term 'meaning-system' is used instead of 'world view', the term he uses. (Alternatives would include such terms as 'ideational system' and, in a common use of the word, 'culture'.)

For Luckmann, the meaning-system is a universal form of religion because it is only by internalizing it that individuals acquire consciousness and a conscience, a self-concept and entry to a community in which members have moral obligations to one another. The meaning-system, embodied in language, is internalized as subjective reality. Individual existence thus derives its meaning from a social meaning-system, a system which transcends the life of the individual and the lives of generations.

In order to be capable of making authoritative sense of the everyday world and of claiming jurisdiction over individual conduct, a meaning-system also needs to provide for an understanding of itself. It needs to incorporate an understanding of whatever confers ultimate significance on existence and gives meaning to those experiences which occur when the routines of everyday life are overborne by events. The part of the meaning-system that fulfils this function may be implicit but can consist of a specific belief system expressed in ritual acts (such as christenings) and sacred images (such as those of the Nativity) but primarily in special uses of language (such as its use in marriages and other ceremonies).

Under a traditional social order, with a simple division of labour, different spheres of activity overlap and interpenetrate. Family life, economic life and political life are not differentiated, and religious norms prevail in all spheres. Society imprints on the minds of its members an existing meaning-system complete with religious representations of an underlying belief system.

Modern industrial society, on the other hand, is the outcome of a long process of institutional segmentation of the social structure. In such society work, for example, gets its meaning from norms that are rational in relation to the functional needs of the economy, rather than from its place in a coherent belief system. The same is true of other institutional spheres. For the individual, life is a series of specialized and segregated roles (worker, parent, party-member) rather than a unified pattern of activity expressing all-encompassing religious norms. From the same processes of segmentation and segregation, argues Luckmann, there emerges for the individual a 'private sphere', the basis for a sense of autonomy. Although actual choices remain a function of social biography, the individual becomes a consumer, free to choose among goods and services, among hobbies and marriage partners, and even among competing belief systems. Religion becomes institutionally non-specialized, a phenomenon of the private sphere, and one that rests primarily on emotions and sentiments. Traditional religious ideas are among the choices available to the individual as constituents of a private belief system, but now these ideas tend to have a rhetorical status rather than a commanding influence over personal priorities. The contemporary belief system bestows a sacred status on the respondent's autonomy in the private sphere. This status is expressed in emphases on self-expression, self-realization, sexuality and familism.

For Luckman, secularization is a process of change not from religion to its absence, but from one form of religion to another: from a form in which religious norms dominate all spheres of activity to one in which religion is relegated to the private sphere. His account seems plausible enough in its treatment of important aspects of the origin and character of religiosity in modern societies, but it does not address important issues about the relationship between individual and society, and the modern status of that social form of religion identified by Durkheim which sees society as the real source of moral authority.

What seems necessary is a synthesis of Luckmann's views with a version of Bellah's (1967) concept of 'civil religion'. Seen as modern society's counterpart of traditional religion, civil religion refers to a belief system manifested periodically in such phenomena as coronations and presidential inaugurations, and more frequently on such occasions as Remembrance Sunday and Thanksgiving Day, and by the support of national representatives in international cultural and athletic contests. It is by such means that a modern society continually affirms a dominant value system, a system embodied in an idealized image of itself. The most vivid demonstration of Durkheim's view of the relationship between individual and society is apparent in appeals to patriotism or nationalism. Such appeals, which are evidently not yet without potency in modern society, presuppose the religious character of the relationship between individual and society that he suggested. The same relationship, it will now be argued, makes a moral obligation of reproduction.

It is curious that the sociology of religion has shown so little interest in human reproduction. That it is sustained by the reproduction of members is a central characteristic of the concept of society. To be a member of society, traditional or modern, is to belong to a community the history of which has depended on the willingness of a sufficient proportion of its members to bear and rear children, and the destiny of which depends on the persistence of this willingness. This demographic truism is implicit in the meaning-system. Individuals know that their links with forebears and living kin have depended on reproduction by former and contemporary members of their own society, that everyone is a son or daughter, grandson or granddaughter, that everyone is a member of a society made up of families which were themselves products of families. For the individual, identification with society is identification with an institution committed to the reproduction of members. To the extent that society is 'the object of a venerable respect', so is parenthood. To the extent that society exercises moral authority over its members, parenthood will be encouraged. It is, of course, precisely the idea of parenthood as a moral obligation that is embodied in the doctrines, images and rituals of institutionalized Christianity.

But does society in fact exercise moral authority over reproductive behaviour in industrialized countries, notwithstanding the value accorded to individual autonomy? Is the collapse of fertility in recent decades not striking evidence to the contrary? These are questions on which different views are held and which, in principle, can be the subject of empirical inquiry.

The first step is to define dimensions of variation in attitudes that could form the basis of measures of the extent to which reproductive behaviour is a matter of obligation. One possibility is a dimension of the potency of obligation in terms of variation in the acceptance of cultural norms about reproductive behaviour. At one extreme of this dimension of variation, the effective exercise of moral authority would be apparent in an absolutist acceptance of specified rules. For example, a Catholic at this extreme would be expected to accept rules proscribing any attempt at fertility regulation. The other extreme would be identifiable in a relativism that rejected these rules. Here, individuals would claim that appropriate reproductive behaviour was entirely dependent on circumstances. Thus one dimension of the acceptance of moral authority would be absolutism–relativism in attitudes to reproductive behaviour.

Another dimension of obligation is that of collectivism–individualism (or holism–individualism), with reference to the acceptance of social norms about reproductive behaviour. At the collectivist extreme, conformity in reproductive behaviour would be an expression of the value placed on the expectations of the community. In contrast, attitudes to reproductive behaviour at the other end of the scale would express the value placed on the preferences of the individual.

The two dimensions are shown as a co-ordinate system in figure 1. The different quadrants formed by the axes imply different attitude syndromes. The top-right quadrant combines absolutism and collectivism, and corresponds

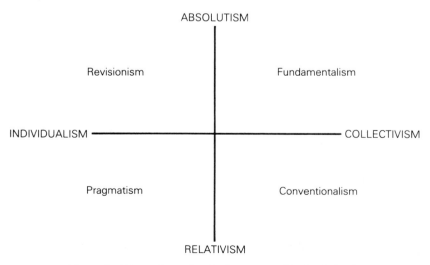

Figure 1   Dimensions of attitudes to reproductive behaviour

to what was described in a previous essay as fundamentalism: 'a particular form of reproductive behaviour is prescribed as sacred whatever its profane meanings' (Simons 1982). However, the degree of fundamentalism implied would be relative to the specific context in which the schema was applied. In one context, the attitudes prevailing in many Moslem societies might be used to exemplify the dimensions of the syndrome. In modern Europe, fundamentalism might be exemplified by couples who believed that they were expected, legitimately expected, to produce at least two children.

The bottom-left quadrant corresponds to what was described in the earlier essay as pragmatism: 'variable ways of accommodating sacred to profane meanings are permitted'. Where this quadrant is dominant, attitudes to reproductive behaviour may be highly responsive to changes in conditions, since neither absolutist convictions nor respect for conventions are an impediment to change.

The bottom-right quadrant, labelled conventionalism, combines collectivism with relativism. Here attitudes will express normative constraints but are likely to be responsive to change in conditions affecting those who act as opinion-leaders or reference groups for society at large. Fertility may be very low where lifestyles are expensive.

Finally, the top-left quadrant combines individualism and absolutism to produce the syndrome labelled revisionism. The absence of social constraints here makes fertility responsive to change in conditions, and subject to absolutist convictions rather than specific rules of behaviour.

It is assumed that reproductive behaviour in any given society, or group within society, may be described, and therefore at least partly explained, by the relative dominance of each of the four syndromes.

The foregoing review of ideas about the nature of the relationship between religion and fertility can be used to identify three different views of the actual relationship found in modern societies, and of its implications for reproductive behaviour in these societies.

First there is the view that the low fertility of modern society is, at least in part, the result of a decline in acceptance of traditional Christian doctrines on reproductive behaviour. According to Lesthaeghe (1983), in the latest of his valuable contributions to this subject, secular individualism ('the pursuit of personal goals devoid of reference to a cohesive and overarching religious or philosophical construct') had become fully legitimate by the last quarter of the nineteenth century. The rationality of the individual had gained supremacy over that of the group, and this shift was exemplified by the marital-fertility transition. Lesthaeghe argues that the transition and recent changes in family formation and procreation should be regarded as successive manifestations of a long-term shift in the Western meaning-system. Using multivariate analyses of regional data for three European countries, he demonstrates a close relationship, lasting over a period of at least a century, between the speed of the marital-fertility transition, the rejection of traditional religious ideas (shown by such indicators as rates of attendance at Sunday Mass) and structural change (using such indicators as the proportion of the population employed in industry). In terms of figure 1, Lesthaeghe is postulating a shift from absolutism to relativism, and from collectivism to individualism. From this standpoint, he holds that the fertility decline since the 1960s is only partly explained by such factors as increasing opportunity costs for women and decline in the relative income of younger generations socialized at a time of substantial economic growth. That the cause also lies in secular individualism is shown, he believes, by 'the legitimation of cohabitation outside marriage, voluntary childlessness, non-conformist sexual behaviour, abortion, and euthanasia'.

A second view on the relationship between religion and fertility in modern society can be developed from Luckmann's thesis that secularization is a process of relegating religion to the private sphere. It is his view, as mentioned above, that the sacred status bestowed by the contemporary belief system on the individual's autonomy is expressed in emphases on self-expression, self-realization, sexuality and familism. He holds that a considerable though incomplete liberation of sexuality from social control permits greater weight to individual preference in determining sexual conduct. The most important catalyst of ideas about ultimate significance and individual autonomy is the family. Like sexuality, the family offers the individual a means of self-transcendence. Unlike sexuality, the family can be the object of sentiments supported without contradiction by traditional Christian rhetoric. On Luckmann's view, the appropriate quadrants for modern society seem to be those labelled revisionism or pragmatism but, in contrast to Lesthaeghe's interpretation, the movement towards individualism is seen as positively encouraging family sentiment. Presumably families may be large or small, their size depending on preferred lifestyle and available resources, but childlessness would be unpopular. Of course it was not Luckmann's purpose to analyse reproductive behaviour in modern society. He was writing as a theorist on religion.

The third and final view to be described is one based on the concept of civil religion and the idea of the social meaning-system as a universal form of religion. It is similar to a view that has been described more fully in a previous essay (Simons 1982). Applied to modern societies, this view sees attitudes to child-bearing as a function of identification of individual with society. In the process of modernization, there is indeed a move towards pragmatism (secular individualism) and a movement in the same direction is likely to be part of the explanation of the recent fertility decline. However, if identification with society implies commitment to the reproduction of its members, a coherent social meaning-system cannot sustain both the legitimacy of this commitment and the legitimacy of ignoring it. Society may be relatively indifferent to voluntary childlessness when this is a choice of the minority, but any general move in this direction would suggest a general decline in the plausibility of the meaning-system and therefore in the perceived legitimacy of norms and values. Such a disintegration may, of course, occur. Other non-conformist behaviour, such as cohabitation and abortion, may be more easily accommodated without risk to the coherence of the system.

In terms of figure 1, the view from the standpoint of civil religion points to the importance of taking into account a fundamentalism about reproductive behaviour that is inherent in the nature of social meaning-systems rather than dependent upon the acceptance of particular religious doctrines. The strong reinforcing-effects of the latter are of course acknowledged. This view is like Lesthaeghe's and unlike Luckmann's in locating religion in the public rather than the private sphere. It is like Luckmann's and unlike Lesthaeghe's in its emphasis on change in the form of religion rather than on loss of the influence of specific religious ideas. It is unlike both in stressing the continuing importance of societal influence over individual conduct.

FAMILISM IN CONTEMPORARY EUROPE

This is an appropriate point to consider some evidence bearing on these different views about the relationship between religion and fertility in contemporary Europe.

To start with, it is important to recall that, less than twenty years ago, Europe was at the peak of a boom in familism, a boom which had its origins in the pre-war period and which was apparent in rising fertility rates, rising marriage rates and a falling age at marriage, together with a shift towards earlier child-bearing and larger families and away from childless and single-child families. From the view based on the idea of civil religion, it can be argued that the boom represented a change in the balance of pragmatism and fundamentalism, in the direction of the latter. An existing account on these lines suggested that the reversal was largely a product of fundamentalist tendencies enhanced by the experience of the Second World War. That interpretation was supported by evidence from England that the fertility movements were associated with similar movements (up as well as down) in the proportions of the population attending Easter Communion in the Church of England (Simons 1982) and becoming converts to Catholicism (Simons 1980). A similar revival of religious sentiment occurred in America and elsewhere. Presumably Luckmann saw the boom in familism as evidence for his thesis that familism expressed the sacred status now bestowed on individual autonomy; he would probably agree that general improvements in income helped to make the boom possible. The evidence on rising rates of religious observance would be more difficult to articulate with his view that religion had been relegated to the private sphere, or with Lesthaeghe's view of the relationship between religion and fertility as one that had been dissolving over a long period.

A new source of evidence on these issues is a set of national surveys of values in European countries conducted under the sponsorship of a charitable foundation, the European Value Systems Study Group. The original aim of the study was 'to analyse and describe the moral and social value systems prevailing in Europe'. A translation of the same questionnaire was used in each country. In each case the respondents were a nationally representative sample of 1200 adults aged eighteen and over. Since 1981, surveys have been conducted in twenty-seven countries, some of them outside Europe. The first publications have been an international report of the study, based on data from nine countries (Stoetzel 1983), and a report on one national survey, in Ireland (Fogarty et al. 1984).

Table 1 European Values Study 1981: national responses of nine European countries to questions on religious and political issues (total fertility rate in 1981 also shown for each country)

	Denmark	Germany (FR)	Netherlands	Italy	Belgium	Britain	Spain	France	Ireland
Total fertility rate	1.4	1.4	1.6	1.6	1.7	1.8	2.0	2.0	3.1
Do you believe in God? Yes (%)	58	72	65	84	77	76	87	62	95
How important is God in your life? Mean value on scale of 1 (=not at all) to 10 (=very)	4.5	5.7	5.3	7.0	5.9	5.7	6.4	4.7	8.0
Apart from weddings, funerals and baptisms, about how often do you attend religious services these days? Once a month or more often (%)	12	37	40	52	38	23	53	18	88
How proud are you to be of your nationality? Very or quite proud (%)	71	59	60	80	71	86	83	76	91
Political orientation Mean value on scale of 1 (=left) to 10 (=right)	5.8	5.6	5.5	4.6	6.1	5.7	4.9	4.9	6.2
Justifiability of abortion Mean value on scale of 1 (=never) to 10 (=always)	6.4	3.9	4.4	4.3	3.5	4.0	2.8	4.9	1.7

Source: values data from Social Surveys (Gallup Poll).

Some of the questions on religious and political issues used in the Values Survey appear in table 1, which shows, for each of nine countries, the aggregate response to each question as a mean scale value or percentage. The total fertility rate in the survey year is also shown. On the evidence of this table, it seems premature to regard traditional religious ideas as a spent force in Europe. Most of these Europeans profess to believe in God, and mean scale values on an index of the importance of God are comfortably beyond the mid-point in most cases. Another conservative tendency is indicated by the fact that six countries have mean values on the right of the political orientation scale. Responses to the question about national pride suggest that nationalism continues to thrive, though the responses for Germany and the Netherlands are notably low.

Some evidence on social differences in beliefs and values that may be relevant to known social differences in fertility is available in Stoetzel's (1983) report on the results of the Values Survey in nine European countries. Although a number of inter-country comparisons are presented in the report, most of the analyses are of social differences within the combined European samples; the number of respondents totalled 12,463. There are no multivariate analyses. A selection of findings is given in table 2. Because, as suggested by the responses to question (e), age usually has a profound effect on values (the older the respondent, the more conservative the response) this source of variation should be borne in mind when considering some of the evidence in table 2. For example, those with higher education are more likely to be young, and the category 'women, not employed' includes those who have retired and young mothers who have temporarily ceased to be employed.

Stoetzel finds that an index of 'permissiveness' (his equivalent of pragmatism is a major discriminating variable at the individual level (see question (a), for example). Those exhibiting most pragmatism were the young, the educated, those who described themselves as left-wing, and non-believers. High income was associated with more pragmatism, home-ownership with less. Apparently, for every rise in level of income, those who did not own their own homes were more pragmatist and those who did were less so. Conversely, the poorer the non-owners, the more fundamentalist they seemed to be. Asked whether they were religious, two-thirds of respondents said they were. Most respondents in the nine countries described themselves as Catholics, 28 per cent as Protestants. Women professed more religiosity than men, but this was much less so with women in full-time employment.

Responses (not shown) to questions about religiosity tabulated by occupation show something like the 'J' shape often found in analyses of completed fertility by occupational category, with relatively low religiosity at the bottom of the non-manual scale. A similar pattern is shown for responses to a question about following instructions at work even if disagreeing with them. Compared with those who completed their education at seventeen years of age or above, the less educated were more likely to appear more religious (question (b)) and absolutist (question (e)).

The existence of a dimension of conventionalism–revisionism also appears to be revealed by the findings, and to be represented by a scale on which respondents were asked to rate their political orientation between left

(= 1) and right (= 10). Stoetzel reports that, compared with those on the right of the scale, those on the left were likely to be more sceptical of authority, more concerned with the interests of the individual, less patriotic, less satisfied with home life, job and financial situation of household, to have less confidence in parliament, the civil service and other institutions except the trade unions, and to be less likely to believe that children were important to the success of marriage (question (d)). Those on the left were also less likely to describe themselves as religious or to assign importance to God in their lives.

Scores on the left–right political scale were found to be normally distributed but around different mean positions in the different countries: a continuous distribution with most people close to the centre, rather than a division into opposed camps on either side of it. The distribution was more concentrated (there was more consensus) the more the mean position was to the right of the scale. Women were to the right of men, but there was little difference between men and working women.

The data are not tabulated by Stoetzel but he gives some information (p. 133) on responses to a question about ideal family size. The mean for all nine countries was 2.52. The figure varied considerably by age and education. He seems to suggest that those with the longest education (graduates presumably) had a higher ideal family size than those with less. Only one person in four believed that a woman had to have a child in order to be fulfilled.

The findings suggest that fundamentalism is positively associated with familist sentiments and (like fertility) negatively associated with urban residence, length of education, low but non-manual socio-economic status, and whether women are employed outside the home. Conventionalism, measured as a political orientation towards the right, seems to be positively associated with familist sentiments, and with income. Thus there is the possibility (subject to an analysis which took account of age effects) that different combinations of fundamentalism and conventionalism could help to explain the socio-economic differentials revealed by national fertility surveys in European countries. An analysis of differentials in these surveys has been reported by Jones (1982).

The foregoing observations assume, on the basis of the correlates reported by Stoetzel, that questions like those on the importance of God in the individual's life and on political orientation are in fact measures of fundamentalism and conventionalism respectively. In order to put this assumption to further test, forty questions thought likely to represent these dimensions were selected from the 269 in the questionnaire, for an analysis of underlying dimensions using principal-components analysis. The data available for this purpose at the time were aggregate responses for thirteen European countries and for twenty-four different age, occupational and other groups in one country, Britain. The computer program used was devised by Slater (1977), and is especially well suited to this kind of exploratory analysis.

In the event, the first dimension produced by the thirteen-country analysis and by the analyses of the British social groups clearly represented fundamentalism. Although there were differences between the two analyses

Table 2 European Values Survey 1981: distribution by social category of individual responses given by a combination of national samples in nine countries[a] to selected questions (figures in parentheses refer to tables in Stoetzel 1983)

Social Category	Subjects of questions and distribution of responses	
	(a) *Permissiveness*[b] (43,48), index	(b) *Importance of God*[c] (45,48), index
Age at completing education		
Under 17 years	2.43	6.26
17 years and over	2.98	5.35
Income level		
High	2.95	5.39
Medium	2.84	5.57
Low	2.55	6.12

	(c) *Belief that sufficient reasons for divorce are:*	
	incompatible personalities %	*either person ceasing to love the other (29),* %
Men	47	58
Women		
Employed	53	67
Not employed	42	54
Political orientation[c]		
Left	59	67
Right	37	54

	(d) *Importance of children to the success of marriage* (28), ratio
Importance of God[c]	
Maximum/minimum	1.18
Political orientation[c]	
Right/Left	1.13

	(e) *Belief that there are absolutely clear guidelines about good and evil* (43, 52), %	(f) *Tending to disagree that marriage is an outdated institution* (53), %
All	26	74
Age at completion of education		
Under 17 years	29	–
17 years or over	21	–
Age		
20	15	64
40	26	76
60	35	80

Table 2 *(continued)*

Social Category	Subjects of questions and distribution of responses
	(g) *Belief that parents should always be loved and respected, whatever their qualities or faults* *(48), %*
Income	
High	51
Medium	63
Low	66

[a]Belgium, Denmark, Spain, France, Britain, Netherlands, Irish Republic, Italy, Germany (FR).
[b]Based on a rating of the justifiability of 22 events, including abortion and divorce, on a scale of 1 (= never) to 10 (= always).
[c]As defined for table 1.

in the questions contributing the dimensions, the fundamentalist pole was produced in each case by positive responses to questions on such matters as the importance of God, belief that there are absolutely clear guidelines about good and evil, and national pride. Also towards the fundamentalist end was the belief that parents should always be loved and respected whatever their qualities or faults. The other, pragmatist, end of the dimension was produced in each case by positive responses to questions about approval of abortion, divorce, and women wishing to be single parents.

The theme of the second dimension produced in each case seemed to correspond well enough to a dimension of conventionalism–revisionism as defined above. In both analyses, the conventionalist pole could be identified by self-rating towards the right of the political scale, belief that one should follow instructions at work even if disagreeing with them, belief that most people can be trusted, and satisfaction with life. The other, revisionist end of the dimension could be identified in both analyses by a tendency to think marriage outdated, and the view that 'sex under age' and extramarital affairs were justified.

The outcome of these analyses, together with Stoetzel's results, suggest that it is reasonable to regard the question on the importance of God and the question on political orientation as summary measures representing the two dimensions of interest. A problem with the latter question is that some 20 per cent of respondents declined to answer it. However, tests on three relevant questions in the British survey (for women of reproductive age only) showed no significant difference in distribution of responses between those who answered and those who declined to answer the question on political orientation.

In showing that the question on national pride is fairly prominent on the dimension of fundamentalism, the analyses also provide some justification for regarding this question as a measure of fundamentalism from the standpoint of civil religion: a measure of the individual's identification with society. Some interesting relationships between the responses to this question

Table 3 European Values Survey 1981: responses of three age groups in the British and Irish surveys to questions on the importance of God, national pride, political orientation and familism

	Britain (age)			Ireland (age)		
	18–24	*25–34*	*35–44*	*18–24*	*25–34*	*35–44*
Importance of God in my life Mean value on scale from 1 (=not at all) to 10 (= very)	4.2	4.8	5.6	6.9	7.5	7.9
Political orientation Mean value on scale from 1 (=left) to 10 (= right)	5.2	5.5	5.4	5.7	5.6	6.0
National pride 'Very proud' to be British/Irish (%)	35	42	48	58	61	64
Whether agree marriage is an outdated institution Tend to agree (%)	19	13	15	16	10	11
Whether approve if a woman wants to have a child as a single parent but not a stable relationship with a man Approve (%)	41	48	31	27	21	12
Importance of children for a successful marriage Very important (%)	43	50	59	46	55	55
Whether agree parents' duty is to do their best for their children even at the expense of their own well-being Agree (%)	63	67	63	62	70	79
Whether agree one must always love and respect parents regardless of their faults Agree (%)	54	52	52	64	74	78
Ideal family size: husband, wife and how many children? Mean ideal	2.43	2.31	2.34	3.86	3.75	3.92
Justifiability of abortion Mean value on scale from 1 (=never) to 10 (=always)	4.7	4.5	4.2	2.2	1.9	1.6

Source: British tabulations: Social Surveys (Gallup Poll); Irish tabulations: Fogarty et al. (1984).

and those to other questions used in the Values Survey have already been demonstrated by Rose (1984). Responses to the question are not measured on a ten-point scale like the other two questions. Respondents are asked to say whether they are very proud, quite proud, not very proud, or not at all proud to be of their nationality. Responses are given the values 4, 3, 2, 1

Table 4 European Values Survey 1981, British sample, women aged 18–44 only: mean scores on measures of importance of God, political orientation and national pride by responses to familism questions

	%	Importance of God[a]	Political orientation[a]	National pride[b]
Do you tend to agree or disagree. 'Marriage is an outdated institution'?				
Tend to agree	13	4.9	4.9	3.2
Tend to disagree	87	5.4	5.5	3.3
How important are children for a successful marriage?				
Very/Rather	78	5.5	5.4	3.3
Not very	23	4.4	5.4	3.2
Whether agree parents' duty is to do their best for their children even at the expense of their own well-being				
Agree	66	5.5	5.5	3.3
Disagree	23	4.7	5.0	3.3
Neither	11	5.1	5.2	3.1
Whether agree that one must always love and respect parents, regardless of their qualities and faults				
Agree	53	5.8	5.4	3.3
Disagree	47	4.9	5.4	3.2
Whether approve if a woman wants to have a child as a single parent but does not want a stable relationship with a man				
Approve	41	4.8	5.3	3.3
Disapprove	36	5.7	5.4	3.3
Depends	23	5.3	5.7	3.2
Ideal family size: husband, wife and how many children?				
0–1	5	4.8	5.4	2.8
2	66	5.2	5.4	3.3
3 or more	30	5.6	5.7	3.2
Justifiability of abortion (1 = never, 10 = always)				
1–3	40	6.1	5.4	3.3
4–6	38	5.2	5.5	3.3
7–10	23	3.9	5.2	3.0
All		5.3	5.4	3.3
No.		365	293	355

[a]Scale as defined in table 1.

[b]Scale: very proud = 4; quite proud = 3; not very proud = 2; not at all proud = 1.

respectively. This difference in format should be borne in mind when comparing results for the different questions.

The next part of the essay reports an investigation of relationships between each of these three measures (importance of God, political orientation, and national pride) and measures of familism. To start with, the effect of age

Table 5   European Values Survey 1981: classification of 13 countries by mean values on measures of the importance of God and political orientation, showing familism index[a] for each country

		Political orientation divided at its mean value for all 13 countries		
		Left of mean	Right of mean	
		Mean scale value 4.63–5.29	Mean scale value 5.30–6.20	
Importance of God				
Mean scale value			*Index*		*Index*
High:	6.60–8.02	Italy	4	Irish Republic	12
				Northern Ireland	11
Medium:	5.30–6.59	Spain	13	Norway	10
				Finland	8
				Belgium	7
				Great Britain	6
				Netherlands	3
				Germany (FR)	1
Low:	3.99–5.29	France	9	Sweden	5
				Denmark	2

[a]The index is rank of country in ascending order by mean rank on the following variables: ideal family size and percentages endorsing the views that children are important for successful marriage and parents should do their best for children even at the expense of their own well-being.

Spearman rank order correlation coefficients: familism index and mean scale value of importance of God, 0.54; familism index and mean scale value of political orientation, 0.26.

on all measures is considered. In table 3, the findings of the British survey are compared with those of the Irish survey.

Irish reponses were, predictably, more fundamentalist and more familist than British responses. In both countries, a majority in all three age groups profess familist views. For the questions on parents' duty to children and childrens' duty to parents, which seem to be directed specifically to familist sentiment, the sharp increase by age in Ireland is not apparent in Britain. The gradient in Ireland may be reflecting a downward trend in fertility.

An analysis using the British data is shown in table 4. Mean scale values on the measures of importance of God, political orientation and national pride are tabulated by responses to the familism questions. Apparently, the importance of God in the individual's life varies positively with familism. There is less variation by political orientation, though such variation as exists is in the expected direction. There is least variation in national pride, though there are noteworthy differences by ideal family size and the justifiability of abortion.

In an attempt to demonstrate international variation in the effects of fundamentalism and conventionalism on attitudes to family-building, national values of the indexes used in the analysis just described and of other measures were used in an analysis of variation among the thirteen countries

Table 6 European Values Survey 1981: classification of 13 countries by mean values on measures of national pride and political orientation, showing familism index[a] and total fertility rate (1981) for each country

		Political orientation divided at mean value for all 13 countries					
		Left of mean			*Right of mean*		
		Mean scale value 4.63–5.29			Mean scale value 5.30–6.20		
National pride Mean scale value			*Index*	*TFR*		*Index*	*TFR*
High:	3.30–3.62	Spain	13	2.0	Irish Republic	12	3.1
					Northern Ireland	11	2.5
					Great Britain	6	1.8
Medium:	3.00–3.29	France	9	2.0	Norway	10	1.7
		Italy	4	1.6	Finland	8	1.6
					Belgium	7	1.7
					Denmark	2	1.4
Low:	2.74–2.99				Sweden	5	1.6
					Netherlands	3	1.6
					Germany (FR)	1	1.4

[a]Defined as in table 5.
Spearman rank order correlation coefficients: familism index and TFR, 0.93; familism index and national pride, 0.71; TFR and national pride, 0.80.

that were the subject of the multivariate analysis mentioned earlier. Because aggregate data only were available for this purpose, any outcome is subject to the important qualification that it may misrepresent characteristics of the generations of reproductive age. Nevertheless, the outcome is interesting.

The thirteen countries were first ranked by national values for ideal family size and for percentages responding positively to questions on the importance of children for successful marriage, and whether parents should do their best for children even at the expense of their own well-being. The rank order of the mean rank was used as an index of familism; ranking was in ascending order so that higher values would represent higher familism. Countries were then classified by their mean values on the importance of God scale, using three approximately equal bands over the observed range, and then by whether they were to the right or left of the mean value for all countries on the political-orientation scale. The result is shown in table 5. Apparently the classification by importance of God, as a measure of Christian fundamentalism, has a modest association with the values of the familism index. Political orientation has little association with the values of the index but separates the mediterranean countries from the others.

In the next analysis, national pride was used in place of the importance of God as a measure of fundamentalism. It is evident from the outcome,

Table 7   European Values Survey 1981: classification of 13 countries by mean values on measures of political orientation and national pride, showing index[a] of approval of non-conformist sexual conduct for each country

				National pride divided at mean value for all 13 countries		
				Low		*High*
				Mean scale value 2.74–3.13		Mean scale value 3.14–3.62
Political orientation Mean scale value			*Index*			*Index*
Right:	5.61–6.20	Denmark	8	Irish Republic		1
		Belgium	9	Norway		2
				Northern Ireland		3
				Finland		4
				Great Britain		6
Centre right:	5.00–5.60	Sweden	5			
		Germany	7			
		Netherlands	11			
Left:	4.63–4.99	France	13	Spain		10
				Italy		12

[a]The index is rank of country in ascending order by mean rank on the following variables: mean scale values for justifiability of sex under legal age and of married people having affairs, and percentage responding positively to question whether marriage is an outdated institution.
Spearman rank order correlation coefficients: index of approval of non-conformist sexual conduct and mean scale value of political orientation, -0.73; the index and mean scale value of national pride, -0.40.

shown in table 6, that this measure is more powerful than the previous one in putting countries into ascending order by familism. Total fertility rate in the survey year is also shown. Its level seems to vary fairly consistently with the level of the familism index.

An attempt to show the relevance of political orientation is presented in table 7. Here countries are assigned by political orientation to one of three approximately equal bands over the observed range, and are divided horizontally into those above and those below the mean value on the national-pride scale. In place of an index of familism, an index of non-conformist sexual conduct was constructed as follows. The thirteen countries were ranked in ascending order by mean scale position on the justifiability of sex under the legal age and the justifiability of married people having affairs, and by the percentage endorsing the view that marriage is an outdated institution. The ranking of the mean ranks was used as an index in the same way that the familism index was used in the previous analyses. There is an obvious tendency for index values to increase (implying more approval of non-conformist sexual conduct) as countries descend the scale towards the left end of the range. In other words, the measure appears to be associated more with approval of non-conformist sexual conduct than with familism, an outcome foreshadowed by the multivariate analyses described earlier.

Taken together, the analyses just described (or more refined versions, using more appropriate parts of the data when available) could be used to nominate countries for the different quadrants of figure 1, according to their relative dominance as indicated by a country's position on the national pride and political orientation scales. Thus fundamentalism seems relatively distinctive of the Irish Republic, revisionism of Spain, conventionalism of Germany, and pragmatism of France. The purpose of making such distinctions is to contribute to explanations of the distinctive characteristics of fertility in these countries, such as the high fertility of Ireland, the rapidly declining fertility of Spain, and the remarkably low fertility of Germany.

One way in which countries in different quadrants might be expected to differ is in their readiness to abandon familist behaviour. The more fundamentalist countries, such as Ireland and Britain, would be expected to be more reluctant to change than would more pragmatist or revisionist countries such as France and Italy. Some evidence that may be relevant here is available from a survey conducted in the nine countries of the European Economic Community in 1979. Respondents were asked whether they would endorse the following statement: 'The future of society is too uncertain to risk bringing children into the world.' The United Kingdom and Ireland had the lowest percentages endorsing the statement: 25 per cent in each case. France and Italy had the highest percentages: 51 and 57 per cent respectively (de la Beaumelle 1979).

SUMMARY AND CONCLUSIONS

The underlying argument of this essay is that the factors which determine the importance to lifestyle of producing children are those which arise from the religious character of the relationship between individual and society. Where the relationship has this religious character, the individual identifies with society as an institution committed to the reproduction of its members. On this view, religion is understood not as a set of doctrines which lose their influence during the process of modernization, nor as a matter of private sentiment, but in the Durkheimian sense as whatever belief system underlies veneration of society and its institutions. In other words, the claim is that it is societal fundamentalism, not Christian fundamentalism, that makes parenthood a moral obligation. Of course, Christian fundamentalism can have powerful reinforcing-effects: the direct effects of doctrine on behaviour, and the indirect effects of encouraging commitment to shared values and thus to societal fundamentalism.

As the basis of a theory which links this view of religion with variation in attitudes to reproductive behaviour, the use of two dimensions of moral obligation were combined to form the attitude dimensions fundamentalism–pragmatism and conventionalism – revisionism. It was suggested that variation on these dimensions could help to explain social variation in fertility.

The fertility boom in Western societies between the 1950s and 1960s, and evidence that it coincided with revivals in religious sentiment, appear to support the proposed theory. Considerably more evidence is available from the findings of the International Values Survey of 1981. The published findings and multivariate analyses of aggregate data (for thirteen countries and for twenty-four social groups in Britain) offer support for the existence of the two dimensions of interest among relevant attitudes. Different combinations of values on these two dimensions suggest a potential explanation of known social differentials in fertility, such as the 'J'-shaped distribution of completed fertility by socio-economic group. In that particular case, the attitudinal evidence would be consistent with an explanation that referred to the relative fundamentalism of manual workers and the relative conventionalism of middle-class groups. A fertility survey that incorporated some of the questions used in the Values Survey would be needed to confirm this interpretation.

For the inter-country analyses reported above, a survey question on the importance of God was used as a summary measure of Christian fundamentalism and a question on political orientation was used as a measure of conventionalism. A third question, on national pride, was used as a measure, admittedly unsophisticated, of the individual's identification with society. The relationship between national values on these measures and values for ideal family size and other measures of familism were investigated, using aggregate data for thirteen countries. The results show that, internationally, responses to the questions on national pride were a better predictor of familism, than the responses to the question on the importance of God. Political orientation (the measure of conventionalism) appeared to be unrelated to familism but to be associated with readiness to endorse non-conformist sexual conduct. Again, the results seem to support the proposed theory of variation, and thus help to explain distinctive characteristics of fertility in different countries.

Earlier it was suggested that a popular class of hypotheses about fertility variation in modern societies could be summarized in the broad generalization that, when deciding whether or when to add to their families, people took into account the likely effects of doing so on other aspects of their projected lifestyles. How are the findings of this essay related to that generalization?

While the analyses generally tend to support the conclusion that much social variation in fertility can be interpreted with reference to fundamentalism and conventionalism, it does not follow, of course, that variation in the costs of maintaining projected lifestyle or in the income available to do so are irrelevant to fertility variation. The conclusion is rather that the perceived implications of costs and income are culturally mediated. For example, women who prefer to stay at home are likely to be more fundamentalist than are those who go out to work, and therefore inclined to put greater value on the importance of child-bearing to projected lifestyle. On the other hand, for women in both categories, the economy determines the lifestyles available and their costs.

Fertility decline over the past two decades has been accompanied by a general decline in church attendance and other indicators of religious practice in European countries. There is also evidence of a decline in national pride.

The Commission of the European Community compared responses to a question on the subject asked in national surveys in five countries in 1982 with responses to a similar question asked in 1970. The level of national pride was lower at all ages in 1982 than it was in 1970 in Belgium, France, Italy and the Netherlands. In Germany the level was similar for all birth cohorts since 1931, but those born between 1931 and 1935 expressed a slightly higher level of pride in both 1970 and 1982 than did the generations immediately preceding and following them (Tchernia 1982).

In contrast to the evidence indicating some decline in fundamentalism, data from the Values Survey suggest that religious sentiment remains important for a majority of Europeans, that levels of national pride are generally high, and that familism is still a dominant feature of social life. Taken as a whole, the evidence implies that, even though there may have been a shift towards pragmatism, fundamentalist attitudes continue to remain influential in most countries.

Low fertility is not inconsistent with familism where expensive life-styles, for offspring as well as parents, are highly valued. However, presumably there is a lower limit of preferred family size beyond which evidence of familism would seem to be wanting. It is difficult to place this limit lower than two children. This is not simply because two is one more than the bare minimum needed to qualify for parenthood. It is because sibling relationships, and both parent–daughter and parent–son relationships are embedded in the concept of the family, motivating familist couples to have two children.

Thus one view of the fertility decline since the 1960s is to see it as an adjustment of fertility, prompted by a shift to pragmatism or revisionism, towards a minimum level consistent with the high value still placed on the family. According to the theory proposed above, any general movement below this minimum level could reflect a decline in familism that had its roots in a low identification of the individual with society. The condition would be reflected in relatively low national values on measures of familism, such as the low index values shown for Germany and some other countries with very low fertility in table 6. (Again, it is necessary to keep in mind the fact that, because they are based on aggregate data – all age groups – the analyses reported above may misrepresent trends in the generations of reproductive age.)

Because it would apply more generally, an explanation of the decline based on the view taken here would have advantages that could not be claimed by appeals to the effect of such specific factors as increases in the proportion of women in the labour force. (For details of the limitations of this factor as a general explanation, see Hohn 1983.) It does not follow that such factors are irrelevant. As well as affecting fertility directly, a shift away from fundamentalism may encourage more women to enter the labour force, if jobs are available and if wage rates are sufficiently attractive. The experience of being in the labour force may in turn encourage a further shift in the same direction. However, the outcome may, as de Cooman et al. (1983) are currently attempting to establish, be more influential on the timing of births than on ultimate family size.

The norms of the consumer society have evidently had their effects on the calculus of choice applied to reproductive behaviour. Families are started late and kept small, to maintain or improve living-standards. However, to the extent that this is merely a change of pattern, it is evidence of the continuing importance of parenthood to the lifestyles of the majority, and of the place of the family in the religions, civil and institutional, of contemporary industrial society.

REFERENCES

Bellah, R. 1967: Civil religion in America. *Daedalus*, 96 (1), 1–21.
Calot, G., and Blayo, C. 1982: Recent course of fertility in Western Europe. *Population Studies*, 36 (3), 349–72.
De Cooman, E., Ermisch, J., and Joshi, H. 1985: *The Next Birth and the Labour Market*, CEPR Discussion Paper no. 37. London: Centre for Economic Policy Research.
De la Beaumelle, S. 1979: *The Europeans and their Children: a survey carried out in the nine countries of the European community*. Brussels: Commission of the European Communities.
Durkheim, E. 1952: *Suicide*. London, Routledge and Kegan Paul. (First published in French, 1897.)
—— 1915: *The Elementary Forms of the Religious Life*. London: Allen and Unwin. (First published in French, 1912.)
Ermisch, J. 1983: *The Political Economy of Demographic Change: causes and implications of population trends in Great Britain*. London, Heinemann.
Fogarty, M., Ryan, L., and Lee, J. 1984: *Irish Values and Attitudes: the Irish report of the European Value Systems Study*. Dublin: Dominican Publications.
Höhn, C. 1983: Participation in economic activity and the changing role of women. In *Proceedings of the European Population Conference 1982*, Strasbourg: Council of Europe, pp. 129–47.
Jones, E. 1982: *Socio-economic Differentials in Achieved Fertility*, EEC Analyses of WFS Surveys in Europe and USA, no. 21.
Lesthaeghe, R. 1983: A century of demographic and cultural change in Western Europe: an exploration of underlying dimensions. *Population and Development Review*, 9 (3), 411–35.
Luckmann, T. 1967: *The Invisible Religion*. London, Macmillan.
Notestein, F. 1945: Population – the long view. In T. W. Schultz (ed.), *Food for the World*: Chicago: University of Chicago Press.
Rose, R. 1984: *National Pride: cross-national surveys*, Studies in Public Policy, no. 136. Glasgow: Centre for the Study of Public Policy, University of Strathclyde.
Schutz, A. 1962: *Collected Papers*, ed. M. Natanson. The Hague: Martinus Nijhoff.
Simons, J. 1980: Developments in the interpretation of recent fertility trends in England and Wales. In J. Hobcraft and P. Rees (eds), *Regional Demographic Development*, London: Croom Helm, pp. 117–38.
—— 1982: Reproductive behaviour as religious practice. In C. Höhn and R. Mackensen (eds), *Determinants of Fertility Trends: theories re-examined*, proceedings of an International Union for the Scientific Study of Population seminar, Bad Homburg, April 1980. Liège: Ordina, pp. 131–45.
Slater, P. 1977: *The Measurement of Intrapersonal Space by Grid Technique*, vol. II: *Dimensions of Intrapersonal Space*. London: John Wiley.
Stoetzel, J. 1983: *Les Valeurs du temps présent: une enquête européenne*. Paris: Presses Universitaires de France.
Tchernia, J. 1982: *The Young Europeans: an exploratory study of 15–24 year olds in EEC countries*. Brussels: Commission of the European Community.

Mortality since Malthus

Stephen J. Kunitz

INTRODUCTION

It is a truth universally acknowledged that death and taxes are with us always: inevitable as the cycle of seasons and the succession of day and night; ineluctable as the ebb and flow of the tides. But every taxpayer knows that, while taxes may be inevitable, who gets taxed, and how much, is by no means a law of nature. It is a consequence of the way states are governed, wealth distributed and armies equipped. And, though death, too, is inevitable, how it happens, and when, are by no means laws of nature either. The burden of death, like the burden of taxes, is distributed in ways that reflect the organization of political, economic and social institutions within nations, as well as the relations among them. That was clear to Malthus. 150 years on it should be even clearer to us.

It is useful to think of mortality as composed broadly of three different sorts of causes: (1) epidemic infectious diseases; (2) endemic infectious diseases; and (3) non-infectious diseases. Among the first category are diseases spread from person to person by direct contact (e.g. smallpox), others spread by intermediate vectors such as mosquitoes or body lice (e.g. malaria and typhus), and still others spread from animal reservoirs to humans (e.g. plague). What these diseases have in common is that – with the possible exception of typhus – they are not made significantly more lethal by undernutrition of the host (Conference participants 1983), and historically their disappearance has been associated with the growth of stable governments, the emergence of disciplined armies, and the expansion and integration of nation states.

In the second category are tuberculosis and a wide variety of respiratory diseases and diarrhoeas which are made more or less lethal by the nutritional status of the host and which are therefore particularly responsive to changes in standards of living. The third category is comprised of such conditions as cancer, cardio-vascular disease, hypertension and the like, whose aetiology is as yet incompletely understood.

I shall use data from Europe and the Americas to suggest that the course of mortality decline since the seventeenth century has been the result of differences in the ways nations have grown and their economies developed, or failed to develop. There seems to have been a more or less regular sequence

Stanley Engerman and Ralph Sell commented on early versions of this essay. I am grateful for their advice, though I have not always made use of it.

in which the epidemic infectious diseases declined first, largely as a result of the emergence of relatively stable governments and the growth and integration of populations. By the late eighteenth century in North-western Europe and North America the epidemic diseases had largely receded, and the endemic diseases were beginning to recede as a result of a general increase in the standard of living. The recession of endemic diseases occurred more slowly in Eastern and Southern Europe and in Latin America, largely as a result of differences in the patterns of economic development.[1]

A striking feature of the decline of endemic diseases in North America and North-western Europe in the nineteenth century is that it was a rural phenomenon. It occurred in nations in which agriculture was mixed dairy and arable practised on family farms of 20–50 hectares and in which surplus rural population was absorbed in industrializing cities or, in the case of Europe, in the Americas. In the high-mortality countries of Eastern and Southern Europe and Latin America, agriculture tended to be based upon single crops grown on latifundia worked by an impoverished peasantry, many of whom also did subsistence farming on minifundia, or even microfundia. That is to say, in Europe in the nineteenth century as in the Americas during most of the twentieth century, national differences in mortality seem to be most clearly related to variations in agriculture. The *Gemeinschaft*-like qualities of peasant life have often been described, but high mortality from endemic diseases suggests a darker side, as does the frequency of peasant wars since the nineteenth century. Only as the standard of living of such nations has improved have their peoples moved to the more benign mortality regime characteristic of advanced industrial nations.

Complicating the picture of mortality decline is the growth of public health and curative medicine in the present century. There is no question that each has had an impact upon mortality, but primarily in the reduction of epidemic infectious diseases. Once that transition has occurred, further progress resulting from the diminution of endemic infectious disease is dependent very largely – but by no means entirely – upon improvements in living-conditions.

Mortality rates are still, with rare and unverified exceptions, one per person. When and how death occurs, however, is highly variable and dependent upon prevailing political and economic patterns. Whether one accepts Malthus's explanations or not, one of his great virtues was that he was explicit about the relationships he thought existed between such patterns and vital processes. In that sense, at least, we have not moved much beyond him in our understanding of mortality. It is the purpose of this paper to make a modest gesture in that direction.

MORTALITY IN EUROPE

Writing at the end of the eighteenth century and during the first three decades of the nineteenth century, Robert Malthus was witness to an historic transformation in European mortality.[2]

[1]This classification owes much to Omran's (1971) useful typology, which, however, is almost empty of political content.

[2]Much of the material in this section is discussed in detail in Kunitz (1983).

I think it appears that in modern Europe the positive checks to population prevail less and the preventive checks more than in past times, and in the more uncivilised parts of the world.

War, the predominant check to the population of savage nations, has certainly abated, even including the late unhappy revolutionary contests; and since the prevalence of a greater degree of personal cleanliness, of better modes of clearing and building towns, and of a more equable distribution of the products of the soil from improving knowledge in political economy, plagues, violent diseases, and famines have been certainly mitigated, and have become less frequent. (Malthus 1960, p. 315)

Indeed, numerous historians are agreed that there was a remarkable diminution in wars, plagues, and famines in the century before Malthus's birth (Flinn 1981, pp. 95–101). There was, first, a change in the organization of armies; a shift to naval warfare; improvements in military hygiene and discipline, and less 'sacking of cities . . . putting whole populations to the sword, and . . . burning of crops'.

Secondly, there were improvements in agriculture, including the settlement of new lands, the spread of new crops imported from the Americas, improved transportation and commercial organization, more sophisticated social administration and 'famine relief', and new crop rotations, resulting in greater productivity.

And, thirdly, throughout the seventeenth century and culminating in the eighteenth there was a progressive reduction in and finally the disappearance of plague from Western Europe. The reasons are not entirely clear, but very likely the increasing ability of nation states effectively to protect their boundaries by the enforcement of quarantine and the establishment (in the case of the Hapsburgs) of a *cordon sanitaire* of 1500 kilometres was of overwhelming significance.

Bubonic plague is a zoonotic disease whose spread can be interrupted by intervening at some point between the small-mammal reservoir and the accidental human host. But changes in Western Europe resulted in the transformation of other causes of morbidity and mortality as well in the century before Malthus's birth. The acute infectious diseases that immunize after a single contact and therefore require populations of substantial size in order to become endemic changed their character during the eighteenth century (Black 1966, pp. 207–11). At the beginning of the century measles and smallpox were epidemic diseases affecting not only children but also young adults. By Malthus's day they were well on the way to becoming childhood diseases as a result of population growth and integration of national economies, which provided a large-enough pool of new susceptibles each year to maintain them in ever-younger age groups. As childhood diseases they tended to be less lethal than they were as epidemics affecting adults as well as children.

Typhus, a disease of filth and famine which had followed in the train of European armies since the fifteenth century, had begun to diminish in severity during Malthus's lifetime and had essentially disappeared from the battlefield by the time of the American Civil War and the Franco-Prussian War. This was presumably a result of improved military hygiene and discipline as well as improvements in transportation, which permitted food to be moved quickly to areas of famine (Zinsser 1960).

In general, the endemic diseases that increased in relative significance by the end of the eighteenth century were made more or less lethal by the nutritional status of the host. Tuberculosis, and the pneumonia–diarrhoea complex affecting infants and young children would have been particularly important. It is because access to food – especially perhaps cows' milk – made an increasing difference in life chances after the decline in epidemics that differences in life expectancy between the English aristocracy and the rest of the population first became evident in the second half of the eighteenth century.[3] This would have been especially important in respect of measles and the pneumonias and diarrhoeas affecting infants and children, among whom the consequences of diminished mortality would have had a particularly large impact upon life expectancy at birth. Presumably, the same divergence between social strata occurred elsewhere in Europe at the same time (Antonovsky 1967, pp. 31–73).

It is also likely that it was in the eighteenth century that the mortality regime of North-western Europe began to diverge significantly from that of Eastern and Southern Europe. Among the major determinants of this divergence were the very different conditions of rural life found in the core and peripheral nations. Agriculture in the former areas was mixed dairy and arable carried out on independently held farms, while the latter areas were characterized by large latifundia worked by a poverty-stricken, servile peasantry, or by minifundia worked by equally poor peasants. Malthus observed, for example,

Russia has great natural resources. Its produce is, in its present state, above its consumption; and it wants nothing but greater freedom of industrious exertion, and an adequate vent for its commodities in the interior parts of the country, to occasion an increase of population astonishingly rapid. The principal obstacle to this is the vassalage, or rather slavery, of the peasants, and the ignorance and indolence which almost necessarily accompany such a state. (Malthus 1960, p. 186)

The mortality decline in North-western Europe was essentially a rural phenomenon. Urban mortality remained high through much of the nineteenth century, and it appears that it was conditions of rural life that distinguished the core from the peripheral nations in respect of their death rates. Among these conditions must be counted as especially important nutritional status and hygienic conditions, both personal and public. It is clear, I think, that (1) medical therapy had very little impact, with the possible exception of smallpox inoculation and – in the late nineteenth century – diphtheria anti-toxin; and (2) the nutritional status of the poor did improve in England, and presumably elsewhere as well, in the course of the century (Floud and Wachter 1982).

---

[3]The editors of this volume have suggested to me that (1) in the eighteenth century the aristocracy separated themselves from intimate contact with their servants, thus perhaps protecting themselves from contact with infectious diseases; and (2) the aristocracy would have been more receptive than others to advice from physicians regarding the virtues of breast-feeding. Both are plausible. The first possibility may be examined by determining whether mortality at all ages decreased significantly or whether it was a reduction in infant and child mortality that was most responsible for improved life expectancy.

Table 1 Mortality in England and Wales, per million

Category	1848–54		1901	
	Rate	%	Rate	%
Air-borne: total	7,259	33.2	5,122	30.2
Respiratory tuberculosis	2,901	13.2	1,268	7.4
Bronchitis, pneumonia, influenza	2,239	10.2	2,747	16.1
Whooping-cough	423	1.9	312	1.8
Measles	342	1.5	278	1.6
Scarlet fever, diphtheria	1,016	4.6	407	2.4
Smallpox	263	1.2	10	0
Other	75	0.3	100	0.5
Water- and food-borne: total	3,562	16.3	1,931	11.3
Cholera, diarrhoea, dysentery	1,819	8.3	1,232	7.2
Non-respiratory tuberculosis	753	3.4	544	3.2
Typhoid, typhus	990	4.5	155	0.9
Other infectious diseases	2,144	9.8	1,415	8.3
Non-infectious diseases	8,891	40.6	8,490	50.0
All diseases	21,856	99.9	16,958	99.8

Source: McKeown (1976a).

By the mid nineteenth century, then, the most significant infectious diseases were endemic. In England and Wales about 60 per cent of the deaths at mid century were caused by infectious diseases, with air-borne diseases being about twice as significant as food- and water-borne diseases (see table 1). From mid century to 1901 mortality from virtually all infectious diseases declined, with the exception of bronchitis, pneumonia and influenza. Deaths from non-infectious causes remained essentially constant and thus contributed proportionately more to mortality as time went by. Almost 44 per cent of the decline related to air-borne diseases and 33 per cent to water- and food-borne diseases. The single greatest contribution to the mortality decline in this period came from the 1–4 age group, which presumably benefited from improvements in milk distribution and processing as well as more general sanitary improvements.[4]

As the infectious diseases have continued to wane in significance in Europe and in non-European industrial nations, the non-infectious diseases have assumed greater relative importance. I shall have something to say about them at the end of the following section, which deals with mortality change in North America.

[4]McKeown's thesis that nutrition was the major determinant of mortality decline may be correct, but primarily for the period for which he has data. Indeed, the very fact that national data exist only from the late eighteenth and early nineteenth centuries is a reflection of the growth of bureaucratic states, the same phenomenon that I am associating with the origins of the mortality decline. It is not surprising, therefore, that national data are not available from periods when nutrition was not the major reason for mortality decline.

Malthus observed of the former British colonies,

> But the English North-American colonies, now the powerful people of the United States
> of America, far outstripped all the others in the progress of their population. To the
> quantity of rich land which they possessed in common with the Spanish and Portuguese
> colonies, they added a greater degree of liberty and equality. Though not without some
> restrictions on their foreign commerce, they were allowed the liberty of managing their
> own internal affairs. The political institutions which prevailed were favourable to the
> alienation and division of property. Lands which were not cultivated were declared
> grantable to any other person. In Pennsylvania there was no right of primogeniture;
> and in the provinces of New England the eldest son had only a double share. There
> were no tithes in any of the states, and scarcely any taxes. And on account of the extreme
> cheapness of good land, and a situation favourable to the exportation of grain, a capital
> could not be more advantageously employed than in agriculture; which, at the same
> time that it affords the greatest quantity of healthy work, supplies the most valuable
> produce to the society.
> The consequence of these favourable circumstances united was a rapidity of increase
> almost without parallel in history. (Malthus 1960, p. 303)

As Malthus observed, the settlement of North America was fundamentally
different from that of Latin America. The contrasts, indeed, are of crucial
importance to the evolution of morality in the Americas. Settlement began
later in North America and was the product of an entirely different colonizing
nation, one for which control of international trade rather than political
domination of European territory had become the most significant feature
of economic life (Lang 1975, p. 221). The settlement of North America by
the British was a commercial venture: 'In its numerous enclaves, the English
colonies incorporated a religious and economic diversity that was the offshoot
of the English Reformation and a growing economic complexity.' In contrast
to the Spanish settlements, 'In English America, local institutions gave
expression to the peculiar economic and social conditions of each colony.
In Spanish America, the diverse conditions of an entire continent had to find
expression in the same set of standard institutions' (pp. 221-2). This is not
to say that the English colonies were less dependent upon England than the
Spanish were upon Spain, but rather that upon achieving independence there
were legitimate political institutions in existence which assumed control
over the new nation's government.

It is particularly important, too, that North American settlement was not
based upon establishing a semi-feudal relationship with an extensive
indigenous agricultural population. The Indian population in the east was
largely destroyed by European diseases and warfare or forced west, and their
land was claimed and farmed by the new settlers. This is fundamentally
different from what happened in large areas of Latin America, where, though
the native population declined dramatically, feudal relationships were
imposed upon the survivors, an issue to which I shall return below.

Mortality in the English colonies in the seventeenth and eighteenth
centuries was not much different from the rates in the mother country at
the same time. There were of course regional differences, with life expectancy

being lower in Maryland than in New England.[5] In general, however, it appears that high levels of mortality from endemic diseases such as dysentery and tuberculosis had superimposed upon them epidemics of infectious diseases such as smallpox, measles, malaria and, in the south, yellow fever. Smallpox and measles began to recede in the late eighteenth century for the same reasons as in Europe: with the growth of population and development of communications, they increasingly afflicted children rather than adults. Malaria receded during the first half of the nineteenth century as settlement shifted from river valleys, as swampy fields were drained, and as travel by rail replaced river and canal boats. Yellow fever was an urban disease which by the beginning of the nineteenth century occurred primarily in the south, to which, evidently, it was continuously imported from the Caribbean and perhaps Africa.

Though there continued to be regional differences in mortality, and though many cities were characterized by wide swings in deaths from year to year, it is thought that nationwide throughout the first half of the nineteenth century life expectancy was remarkably stable, neither fluctuating widely nor dropping steadily (McClelland and Zeckhauser 1982). This is probably because the population was sufficiently large and communication sufficiently developed for the density-dependent crowd diseases to become childhood diseases, and sufficiently rural for high and fluctuating urban mortality to have relatively little impact on overall mortality. Furthermore, inferences based upon the terminal heights of various populations suggest that nutritional status was remarkably good and better among farmers than among urban labourers (Fogel 1984). Thus by the time of the Civil War the infectious diseases that afflicted the population significantly were endemic rather than epidemic in nature.

From the Civil War to the First World War, a major change occurred in the United States: despite massive waves of immigration from the high-mortality countries of Europe, mortality began to decline. Valid information on cause of death is not widely available for the second half of the nineteenth century. In table 2 I have displayed data from Massachusetts from 1856–60 and 1891–5. Unfortunately, using crude mortality rates obliterates the decline which took place. None the less, the cause-of-death data are useful as they represent the entire state rather than simply an urban area. The data are presented in the same format as table 1 to facilitate comparisons.

Considering the span of years involved and uncertainties with regard to the validity of many of the diagnoses, it is striking that the contributions of air-borne and food- and water-borne diseases are so similar in Massachusetts and in England and Wales in the last half of the nineteenth century. As in Europe, despite significant declines the important infectious diseases that remained by the end of the nineteenth century were respiratory tuberculosis and the non-specific pneumonias and diarrhoeas, all of which are particularly sensitive to nutritional status (McDermott 1966).

At this juncture I may summarize by saying that the historic decline in mortality in North-western Europe and North America in the two centuries

[5]Much of this section is based upon data to be found in Kunitz (1984).

Table 2   Mortality in Massachusetts, selected causes, crude rates per million

Category	1856–60 Rate	%	1891–5 Rate	%
Air-borne: total	6,910	38.5	5,354	25.9
Smallpox	130	0.7	4	0
Measles	150	0.8	70	0
Scarlet fever	1,050	5.8	240	1.2
Diphtheria and croup	490	2.7	640	3.2
Consumption	3,890	21.6	2,310	11.6
Whooping-cough	240	1.3	120	0
Food- and water-borne: total	2,020	11.2	1,530	7.7
Typhoid fever	800	4.4	320	1.6
Dysentery	580	3.2	90	0
Cholera infantum	640	3.5	1,120	5.6
Other				
Childbirth	200	1.1	140	0.7
Cancer	230	1.2	640	3.2
Kidney diseases	40	0.2	690	3.4
Heart diseases	510	2.8	1,490	7.5
Brain diseases	1,020	5.6	2,080	10.4
All causes: total	17,940		19,830	

Source: Abbott (1897).

bracketing Malthus's lifetime followed roughly this sequence: in Europe plague (which never seems to have been important in the Americas) declined as nation states evolved and were increasingly able to control their armies, their boundaries, and their internal affairs; typhus declined as military discipline became more rigorous and as famines were averted; concurrently, the growth of population (in both Europe and North America) led to a transformation in the acute infectious diseases (particularly smallpox and measles) from epidemics affecting susceptibles at all ages in periodic waves to endemic childhood diseases, and malaria (in North America) receded as a result of improvements in rural areas; finally the infectious diseases that seem especially sensitive to the nutritional status of the host declined in the course of the nineteenth century but still remained significant by the beginning of the present century.

It seems reasonable to propose that this sequence was the result of the growth of stable states which were able not only to control their boundaries and armies but also to encourage industry and transportation, redistribute resources during occasional periods of want, and assure at least secure subsistence to an increasing proportion of their populations. I would suggest further that as a consequence of being hedged round by such societal supports, individual behaviour determined largely by social class and subcultural characteristics began to assume greater relative importance in explaining the incidence of important causes of mortality and morbidity. Presumably, this explains the very large differences in infant mortality among equally poor immigrant groups in both the United States and England in the early decades of the present century (Ashby 1922, Woodbury 1926). Rene Dubos has written (1965, p. 165),

The sciences concerned with microbial diseases have developed almost exclusively from the study of acute or semi-acute infectious processes caused by virulent microorganisms acquired through exposure to an exogenous source of infection. In contrast, the microbial diseases most common in our communities today arise from the activities of microorganisms that are ubiquitous in the environment, persist in the body without causing any obvious harm under ordinary circumstances, and exert pathological effects only when the infected person is under conditions of physiological stress.

By the turn of the present century, then, both the levels and structure of mortality in North-western Europe and North America had been transformed to a pattern new in human history. Infectious diseases were rapidly receding in demographic significance, to be replaced by non-infectious causes of morbidity and mortality. And one of the great frustrations for anyone concerned with the evolution of disease is to explain what has happened since, for there is no theory of non-infectious diseases as satisfactory and broadly inclusive as the germ theory of infectious diseases. This is not to say that no theories have been offered. The so-called diseases of civilization – primarily cancer and cardio-vascular diseases – are attributed to a wide range of factors: the stress of modern life, environmental and occupational exposures, unemployment, full employment, the absence of meaningful relationships and social support, dietary indiscretions, inadequate exercise, and so on.[6]

Thinking of non-infectious diseases as diseases of civilization may result from our thinking of modernization as a unilinear process with in-built sociological and epidemiological imperatives. There are several reasons for believing that this is not the case.

First, the very considerable differences in life expectancy among European populations and the rapidly changing incidence of such causes of death as cerebro-vascular and cardio-vascular diseases suggests that the only common factor amongst modern industrial nations is that infectious diseases are no longer the leading causes of death. The non-infectious diseases seem to vary widely and rise and fall for reasons that are only incompletely understood. (Junge and Hoffmeister 1982, Van Poppel 1981, Marmot 1980, Townsend and Davidson 1982).

Second, considering cancers of all sorts, 'Whereas the total . . . incidence varies less than four-fold from one part of the world to another, the incidence of cancer at individual sites may vary a hundred times or more' (Doll and Armstrong 1981, p. 93). Though the molecular mechanisms are not known, inferences based upon ecological and individual correlations implicate different risk factors for different cancers, and these may increase or decrease with 'modernization'. Table 3 lists some common cancers that seem to vary

---

[6]See, for instance, Berkman and Breslow (1983).

Table 3   Suspected causes of the changes in incidence of common cancers which occur with economic development

Expected change with economic development:

	Increase		Decrease
Cancer	Suspected cause of change[a]	Cancer	Suspected cause of change[a]
Colon/rectum	Dietary meat or fat Decreased dietary fibre	Mouth	Improved oral hygiene Decline in some forms of tobacco use (e.g. chewing)
Pancreas	Cigarette-smoking Dietary fat (?)		Decline in alcohol consumption
Lung	Cigarette-smoking Some occupations Air pollution	Oropharynx/ oesophagus	Decline in some forms of tobacco use Decline in alcohol consumption Improved diet (?)
Breast	Declining fertility Dietary fat or total energy	Stomach	Vitamin A or C (?) Improved preservation of food (?)
Corpus uteri	Dietary fat or total energy Oestrogen therapy	Liver	Improved hygiene Improved food quality and storage
Ovary	Declining fertility	Penis	Circumcision Personal cleanliness
Prostate	Dietary change (?)	Cervix uteri	Delayed intercourse Reduced promiscuity Improved sexual hygiene (?)
Bladder	Cigarette-smoking Some occupations		Improved diet (?)

[a] (?) Indicates speculative associations.
Source: Doll and Armstrong (1981).

with level of economic development. As Doll and Armstrong observe (p. 106), 'Westernization is not . . . an indivisible package. There is no necessary set of cancer outcomes that must follow economic development. Depending on the presence or absence of individual components of Western lifestyle, the overall incidence of cancer may either rise (as it has in Black Americans) or fall (as it is now doing in Japan).'

Third, at a more general sociological level it has been common since the nineteenth century to think in dichotomies which describe the transformation from traditional to modern: from *Gemeinschaft* to *Gesellschaft*; from status to contract; and from folk to urban (Nisbet 1966). These notions have had a profound influence upon the social sciences and through them upon much contemporary epidemiology which is concerned with the health consequences of social and cultural change (Cassel et al. 1960, Cassel 1976). The *Gemeinschaft*-like qualities of pre-industrial communities are thought to be conducive to good health, while the *Gesellschaft*-like qualities of urban life are considered damaging to health, physical as well as psychological. Coronary-artery disease and hypertension are the conditions which have been linked most frequently to the change from rural to urban life, but it is by no means clear that it is the quality of social relationships that is of most explanatory value (Beaglehole et al. 1977). Nor is it clear how new a phenomenon it is. Bichat observed atherosclerosis in 70 per cent of autopsied cases seventy years of age and above in Paris in the early nineteenth century (Ackerknecht 1967, p. 56).

Moreover, under the rubric 'traditional' is listed everything that is not urban and industrial, from forest-dwelling hunter–gatherers to agricultural peasants. The differences among them may be every bit as great as between any of them and so-called modern societies. In respect of peasant societies in particular, arguably the typology entirely misinterprets the characteristics of social relationships (Foster 1960–1).

Finally, the distinction between folk communities and urban societies encourages us to forget that it is the latter which have the lowest mortality rates in human history. And I have suggested above that low mortality seems to be associated with a relative increase in the degree to which individual behaviour and choices determine morbidity and morality. I emphasize *relative* because such freedom is not, and never can be, absolute. Innocent victims of accidents and exposures to occupational and environmental hazards, for example, can hardly be described as responsible for what befalls them. And the degree to which even cigarette smoking is entirely a matter of free choice is also arguable when private industry and governments all benefit from the sale of tobacco (Townsend and Davidson 1982, Cooper and Schatzkin 1982). None the less, education regarding diet, exercise and many hazardous exposures, and screening for, and early treatment of, such risk factors as hypertension, have led individuals to change their behaviour and so lower their chances of dying prematurely. Being subjected to advertisements from cigarette companies is different from being subjected to plague and famine. As the following discussion of Latin America will suggest, the poverty of peasant life creates a more rigid structure of mortality than exists in technologically developed societies.

LATIN AMERICA

Toward the end of his life, Malthus observed that

The countries most resembling the United States of America are those territories of the New World which lately belonged to Spain. In abundance and fertility of soil they are indeed superior; but almost all the vices in the government of the mother country were introduced into her colonial possessions, and particularly that very unequal distribution of landed property which takes place under the feudal system. These evils, and the circumstances of a very large part of the population being Indians in a depressed state, and inferior in industry and energy to Europeans, necessarily prevent the rapid increase of numbers which the abundance and fertility of the land would admit. But it appears from the instructive and interesting account of New Spain, which Mr Humboldt has not long since given to the public, that for the last half of the eighteenth century, the excess of births above the deaths, and the progress of the population have been very great. (Malthus 1982, p. 234)

As Malthus noted, the Spanish introduced feudalism into Latin America. 'Spain alone, of all the nations that came to the Americas, conquered an extensive agricultural society' (Lang 1975, p. 220). On this they superimposed their own system of domination and control, extracting tribute from the native population. Whether this was feudalism or capitalism is a matter of debate which I shall not attempt to resolve (Frank 1969). Whichever it was, it differed from the pattern in North America.

In America, as in Iberia, unity was the creation of the political determination of the Spanish state. The comprehensive institutions that Spain cast upon the Americas – the church, the state bureaucracy, and the Inquisition – provide a measure of strength of state participation in the formation of Hispanic culture. . . . Men of influence, even if that influence was of purely local significance, typically had a foot-hold in the bureaucratic structure. Wealth, status, and power were bound to the instruments that tied Spain to America. (Lang 1975, pp. 219–22)

Trade between Spain and America was a royal monopoly, and, because Spanish industry could not supply all the needs of the colonies, industries began to develop locally as early as the seventeenth century. But local and Spanish-made goods could not compete with first Dutch and then English products smuggled in increasingly during the seventeenth and eighteenth centuries, especially after the Bourbon commercial reform of the late eighteenth century. Textile production continued to grow, however, only to be destroyed by the introduction of inexpensive British goods in the early nineteenth century (pp. 81–2).

The Bourbon reforms also weakened the existing bureaucracy by attacking the 'traditional role of privileged groups' (p. 98), and, when Napoleon seized the Spanish throne, this already weakened institutional structure collapsed. Thus, when independence was achieved in the wake of this bureaucratic collapse, there were no alternative existing structures upon which to build stable governments. 'The revolutions produced weak states whose resources were soon engrossed by Anglosaxon entrepreneurs' (p. 235). Engrossment continued throughout the nineteenth century, resulting in the failure of large areas of Latin America to develop significant locally owned industry.

This brief sketch has ignored substantial differences within Latin America. For example, not all of Mexico and South and Central America was occupied by extensive indigenous agricultural societies, and where mobile hunting-gathering tribes were found, domination was much more difficult – even impossible – to impose. In vast areas of tropical forest in northern Brazil no European settlements were established. In some tropical areas slaves from

Africa were introduced, primarily into the Caribbean islands and along the north-east and northern Pacific coasts of South America (Sanchez-Albornoz 1974, p. 138). Grassland areas in what became Argentina, Uruguay and southern Brazil had no extensive indigenous agriculture and hence did not attract early Spanish settlement. As Oveido, a Spanish chronicler, commented, 'The Indies are worth nothing without the Indians' (Crossley 1971, p. 401). Indeed, it was these areas which attracted the greatest amount of European immigration during the late nineteenth century (Sanchez-Albornoz 1974, p. 154).

Turning now to patterns of mortality, it is not entirely clear which of the infectious diseases affected pre-Columbian populations. Certainly the very large urban populations found by the first Spaniards to arrive could well have supported specifically human-adapted acute viral infectious diseases, but if they existed they are as yet unknown (Newman 1976, Strong 1915). On the other hand, there is now quite good evidence that tuberculosis existed in pre-Columbian populations, though there is no evidence that it was a widespread cause of death until the poverty and malnutrition of the colonial and subsequent periods exacerbated the situation (Buikstra 1981). Yellow fever was almost certainly an African import, and malaria too was probably introduced as a result of contact with Africans.

Though the size of the indigenous population on the eve of conquest is a matter of debate, it is generally agreed to have been very substantial. In the urban areas of the Aztec empire sophisticated public-health measures and hospitals were found by the first Europeans, and nutrition is thought to have been adequate (Schendel 1968, Cook and Borah 1979, p. 129). Both factors undoubtedly contributed to what must have been by European standards fairly low mortality rates. Indeed, it has been suggested that massive sacrifices of captives by the Aztecs in the *guerras floridas* as well as the sacrifice of young children practised by the Santamariana culture of northern Argentina were both responses to population pressure (Sanchez-Albornoz 1974, p. 28).

The result of the introduction of European diseases into this virgin-soil population is well known. As in North America, the number of Indians declined enormously, though the magnitude of the catastrophe is not known with certainty. Measles, smallpox, influenza, typhus and perhaps even plague contributed to the destruction of indigenous peoples and their societies in the sixteenth, seventeenth and eighteenth centuries (Dobyns 1963). It is likely that densely settled agriculturalists suffered most, while nomadic hunter–gatherers were relatively unaffected. Even today these latter populations show evidence of continuing isolation from the diseases that decimated earlier peoples and are prevalent among contemporary metropolitan populations (Black et al. 1974, Neel 1970).

Malthus observed that, by the mid eighteenth century, population in Latin America had begun to recover. Epidemics were still common, but on nothing like the same scale as in the sixteenth century. The epidemics of the late eighteenth and early nineteenth centuries seem to have been primarily smallpox and typhus. The contribution of increasingly powerful centralized governments in Northern Europe to a decline in mortality there was not

Stephen J. Kunitz

echoed by the bureaucratic institutions of Latin America. Indeed, it is largely to bureaucratic ineptitude and powerlessness that Cooper (1965, p. 189) attributes the epidemics which afflicted Mexico City between 1761 and 1813. Laws regarding quarantine and sanitation were continually disregarded by governors and governed alike.

Epidemics were superimposed upon high levels of endemic diseases. In the urban captaincy of São Paulo, Brazil, between 1777 and 1836, crude mortality ranged between 21.2 and 28.9 per 1,000, less than in New Orleans at about the same time, and probably an underestimate. Infant mortality at the end of the eighteenth century was about 288 per 1,000 live births, and life expectancy at birth is estimated to have been about 38 years. (Sanchez-Albornoz 1974). By way of contrast, average annual crude mortality in Havana between 1801–10 and 1821–30 ranged between 36 and 46 per 1,000 (Diaz-Briquets 1983).

In Mexico, population began to recover by the mid seventeenth century. Indeed, from 1651 to 1850 the ratio of births to deaths ranged between 1:1 and 2:1 (Cook and Borah 1974, pp. 338–57). Since birth rates are estimated to have been very high during this entire period, of the order of 40–50 per 1,000 (pp. 289–90), mortality must have been generally high but fluctuating. Based upon these sketchy figures, it appears that during the 200 years prior to the mid nineteenth century, mortality generally was in the range of 30 or more per 1,000, often going higher during epidemic years but never remaining high enough to keep the population from growing. Of course, there must have been very wide regional differences, but we have as yet little accurate knowledge of these before the late nineteenth century (McGovern-Bowen 1983).

Life-table estimates are available from the middle of the nineteenth century for all Latin America excepting Argentina, Uruguay and Cuba. From 1860 to 1900, life expectancy at birth increased from 24.4 to 27.2 years (Arriaga 1970, p. 19). In fact, these average figures mask differences among countries. The Dominican Republic, Guatemala and Nicaragua had lower life expectancy in 1900 than Brazil, Chile, Columbia, Costa Rica, Mexico and Panama had in 1860.

Even within nations there was considerable heterogeneity. In Mexico the proportionate contribution of the infectious diseases to mortality was over 70 per cent in Oaxaca in the last quarter of the nineteenth century, between 60 and 65 per cent in Jalisco, and between 54 and 65 per cent in Guadalajara. During the present century the differences widened very considerably, with mortality from infectious diseases remaining high in Oaxaca and dropping precipitously in the other two areas (Cook and Borah 1974, p. 415). It is significant that Oaxaca is an area of dense Indian settlement as compared with the other two, more northerly areas (Fox 1976, pp. 56–62) – which is to say, it is one of those areas in which the Spanish established their most exploitative relationships with the native population, a relationship whose legacy persists to the present (Wolf 1968, pp. 3–45).

Table 4 displays average annual crude mortality rates from 1900–4 through 1950–4 from a number of Latin American countries. The pattern in the early years of the century follows the pattern of Spanish domination noted above.

Table 4 Crude mortality rates, Latin America

Country	1900–4	1910–14	1920–4	1930–4	1940–4	1950–4
Uruguay	13.2	13.5	12.6	11.5	10.3	8.5
Argentina	20.0	15.6	13.8	12.2	10.5	8.8
Cuba	23.7	21.4	19.3	13.3	10.9	11.3
Panama	21.0	19.0	17.3	15.1	12.7	9.1
Costa Rica	28.8	27.2	25.2	21.5	17.4	10.7
Guatemala	35.4	33.0	33.7	31.7	28.5	23.4
Mexico	33.4	46.6	28.4	26.7	21.8	15.4
Venezuela	29.1	28.3	26.0	21.9	18.8	12.3
Columbia	26.6	26.0	23.7	22.5	20.3	18.4
Chile	31.6	31.5	31.3	24.5	20.1	13.7

Source: Sanchez-Albornoz (1974).

Uruguay and Argentina had the lowest rates. Costa Rica, Guatemala, Mexico, Venezuela, Colombia and Chile all had substantially higher rates. Cuba and Panama were intermediate and are especially interesting as they were both outposts of United States interests in which public-health research and sanitary reforms played a very prominent role (Diaz-Briquets 1983).

By the 1950s, then, mortality in much of Latin America had declined quite substantially. Living-standards had not improved dramatically and medical care of individuals had not become widely available. Arriaga has suggested that mortality was generally high in the late nineteenth and early twentieth centuries, with differences that were attributable to level of economic development. Beginning in about 1930, however, mortality in all nations began to improve rapidly and to converge. Arriaga maintains this was the time when public-health improvements became uncoupled from economic factors, since they were transferable by private and government agencies (Arriaga 1971, Robinson 1971, p. 227, Mandle 1970). This position gains some support from the aforementioned data from Panama and Cuba. The presence of the US Army and its imposition of sanitary reforms – as well as the research it supported into the aetiology of yellow fever – seem to have had a profound impact upon mortality in these relatively small nations.

With respect to causes of death, Diaz-Briquets has shown (1983, pp. 29–30) that in Cuba mortality was high and fluctuating throughout the nineteenth century from a combination of epidemics of cholera, smallpox and yellow fever, which were superimposed upon high levels of endemic infectious diseases. Especially prominent among the latter were tuberculosis and the diarrhoeas. As a result of the sanitary reforms introduced by the US Army at the turn of the century, the epidemic diseases declined precipitously, to be followed by a more gradual decline in the endemic diseases over the next half century. Between 1901 and 1953 21 per cent of the mortality decline related to tuberculosis, 16.5 per cent to other infectious and parasitic diseases (malaria, enteric fever, non-respiratory tuberculosis, meningitis and tetanus), 20.7 per cent to cardio-vascular diseases (of unknown aetiology but presumably infectious in origin) and 21.5 per cent to diarrhoea, gastritis and enteritis (Diaz-Briquets 1983, pp. 60–1). A similar pattern was observed in

Chile between 1939–41 and 1959–61 (Behm and Gutierrez 1967). With a few rare exceptions, it was not until the 1940s that effective therapy for the most infectious diseases became available, and most of the decline is thus attributable to other factors: primarily, improved sanitation, including mosquito control, and improved nutrition.

All these data indicate that in Latin America throughout the nineteenth century, and in some countries into the present century as well, mortality from both endemic and epidemic diseases was very high. As late as the 1920s and 1930s, for example, studies in Guatemala and the Yucatán Peninsula found that infant mortality reached extraordinary levels, that malnutrition was common, that enteric diseases were caused by a bewildering assortment of micro-organisms, and that malaria was epidemic. (Shattuck 1933, 1938). The causal relationship between malnutrition and endemic diseases was not elucidated until later, however, in a series of important studies carried out in Maya Indian villages in the Gutemala highlands in the late 1950s and early 1960s (Gordon et al. 1968; Scrimshaw et al. 1968). In addition to working out this by-now well-known relationship, it was shown that medical care and public-health measures – such as digging pit privies and protecting water sources – were not sufficient to prevent or abort an epidemic of diarrhoeal disease but were able to reduce the case–fatality ratio.

This research was done in an area of free villages which had escaped land enclosures (Fox 1971b, p. 121). None the less, population growth and presumably the local system of social stratification had resulted in the division of property into dwarf holdings and necessitated labour migration – often to lowland coffee plantations – to supplement local subsistence agriculture. This situation is not unique to highland Guatemala. Oscar Lewis has pointed out (1951, pp. 126–7) that Mexican history has often been conceived of as a conflict between haciendas and free villages; that even in free villages there has been a high proportion of landless peasants; and that even those with land have often had holdings so small that they have needed to find other sources of income as well.[7]

Moreover, landlessness, labour migration and rural poverty are associated with high mortality throughout much of Latin America. In general rural mortality is higher than urban in all countries for which data have been published (UN 1982), the reverse of the nineteenth-century North American and North European patterns. And a number of studies suggest that (1) the nutritional status of children in primarily Indian rural communities has not improved over the past several decades (Malina and Himes 1978, Bogin and MacVean 1984); and (2) involvement in agricultural wage labour is associated with higher rates of morbidity and mortality than is relatively greater dependence upon subsistence farming (Laurell et al. 1977, Victoria and Blank 1980).

---

[7]It was in this book that Lewis took issue with Redfield's interpretation of life in the same village, which he had studied seventeen years earlier. Based upon this and other field studies, Redfield had formulated the concept of the folk–urban continuum, which is of a piece with other contrasts between traditional communities and modern societies, and which, as Lewis pointed out, may have misinterpreted peasant life. See, Redfield (1930).

Table 5   Economy and life expectancy in Latin America

Country	% of labour force in agriculture		Life expectancy		GNP per capita ($)	Adult literacy (%)
	1960	1980	1960	1981	1981	1980
Haiti	80	74	44	54	300	23
Bolivia	61	50	43	51	600	63
Honduras	70	63	46	59	600	60
El Salvador	62	50	46	57	650	62
Nicaragua	62	43	47	57	860	90
Cuba	39	23	63	73	–	95
Guatemala	67	55	47	59	1,140	–
Peru	52	39	47	58	1,170	80
Ecuador	57	52	51	62	1,180	81
Jamaica	39	21	64	71	1,180	90
Dominican Republic	67	49	51	62	1,260	67
Columbia	51	26	53	63	1,380	81
Costa Rica	51	29	62	73	1,430	90
Paraguay	56	44	56	65	1,630	84
Panama	51	27	62	71	1,910	85
Brazil	52	30	55	64	2,220	76
Mexico	55	36	57	66	2,250	83
Argentina	20	13	65	71	2,560	93
Chile	31	19	57	68	2,560	–
Uruguay	21	11	68	71	2,820	94
Venezuela	35	18	57	68	4,220	82

Source: World Bank (1983).

Cross-national data support the existence of a relationship between agriculture and mortality. It would be ideal to have information on the degree to which the labour force works on micro- and minifundia, intermediate-sized family farms, and latifundia (Furtado 1976, p. 74). In the absence of such data, however, I have had to make do with the data displayed in table 5: proportion of the labour force employed in agriculture in 1960 and 1980, life expectancy at birth in 1960 and 1981, and gross national product per capita and adult literacy in 1981 for twenty-one Latin American and Caribbean nations.

There has generally been a decline in labour-force participation in agriculture over the two decades, though the correlation between the proportions in each year is very high (Pearson's $r = 0.94$). In each year, too, the correlation between participation in agriculture and life expectancy is high, inverse and virtually identical ($r = -0.81$ and -0.82). And, finally, GNP per capita is inversely correlated with both proportion of the labour force in agriculture in 1980–1 ($r = -0.77$) and with life expectancy at birth in 1981 ($r = -0.77$). Thus high labour-force participation in agriculture is associated with low income and low life expectancy at birth.

It has often been observed that infant and child mortality are inversely related to educational attainment, and at the individual level one can well understand why this might be the case: better-educated mothers are more likely to use medical and nutrition services than those who are less well educated, and they may do other things differently as well. But this ignores the question of why the child of a mother with seven to nine years of education is almost four times more likely to die before the age of two in Bolivia than in Cuba. Palloni has argued (1981, p. 642), correctly I believe, that

The extent of illiteracy in a society reflects not only the limitations of individuals but, more importantly, the capacity of a system to organize and mobilize to fulfill societal necessities. From this point of view the proportion illiterate in a population is less an indication of the fraction of mothers with inadequate knowledge to treat and feed a sick child or to challenge the authority of elders than a reflection of the degree of social and political maturity of the system above and beyond the wealth at its disposal and the degree of equality of its distribution.

The data in table 5 indicate that literacy is weakly correlated with per-capita GNP ($r = 0.54$) but strongly inversely correlated with the proportion of the labour force involved in agriculture ($r = 0.82$) and, not surprisingly, positively correlated with life expectancy ($r = 0.72$). Thus at this level of analysis it appears that illiteracy, dependence upon agriculture, and low life expectancy are all related. It is reasonable to infer that rural backwardness, the result of a historic pattern of landholding and production for the international market, is the major determinant of the mortality patterns observed in Latin America.

Under the conditions of rural poverty I have been discussing, how effective can medical care be in reducing mortality? The community study in the Guatemala highlands which was mentioned above showed that preventive and therapeutic measures were unable to stop an epidemic of diarrhoeal disease but that therapy was able to reduce the case–fatality rate. Other work has shown that a clinic may fail owing to the opposition of threatened local elites; local people may be unwilling to boil their water because to do so conflicts with their hot–cold theories of disease, or they may not use new services because of suspicion of the motives of outsiders; and health workers may not understand local beliefs and accommodate to them. (Paul 1955, McCormick et al. 1979). On the other hand, there is quite good evidence that primary health care may have a very considerable impact upon mortality when it is provided in an acceptable fashion (Berggren et al. 1981).[8] Such intensive and carefully established programmes are all too rare, however, and it is almost certainly the case that primary health care has not been responsible for a large share of the decline in mortality that has occurred in Latin America over the past sixty years, though it could make a substantial contribution in the future.

The studies of the difficulties and failures of innovations at the local level support the suggestion that the decline in mortality which began in the first few decades of this century was primarily the result of innovations in public health that were not dependent upon individual beliefs and practices.

---

[8]Oral rehydration may be a therapeutic modality that will have a significant impact on mortality from diarrhoea among infants and children.

Governments, international agencies and private organizations have been able to effect truly remarkable reductions in mortality from diseases that can be prevented by quarantine, spraying and vaccination. Malaria control, for example, seems to have been associated with much of the decline in mortality since 1950, and indeed even earlier (Palloni and Wyrick 1981, Giglioli 1972).

Diarrhoea, now the major cause of death among infants and children, is much more responsive to other measures, however, particularly to improvements in standards of living. Historically, declining mortality has been associated with a diminution in the differences in mortality rates among social classes. The same pattern is observed spatially in Latin America, where in high-mortality countries differences in education are related to greater differences in child mortality rates than they are in low-mortality countries (UN 1982). It appears that, after epidemics have declined, social-class distinctions in mortality become more obvious as access to resources increasingly has an impact upon survival from the endemic infectious diseases that are particularly sensitive to nutritional status. Subsequently, class distinctions in mortality diminish as the general standard of living improves and overall mortality declines, and this may happen either as a result of an expansion of the entire economy – which may not, however, affect the distribution of wealth – or as a result of a redistribution of wealth with little or no increase in average per-capita income.

Complicating the evolution of mortality in Latin America is the issue of international indebtedness. It seems entirely plausible that the assumption of external debts has in many nations resulted in economic improvements which have led to reduced mortality. Within the past decade or so, however, the problems of repayment, rescheduling and default have loomed ever larger (Payer 1976). When the International Montetary Fund intervenes to forestall default, it requires substantial changes in the economic policies of the debtor countries, and such changes involve, among other things, reduction in government spending and price supports. It is likely that these changes will be reflected in a slowing – or perhaps even reversal – of the mortality decline in recent decades.

The economic impact of the debt burden and the belt-tightening measures that accompany IMF lending can be quickly summarized in aggregate terms. The year-end estimate was that, for Latin America as a whole, gross national product (GNP) declined by 3.8 percent in 1983, adjusted for inflation. Per capita income fell for the third straight year in 1983, to a level eight percent below its peak in 1980. On present prospects, even if growth picks up after 1983, per capita income will not return to the 1980 level before the end of the decade. (Roett 1983–4, p. 699)

Thus, at a time when the most prevalent diseases have become those that respond to improvements in the standard of living, poverty is increasing. The prospects for continuing rapid decline in mortality in the near future are not great (Gwatkin 1980).

CONCLUSIONS

The points I have wanted to make in this essay are as follows. First, historically stable governments that can exercise control over their borders, discipline their armies and enforce sanitary regulations have been necessary in order to bring epidemics under control. Capitalist and socialist[9] governments as well as armies of occupation have all been able to accomplish this. By the twentieth century, however, public-health techniques had evolved sufficiently for even relatively weak governments, as in Latin America, to control epidemics.

Second, endemic diseases – especially the unholy trinity of pneumonia, diarrhoea and malnutrition – are not as likely to be controlled by administrative means. They are far more responsive to patterns of social stratification and exploitation. Among the peoples I have been considering, it is peasants enmeshed in agricultural wage labour who seem to account for the greatest cross-national differences in mortality once epidemic diseases have been eliminated.

Third, economic development – usually meaning the growth of industry – was in its early phases associated with increased poverty and mortality but in the long run has raised living-standards sufficiently to eliminate the endemic infectious diseases as a significant cause of death. The results have been that non-infectious diseases have assumed relatively greater importance than in the past in the industrial nations, and that levels of mortality are lower than ever before in human history. The aetiology of these diseases is not yet completely understood, but enough is known to allow us to say that economic development does not embody an epidemiological imperative requiring that we all die of cardio-vascular disease or cancer. Whether we shall all live our allotted four-score and five and then collapse like the one-hoss shay is as yet unknown, however (Fries and Crapo 1981, Manton 1982).

Finally, the role of medicine in the mortality decline has been a topic of considerable debate, not simply as an interesting intellectual exercise but because of its very immediate political and economic relevance.[10] If, after all, in a time of constrained resources, it can be shown that the effects of medical care have been over-sold, then a powerful argument exists for reduced spending. That therapeutic medicine – that is to say, the treatment of individuals – had little impact upon the historic decline of mortality in Europe and North America until the present century seems clear. That it has been entirely without value among the poor in Europe and North America as well as in Latin America is arguable. That it will be without benefit in the control of non-infectious diseases is an assertion of faith more than a statement of fact.

---

[9]For example, the Soviet Union during the 1920s.
[10]See McKeown (1976b), Beeson (1977), Godber (1977), Hart (1977), Holland (1977), Dollery (1981) and McDermott (1981, 1982).

Political calculators have been led into the error of supposing that there is generally speaking, an invariable order of mortality in all countries: but it appears, on the contrary, that this order is extremely variable; that it is very different in different places of the same country, and within certain limits depends upon circumstances which it is in the power of man to alter. (Malthus 1960, p. 154)

Now, even more than in Malthus's time, death, though still inevitable, is in the power of man to alter. He knew that mortality patterns were the product of social systems and that civilized societies had much reduced the spectre of death. That has continued to be true in the 150 years since he died. Let us hope it remains so in the future.

REFERENCES

Abbott, S. 1897: *The Vital Statistics of Massachusetts: A Forty Years' Report, 1856-1895,* Twenty-eighth Annual Report of the Massachusetts State Board of Health, Public Document no. 34. Boston, Mass.
Ackerknecht, E. H. 1967: *Medicine at the Paris Hospital 1794-1848.* Baltimore: Johns Hopkins University Press.
Antonovsky, A. 1967: Social Class, life expectancy and overall mortality. *Milbank Memorial Fund Quarterly,* 45, 31-73.
Arriaga, E. E. 1970: *Mortality Decline and its Demographic Effects in Latin America,* Population Monograph series, no. 6. Berkeley, Calif.: Institute of International Studies, University of California.
—— and Davis, K. 1969: The pattern of mortality change in Latin America. *Demography,* 6, 223-42.
Ashby, H. T. 1922: *Infant Mortality.* Cambridge: Cambridge University Press.
Beaglehole, R., Salmond, C., Hooper, A., Huntsman, J., Stanhope, J. M., and Cassel, J. C. 1977: Blood pressure and social interaction in Tokelauan migrants in New Zealand. *Journal of Chronic Diseases,* 30, 808-12.
Beeson, P. B. 1977: McKeown's *The Role of Medicine:* A clinician's reaction. *Milbank Memorial Fund Quarterly,* 55, 365-71.
Behm, H., and Gutierrez, H. 1967: Structure of causes of death and level of mortality. In *Proceedings of the World Population Conference,* New York: United Nations, vol. II.
Berggren, W., Ewbank, D. C. and Berggren, G. 1981: Reduction of mortality in rural Haiti through a primary-health-care program. *New England Journal of Medicine,* 304, 1324-30.
Berkman, L. F., and Breslow, L. 1983: *Health and Ways of Living.* New York: Oxford University Press.
Black, F. L. 1966: Measles endemicity and insular populations: critical community size and its evolutionary implications. *Journal of Theoretical Biology,* 11, 207-11.
—— Hierholzer, W. J., de Pinheiro, F., Evans, A. S., Woodall, J. P., Opton, E. M., Emmons, J. E., West, B. S., Edsall, G., Downs, W. G. and Wallace, G. D. 1974: Evidence for persistence of infectious agents in isolated human populations. *American Journal of Epidemiology,* 100, 230-50.
Bogin, B., and MacVean, B. B. 1984: Growth status of non-agrarian, semi-urban living Indians in Guatemala. *Human Biology,* 56, 527-38.
Buikstra, J. E. (ed.) 1981: *Prehistoric Tuberculosis in the Americas,* Scientific Papers, no. 5. Evanston, IU: Northwestern University Archaeological Program.
Cassel, J. 1976: The contribution of the social environment to host resistance. *American Journal of Epidemiology,* 104, 107-23.

Cassel, J., Patrick, R., and Jenkins, D. 1960: Epidemiological analysis of the health implications of cultural change. *Annals of the New York Academy of Science*, 84, 938–49.

Conference participants 1983: The relationship of nutrition, disease, and social conditions: a graphical presentation. *Journal of Interdisciplinary History*, 14, 503–6.

Cook, S. F., and Borah, W. 1974: *Essays in Population History*, vol. II. Berkeley, Calif., and Los Angeles: University of California Press.

—— 1979: *Essays in Population History*, vol. III. Berkeley, Calif., and Los Angeles: University of California Press.

Cooper, D. B. 1965: Epidemic Disease in Mexico City, 1761–1813. Austin: University of Texas Press.

Cooper, R., and Schatzkin, A. 1982: The pattern of mass disease in the USSR: a product of socialist or capitalist development? *International Journal of Health Services*, 12, 459–80.

Crossley, J. C. 1971: The River Plate countries. In H. Blakemore and C. T. Smith (eds), *Latin America: geographical perspectives*, London: Methuen.

Diaz-Briquets, S. 1983: *The Health Revolution in Cuba*. Austin: University of Texas Press.

Dobyns, H. F. 1963: An outline of Andean epidemic history. *Bulletin of the History of Medicine*, 37, 493–515.

Doll, R., and Armstrong, B. 1981: Cancer. In H. Trowell and D. Burkitt (eds), *Western Diseases*, Cambridge, Mass.: Harvard University Press.

Dollery, C. 1978: *The End of an Age of Optimism*. London: Nuffield Provincial Hospitals Trust.

Dubos, R. 1965: *Man Adapting*. New Haven, Conn.: Yale University Press.

Flinn, M. W. 1981: *The European Demographic System 1500–1820*. Brighton, Sussex: Harvester Press.

Floud, R., and Wachter, K. W. 1982: Poverty and physical stature: evidence on the standard of living of London boys. *Social Science History*, 6, 422–52.

Fogel, R. W. 1984: *Nutrition and the Decline in Mortality since 1700: some preliminary findings*, Working Paper no. 1402. Cambridge, Mass.: National Bureau of Economic Research.

Foster, G. M. 1960–1: Interpersonal relations in peasant society. *Human Organization*, 19, 174–84.

Fox, D. J. 1971a: Mexico. In H. Blakemore and C. T. Smith (eds), *Latin America: geographical perspectives*. London: Methuen.

—— 1971b: Central America, including Panama. In H. Blakemore and C. T. Smith (eds), *Latin America: geographical perspectives*. London: Methuen.

Frank, A. G. 1969: *Capitalism and Underdevelopment in Latin America*. New York: Monthly Review Press.

Fries, J. F., and Crapo, L. M. 1981: *Vitality and Aging*. San Francisco: H. Freeman.

Furtado, C. 1976: *Economic Development of Latin America*, 2nd edn. Cambridge University Press.

Giglioli, G. 1972: Changes in the pattern of mortality following the eradication of hyperendemic malaria from a highly susceptible community. *Bulletin of the World Health Organization*, 46, 181–202.

Godber, G. E. 1977: McKeown's *The Role of Medicine*: comments from a former Chief Medical Officer. *Milbank Memorial Fund Quarterly*, 55, 373–7.

Gordon, J. E., Ascoli, W., Mata, L. J., Guzman, M. A., and Scrimshaw, N. S. 1968: Nutrition and infection field study in Guatemalan villages, 1959–64: VI. acute diarrheal disease and nutritional disorders in general disease incidence. *Archives of Environmental Health*, 16, 424–36.

Gwatkin, D. R. 1980: Indications of change in developing country mortality trends. *Population and Development Review*, 6, 615–44.

Hart, J. T. 1977: McKeown's *The Role of Medicine*: advancing backwards. *Milbank Memorial Fund Quarterly*, 55, 383–8.

Holland, W. 1977: McKeown's *The Role of Medicine*: the view from social medicine. *Milbank Memorial Fund Quarterly*, 55, 379–82.

Junge, B., and Hoffmeister, H. 1982: 'Civilization-associated' diseases in Europe and industrial nations outside of Europe. *Preventive Medicine*, 11, 117–30.

Kunitz, S. J. 1983: Speculations on the European mortality decline. *Economic History Review*, ns. 36, 349–64.

—— 1984: Mortality change in America, 1620–1920. *Human Biology*, 56, 559–82.

Lang, J. 1975: *Conquest and Commerce: Spain and England in the Americas.* New York: Academic Press.

Laurell, A. C., Gil, J. B., Machetto, T., Polomo, J., Ruffo, C. P., Chavez, M. R., Urbina, M. and Velazquez, N. 1977: Disease and rural development: a sociological analysis of morbidity in two Mexican villages. *International Journal of Health Services*, 7, 401–23.

Leibowitz, J. O. 1970: *The History of Coronary Heart Disease.* London: Wellcome Institute for the History of Medicine.

Lewis, O. 1951: *Life in a Mexican Village. Tepoztian restudied.* Urbana: University of Illinois Press.

Manton, K. G. 1982: Changing concepts of morbidity and mortality in the elderly population. *Milbank Memorial Fund Quarterly*, 60, 183–244.

Marmot, M. G. 1980: Affluence, urbanization and coronary heart disease. In E. J. Clegg and J. P. Garlick (eds), *Disease and Urbanization*, London: Taylor and Francis.

McClelland, P. D., and Zeckhauser, R. J. 1982: *Demographic Dimensions of the New Republic*, Cambridge: Cambridge University Press.

McCormick, M. C., Shapiro, S. and Horn, S. D. 1979: The relationship between infant mortality rates and medical care and socio-economic variables, Chile 1960–1970. *International Journal of Epidemiology*, 8, 145–54.

McDermott, W. 1966: Modern medicine and the demographic-disease pattern of overly traditional societies: a technological misfit. In H. van Zile Hyde (ed.), *Manpower for the World's Health*, Evanston, Ill.: Association of American Medical Colleges.

—— 1981: Absence of indicators of the influence of its physicians on a society's health. *American Journal of Medicine*, 70, 833–43.

—— 1982: Social ramifications of control of microbial disease. *Johns Hopkins Medical Journal*, 151, 302–12.

McGovern-Bowen, C. G. 1983: Mortality and crisis mortality in eighteenth-century Mexico: the case of Patzcuaro, Michoacan. Department of Geography Discussion Paper, 82, Syracuse, NY: Syracuse University.

McKeown, T. 1976a: *The Modern Rise of Population.* New York: Academic Press.

—— 1976b: *The Role of Medicine: dream mirage, or nemesis.* London: Nuffield Provincial Hospitals Trust.

Malina, R. M., and Himes, J. H. 1978: Patterns of childhood mortality and growth status in a rural Zapotec community. *Annals of Human Biology*, 5, 517–31.

Malthus, T. 1960: *Essay on the principle of Population*, 2nd ed., 2 vols. London: J. M. Dent (First published 1803.)

—— 1982: *A Summary View of the Principle of Population.* Harmondsworth: Penguin. (First published 1830.)

Mandle, J. R. 1970: The decline in mortality in British Guiana, 1911–1960. *Demography*, 7, 301–15.

Neel, J. V. 1970: Lessons from a 'primitive' people. *Science*, 170, 815–22.

Newman, M. T. 1976: Aboriginal new world epidemiology and medical care, and the impact of old world disease imports. *American Journal of Physical Anthropology*, 45, 667–72.

Nisbet, R. A. 1966: *The Sociological Tradition.* New York: Basic Books.

Omran, A. 1971: The epidemiological transition: a theory of the epidemiology of population change. *Milbank Memorial Fund Quarterly*, 49, 509–38.

Palloni, A. 1981: Mortality in Latin America: changing patterns. *Population and Development Review*, 7, 623–49.

—— and Wyrick, R. 1981: Mortality decline in Latin America: changes in the structure of causes of death, 1950–1975. *Social Biology*, 28, 187–216.

Paul, B. D. (ed.) 1955: *Health, Culture, and Community: case studies of public reactions to health programs*. New York: Russel Sage Foundation.

Payer, C. 1976: Third world debt problems: the new wave of defaults. *Monthly Review*, 28, 1–19.

Redfield, R. 1930: *Tepoztian, a Mexican Village: a study of folk life*. Chicago: University of Chicago Press.

Robinson, D. J. 1971: Venezuela and Columbia. In H. Blakemore and C. T. Smith (eds), *Latin America: geographical perspectives*, London: Methuen.

Roett, R. 1983–4: Democracy and debt in South America: a continent's dilemma. *Foreign Affairs*, 62, 695–720.

Sanchez-Albornoz, N. 1974: *The Population of Latin America: a history*. Berkeley, Calif., and Los Angeles: University of California Press.

Schendel, G. 1968: *Medicine in Mexico*. Austin: University of Texas Press.

Scrimshaw, N. S., Guzman, M. A., Flores, M. and Gordon, J. E. 1968: Nutrition and infection field study in Guatemalan villages 1959–64: V. *Archives of Environmental Health*, 16, 223–34.

Shattuck, G. C. 1933: *The Peninsula of Yucatán: medical, biological, meteorological and sociological studies*. Washington, DC: Carnegie Institute of Washington.

—— 1938: *A Medical Survey of the Republic of Guatemala*. Washington, DC: Carnegie Institute of Washington.

Strong, R. P. 1915: *Report of the First Expedition to South America, 1913*. Cambridge, Mass.: Harvard University Press, Harvard School of Tropical Medicine.

Townsend, P., and Davidson, N. 1982: *Inequalities in Health*. Harmondsworth: Penguin.

United Nations 1982: *Levels and Trends of Mortality since 1950*. New York: United Nations, Department of International Economic and Social Affairs.

Van Poppel, F. W. R. 1981: Regional mortality differences in Western Europe. *Social Science and Medicine*, D, 15, 341–52.

Victoria, C. G., and Blank, N. 1980: Epidemiology of infant mortality in Rio Grande do Sul, Brazil. *Journal of Tropical Medicine and Hygiene*, 83, 177–86.

Wolf, E. A. 1968: *Peasant Wars of the Twentieth Century*. New York: Harper Torchbooks.

Woodbury, R. M. 1926: *Infant Mortality and its Causes*. Baltimore: Williams and Wilkins.

World Bank 1983: *World Development Report 1983*. New York: Oxford University Press.

Contributors

ESTER BOSERUP, a Danish economist of longstanding international repute, has held various administrative and research positions with the Danish government and with the United Nations. Her publications include *Conditions of Agricultural Growth* (Allen and Unwin, 1965), *Women's Role in Economic Development* (St Martin's Press, 1970) and *Population and Technology* (Basil Blackwell, 1983).

DAVID COLEMAN is Lecturer in Demography at Oxford University. He is the author of many articles on the demography of ethnic minorities and ethnic marital choice in developed societies, and the editor of *The Demography of Immigrants and Minority Groups in the United Kingdom* (Academic Press, 1982). He is currently preparing (with J. Salt) a study of the population of Britain.

NANCY HOWELL is Professor of Sociology at the University of Toronto and author of *The Demography of the Dobe !Kung* (Academic Press, 1979).

PHILIP KREAGER teaches demography and social anthropology at the Pauling Centre for Human Sciences, Oxford University, and is currently Temporary Lecturer in Population Studies at the London School of Economics and Political Science.

STEPHEN J. KUNITZ is Associate Professor of Preventive, Family and Rehabilitation Medicine at the University of Rochester School of Medicine and Dentistry, and Associate Professor of Sociology at the University of Rochester College of Arts and Sciences, Rochester, New York. He is the author of *Disease Change and the Role of Medicine, The Navajo Experience* (University of California Press, 1983).

RONALD DEMOS LEE is Professor of Demography and Economics at the University of California, Berkeley. He has published extensively in the fields of economic, mathematical and historical demography, is the editor of three volumes on historical demography and determinants of fertility and author of *Econometric Studies of Topics in Demographic History* (Arno Press, 1978).

R. LESTHAEGHE is Professor of Sociology and Demography at the Vrije Universiteit in Brussels and Director of its Centrum voor Sociologie. He is co-editor (with H. J. Page) of *Child-spacing in Tropical Africa. Traditions and Change* (1981) and author of several works dealing with the fertility transition in Europe and Africa.

ROGER SCHOFIELD is the Director of the Cambridge Group for the History of Population and Social Structure and a Fellow of Clare College, Cambridge. He is an editor of *Population Studies* and *Local Population Studies* and is currently President of the British Society for Population Studies. He is the author of numerous articles on English demographic history and a co-author (with E. A. Wrigley) of *The Population History of England 1541–1871* (Edward Arnold, 1981).

JOHN SIMONS is a Senior Research Fellow at the Centre for Population Studies, London School of Hygiene and Tropical Medicine, and studies cultural influences on fertility in developed and developing countries.

RICHARD SMITH is a Fellow of All Souls College, Oxford and University Lecturer in Historical Demography at the University of Oxford. He has published many articles on the demographic and family history of medieval and early modern Europe, is co-editor of *Bastardy and its Comparative History* (Edward Arnold, 1980) and editor of *Land, Kinship and Life-cycle* (Cambridge University Press, 1985) and *The World We Have Gained* (Basil Blackwell, 1986).

RICHARD STONE is Professor Emeritus at Cambridge University. Author of numerous books and articles on economic and social accounting, demand analysis and economic modelling, he was awarded the Nobel Memorial Prize in Economic Science in 1984.

G. N. VON TUNZELMANN is Reader in the Economics of Science and Technology at the Science Policy Research Unit, University of Sussex. He has worked extensively on quantitative economic history (especially in the field of technological change) and economic dynamics. His publications include *Steam Power and British Industrialization to 1860* (Oxford University Press, 1978).

E. A. WRIGLEY is Professor of Population Studies at the London School of Economics and a director of the Cambridge Group for the History of Population and Social Structure. He is the author of numerous articles, in addition to *Industrial Growth and Population Change* (Cambridge University Press, 1961), *Population and History* (Weidenfeld and Nicolson, 1969) and (with Roger Schofield) *The Population History of England 1541–1871* (Edward Arnold, 1981).

Index